# Investigative Reporting in Canada

*280101*

## Case Studies

Maxine Ruvinsky

OXFORD
UNIVERSITY PRESS

# OXFORD
### UNIVERSITY PRESS

70 Wynford Drive, Don Mills, Ontario M3C 1J9
www.oup.com/ca

Oxford University Press is a department of the University of Oxford.
It furthers the University's objective of excellence in research, scholarship,
and education by publishing worldwide in

Oxford    New York

Auckland    Cape Town    Dar es Salaam    Hong Kong    Karachi
Kuala Lumpur    Madrid    Melbourne    Mexico City    Nairobi
New Delhi    Shanghai    Taipei    Toronto

With offices in

Argentina    Austria    Brazil    Chile    Czech Republic    France    Greece
Guatemala    Hungary    Italy    Japan    Poland    Portugal    Singapore
South Korea    Switzerland    Thailand    Turkey    Ukraine    Vietnam

Oxford is a trade mark of Oxford University Press
in the UK and in certain other countries

Published in Canada by Oxford University Press

**Library and Archives Canada Cataloguing in Publication**

Investigative reporting in Canada : case studies / Maxine Ruvinsky.

Includes bibliographical references and index.
ISBN 978-0-19-542381-5.

1. Investigating reporting—Canada—Case studies—Textbooks.
2. Journalists—Canada—Interviews—Textbooks. I. Title.

PN 4914.I58R88 2007    070.4'30971    C2007-904428-X

Cover image: Emrah Turudu/iStockphoto
Cover design: Erin Thomas

1 2 3 4 – 11 10 09 08
This book is printed on permanent (acid-free) paper ∞
Printed in Canada

# Contents

## Part Three
## Talking Investigative Journalism

# Preface

This book addresses the subject of investigative reporting in Canadian newspapers through a series of thirteen case studies. The choice of stories is completely and quirkily individual: I went after the investigative tales that intrigued me, without worrying much about fitting them into a larger framework. In fact, it was only while writing that I began to see the common threads in my impulsive choices.

Aimed largely at inspiring journalism students, *Investigative Reporting in Canada* features in-depth interviews with the authoring reporters and so provides a kind of personalized instruction manual—a look at the stories behind the stories. The text aims to teach the skills and inculcate in young journalists the intellectual qualities that have made the institution of 'the press', now so beleaguered, worth the saving. It includes, in addition to the thirteen case studies, supplementary interviews (in Chapter 14, 'Conversations with Canadian Journalists') with four senior journalists who discuss their own work, comment on the state of investigative journalism generally, and speculate on its future.

Each chapter's case study employs the same format: first, a summary of the story or series being scrutinized, followed by interviews with the journalists who wrote them, and last, a brief commentary section to extract the essential lessons of the reporters' work. How did the story originate and how was it nailed down? What does it show us about the practice of investigative reporting? And what do I need to learn to be able to write this kind of story instead of just read about it?

I began to collect the stories in preparation for this book in 2002, when I served as a judge in the investigative category for the gold standard National Newspaper Awards. I had originally intended to look at stories from a single year, 2001, but one thing led to another and I ended up with nine stories written in 2001. As the project progressed, I added two more from 2002, and one each from 2003 and 2005—the latter a series called Blind Faith that fell decidedly outside my planned time frame for the book but was just too good to resist. I wanted to limit the choice of stories to a particular period of time partly in order to be able to judge the longer-term impact of the work, not just the immediate reactions.

After choosing the stories, all from a handful of the country's newspapers, I interviewed the journalists who wrote them, putting to each the same series of questions. How did the stories arise, and how did the reporters map out and conduct their research? What obstacles did they face and what aspects of the stories surprised them? I also queried the writers on the impact of the stories: Had they 'done any good'? Finally, I asked these journalists—some of the country's finest investigative reporters—how they entered the newspaper business, how they became interested in investigative work, and what advice they would offer to aspiring reporters. The book proceeds in three parts.

# Part One: Tracking the Truth: The Literature of Exposure

Part One presents eight case studies of the classic 'crusading' variety—stories meant to comfort the afflicted and afflict the comfortable.[1] This is investigative journalism aimed at protecting society's most vulnerable and exposing victimization that continues under cover of collective ignorance (to the selective advantage of the victimizers). This kind of investigation tries to alert the public and ultimately to so outrage its collective conscience as to force remedial action to right the wrong, now no longer shrouded from public view. In less dramatic form, it seeks as well to 'wise up the marks'—to let people know, for example, that the most expensive bottled water may in fact be of poorer quality than the stuff that comes out of the tap, or that the funds they so generously provide to a given charity may not be supporting the cause to which they felt compelled to contribute.

The first section opens with one story that's really in a class by itself (the case of the prostitutes going missing from Vancouver's Downtown Eastside) because it grew from ordinary crime reportage on the police beat. Three chapters on environmental stories follow; a major criterion for their inclusion in the book was that by their thoroughness they tend to counteract the widespread acceptance of environmental degradation as 'normal'. All three bring home a sense of individual responsibility—and empowerment—for the state of the Earth, fostering greater awareness and encouraging proactive responses.

The last four chapters of Part One map some thorny issues. They address emerging trends and the pathways of public opinion, challenging the roots (and often intransigence to contrary evidence) of widely held assumptions. They deal, in other words, with cultural politics: the subtle shifts in public perception and sentiment on the issues and controversies of the day. Reporters who engage in this kind of investigative journalism can act as early warning systems for emerging threats to democracy.

# Part Two: Documenting the Truth: Computer-Assisted Reporting

The advent of computer-assisted reporting (CAR) represents the latest—and hottest— advance in the techniques of investigative journalism. It frees reporters from the 'he-said-she-said' format, allowing them to use data analysis to independently uncover patterns and trends. Understand that computer-assisted reporting doesn't change the essential nature of investigative work—it's still aimed at comforting the afflicted and afflicting the comfortable—but it can amplify the power of such reportage in the public interest. This second section presents five classic CAR investigations: three from the *Toronto Star* and two from the *Hamilton Spectator*.

These stories show how spreadsheet and database programs are being used to advance investigative journalism, and how CAR can facilitate the bringing of stories to print that beforehand would likely have perished under the sheer weight of required number crunching. As the newest gadget in the reporter's toolbox, CAR can't take the place of a lively curiosity or strong social conscience (the only irreducible prerequisites for aspiring investigative reporters), but it can certainly further the efforts motivated by these. Interestingly, many CAR stories, which involve computer analysis of critical data, began life as frustrated access-to-information (ATI) requests. Reporters often spent years battling bureaucratic or official intransigence to get the necessary documents released.

# Part Three: Talking Investigative Journalism

The final section considers investigative journalism (whether broadcast or print) and features interviews with four prominent Canadian journalists—two from the CBC (Cecil Rosner and David McKie) and two independents (Elaine Dewar and Julian Sher). The inclusion in Part Three of interviews with broadcast journalists and independents helps to broaden the book's focus and to underline the common elements of all investigative reporting, regardless of medium.

Julian Sher is the creator and webmaster of the blockbuster JournalismNet,[2] the author of several best-selling investigative books, and the producer of award-winning documentaries. As a producer for CBC Television's *The Fifth Estate* from 1990 to 2000, he covered some of the major stories of the decade around the world. His documentary and book about the famous murder trial of Steven Truscott were instrumental in getting the case reopened.[3] His most recent book, co-written with the *Gazette* (Montreal)'s William Marsden, blew the lid off the criminal activities of the Hells Angels motorcycle gang.[4] He has also worked as an Internet trainer and media consultant worldwide.

Cecil Rosner, managing editor for CBC Television and Radio in Manitoba, has long been associated with investigative journalism in Canada, both as practitioner and critic, and created the hard-hitting current affairs program *Disclosure* (2001–4). Rosner began his career in the mid-'70s as a reporter and editor for the *Winnipeg Free Press* and now teaches a course in investigative reporting at the University of Winnipeg. He is co-author of *When Justice Fails: The David Milgaard Story*.[5] In 2004, he received a Michener-Deacon Fellowship to research the history of investigative reporting in Canada and is currently working on a book on the same topic.

Elaine Dewar is an award-winning journalist and author based in Toronto whose work has earned her accolades as a fearless iconoclast and a brilliant writer. She began her journalistic career at *Maclean's*, working as a contributor, editor, and finally associate editor. Dewar also wrote for television in the mid-'80s (the critically acclaimed *Lorne Greene's New Wilderness*), and is an occasional lecturer. The legendary journalist and author Peter C. Newman, once Dewar's boss at *Maclean's*, called her 'the Rachel Carson of Canada'.[6] Dewar's latest book, *The Second Tree: Of Clones, Chimeras and the Quest for Immortality*, won the Pearson Writers' Trust Non-fiction Prize.[7]

David McKie, a leading member of the CBC's investigative unit in Ottawa, was instrumental in some of the national broadcaster's most stunning recent investigative reports (including Faint Warning, Prescribed to Death, and Dying for a Job). With Jim Bronskill of the Canadian Press, he teaches a research methods course at the Carleton University School of Journalism and has travelled across this country to give workshops in his specialty, computer-assisted reporting. He is also the author, along with Fred Vallance-Jones, Robert Cribb, and Dean Jobb, of the excellent research-methods text, *Digging Deeper: A Canadian Reporter's Research Guide* (Oxford University Press, 2006).

# Author's Note

In *Investigative Reporting*, I've sacrificed breadth for depth. The thirteen case studies presented here consider investigative reporting in Canadian newspapers. The book does not consider such reporting in broadcast or online media, nor does it try to assess the overall state of the art. Such an attempt would require a work in many volumes.

The offerings are limited in time and number. Only five newspapers are represented, and four of them are in Ontario. Only one of the five papers serves a medium-sized market (the valiantly can-do *Hamilton Spectator*). The others are major, big-city dailies (the *Vancouver Sun*, the *Ottawa Citizen*, the *Globe and Mail*, and the inimitable *Toronto Star*) that you might well expect to find at the head of the pack.

I certainly do not, however, mean to suggest that investigative reporting is only for the largest and richest papers—a point well made repeatedly by the journalists I interviewed. Investigative work flourishes wherever the reportorial will and the management support for it exist. To underscore that point, throughout the text I briefly reference work done at much smaller venues. Students are encouraged to follow up these references to investigative work done by reporters at smaller papers.

I exclude political reporting, because it is such a large sub-genre of reportage with unique elements that render it in some senses almost anti-investigative. Political reporters rely on contacts and inside information hard won through the auspices of those same contacts. Like the police beat reporter, the political reporter cannot 'hit and run' but is in it for the long haul, where the tips (in plain brown envelopes or otherwise) go only to the trusted. Thus I do not deal directly with some of the most important political news stories and greatest political reportage of recent years—for example, Andrew McIntosh's pieces about Shawinigate[8] or Daniel Leblanc's work on the federal sponsorship scandal that sparked an inquiry and helped topple a government.[9]

I do, however, refer in passing to political reportage, and ironically, one journalist featured in this book proffered a theory of political reportage that mirrored my own reasoning in deciding to exclude it in the first place. 'I never worked the political circuit,' said Paul McKay, 'because I figured my job, in a way, was to make enemies.'[10]

I do not address at all the business aspects of investigative journalism, the possible financial underpinnings or necessary corporate infrastructure for such an avowedly idealistic venture to thrive. In other words, I do not argue from a business perspective that such journalism will lead to greater media profits, even though most forward thinking media owners and managers recognize that good journalism and corporate profit are hardly mutually exclusive categories. In fact, most newspaper moguls are already poised to adopt (and invest in) whatever means necessary to stem, and then reverse, the tide of declining readership. Practising journalists, for their part, have little choice but to address on a daily basis the problems (such as diminished newsroom resources and an eroded journalistic base) engendered by concentrated media ownership and (erstwhile galloping, recently stalled)[11] media convergence.

Finally, I avoid entirely the business of journalism awards.[12] Though virtually all of the journalists who appear in these pages are award winners, none is motivated to pursue the work by the promise of an award. Moreover, the judging of awards is a subjective business, however you slice it, and each year sees more deserving stories than there are awards to go around.

# Endnotes

1. With apologies to Finley Peter Dunne, a Chicago journalist who died in 1936. Dunne coined the famous line ('The job of a newspaper is to comfort the afflicted and afflict the comfortable.'). But according to Dr. Ink of the Poynter Institute Online, Dunne meant the phrase as a putdown of the press, a way of calling attention to its arrogance. 'Dunne's argument was that the power of newspapers was out of proportion, that they exerted influence where they had no legitimate business. They even had the arrogance to think they can afflict the comfortable and comfort the afflicted.' Going Dunne one better, Dr. Ink claimed that 'the worst journalism comforts the comfortable and afflicts the afflicted.' Journalists, he insists, should be watchdogging the powerful and getting at the truth. 'So let's absolve them of the responsibility of charity or iconoclasm. If journalists want to comfort the afflicted, they should send money to the Red Cross.' See www.poynter.org/column.asp?id=1&aid=2852.

2. Julian Sher was at the leading edge of the Internet explosion in Canadian journalism. Much in demand as an Internet trainer, Sher pens a regular column on the subject in the Canadian Association of Journalists' *Media* magazine. In the mid-'90s, he predicted the steep rise of the Internet as a journalistic tool and medium. See 'A beginner's guide to the Internet: Phobia, hype . . . and help', *Media* 2.4 (Winter 1995), 7.

3. Julian Sher, *'Until You Are Dead': Steven Truscott's Long Ride into History* (Knopf Canada, 2001).

4. Julian Sher and William Marsden, *Angels of Death: Inside the Bikers' Global Crime Empire* (Knopf Canada, 2006).

5. Carl Karp and Cecil Rosner, *When Justice Fails: The David Milgaard Story* (McClelland & Stewart, 1991).

6. Two of Dewar's books dealt with environmental politics. See *Cloak of Green* (James Lorimer & Co., 1998) and *Bones: Discovering the First Americans* (Random House Canada, 2001).

7. Elaine Dewar, *The Second Tree: Of Clones, Chimeras and the Quest for Immortality* (Random House Canada, 2004).

8. Andrew McIntosh, 'The story that Jean Chrétien can't seem to shake', *Media* 8.2 (Summer 2001), 10–11. McIntosh, formerly of the *National Post* (and now in California with the *Sacramento Bee*), wrote a series of stories about former prime minister Jean Chrétien's part-ownership of a golf club in his home riding of Shawinigan, Quebec. The series, which exposed Chrétien's potential conflict of interest, raised questions about political

patronage vis-à-vis some four million dollars of federal funds for job creation grants and loans, and ultimately triggered an RCMP investigation. The series ran in the *National Post* in 1999 and 2000.

9.  Daniel LeBlanc and Campbell Clark, 'Ottawa can't find $550,000 report', *Globe and Mail* (11 March 2002), A1. The scandal (often referred to as AdScam) involved millions of dollars in public funds paid out in commissions to Quebec advertising agencies and revealed massive mismanagement of the public purse. The series originated with a federal audit and sparked an inquiry (the Gomery Commission) into the affair. For an analysis of the aftermath of these stories and their impact, see Dean Jobb, 'Gomery has important lessons: The sponsorship scandal should spark overdue reforms of the federal Access to Information Act', *Media* 11.4 (Winter 2006), 14–15.

10. Interview with Paul McKay, 12 April 2006.

11. Tim Pritchard, 'On Convergence', in *Textual Studies in Canada: The Journalism Issue* 16 (Fall 2002), 45–8.

12. Canada's daily newspapers compete annually for three major awards: the National Newspaper Awards, sponsored by the Canadian Newspaper Association, is the largest. The Michener Foundation presents a single annual award to a news organization (not restricted to newspapers) for meritorious public service journalism. The newest awards, from the Canadian Association of Journalists (CAJ), are distinguished by the fact that the judges are all former journalists. For a sense of the angst that attends the awarding of journalism prizes, see Michelle MacAfee's 'The politics of journalism awards: Some media outlets complain that they are frequently overlooked', *Media* 11.2 (Spring 2005), 12–13.

# Introduction

When I first envisioned this book, I had an airtight plan. Fond of long, clean surfaces and tight right angles, I plotted three chapters in each of four categories (the people, the planet, cultural politics, and computer-assisted reporting) for a judicious total of twelve. To each of the chosen interviewees, I would put the same ten questions. From their responses (in taped telephone interviews later transcribed), I would reconstruct the narrative of 'the story behind the story'. Then I would extract principles of investigative reporting and conclude with the reporters' advice to aspiring sleuths.

By the time I started drafting my manuscript, the journalists and their stories had burst the seams of my neat little scheme, forcing me to revise it to fit the actual cases. The reporters, too, evinced a passionate individuality that resisted categorization and instead demanded one-by-one treatment.

The trouble began with roughly half of the investigative reporters I interviewed refusing the moniker. 'I'm just a reporter,' said some. 'All good reporting is investigative,' said others. Moreover, wide disagreement prevailed among them over what does and does not constitute investigative reporting. It amounts to 'just asking another question', said Kevin Donovan. It's about going after 'the people that deserve to be exposed, the bad guys', said Robert Cribb. Even the Canadian Newspaper Association has waffled between *enterprise* and *investigative* in choosing how to name the category of National Newspaper Award given for the kind of in-depth reportage analyzed here.

Clearly, some extended definitions of the term *investigative journalism* as a sub-genre of the reporter's craft are in order here. Fortunately, there is no dearth of published opinion (or of disagreement) on the fundamental nature of the beast.

Aimed at exposing wrongdoing or injustice, investigative journalism usually involves scouring documents for leads and contacts, withstanding editorial pressure to abandon the long-term (and expensive) project, and cultivating sources who are often reluctant to talk for fear of repercussions.

For US scholar John Ullmann, who defines investigative reporting as 'journalism that counts', such reportage faces its most difficult hurdles not among external sources but inside the newsroom. Writing in 1995, Ullmann claimed that

> . . . the toughest, most difficult barriers for a reporter to overcome are those hurdles placed in his or her path by the people in the newsroom. Without question, and with few exceptions, the current crop of editors/managers at daily newspapers will be judged in decades to come as being generally bad for journalism and probably bad for newspapers specifically. . . . Everywhere I go . . . reporters say it has become harder to get ambitious enterprise articles in the newspaper.[1]

Still, Ullmann maintained, devotion to the field remains, because investigative stories 'have the opportunity to benefit a public increasingly removed from managing our democracy'.[2]

One British commentator defines investigative reporting as a discipline that 'seeks to gather facts which someone wants suppressed'. The investigative reporter searches out

> . . . not just the obvious informants who will be uncontroversial or economical with the truth, but the less obvious who know about disturbing secrets and are angry or disturbed enough to divulge them.[3]

Another divides the journalistic universe in three: the generalists, who merely 'transcribe' reality (the old just-the-facts gang); the specialists, who explicate or interpret, reporting in-depth to elucidate the meaning of the news; and the investigative journalist, who does both of the above but then goes one essential step further to secure the evidence that will implicate the wrongdoer or document the injustice.[4]

Northwestern University journalism professor David Protess defined the art as 'the journalism of outrage'[5] and US journalist and author Bruce Shapiro concurred. Discussing the professor in his own book on investigative journalism, *Shaking the Foundations: 200 Years of Investigative Journalism in America*, Shapiro noted that Protess practised what he preached:

> In 1998, Illinois death-row inmate Anthony Porter, with an I.Q. of fifty-one, was two days away from execution for a double murder sixteen years earlier. A federal judge ordered a stay to consider whether Porter's mental retardation should have barred him from execution. In the time brought by the stay, Northwestern University journalism professor David Protess assigned his students to investigate Porter's case. The student reporters learned that the only witness against Porter had been threatened by police; they located the actual killer and secured

his confession on videotape. . . . Porter's case—Illinois's tenth exoneration of a death-row inmate—shocked the state.[6]

Investigative reporting, then, is meant to effect change. That distinguishes it from the more ubiquitous standard daily reportage, which is intended instead to act as a kind of social glue and maintain a common view among the public at large, preserving the status quo in all its guises without drawing excessive attention to the fact that a status quo exists. But the job of the investigative reporter entails more than documenting individual wrongs; the point is to present a *pattern* of wrongdoing.

> The presentation of the pattern provides a compelling display of both multiple and structural corroboration for these fundamental moral facts: a public system has *failed*; *innocent* citizens can be, and have been, its *victims*; and the *guilty* officials ought to be held *accountable* not only for *malfeasance* but also *indifference* and *hypocrisy*.[7]

So central is the idea of impact to investigative reporting that some critics believe it ought to be the major factor in assessing the value of an investigative report. Yet investigative work can also effect change in subtler ways, altering in the longer term the way people think about an issue. While investigative reporting can bring injustice to light and wrongdoers to account, it can also provoke a readership to more independent and critical thought.

Investigative work requires 'mastery in the journalistic craft'; it demands 'knowledge that must be learned but cannot readily be taught and methods that must be practised but cannot easily be analyzed.'[8] That mastery is itself something of a mystery, perhaps even to highly skilled practitioners, since the pedestrian 'objectivity' of the press and its attendant rules of engagement don't apply seamlessly to the investigative story. The only reliable rule for investigative reporters is to be ready to eschew the everyday conventions of daily reportage and even to break the rules that govern its execution.

The investigative reporter is a critical thinker supreme, one who exhibits 'a tolerance for uncertainty, an acceptance of risk and a commitment to caring for truth.'[9] He or she is able to see the pattern in the forest of facts and to discern its meaning. Investigative reporters almost invariably refer to a kind of sixth sense that provides the impetus to proceed with a story and guides their efforts throughout the complex process of shaping it. Many of the reporters I interviewed for this book claimed they could 'feel' a story, and this sensation propelled them forward even when no one else in their newsrooms shared their intuitions or concerns.

Some commentators believe that investigative reporting relies on two primary sets of skills: people skills (getting sources to open up and reveal what they know about the story) and documentary research skills (being able to comb records and extract the relevant facts). The first is as old as journalism itself, but the second 'has grown vigorously in recent years' to the point where 'the computerized retrieval of documents and analysis of quantitative data are now crucial skills of the investigative reporter.'[10]

Investigative reporters also need confidence in their own judgment and the courage to follow hunches, especially at the earliest (and loneliest) stages of the work. Yet no matter how skilled or well-prepared the reporter, investigative journalism remains a dicey and often dangerous proposition. And going beyond the familiar fence-sitting, 'he-said-she-said' format of daily journalism, investigative reporting may also be defined by what it is not:

> Investigative reporting goes beyond allegation and denial to establish facts, which, if possible, decide the issue one way or the other. . . . [It] is . . . not impartially balanced between allegation and reply. It expresses a judgment based on the facts unearthed.[11]

According to some, that's a defining characteristic lost on too many journalism graduates who 'come out of university with the feeling that journalism is about sitting in the middle of the issues.'[12] A well-known British investigative reporter at *The Sunday Times* (London) believes that 'all reporters should do what so-called investigative reporters do: check facts, never take anything on trust, never take anything on trust from people who have an interest in pushing a particular view.'[13] Investigation, this practitioner maintained, is the very heart of the journalistic project:

> What makes the contents of a newspaper different from those of an advertising brochure is that they say something which the newspaper staff have discovered by their own efforts. Journalism is not about asking important people what happened. It is all about finding out yourself.[14]

The one sure common element in definitions of the craft is their grounding in a moral dimension: Investigative journalism is a form of moral discourse. The reporter's task is a moral one—to expose injustice and thereby arouse the outrage of its audience—an objective as old as that of the Old Testament prophets. But how does this passionate morality align with journalism's attachment to verifiable fact, its prime requirement that personal opinion or sentiment be excised from the journalistic account? The 'facts', some scholars would argue, are themselves based in morality; they would be indiscernible if not for a pre-existing moral stake in the matter:

> The events that are actually recorded in the narrative appear real precisely inso-
> far as they belong to an order of moral existence, just as they derive their mean-
> ing from the placement in this order of moral existence. It is because the events
> described conduce to the establishment of social order or fail to do so that they
> find a place in the narrative attesting to their reality.[15]

By exposing activities or events that depart from the articulated communal 'good', journalists don't simply reflect or reinforce a given moral order. Their role is more seminal. They help to conceptualize and articulate the moral reasoning of a given society by defining the moral code and transgressions against it. To be sure, journalists, including investigative ones, steer clear of making explicit moral judgments in their stories, but that doesn't negate the foundational role moral judgment plays in recognizing the story and bringing it to light.

Doesn't the law of the land, and not the institution of the press, bear responsibility for monitoring unethical or anti-social behaviour? And doesn't the same law punish the code's transgressors? Not necessarily: 'The legal edge may be the sharpest edge among the journalist's tools, but because so much that is wrong is nonetheless legal, the law cannot be the only tool of moral craftwork.'[16]

The investigative story is a moral endeavour by definition, and a kind of litmus test for the values actually held in common by a given community (not just those paid heavy lip service). Perhaps this helps to explain the persistence of investigative reporting. Despite repeated dire predictions of its imminent demise, investigative reporting continues to be practised (in Canada, as in the United States, Britain, and elsewhere) and commitment to it remains strong.[17]

# Just-the-Facts Journalism Versus Investigative Reporting

In objective daily reporting (just-the-facts journalism), the reporter proceeds with a fairly naive or innocent notion of 'truth' as a direct representation of reality, as if reportage could work as transparently as a pane of glass to reveal 'reality'. The truth about reportorial method, of course, is that journalists gather and relay evidence of reality, but what those facts reveal or add up to is a matter of interpretation. Investigative reporters also ground themselves in 'common-sense' variations on the truth as re-presentation. Yet, fortunately, what the investigative reporter may lack in terms of a philosophical understanding of truth and truth telling, he or she compensates for with peer- and time-honoured techniques of verification. Seeking practical rather than philosophical verities, the journalist has a ready answer to the lofty question, 'What is the truth?' The answer is another question: 'About what?'

But if for the investigative journalist the truth about something amounts to a collection of facts, how does the reporter discern those facts in the first place? How does he or she know what facts to seek, or even what to count as fact? It is done through story. The attempt begins and ends with story, because whether or not reporters acknowledge (or even contemplate) it, no fact is value-free and no value is without factual basis. The two concepts inhere in each other.[18]

> Despite the protestations of investigative reporters about facts speaking for themselves and readers or viewers deciding for themselves . . . the actual work of investigative reporting is to compel the facts to speak—and, what's more, to speak in a way that urges a public decision about right and wrong. Investigative journalism is indeed an exercise in public conscience despite itself.[19]

Reading the press as discourse, as a kind of ideological battleground in which newspaper writers debate each other, it seems clear that without the participation of a reading public, the press becomes just another elite claiming special privileges. And if the job of the press is to get the facts right, then reporters who fail to question or challenge existing authority are reduced to aping it.[20]

Studies of news as social knowledge point out that daily reporters don't usually have to take as much responsibility for deciding what they think about the ultimate dilemmas raised by the events and issues they cover.[21] The daily reporter delivers the (supposedly value-free facts) and leaves the 'editorializing' to the reader. 'Here are the cold, hard facts,' the reporter says. 'You decide what they mean.'

The demands of objectivity require the daily reporter to remain detached and present to readers 'just the facts'. But to write the story in the first place, the reporters themselves have to be not only in possession of facts (that is, to believe the facts to be true), but also convinced in some framework or other that the facts matter. If not, encyclopedias could serve as well as newspapers to impart facts.

For investigative reporters, decisions about meaning and values form an integral part of the work from the beginning. The daily reporter tells us how things are; the investigative reporter can't avoid the implicit suggestion that things ought to be otherwise. The former provides a kind of transcription of reality but eschews, in the name of objectivity, further commentary. Where the daily account tells what happened, the investigative one tells what should have.

> Here, then, is a model journalism that is guided, if not by an internal moral compass or some new theory of credibility, then at least by a set of operating procedures more compelling than the objectivity of daily reporting. If journalism is to

initiate dialogue and sustain deliberation, investigative journalism offers some
ideas for deciding what's worth thinking and talking about.[22]

Beyond the obvious differences (the investigative report, for instance, cannot be
dispatched within a single, daily, news cycle), where the daily reporter gathers facts
handed out at news conferences or relayed by expert or eyewitness sources, the investigative reporter seeks the emergent facts at the centre of an issue or controversy.
These facts are often unearthed against the fierce resistance of those who would prefer to keep them buried. Where the daily reporter accepts a certain level of fact from
authorized sources, the investigative reporter approaches such information as a mere
starting point, questioning the facts to arrive at a deeper though still verifiable truth.
While the daily reporter can get by with brief definitions of difficult concepts, the
investigative reporter must burn the midnight oil to stay current on the background
and vocabulary of the issues at hand. The news writer relays existing fact and commentary; the investigative reporter questions both. While for a 450-word daily
report, several sources will suffice, for an investigative project, numerous sources
must be consulted (even though many of them may never be quoted or otherwise
appear in the final story). Where daily reporters' research may be limited to previous
articles available in the newsroom's archives (the 'morgue' in newspaper parlance), or,
increasingly, online, investigative reporters may have to travel far back in time and
avail themselves of the historian's approach to do the story justice.

And finally, while objective daily reporting bolsters the status quo, as per the
'social glue' theory of the function of the press (with no conspiracy implied or
required), the investigative report tends to upset the apple cart. 'General reporting
accepts the chairman of whatever as reputable and likely to be right,' wrote one critic.
'Investigative reporting pursues the whisper that he could be wrong.'[23]

## The Press and the Status Quo

The common wisdom among some critics says the press is a status-quo-saturated
institution that cannot help but reflect, reinforce, and legitimate the dominant culture. But investigative reporting can also work as an antidote to the rule of the dominant (in some ways that is precisely its purpose). It can work to subvert the reigning
ideologies that authorize a range of acceptable opinion. In their book, *Custodians of
Conscience: Investigative Journalism and Public Virtue*, scholars James S. Ettema and
Theodore L. Glasser reached a similar conclusion about the state of investigative
reporting in the United States. They diverged sharply, they wrote, from the 'classic

theorists of social legitimation . . . who maintained that the mass media uncritically reflect and thus unrelentingly legitimize the existing order.'

> In accord with Hallin and others whose understanding of legitimation derives from Habermas, we argue that journalism can achieve no complete or lasting ideological closure. It can serve as an agent of legitimation for dominant values, but there is also reason to believe that it can serve as an agent of change for those values—change that may be, but is not inevitably, for the better.[24]

Such potential, however, is weakened by a lack of public participation. Newspaper readership has been declining for decades along with public interest in 'the news' as a kind of communal repository of shared knowledge and values. As people continue to abandon newspapers (and perhaps interest in 'the news' as such), they leave governments and other powerful entities freer to evade accountability. In terms of the way a social order and social mores evolve, the long-term effects of such wholesale abandonment pose threats to democracy itself. Given public disenchantment with the press, a rigid adherence to the dictates of traditional objectivity may mean further alienation of the public from the press that proposes to represent its right to know. That is, objective journalism, instead of alerting the public or pricking its collective conscience, may instead be stoking—and ultimately legitimating—the apathy of that elusive entity, the average citizen. What, one might ask, has the press done recently for democracy writ large?

> Why should anyone still believe in a role for journalism in the furtherance of democratic ideals? After all, several generations of irascible media theorists, from Horkheimer and Adorno to Herman and Chomsky, have insisted that the news is more likely the means to hegemonic power than democratic empowerment.[25]

Investigative reporting presents an alternative to journalism that goes along to get along, but it's expensive—a fact not lost on those who own and manage Canada's newspapers. The increasing commercialization of the press, along with declining newspaper readership, has fuelled many a dark prediction about the future of investigative reporting for print and indeed about the future of newspapers themselves. Yet investigative reporting continues, and its defenders are far from giving up the fight.

In a 2004 article for *Media* magazine, editor David McKie laid down the gauntlet, vowing his publication would take up the challenge and do more to support and encourage investigative journalism.

> If investigative journalism isn't given the proper support structure, which includes favourable court rulings that allow reporters to protect sources, and the courage

of media outlets to stray from the pack and pursue topics of public interest, then institutions such as governments will continue to be unaccountable to the people they're supposed to serve.[26]

Investigative reporting hasn't had as long or stellar a history or been as roundly celebrated in Canada as it has in the United States.[27] This state of affairs, however, may be starting to change, with investigative reporters from both countries facing unprecedented challenges and beginning to make common cause. At a 2002 conference on investigative reporting, jointly sponsored by the Canadian Association of Journalists and the US group, Investigative Reporters and Editors, Inc., reporters from both countries learned that they faced similar problems trying to wrest information from their respective and reluctant governments.[28]

Called 'Crossing the 49th: Investigative Journalism Techniques from Both Sides of the Border', the inaugural conference was aimed at sharing techniques and strategies to overcome increasing government secrecy, an apparently international phenomenon superbly documented by Alasdair Roberts in his book, *Blacked Out: Government Secrecy in the Age of Information.*[29] Roberts's book explains how, despite the growth in information technologies, nominally democratic governments around the globe have moved to keep information from becoming widely available and have often taken steps to shore up government secrecy and deny the openness that is supposed to characterize democracies. Worse, Roberts opined, was a public 'ethic of detachment' that makes government secrecy seem innocuous.[30]

Does investigative journalism have a future in Canadian newspapers? Severely concentrated ownership in the Canadian newspaper industry, public disenchantment with the press, legal restrictions on reporting, and the cat-and-mouse tactics employed by the access-to-information regimes of the provincial and federal governments all point to troubled times for investigative reporters in the future.

On the other hand, the advent of computer-assisted reporting, the sea changes in the financial underpinnings of the newspaper industry, the ubiquity of Internet communications, and the rise of the blogger as would-be journalist all point to a future that's open to numerous possibilities—some of them positive. I'm not convinced that investigative reporting will find its home in the kind of hard-copy newspapers that currently support it. I'm not sure the media future even includes the old-style newsprint broadsheets and tabloids.

In order for the effects of investigative reporting to 'take', journalists must follow up on the wrongdoing they've uncovered; the efforts of a democratic press are more like a team relay than a race of individuals. The view of newspapers (and media generally) as part and parcel of a corporate monolith, one without potential for social change, is widely held. But the press is not a monolith and its potential for truth telling is well documented. The case studies that comprise this book help attest to that.

Like a rogue reformer, investigative journalism lives perpetually on the edge. Perhaps the edge is not such a bad place to be, though: the edge of possibility, of renewal, of redemption. (An African proverb says that those who do not live on the edge are taking up too much room.) I, for one, am convinced that investigative journalism will survive and ultimately prevail—not because I believe in the benevolence of governments and corporations (I don't), but because of the strength of conviction I've met with in the reporters who populate the pages of *Investigative Reporting in Canada*.

# Thirteen Case Studies in Point

## Chapter 1: The Case of the Disappearing Women (*Vancouver Sun*, 2001)

Three reporters shattered the silence that shrouded the endemic violence against prostitutes that marked Vancouver's notorious Downtown Eastside. Their work led to the arrest of a man (Robert Pickton) in what is now acknowledged as the worst case of serial killing in Canadian history. The story began with a single reporter on the police beat who refused to give up and was later joined by two other reporters on the story. Does anyone imagine that the *Vancouver Sun*'s Lindsay Kines, Lori Culbert, and Kim Bolan spent long evenings among the disenfranchised of the city's Downtown Eastside, getting their stories and provoking an expanded police investigation that led quickly to the arrest of a suspect in Canada's worst case of serial killing, simply for the sake of loyalty to a corporation (their newspaper) or merely in order to collect a paycheque?

## Chapter 2: Reinventing Our Wheels (*Ottawa Citizen/Vancouver Sun*, 2001)

In a summer-long series for the *Ottawa Citizen*, long-time investigative reporter Paul McKay tackled the cultural icon of the car, showing how long the current environmental crisis has been in the making and how central auto emissions have been to the problem. The series then turned to possible solutions. The research took McKay far afield in time (back to the beginning of the twentieth century) and space (to Boulder, Colorado, home to the continent's most progressive public transit system). McKay came up with the inspired idea for the series in his usual way (he'd been thinking things over) and then formulated his analysis using characteristic finesse and superb pacing. Could anyone believe that the capacity for independent thought evinced by reporters like Paul McKay has anything to do with an overarching need to conform to pack behaviour?

## Chapter 3: Death Wish (*Globe and Mail*, 2001)

Alanna Mitchell visited four of the planet's environmental hot spots for a study destined to change her life and draw unprecedented response from her readers. In introducing her readership to the theory of a sixth extinction (one that would put an end to human rule of the planet as quickly as a previous extinction ended the reign of the dinosaurs), Mitchell posed a profound question: Do humans have a death wish? Despite the alarming query, the beautifully written series ended on a note of hope, preferring the belief that even a death wish can be reversed, that it may not, after all, be too late. The four-part series was well played and expertly laid out, but its genesis was the personal conviction of the reporter. Mitchell was propelled by her own need to sound the alarm. She braved numerous physical challenges and dangers to bring readers a seminal volley in the battle for an environmental future. Could anything less than her devotion to the story have motivated the work?

## Chapter 4: Asbestos, Again (*Toronto Star*, 2003)

Peter Gorrie could easily have avoided covering the convoluted campaign launched by the asbestos industry, in concert with government, to 'rehabilitate' the deadly mineral—after all, the rest of the media had. But once he received a news release printed on 'chrysotile paper', the long-time *Toronto Star* reporter knew he had a story. Asking questions no one else had posed, Gorrie uncovered the plan to begin calling asbestos by the name *chrysotile* in a bid to win public acceptance of a substance long infamous for its lethal effects on human lungs. The campaign suggested that deadly asbestos had somehow been rendered harmless (especially for export to poor countries with minimal industrial infrastructure) by a name change. An important story saw print because a single reporter had the background, smarts, and sense of responsibility to challenge the party line of industry and government. Would anyone argue there aren't easier ways to make a living as a reporter?

## Chapter 5: Criminalizing Dissent
## (*Ottawa Citizen*/Southam News, 2001)

Jim Bronskill and David Pugliese exposed a national RCMP campaign to track, discourage, and ultimately criminalize Canadian citizens who dared to exercise their democratic right of dissent. They reported that police agencies across the country had been co-operating for years to marginalize those individuals (including Svend Robinson) and groups (like the Raging Grannies) who disagreed openly with government policy or held and espoused alternative views. In the process, the reporters also discovered that all too many Canadians viewed police tactics (like the intercepting of private emails) as acceptable, assuming that anyone who had attracted police attention must have been up to no good in the first place. Does anyone imagine such hard-hitting journalism originated with an assignment from the city editor or a rewritten press release on a slow day?

## Chapter 6: Dialling for Dollars (*Toronto Star*, 2002)

In classic investigative fashion, the *Star*'s Robert Cribb and Christian Cotroneo went undercover to expose hundreds of fraudulent telemarketing companies whose unscrupulous 'salespeople' set up shop in Toronto and legally ripped off thousands of consumers with telephone sale scams. The reporters risked their personal safety to expose the workings of the so-called boiler rooms, and in the end forced them out of town. They exposed a deeper truth as well: the hyper-capitalist context that made the fraud seem something less than immoral to successful boiler room employees, whose basic attitude toward their marks went something like this: 'If they're stupid enough to fall for the scam and give their credit card numbers over the phone, they deserve to be ripped off'—an attitude apparently not uncommon under consumer capitalism. Is this the work of journalists concerned only with their own good and in thrall to the demands of competitive status?

## Chapter 7: Under Siege in the Ivory Tower
## (*Globe and Mail*, 2001)

When Anne McIlroy told the story of respected psychiatrist and researcher David Healy, targeted for his anti-corporate views of the hard-sell pharmaceutical industry, she did more than go to bat for a single victim of corporate malfeasance. She uncovered the larger issues of academic freedom in an academy shorn of government funds and increasingly dependent on the pharmaceutical industry itself for research dollars. The science specialist had first to overcome her own reluctance to believe that researchers at the University of Toronto would be willing to compromise their integrity and that of their work for fear of losing those same research dollars. McIlroy used her consummate reportorial skills to explicate the hold of the pharmaceutical companies on academic freedom. Is this the mark of a reporter or a newspaper that lives only to legitimate existing power structures?

## Chapter 8: Blind Faith (*Hamilton Spectator,* 2005)

*Hamilton Spectator* reporters Steve Buist, Luma Muhtadie, and Joan Walters exposed the local face of a national and international issue when they decided to investigate the relationship between medical researchers at Hamilton's McMaster University and the giant pharmaceutical companies that fund their research. The *Spectator* series revealed that since 1994, consumer drugs had been withdrawn from the market for safety reasons twice as often as in the previous thirty years. It underlined the potential for disastrous conflict-of-interest situations inherent in having drug companies fund the very researchers who conduct the clinical trials required for drugs to be marketed in Canada. Researchers found themselves evaluating yet-to-be-approved drugs with laboratories and equipment paid for by the very pharmaceutical companies seeking approval. If corporate power were a seamless monolith, why would the *Spectator*—faced with fierce resistance from McMaster—have supported the investigative project to begin with?

## Chapter 9: Nowhere to Go (*Toronto Star,* 2001)

In a groundbreaking series, Kevin Donovan explored the lives of developmentally handicapped people left stranded after the death or incapacitation of parents or other caretakers. The series unearthed widespread and extreme abuse in Ontario's group homes and foster-care system as well as deep inequity in government funding for families who had chosen to care for their handicapped children at home. It took the *Star* sixteen months to win a freedom-of-information battle for the right to access three hundred records detailing the personal stories of those affected. A major lesson here is that the coils of the country's access-to-information laws are worth navigating, despite the difficulties clearly entailed. Donovan managed not only to take the lid off a scandalous situation but also to trace the problem back to its origins in government policy. It took courage and uncommon compassion to see this series through. How many corporate lackeys do you know who could or would have withstood the stress entailed in such emotionally searing reportage?

## Chapter 10: Nobody's Children (*Toronto Star*, 2001)

Three reporters—Leslie Papp, Tanya Talaga, and Jim Rankin—collaborated on this series about the country's epidemic of Canadian children (an estimated twenty thousand in 2001) being raised as wards of the state. They exposed the government policy and lack of accountability that were actively preventing those wards from finding homes with the many childless Canadian couples wishing to adopt. The series involved some database work, but the reporters were provoked to undertake the project by the urgings of conscience, not the availability of data. In fact, the reporters had to build their own database in order to analyze the adoption system's failings. Full of heart and soulful perseverance, the stories exposed Canada's dismal record in finding homes for kids, sparking massive reader interest and institutional change. Would anyone care to argue that the project was fuelled by something other than compassion for the children and a devotion to journalism that counts?

## Chapter 11: Reservations: Recipe for Disaster (*Hamilton Spectator*, 2001)

Using electronic records of the city's restaurant inspections from 1995 to 2001, supplemented by more than fifty interviews and thousands of pages of hard copy from the city's health department, Fred Vallance-Jones uncovered dangerously dirty restaurants supported by an inadequate food-safety inspection system. A specialist in document research and computer-assisted reporting, Vallance-Jones thereby managed to identify some of Hamilton's worst offending restaurants. The *Spectator* put online the database of restaurant inspections (won only after an eighteen-month freedom-of-information battle) and sparked unprecedented reader response.

Restaurant advertisements and reviews mean revenue to newspapers, but the *Spectator* braved the possibility of angry restaurateurs and lost ad dollars in an attempt to protect Hamiltonians from unscrupulous eateries and a broken (if not corrupt) restaurant-inspection system. What argument for media as monolith, what ulterior motive, could discount or devalue this clear evidence of journalism conducted in the public interest?

## Chapter 12: Drive Clean Smokescreen (*Hamilton Spectator*, 2004)

When rumours circulated about Drive Clean, Ontario's anti-car-pollution program, Fred Vallance-Jones determined to check them out. It took the veteran investigative reporter three years to wrest the evidence (over twelve million Drive Clean test results between 1999 and 2004) from the government bureaucracy that supervised the program. With the database secured, Vallance-Jones and *Spectator* colleague Steve Buist crunched the numbers, did the legwork, and uncovered a system riddled with fraud. The program had cost Ontario taxpayers millions but done little to clean the air. In the largest data investigation ever undertaken by the paper, the series exposed precisely the kind of scheme that would normally enjoy easy invisibility under the 'common-sense' culture (à la Roland Barthes) of consumer capitalism. How does this square with the idea of newspapers as nothing but corporate entities bent on legitimating profit at the expense of people, or with reporters as glorified stenographers at the beck and call of their corporate masters?

## Chapter 13: Singled Out: An Investigation into Race and Crime (*Toronto Star*, 2002)

Five ace reporters tackled a difficult story when they set out to ascertain the truth of decades-old allegations about institutionalized racism in the city's police force. The team—Jim Rankin, John Duncanson, Scott Simmie, Michelle Shephard, and Jennifer Quinn—investigated charges from Toronto's black community that police routinely discriminated against blacks, meting out harsher treatment for everything from lapsed licences to drug possession. In fearless pursuit of the truth, the group would end by documenting the discrimination. Using the police department's own massive database of nearly half a million records—obtained after a two-year access-to-information battle—the reporters uncovered ample evidence of racial profiling. Management support for the series never wavered, even after the police union launched a $2.7 billion libel lawsuit against the paper. Is this the kind trouble that a managing editor without a social conscience would countenance, never mind support?

No, none of the reporters depicted in this book wrote their stories 'on assignment'. None was guaranteed that a story even existed, and that pursuing it at all wouldn't mean wasted company time. Each, in his or her own way, had to cope with the tremendous pressure the pursuit of an investigative story entails—the weeks and even months of checking and double-checking, estimating and second-guessing, interviewing and analyzing. Pressure of this sort, especially when it extends over time, takes a special kind of personality to bear. And even though reporters often mention 'lucky breaks' when explaining how their stories arose and how they were nailed down, the truth is that such work takes uncommon dedication. It's dedication—and not some mysterious luck—that saw these reporters through.

# Investigative Journalism: An Interested View

For the purposes of this text, I define *investigative work* in the first instance as that which proceeds against the odds, and—like Robert Cribb—I believe it is supposed to identify culprits, whether these be individuals, or an entire system working under cover of 'normalcy'. Investigative work is in-depth; it requires more time and intellectual energy than daily reportage (perhaps not a defining characteristic, since other forms of long narrative reportage, such as literary journalism, also delve beneath the surface). Investigative work uncovers patterns, not simply isolated incidents. It gets the facts straight, but goes beyond them to explicate the context and gain insight into the larger whole. In a sense, the investigative report contests old facts and seeks to establish 'new' ones, facts that may prove distasteful to the public at large, but that are made by exposure difficult to deny or ignore.

A closely related term used throughout the text is *issues journalism*, by which I mean the underlying issues of public importance that form the ground for investigative reporting: A matter becomes 'visible' and so worth investigating when it represents, reflects, or unearths a larger social problem or injustice. The two work hand in hand: Issues journalism provides a larger context for investigative reports and investigative reports explicate the issues and advance the debate.

Investigative reporters are strong-minded, because it takes strength to withstand the kind of pressure that invariably opposes the exposé of unwanted facts or the offering of countercultural views. Perhaps most important, investigative reporters are after results. There's a bit of the rebel in every investigative reporter, and the purpose of the classic investigative report is to provoke change, not just disagreement.

Sometimes, just the news that a groundbreaking piece is about to appear in a major paper is enough to elicit an initial reaction from the appropriate authorities, often including the promise of action to redress the problems or injustice uncovered. But promises may also go unfulfilled, especially as the news of subsequent days forces the investigative report to the back burner of the public mind (and the reporter's assignment schedule). Impact—what occurred in the wake of the story to right the exposed wrong—is, of course, a defining characteristic of the investigative report. Yet the societal impact of a given story or series is often difficult to assess, especially over the long term. In terms of public perception of and appreciation for investigative reporting, such uncertainty presents a difficulty—what I think of as the 'so-what syndrome' that I address in the book's final chapter.

## Investigative Reporting and the Press

To say that the Canadian newspaper industry is in flux understates the obvious. Any journalism educator who's concentrating exclusively on how things were done in the past, before the Internet explosion, before an oligopolistic ownership structure overtook the newspaper industry, will perforce be misleading students. No one knows how the dust will finally settle or even when. Will broadsheet and tabloid newspapers disappear, replaced by on-screen and online versions of themselves? Will newspapers give up on making money online? Will they give up on trying to make people pay for what they've been getting for years free of charge? For all the intelligent (and not so intelligent) commentary and armchair prophecies, the fact is no one knows.

But the real question is, Does this matter? Isn't the important thing about a 'free press' precisely its content, not its carrier? It doesn't matter (to the public interest) whether we read the news on paper or on a screen (eschewing, for the moment, environmental questions). What matters is that there be journalism conducted in the public interest and inspired by the ideals of a free press in a democratic society. It is only logical that private interests seek private gain; but if no one stands for the public interest, then democratic and free press ideals will be lost by default. The important question is how to use traditional and new technologies to strengthen, preserve, and encourage investigative reporting in Canada.

However the dust settles, whatever old forums pass away and whatever new ones arise for the dissemination of news and commentary; however the journalistic tradition evolves in order to survive—survive in some form, it will. And its future still belongs to those who have learned to think independently and critically, to research creatively and with assiduous focus, to report fearlessly, and to write well.

I hope *Investigative Reporting in Canada* encourages journalism students to go the distance on difficult stories, and that it inspires them to see the role of creative or critical thinking in a craft long ostensibly concerned with just the facts. I hope, too, that it contributes to a movement in newsrooms and journalism schools toward the unabashed return of high ideals and social conscience to the practice of public-spirited and socially conscious investigative journalism.

# Endnotes

1.  John Ullmann, *Investigative Reporting: Advanced Methods and Techniques* (New York: St. Martin's Press, 1995), viii.

2.  Ibid., 176.

3.  David Spark, *Investigative Reporting: A Study in Technique* (Oxford: Focal Press, 1999), 6.

4.  David Murphy, quoted in Spark, *Investigative Reporting: A Study in Technique*, op. cit., 5–6.

5.  David Protess, *The Journalism of Outrage: Investigative Reporting and Agenda Building in America* (New York: Guilford Press, 1991).

6.  Bruce Shapiro, *Shaking the Foundations: 200 Years of Investigative Journalism in America* (New York: Thunder's Mouth Press/Nation Books), 474.

7.  James S. Ettema and Theodore L. Glasser, *Custodians of Conscience: Investigative Journalism and Public Virtue* (New York: Columbia University Press, 1998), 156.

8.  Ibid., 20.

9.  Ibid., 23.

10. Ibid., 37.

11. Spark, *Investigative Reporting*, op. cit., 1–2.

12. British journalist Tony Collins, quoted in Spark, *Investigative Reporting*, op. cit., 2.

13. Ibid.

14. Ibid.

15. Hayden White, *The Content of the Form: Narrative Discourse and Historical Representation* (Baltimore: Johns Hopkins University Press, 1987), 23. Cited in Ettema and Glasser, *Custodians of Conscience*, op. cit., 132.

16. Ettema and Glasser, *Custodians*, op. cit., 74.

17. 'In 1984, *Editor and Publisher* magazine reported the "death" of investigative reporting. This prognostication proved to be unnecessarily gloomy.' Ullmann, *Investigative Reporting*, op. cit., 187.

18. As philosopher Hilary Putnam put it, 'Every fact is a value-loaded and every one of our values loads some fact.' *Reason, Truth, and History*, 201. Cited in *Custodians*, op. cit., 181.

19. Ettema and Glasser, *Custodians*, op. cit., 180–1.

20. French literary theorist Roland Barthes argued long ago that facts are rhetorical devices. They work by burying the traces of their production '. . . under a self-evident appearance of eternity; it is a counter-explanation, the decorous equivalent of a tautology. . . . The foundation of the bourgeois statement of fact is common sense.' See Roland Barthes, 'Myth Today', in *Mythologies* (London: Paladin, 1973), 154–5.

21. See Gaye Tuchman's *Making News: A Study in the Social Construction of Reality* (Free Press, 1968) and Mark Fishman's *Manufacturing the News* (University of Texas Press, 1980), both cited in *Custodians*, op. cit., 159.

22. *Custodians*, op. cit., 193.

23. Spark, *Investigative Reporting*, op. cit., 6.

24. *Custodians*, op. cit., 83.

25. *Custodians*, op. cit., 85.

26. David McKie, 'Read all about it: Media magazine will resume doing its part to support investigative journalism', *Media* 10.3 (Spring 2004), 4.

27. 'The pioneer press of British North America . . . provided a useful service in an emerging colony, but it was only a tame and crude herald of things to come. A more exciting period arrived when conditions in British North America reached a stage similar to those of the American colonies three quarters of a century earlier. The press had to free itself from subservience to colonial governments, commerce had to provide a financial base for independent editors, and the society itself had to go through a ferment of political ideas before there was any hope of a press in Canada equal in vigour and effectiveness to the New England papers which had earlier fought "The Newspaper War on Britain"—as Arthur M. Schlesinger calls it in his *Prelude to Independence*.' From Wilfred Eggleston's preface to W.H. Kesterton's *A History of Journalism in Canada* (Toronto: McClelland & Stewart, 1967), vii.

28. Anita LaRoche, 'Taking notes during a reconnaissance mission!: Anita LaRoche was intrigued to learn that investigative journalists on both sides of the border encounter similar and surprising obstacles in a bid to tell stories that matter'. *Media* 10.2 (Fall 2002/Winter 2003), 12–13.

29. Alasdair Roberts, *Blacked Out: Government Secrecy in the Age of Information* (New York: Cambridge University Press, 2006).

30. A fourth Global Investigative Journalism Conference took place in spring 2007 (24 to 27 May in Toronto; www.caj.ca/events/conf-2007/index.html), following a 2005 meeting in Amsterdam that drew four hundred journalists from around the world.

Part One

# Tracking the Truth:

# The Literature of Exposure

# Chapter 1

# The Case of the Disappearing Women

For a 2001 series in the *Vancouver Sun*, reporters Lindsay Kines, Lori Culbert, and Kim Bolan ventured where police hadn't to investigate a situation that festered for years before it finally made grisly headlines: the disappearance (and, as it would turn out, murder) of dozens of young women in Vancouver's crime-ridden Downtown Eastside. The reporters began with only what the police had revealed: twenty-seven female prostitutes had gone missing from the notoriously down-and-out district. Four months later, their reportorial scrutiny sparked a strengthened police investigation that identified many more missing women and ultimately led to the arrest and trial of a suspect in what is now described as the worst case of serial killing in Canadian history.[1]

This story can actually be said to have begun as early as 1997, when Lindsay Kines, as the police beat reporter at the *Vancouver Sun*, first received a call from a woman concerned about her sister, who had apparently disappeared from the Downtown Eastside—an area home to drug addiction, violence, and the sex trade. She would turn out to be one of many sex trade workers who had gone missing from the district and whose disappearance had remained unsolved—indeed almost unnoticed—until police established an investigation in 1998.

Kines broke the story in the summer of 1998, in an article that revealed police were targeting an increase in the number of missing women, and had added a second detective to the case.[2] Police reported they had files on ten sex trade workers who had gone missing in the previous two years (sixteen over a decade, if earlier cases were counted). Community activists and advocates for the area's poor and addicted confirmed they had noticed spiking violence in the district in recent years. Police noted that crimes such as these were the hardest to solve because of the large number of potential suspects.

At this point, police regarded the various disappearances as incidents independent of each other. They did not suspect a serial killer. In fact, one official described violence against prostitutes in the city's Downtown Eastside with a single word: pandemic. Some said that violence against prostitutes generally (regardless of district) is so common that no single serial killer would be required to account for those missing from Vancouver's red-light district.

Another story followed in the fall, this one with the news that Vancouver police were beefing up their investigation, which was now reviewing forty unsolved cases of missing women dating back to 1971; sixteen of those represented sex trade workers who had gone missing from the district since 1995.[3] Police said they hoped to dispel rumours about the disappearances, which in the absence of hard information were circulating freely. They noted that the first order of police business would be to compile an accurate list of the missing, for they had, in fact, no evidence to suggest that a killer was at large, or even that the missing women were dead.

Nearly six months passed before the next stories on the issue. In March of 1999, the paper published two articles, one a front-pager updating the police review. Police now spoke of twenty cases since 1995; the announced increase was met with public demands for action.[4] The story had local prostitutes calling for a $100,000 reward to help catch the person responsible for the disappearances. Police tried to counter full-blown rumours of a serial killer by reiterating that they had no evidence to that effect. Protestors and critics meanwhile urged police to up the investigation by assigning more officers (at this point there were two) to work the case.

The second piece was a two-part feature that went straight for the heartstrings and hit its mark. In the first part of 'Missing on the Mean Streets', Kines told the poignant story of one of the missing women: how despite her advantages—a good home, good looks, and talent—she had become mired in the life of the red-light district, and gone missing from it at the age of 28, leaving behind two small children.[5] The piece opened with excerpts from the woman's diary and included interviews with her family members and friends.

Then the feature opened on to the issues, detailing the desperation of the area's drug-addicted sex trade workers. It profiled some of the cases, and quoted street workers and social critics saying society had refused its responsibility by not doing more to help the women escape the cycle of prostitution, drugs, and violence that was their lot on the Downtown Eastside. When police confirmed the number of missing at twenty since 1995, they also acknowledged that the number was continuing to grow.[6] Critics again urged police to set up a special task force.

It was at this point that a larger issue began to emerge from the news reports, and some critics began to suggest that little was being done *because* the women were sex trade workers. Such commentary pricked the public conscience by questioning whether female college students gone missing from campus wouldn't have elicited more and speedier police attention.

Kines's March 1999 stories had turned the heat up, but only briefly, and in the following years, the issue and the story languished for lack of hard evidence to link the disappearances.

Then came 2001, when the *Vancouver Sun*, frustrated by the lack of progress on the story, and led then by the legendary Neil Reynolds, took the gloves off. Reynolds assigned two more reporters to work with Kines on the story: Kim Bolan, the long-time *Sun* reporter famed for her courageous, insightful, and decades-long coverage of the Air India affair and its aftermath,[7] and Lori Culbert, the newest member of the *Sun* newsroom on the team—a woman with a flair for features and a soft-spoken and gentle manner that belie an iron will.

The A-team of reporters worked the story for four months. That's an eternity in the world of daily newspapers, and an expensive commitment, especially considering that it might not have panned out—always a risk in investigative work. But the reporters delivered, producing a hard-hitting series that consisted of two week-long runs, in September and November 2001.

Soon after the three-strong investigative team was assigned to the story, Kines conducted a breakthrough interview with Vancouver police that led to the lead story in the September 2001 series. The article reported that officials were establishing a joint RCMP–Vancouver Police task force to replace the initial 1998 Vancouver police team. There would be more resources available, and the new team would include specialized and experienced officers.[8] Police were now reviewing thirty-one missing-women cases, and looking at more than a dozen new ones, the article reported. Though they still had no hard evidence (no bodies or crime scenes), police nevertheless now allowed that the disappearances fit a pattern, that the missing women were feared dead, and that a serial killer on the loose in the Downtown Eastside was a 'strong possibility'. The story also referred to the never-caught, so-called Green River Killer, who murdered forty-nine prostitutes in the state of Washington.

The newspaper series continued through the week with revelations of how flawed the initial police investigation had been and with reaction from various sources, including friends and family members of the missing women. It ended with official promises of action to address the problems uncovered.

On 23 November 2001, the second instalment of the series opened with a report that included official police speculation about the perpetrator (now assumed). Police surmised that the killer had refined his technique and become more careful about concealing evidence. The next day saw a two-part profile by Lori Culbert on one of the missing women and a front-page story about Vancouver police meeting with detectives who had worked on the case of the Green River Killer.

The week's offerings continued to carve a wide swath of reports about police progress on the file; they included one feature about a convicted prostitute killer and another about how anxiety among sex trade workers in the Downtown Eastside was rising along with the reported numbers of the missing.

The November series ended on the 28th, with two forward-looking pieces: one about plans for a long-term detox centre for the women of the Downtown Eastside, and the other about Canadian prostitution laws, which some critics considered a major part of the problem.

Only months after the series ended, early in 2002, police arrested a suspect—Robert William Pickton, a Coquitlam pig farmer—in what was finally recognized as a case of serial killing and not a spate of unrelated crimes. In the summer of 2002, police began digging up the Pickton farm in search of evidence. Initially, Pickton was charged with two counts of first-degree murder, but as the months passed and the gory evidence mounted, more charges were added. When trial proceedings began in 2006, Pickton faced twenty-six counts. The Downtown Eastside's missing women now numbered sixty-eight.

Many articles comprised the ongoing coverage of the story, but here we'll focus on the September–November 2001 stories by Kines, Culbert, and Bolan, since these are the ones that led to an arrest in a case that had long been stuck in a wrong assumption: that the disappearances were not related and no single individual was responsible for them.

I interviewed the three reporters in the spring of 2006, nearly five years after they had written the series. That June, the Pickton trial was still hearing legal arguments on admissibility of evidence.[9] Lori Culbert was covering the trial; Kim Bolan was still at the *Sun* but had moved on to other stories; and Lindsay Kines was now at the *Victoria Times-Colonist* covering provincial politics.

# The Interview: **Lindsay Kines**
(4 April 2006)

The missing-women case began for Lindsay Kines in 1997, when as the *Vancouver Sun*'s police reporter, he got a call from a woman worried about her sister who had gone missing from the Downtown Eastside. Kines wrote a story, and then a follow-up about a year later, when another person contacted him to tell of a friend missing from the city's red-light district. The source said he'd heard about still others who had gone missing from the area. Kines started digging.

> I began checking with sources I'd developed on the police beat, and before that, while covering social services stories on the Downtown Eastside. A short time later, I did the first story [3 July 1998] on police looking at a large number of missing women from the Downtown Eastside.
>
> In the months and years after that, I did numerous other stories. As the numbers and the investigation grew, I realized the police were looking at a large number of missing women. But as the police said, people do go missing and aren't necessarily the victims of serial killers. It just looked at that point like individual stories. The police responses were also convincing: that there was nothing to suggest these cases were all linked; that they had no evidence of foul play; there were no bodies, no crime scenes.

At the time of the 1998 stories, police were investigating as many as forty disappearances dating back as far as 1971. After that, the list of the missing 'kept growing and growing'. The word on the street, Kines learned, was that women had been disappearing from the Downtown Eastside for years. Much anger was directed at police for not doing more about the situation, and some suggested the police simply didn't care about missing prostitutes. But Kines doesn't blame police.

> There were police officers concerned about this, and . . . that fuelled a lot of our stories. So, I don't want to say the police wouldn't have done this without our persistence. . . . I don't want to say that the police didn't care, because there were lots—many were my sources—who did care. And they were the ones giving me the information that fed the stories.

Although the story involved database work, court documents, and access-to-information requests, the research began as it often does in journalistic work—with people.

> We did use court records, freedom-of-information requests, and our own rudimentary database of missing and murdered sex trade workers, [but the story] was driven largely by human sources.

The reporters began by interviewing the families and friends of the missing women, as well as Vancouver police and official sources. More sources (family and friends of other missing women) began to come forward after the initial stories ran, but the reporters tended to get most of their information about the missing women from police.

The story, like so many investigations, mushroomed over time. We looked at how police conducted serial murder investigations in other jurisdictions such as Seattle and Poughkeepsie, New York. We looked at previous murder cases in BC. We mined court records for reports on attacks on sex trade workers. Operating on the principle that some of the women may have been murdered and their bodies hidden, we also put together a database of all the missing women, as well as solved and unsolved murders of sex trade workers in BC, to see if we could spot any patterns. And we filed a freedom-of-information request that paid dividends with a confidential report showing how strapped the Vancouver Police Department [VPD] was for resources throughout the missing-women investigation.

    I was thinking, 'This is an amazing story . . . the numbers are so much higher than we'd been told.' And Lori did amazing work in tracking down some of those family members. . . . I essentially got leaked some names, and then we went about trying to track down that, in fact, they were missing, and that the police were looking at them. The names were from many different police sources . . . cases had been reported to other detachments that had never been forwarded to the Vancouver Police Department—those were just some of the jurisdictional problems of that investigation.

The defining moment for Kines came with a breakthrough interview in September of 2001, when he contacted a police source who agreed to discuss all the problems with the VPD's initial handling of the case.

    My call seemed to catch the source at the right moment, of frustration with the case, and ready to talk. The first meeting lasted about four hours, and provided the basis for one of the key stories in our series that exposed serious problems with the police handling of the file. . . . My having been on the beat for a long time, having been on that story for a long time—it established some trust. They wanted to spill the beans . . . I just happened to call at the right time.

The interview allowed Kines to write the lead stories to the 2001 series. Before the interview, the reporters were still looking for a way to break the story.

    We had been assigned to do this project, and we actually didn't know what the focus of the project was going to be. We wanted to do more on the missing-women case, but we didn't know what sort of tactic, what angle it was going to follow. It was a matter of calling around to sources and saying, 'Can we sit down and talk?'

    I could tell right away from this one call [to the Vancouver police source] that there was something more there than just an update on the case. I was stunned after that meeting, at some of the revelations. I just had no idea that there were so many problems with that initial investigation. So, that was the big one, the one that led to the main story of the series . . . about how the police investigation was flawed.

Some of the major obstacles the story presented were the same ones faced by police investigators.

> There was no proof that any of the women had met with foul play. There were no bodies, no crime scenes. Police would frequently say there was no evidence that a serial killer was at work, and it was difficult to refute that claim. It also made it difficult to generate new angles on the story, since each disappearance followed a similar pattern. I think that tended to undermine interest in the story among editors, because it was often as if you were telling the same story over and over again about families that hadn't heard from their daughter or sister for a long time, about police efforts to find her, always with the line that they had no proof she had met with foul play.

Another burden imposed by the story was one of conscience.

> The story does weigh on your conscience . . . because it's also not the sole story you're working on. I wasn't an investigative reporter assigned to this exclusively—I was a police beat reporter. So you're doing any number of other stories. Meanwhile this case is in the back of your mind.

If he had it all to do over again, he would have been less accepting of official information from authorities.

> I would have more closely scrutinized what, exactly, the police were doing and what resources they were devoting to the case. Later, I learned from police sources that their investigation was not nearly as comprehensive as they made it out to be. A number of the people working on the investigation were inexperienced. Some were holding more than one job. And they simply didn't have the resources to devote to such a complex case. But I didn't know that early on, and knowing what I know now, I should have asked some tougher questions: What is the experience of these people? How many [officers] do they have? Are they working on this full time? Questions that seem obvious in hindsight.

The question of the right approach on this story continues to haunt him.

> I'm still torn on this one. If I'd come on as some sort of pit bull, maybe I wouldn't have developed the trust with these people and later on maybe they wouldn't have given the information they gave me. I'm at the leg now[10] and I do take more of this adversarial role, maybe because of that experience—you know, grilling these politicians. But I also feel that because they see you as an adversary, it's

much tougher to develop sources. I don't think I've been nearly as effective here at developing inside sources as I was on the police beat.

So, I don't know that I've found the perfect balance. It's almost like there are two ways of approaching it: you can be this soft-spoken, self-effacing person that slowly builds trust, or you can come on as the pit bull. I think you can get stories both ways. It's easier with politicians: they do have to come and talk to you each day because they want to get elected. It's tough to do that with the cops, because they just freeze you out. If they knew you as a pit bull, they probably wouldn't have sat down with you either.

The follow-up to the missing-women story is bound to be at least as compelling as the tale itself, but it won't begin in earnest until the Pickton trial has concluded.

If he [Pickton] is convicted, the obvious question to be pursued is why he eluded police for so long. Our investigation determined that he had surfaced as a suspect early in the police investigation, but for whatever reason—possibly a police jurisdictional battle—he wasn't arrested until years later. The police really need to explain how that happened, as a number of women died in the intervening years.

A lot was made of the idea, seized on by frustrated critics, that because the women were prostitutes, they didn't matter to police, to the press, or to the public at large. Kines holds a different view.

I never met any police officers who felt that way; the reporters certainly didn't feel that way. But you know, institutionally, I think there's probably some truth to that. I think, culturally, there is some truth to that. If you had a whole bunch of women going missing from a different sector of society, from suburbia, say, then there might have been more attention paid to it earlier and more resources put into it. The counter-argument [is that] there are more possible explanations for someone to go missing from the Downtown Eastside than from suburbia, given the level of violence and crime. . . . But we did find that was a sort of myth as well—these women did have connections with family, they did have friends who knew about their whereabouts and noticed that they weren't around.

The stories ultimately prompted authorities to allocate more staff, time, and other resources to the police investigation. Kines also believes that 'police became more attentive in their dealings with family members following our reporting.'[11]

One thing I've never been able to assess is what the impact of our series was on the police, but I've heard from people behind the scenes that they certainly believe it did result in getting more resources for their task force, or at least not losing the ones they had. I've heard from police sources that the stories made a difference. The task force was up and running by the time our series of stories ran. But I think they were able to secure more resources, get what they needed to stick with it.

It's always hard to measure what comes first, but I know that the Vancouver Police Department and the RCMP were already working together. From the spring of that year, they had decided they needed to do more; our series ran in the fall.

The initial Vancouver Police Department investigation had been badly flawed, and once the new joint task force with the RCMP was struck in the spring of 2001, detectives determined not to repeat early errors.

I think they were much more careful about wanting to do it right. Certainly they said that to us the second time around. They said, 'Look, we want to make sure we do this thoroughly and properly.'

In the fall, I think they were expecting it be a long, long haul to try to find a suspect. So, I think it was partially a fluke and partly good preparation that they were able to identify a suspect so quickly. [Pickton was initially charged with two counts of first-degree murder in February 2002, only months after the newspaper series ran.]

An article the *Vancouver Sun* ran online on 6 November 2002, entitled 'How Lindsay Kines and *Sun* reporters broke the missing-women story', says the reporters eventually identified forty-five missing women, though when they began reporting, police had announced an official count of only twenty-seven.[12] But Kines explained that the situation was more complex than the summary article might suggest.

I think that note is maybe a bit misleading. We came out with a list, this expanded list, before the police did, but much of that information came from the police; it came from sources that said they were looking at more names. Then we managed to get some of the names, track down the families, and confirm that they were missing, or confirm that they had been found or located or whatever. So I think the police knew about all the names, but they hadn't officially released them. We were able to break it before they released it, which I think put more pressure on them as well.

Kines eschews the term *investigative reporter*. He does not consider himself one, and he believes it was his beat expertise, not his investigative skills, that allowed him to break the missing-women story. Underestimating the power of beat reporting, Kines further maintains, is a common error in newsroom management.

I've never called myself an investigative reporter. I'm just a reporter. But I believe that any good reporting, by definition, should be investigative. Covering the police beat improved my reporting immensely, because that's where I first learned how to develop and work with sources.

The police beat is good training, because you have to earn the trust of police officers by producing fair and accurate reports over a period of time. Once they see that you can be trusted, you start getting greater access to information, including information that may be critical of their own organization. If I hadn't been covering the police for six years, I don't believe officers would have trusted me enough to tell me about the myriad problems with the original missing-women investigation.

I regard this story as investigative because it required that the reporters work consistently and for a prolonged period in the face of potentially hostile establishment forces and against the odds. At the same time, the work clearly stemmed from police-beat reporting. Kines agrees that the story required 'working for a long time and consistently' but 'on a particular beat,' which is what 'enabled me to develop the sources.'

I didn't develop the sources working specifically on the missing-women case; it was from working about six, seven years, on the police beat itself. Over that period of time, if people see that you at least try to be fair, accurate, and balanced, they'll call you. Many of the sources I used on the missing-women stories, I developed on other stories completely unrelated to the missing-women case, and much earlier in my time on the beat.

Keeping in touch with sources over time is critical, because the minor official that acts as a source on one story may become a major official a decade or two later, and so be in a position to help out a trusted reporter.

Particularly on the police beat, it's really important [to maintain contacts] because if you do a feature on a constable, ten years later he or she's maybe a sergeant or an inspector, with access to a lot more inside information, and that's exactly what happened. Some people whom I had interviewed and got to know on completely unrelated stories were eventually in positions where they could feed me a lot more information.

There's a reason for the beat system at newspapers, most reporters agree. It's been around 'for a long time and for good reason'.

It's the best way, I think, to develop good sources and to get good story ideas, particularly on the police beat. I think one of the mistakes newspapers make is they move people off it too quickly. I think it takes a minimum of five years to develop really good sources on that beat. Cops take a long time to learn to trust you. You have to have a really good reputation, and that will start opening doors for you. And you want a lot of sources so that they can't trace it back to one. They don't know where it's coming from. That takes a long time to do. [The police beat] is an especially rich source that by its very nature often defines many of the front-page stories.

Another essential ingredient in getting the missing-women series to run in the *Sun* was management support at the highest levels.

We would not have got that story if we hadn't had an editor at the time, Neil Reynolds, who was willing to free up reporters for long periods of time. You have to have a little bit of breathing time in order to go and meet with somebody on the prospect that you might not have a story at the end of it. It's increasingly rare in newspapers to be given that kind of time. And if you have to turn a story around each time, I don't know if you'd be able to do that at most places. Neil Reynolds freed three reporters up for essentially four months at that paper.

We didn't have those stories or angles or information when that started; we essentially had nothing. It was a bunch of calling around and trying to figure out where to go with this—just calling on everybody I knew associated with the case. It's partially luck, but partially just being given the time to dig. We wouldn't have done that without Neil Reynolds, and Noreen Rasbach [since moved to *The Globe and Mail*], who was the most hands-on editor. But Neil was certainly the one who gave the word to free up three reporters for four months. I mean we just wouldn't have done that work while juggling other stories at the same time—it just wouldn't have happened.

Kines is from a small town in Manitoba called Birtle. He knew from his teenage years that he wanted to be a journalist.

I knew very early, like in high school, that that's what I wanted to do. I think it was, frankly, from reading a fiction book about a reporter, and I was just intrigued by that ability to hold people to account through writing and reporting. I went to Red River Community College in Winnipeg; they had a creative communications program, and as you can imagine, it was sort of a broad spectrum. But you could specialize in the second year, and I specialized in journalism.

I had a summer job at the *Russell Banner*. It was a weekly paper near my hometown, and I was fortunate because the college program had a work-experience, on-the-job training. The training lasted about four weeks—two two-week stints—and I took both of mine at the *Brandon Sun*, which was a good little independent paper and family owned. I didn't realize at the time how fortunate I was, that [such a paper] was a dying breed. The *Sun* was a small paper; it had a circulation of, I think, only about eighteen thousand. But we had seven or eight city-side reporters—it was fantastic.

When I look back, I was so fortunate to start there. We had a really supportive editor. I mean, my first two-week stint at the *Brandon Sun*, it was all young reporters, we were all in our early twenties, and everybody was just out of college. And I thought, 'I have to be here, I have to get back here' . . . So I stayed there for about six years and then went to the *Vancouver Sun*.

Kines offers some advice to aspiring journalists:

I've learned to trust my gut more, and stick with a story even if, early on, editors, friends, and colleagues don't think it's as important as I do. If you think there's a story there, stay with it, keep pushing and writing stories. I've learned that officials can easily ignore one story—even a big one. But it's much more difficult for them to ignore a flood of stories generated by a reporter doggedly pursuing something that he or she believes is important.

There's an aftermath benefit as well: good stories boost morale in the newsroom.

I think that reporters take pride in their paper; they want to believe their paper is out in front . . . even if there are petty jealousies and things within the newsroom, I think you want to believe that you're working for a good paper that has its heart in the right place.

Like many of the ace reporters interviewed, Lindsay Kines is motivated largely by the desire to make a difference. At the time of our talk, he had been working on stories about BC's child-protection system, which came under intense scrutiny after a series of stories about children who had died while in care arrangements financed or subsidized by the provincial government.[13] It's an area of reportage that Kines feels is important to pursue, and Kines is a reporter who knows the value of persistence. He learned it the journalistic way.

I think we [he at the *Times Colonist* and Lori Culbert at the *Vancouver Sun*] did more than seventy stories last year on the Sherry Charlie case[14] and child protection, over about nine months. And I think our pressure led to a number of, or at least influenced, a lot of these reviews that have been launched into child protection. So that would be one recently that made a difference.

# The Interview: **Kim Bolan**
(6 March 2006)

Kim Bolan is the reporter famous for her courageous (death-threat-defying) coverage of the 23 June 1985 story on the Air India bombing—work that earned her the 1999 Courage in Journalism Award. Bolan had just joined the *Vancouver Sun* newsroom the previous year when she began working on Air India in 1985. She is the author of *Loss of Faith: How the Air-India Bombers Got Away with Murder* (McClelland & Stewart, 2005). She largely deferred to Lindsay Kines on the missing-women story, pointing to his critical role in keeping the story alive. She said the lion's share of credit for the series belongs to Kines, whose commitment to the case never flagged.

> Lindsay is the man on the missing women. It was just unbelievable how committed he was to the story, long before anybody else cared about it—literally four or five years before.

By the time she was assigned to the team investigating the missing-women story, Bolan had established herself as a senior reporter with her coverage of the Air India case. That experience taught her a lot about the craft of journalism and about herself.

> Air India has taught me that the story is much bigger than the petty competitive bitches. And it's actually fun, on investigative stories. It's actually fun to work with other people. Also it was a stressful topic, because both of us ended up getting lots of regular calls from really marginalized people who were friends of the women or women working the streets themselves or family members. When they're calling you night and day and it gets stressful—you have somebody else you can talk to about the issues. And then, when it got gory, when we actually knew what was found on the farm . . .

Bolan may have earned her stripes with her coverage of the Air India bombing, but like all reporters, she knows she's only as good as her last story. She's far from resting on her laurels, or even slowing down. 'Air India is extraordinary because most stories don't go on for twenty years,' she said. 'But, you know, I'm sticking with it.'

When we spoke in the spring of 2006, Bolan had just returned from addressing students at Toronto's Ryerson University about *guerrilla journalism*—her term for reportorial work that pushes the envelope of journalistic conventions.

> Because I've carved out a niche for myself and have officially accomplished a lot journalistically, I do have more freedom [than newer or less-accomplished col-

leagues]. But I always have to fight. You fight for time, you fight for space, you fight for commitment to an issue or story.

Has it got harder to practise guerrilla journalism at newspapers in the last ten or twenty years?

Sometimes it's harder, but if I didn't think there was room there, I wouldn't work in this job. Reporters are, I think, by our nature—we spend a good chunk of our time miserable. It's just part of the way we are, the Eeyores of the profession.[15]

But, if you feel like you're successful ten, twenty per cent of the time, that's still worth it. And I do think you have to take the good with the bad. I try to be a very hard-working person. Some people when they get discouraged or demoralized, they don't put the energy [into stories] that they used to.

I think it is harder to do investigative journalism; people are worried about the legal liabilities, the stress, but it's still being done. Also, in some ways, it's easier because we have access to so much more information than we've ever had before. So maybe there's a trade-off: you don't get as much time to do it, but with access to information and the Internet, et cetera, you can stumble across much more stuff.

And also, reporters need to be prepared to go out, because you can't do this job strictly by telephone—it's never as good. I do my share of phone stories, like this one I did yesterday. It came in as a news tip last week. There was this guy [a priest], he used to work at this Catholic group home for mentally challenged people in Burnaby, BC, and he'd been charged [with abusing children] and nobody seemed to know, and now he's working for the church with kids in Bellingham.

So you think, this seems interesting, and you follow it up and you get documentation, and then you say, 'Oh my god, the church has been covering this up—this is unbelievable.' I had most of the story in hand Friday, through documents that somebody faxed me, but I still had the sense that it would be better if I went to Bellingham and confronted this priest at mass on Sunday.

That's exactly what she did.

I didn't have to do that; in fact, they probably won't pay me for working Sunday [here she gives a deep, throaty chuckle], but it sure was a lot better story because I did that. I got a sense of this guy, where he lived, his house, and everything else. So sometimes the difference between a good story and a great story is just going that extra distance.

For Bolan, much of what can be said about investigative reporting depends on how the term is defined or understood.

I've sort of developed a new theory about these things in terms of what has the most impact. The volume of stories that sometimes are played less prominently, that may unfold over a long period of time, I think can have more impact than the kind of pre-packaged investigative journalism.

My prime example is Air India, where you just stay on it for twenty years. I would categorize a good portion of the work I've done as investigative work. Sometimes you're doing fifteen-inch stories; sometimes they're buried. But there are developments, and the fact that you're on it all the time makes you more influential in bringing about change, bringing the full truth out, which to me is the ultimate goal of a journalist: having the whole story come out, not just a chunk of it on a given day.

She believes that guerrilla journalism offers more scope and covers more potential territory than much of what is called investigative journalism.

What I'm calling guerrilla journalism is something that can be practised by smaller papers, digging into a story. And it can also be practised when a story may not be the kind of sexy issue that does get the investigative reporting dollars at a bigger paper. Because I just did that talk [at Ryerson] two weeks ago, I've been thinking a lot about this. I even had some Sikh spies [people linked to a Canadian Sikh federation] come to Ryerson. It was quite funny, it was all set up in advance, I found out later. I got like ten pages of new Internet death threats.

You realize you're in a war to get the truth out, and sometimes your opponents are the people that don't want you reporting on them; sometimes they're the limitations of the corporation for which you work; and sometimes they're your own editors who get really tired of the story and want you to quit. But you just don't do it; you come up with creative ways to keep the story alive. So it's guerrilla in the sense that you have to adopt creative tactics—non-traditional tactics and means—sometimes to do your job. And that would be the thinking-on-your-feet part. I'll go out and meet anybody or talk to anybody at any time, even if they seem to be slightly insane.

Whether you call it investigative or guerrilla reporting, this kind of in-depth work takes a personal toll. For most reporters, it gets hard at times to draw a line, to know where their responsibility ends. Bolan recalled writing a recent story about a disabled trucker who had been fighting the Workers Compensation Board for eight years, and finally ended up committing suicide. For weeks afterward, people with WCB problems were calling Bolan, asking her to write *their* stories, and some of them even threatened suicide.

I'm not a mental health professional, but you know, the reality is you do offer hope to people when you wade into these issues. I mean what kind of moral and community responsibility *do* you have to follow up afterwards? So I do find it really, really hard. And there are lots of times when I think, oh my, I don't want to do this.

What keeps her going is a sense of social obligation, something else learned and honed on the Air India story.

I think I have a sense of duty, which is, it's kind of corny . . . I call it my *sewa* because that's what the Sikhs have always told me: it's your *sewa*. In Sikhism, *sewa* is a tenet of the religion; you have to serve selflessly, without any gain coming back to you, and that's your service—your *sewa*. They used to say that to me whenever they phoned me on my day off. I'd say, 'But it's my day off,' and they'd say, 'But it's your *sewa*; you have to do this.' So I use *sewa* to describe it, regardless of whether it's a Sikh story or not. I do have a sense of service toward my community. And sometimes it's in conflict with my employer, too, because I feel that I'm writing my stories for my readers, not for CanWest Global.

Like Kines, Bolan dislikes the term *investigative journalism* because 'all journalism is investigative'. She sees herself performing the role of 'midwife' to the truth, ensuring that it emerges whole.

I'm just trying to help the truth come out. Let's face it: there are a lot of people who would rather have us not report certain things or have us let something go.

## The Interview: **Lori Culbert**
(12 May 2006)

Lori Culbert, like Kim Bolan, came aboard the missing-women story in 2001.

Lindsay had been writing about women disappearing from the Downtown Eastside since the late 1990s, and he came to me in early 2001 and asked if I'd be interested in working on a project with him about it. We talked to our bosses and they were very supportive, but it came mainly from Lindsay and then we jumped on board, Kim and I.

In 2001, after the early stories by Kines, all that the members of the investigative team had to go on, aside from police updates, were rumours of foul play that went back years. The rumours turned out to be a good place to start digging.

There was talk in the Downtown Eastside about a pig farmer who was picking up women, but the women never returned. We can't pin it down exactly [how long these rumours had been circulating], but certainly there are advocates and there are relatives who say they started hearing rumours in the late '90s. Now, it's really hard to substantiate that.

I would say the other advantage was Neil Reynolds. It's interesting, because Neil, whom I very much admire for his love of long-narrative journalism, had said to us that he wanted as part of the package an extremely long exposé, a look at one of the women's lives. That kind of fell into my lap, and at the time, one of the women who were missing was Dawn Crey, the sister of a fairly vocal Native activist in BC, Ernie Crey. And I thought, 'Well, I know Ernie. Ernie's very familiar with the media. Okay this is a good place to start. He can help me track things down.'

I was so naive going into this thinking that I could turn around such a long story in a short period of time. It probably took me about three months to piece together.[16] Dawn was about four years old when social services came in and removed her and the other six or eight siblings in the family from their home and put them, scattered them, in white foster homes throughout the region. She jumped from foster home to foster home to the street to all these various places. She was 45 when she finally disappeared. It took me so long; I was going through old city hall records about where people lived and phone numbers and that kind of thing, to try to track down where she was in different parts of her life, because no one knew.

No one knew where she was at a certain time. No one was tracking her life. It's just so sad. If I went missing, my mother or my husband or someone would know where I went to school and where I lived in certain years. It was this massive puzzle to try to fit all the pieces together, going through old archived court records to figure out when she was in jail and when she wasn't. It was really a huge exercise, but I think in the end, I know that the family was really pleased to have it, because there were just so many questions about where her life had taken her.

So I walked into that being pretty naive. I thought it was going to be something that wouldn't take a lot of research—and it really did take a long, long time.

Culbert was moved by the plight of the women, and worked hard to make apparent to readers what was beginning to take powerful shape in her own mind: essentially a variation on 'there but for fortune go you and I'. She said she wanted to get across in the story that tough breaks and hard times afflict humans with largely indiscriminate regularity. She learned that the sex trade workers of the Downtown Eastside, for all the severity of their problems, were pretty much like people everywhere else.

They are not in a situation that they wanted to be in, and they would so love to be in a different situation. But it's a struggle for them to get out.

The research was intensive and what it was uncovering was potentially explosive. So the timing of the stories in the series was crucial.

> It was very sensitive information that we had, obviously, and we really didn't want—oh, how can I say this properly—we wanted to try to keep as much under wraps as possible about what we were uncovering until publication date. We were concerned that if the police found out the avenues we were investigating, there might be some effort on their part to talk to our bosses about not publishing it. So we made the decision that the day before the first part of our series was to run would be the day that I would start trying to find the families. We just wanted to limit the number of people we were interviewing who might have a communication line back to people who might not want this series published.
>
> We had it through police sources, a list of about twenty-five women who the RCMP/Vancouver police review team thought might be added to the list of missing women. And the list of missing women at that point stood at twenty-seven. I had done as much background work as I could prior to the day before.
>
> I was trying to track down [from this list of twenty-five new names] relatives and friends, people who might know them, so that on the day before, I could start phoning and try to determine whether or not these women truly were missing, or if they were missing, if they fit the profile of the other women on the list. So that day we whittled the twenty-five down to eighteen—what we considered to be eighteen women who were truly missing and who truly fit the profile of the other women who had gone missing from the Downtown Eastside.
>
> And it turns out, our number was accurate, because the police came out—we ran in September—in December and confirmed that they were adding eighteen names to the list. It's funny: police obviously do their investigations in a different way, but some of the women who were on that list of twenty-five weren't actually missing any more. They had been reported missing, but it took a phone call or two to determine that they were alive and well and somewhere else. There was another woman who had disappeared from Victoria, but in speaking to different people who knew her there, [I learned] she had never been a sex trade worker and it didn't appear that she should be on that list of missing women.
>
> There were other women whose family and friends I contacted where it was very clear that they had made reports to the Vancouver police in the 1990s and that very little had been done, that they felt that their loved ones who were last seen on the Downtown Eastside should be on the list, and probably should have been on the list for many years earlier.

Culbert was covering the Pickton trial at the time of our interview; she was in a tight spot with regard to some of my questions about the story, especially since the trial was then in its *voir dire* stage (when the court, without a jury present and before the trial proper begins, determines whether evidence is admissible). In short, she knew more than she was at liberty to disclose.

> I'm in a difficult position. I know the answers to some of these questions now because I'm covering Pickton's *voir dire*, but everything in it is covered by a publication ban on all the evidence that we're hearing. So I know more than I'm allowed to say at this point. I can really speak only to what I did know in 2001.

The 2001 research took the reporters to the heart of the story: the mean streets of Vancouver's Downtown Eastside. Culbert was pregnant at the time of the series; in fact, she gave birth before the last of the stories ran.

> Kim, Lindsay, and I—we were out in the Downtown Eastside, on the stroll, at midnight, at one in the morning, talking to women. And I was massively pregnant, and just thinking at the time how different the situation was for me personally [from what] it was for the women we were writing about.
>
> I was embarking on having my first child. It was very exciting. And these women, this one woman in particular that Kim and I spoke to quite a bit, who was . . . a sex trade worker, and her daughter and niece were, too. She was looking over them, watching out for them. Their lives were so much different from my life. Even though you tell yourself that you're doing good work that will maybe one day help them, it's still really tough.
>
> The one thing about the women who work on the street is that society can turn a blind eye; they can think, 'Oh you know that isn't my relative, that isn't my friend.' But I tell you, you meet these women, and you get to know them and, they're people obviously with hopes and dreams not unlike your own. They're women who never planned to be where they ended up, women who have the most amazing strength and courage to endure the abuse that they do. And who feel that there's no one in society who's listening to them, looking out for them.

Culbert had a chance to do some research further afield in an attempt to understand how other police forces coped with such cases.

> Kim and I travelled to Seattle and we talked to a couple of different police agencies in Washington about how they handled serial killer cases involving sex trade workers. And one of them was the Green River Killer, [a case that] Gerry Ridgeway, of course, has been recently convicted on. It was very interesting to talk to them about some of the different techniques that the police in the States used and compare them to the techniques that were being used in Vancouver. I think those series of stories were also really helpful to show that there were different ways to approach cases like this, and other police agencies had had success in other cities with different approaches.

She agrees that the defining moment for the series as a whole was the breakthrough interview that Kines had with a VPD police officer. It allowed the team to launch the series and set the stage for the major revelations that then ensued. That's when

Culbert began to feel the weight of the story. The discrepancy between the initial numbers of the missing that police had announced and the large jump in that number was an eye-opener for Culbert—that was when she understood how important the work was.

> Because of Lindsay's reputation—he's a reporter who can be trusted and the police knew that—the [interview] was absolutely the biggest, biggest break into this case. I think one of the issues was just working on that list of twenty-five and feeling like we were getting close to proving that the list was much longer than the police had ever publicly said. It made us feel that we were pursuing a story that was so important, because to say that there are twenty-seven missing women versus forty-five—I mean the jump just seemed so huge and so important for the public to know. Knowing that, we put months and months of work into a project that actually was going to show the number of women missing—it just seemed such an important thing to be doing.

The reporters were worried about revealing too much, and tried to strategize the scheduling of the work so as to avoid as much as possible the chance of outside interference with their work (a dilemma Kines also referred to), at least until they could nail down the story.

> It's not that we would have ever thought that our bosses would have caved under police pressure not to run it. I'm not saying that, I'm not passing any kind of judgment on current or previous bosses. It's just that we felt that we were investigating in an area that was fairly sensitive and the task force was in the past and continues to be today extremely sensitive about the information that is released to the public. We had done some sit-down interviews with the higher-ups in the task force, but we just thought that it would be wise to keep what we knew as close to just as few people knowing as possible. And you have to keep in mind, too, for a story like that, we were relying on sources within police departments. So if there's pressure within a police department to refrain from talking to us— either on or off the record—that makes things complicated.

Other obstacles included finding the families of the missing women, and gaining their trust.

> These were family members who had been ignored in some cases for years by the establishment, not only by police or politicians but also by the media. They, I'm sure, phoned newsrooms and asked that we publicize the fact that their loved one was missing, and newspapers weren't giving the kind of attention to a missing sex trade worker as they would have to a missing college student, or something comparable. It definitely was challenging to try to get them to want to talk after all those years.

> The ones who did speak with us, I think for some of them it was suddenly so much so quickly. You know, they had gone for years and years in obscurity and no one was listening and then suddenly we were writing all these stories and running pictures of their loved ones, and I sometimes wonder if we couldn't have done a better job of preparing them for that. Because we know as journalists that we're working on this massive project and we're talking to these people, but it all happens so quickly. I think for some of them it was a really good process, and I think for others it was really hard to go through.
>
> As far as how did I do it, I guess it's just something I've built up over the years. Different journalists are good at different things, and I guess one of the things that I've learned to do over the years is to talk to people in a compassionate way and try to talk to them about the pros and cons of being in the paper and getting their story out there.

It's important to report thoroughly and not be squeamish, but it's also important not to come on like a pit bull, especially with stories as source-dependent as this one.

> For the series and since the series, we have really relied on the families. They're a tremendous resource for us. You need to be compassionate when you're dealing with them. There are people in some cases who have a loved one who is now confirmed dead, and in other cases—you know there are still thirty families who don't have answers and they're almost in a more difficult situation because they just have no idea, and may never know in some of the oldest cases.

Culbert would have done only one thing differently: better prepare the families who did consent to talk to reporters for the coming onslaught of media attention.

> There were a couple of family members I just wish we had spent more time preparing for the massiveness of the project. Because not only did we have the pictures of the new eighteen women splashed across the *Vancouver Sun*, but then of course every media outlet in the city and most national outlets were starting to pick up on the story. I think they were inundated with media requests and that's not always a positive experience. Some of the families I heard from afterward were just feeling shell-shocked about the whole thing and I think that's one of my regrets, that there wasn't more time. I think that's something very valuable that I've learned: when you're dealing with very vulnerable people, you need to spend a bit more time preparing them for what's to come.

When Pickton was arrested in February 2002, Culbert was supposed to be enjoying her maternity leave with her first child.

> It should have been a time that I was thrilled to be at home, but I just wanted to be at work, because after our second series ran in November, it was really only

three months, well less than three months, two and a half months, before Pickton was charged. So it was a time that the resources of the task force were increased substantially, officers were put on to the task force, the list of missing women continued to grow. Publicly, the police were saying that there were more and more women on the list, and then suddenly we've got a suspect. It was really—I'm trying to find the right word—it was really an exhilarating time, watching the fruits of our labour take shape.

Some years after the 2001 stories ran, Culbert gave birth to a second child. At the time of our interview, she was back on the beat, covering the Pickton trial.

I've now had my second child, so I've gone on a couple of mat leaves since all of that. But I'm now back and I'm predominantly writing about Pickton and the missing women. Since the *voir dire* started in January, my paper has been very, very good about setting me aside on covering Pickton. I'm also writing as much as I can about the missing women, the families, the families that still don't know where their loved ones are, and about some of the issues of the Downtown Eastside. My paper's been very good about letting me do that. I think we're all aware of the fact that this is still an ongoing issue in our community and that the arrest of one man does not make all the other problems go away.

That's a critically important point, and the reporters I interviewed made it repeatedly. A great investigative story can make an essential difference to the problems it uncovers, but it cannot, by itself, solve the problems. As Culbert noted, the problems of the Downtown Eastside remain.

I just got an email [in early May 2006] from an activist on the Downtown Eastside, and she said she's counted thirty posters of missing sex trade workers back up, taped all over hydro poles in the Downtown Eastside. She's saying that it's still happening. Now, perhaps it's the work of another serial killer or it's the problems that we have in society of not supporting these women to help them get off the street, and drifting for whatever reason. But this is certainly an issue—from small children who are in social services who when they become adults are most vulnerable to hit the streets—those are all issues that I think are so important for a newspaper to cover and investigate.

It would be lovely to imagine that the stories somehow 'fixed' what was wrong in the city's red-light district, but of course, the stories can only explicate the problem, they cannot do the fixing. How, then, does this reporter see her role in the aftermath of the story, covering the trial and its eventual outcome?

I'm in a courthouse four days a week, taking copy and writing, stockpiling stories that can't run until we don't know when. But it's so important that we're there. Because we're chronicling, and, quite frankly, at this point what Pickton is alleged to have done is almost not the most important thing of what we're learning in this courtroom. It's how the system went wrong; it's how the police investigation started, what happened, what kind of resources were there, how this case was approached from the beginning. Those are really the issues that we need to be learning more about so that police resources can be properly funded in the future.

Culbert came to the newspaper business after earning an English degree from Queen's University in Kingston and then a journalism degree at Humber College in Toronto. The story of how she broke in to the newspaper business reflects the same kind of quiet determination that sees her through difficult stories. And like her colleagues Kines and Bolan, Culbert doesn't consider herself an investigative reporter. 'I mean it sounds so snobbish or elitist or something,' she said. 'And I do overnight stories like everybody else at my paper.'

As for what great reporting requires, Culbert hesitates to propound any theories. She sees herself motivated by curiosity, by wanting to dig and find out more. And like so many reporters, she didn't plan to be a journalist; it was more as if she fell into it, and then discovered after the fact, like a delayed reaction, that she'd found her calling.

If you want to know the truth, I graduated from Queen's, and as most Queen's grads, you fall out of the bubble of Kingston and think that the world's at your feet, like they taught you at Queen's. And then I got essentially a secretary's job in Toronto for $17,000 and realized I had no skills. So, I phoned up Ryerson and they laughed at me because I was so late in applying.

Ryerson's loss turned out to be the gain of Humber College, where Culbert did apply and was able to register.

I have to say it was the best thing I've ever done. I got an internship at the *Toronto Star* in my second year. I got great clips at the *Star* and you know that's what you need in journalism—you need to get published. It was a crime reporter position at the *Star*, then it just kept going. But when I was in university, I didn't know what I wanted to do.

Culbert may not call her reporting investigative, but she does distinguish the everyday reportage from the stuff that makes her proudest of her line of work.

I look at work that Lindsay did in Victoria and that we did at our paper on the child protection system in BC. And I just don't know how long this would have continued in a fairly marginal system if there hadn't been some sort of public outcry. I'm just so proud to be a reporter on days like that. You feel as if you forced the government to make some changes.

Call it whatever you like, says Culbert. What it all amounts to is impact: a difference made. And the profession offers no recompense quite like knowing that you have helped to make that difference.

It was pretty exciting being in Victoria in the budget lockup when they announced the hundred million dollars for child welfare issues and called it the 'children's budget'—that's when it feels great. You're doing your job well and you're serving the public, at least a little bit.[17]

Beneath the surface of the ever-humble Culbert, hesitant to offer advice from on high or even call attention to herself, is a quiet but iron-willed determination to make that difference, to be part of the solution and not the problem. A case in point is the story of how she got her first job in the newspaper business.

I guess I ended up in Vancouver because I irritated the deputy managing editor so much. I was emailing and faxing him story ideas every day for about three months, and he finally said to me, 'If I give you a job for three months will you stop writing to me?' That was in 1996. I was at the *Edmonton Sun*, and I had been in Edmonton for two years. I only wanted to be there for a year.

I was determined to get onto a broadsheet. And it was at a time when there weren't a lot of newspapers hiring. So I just kept sending them story ideas and I would critique the paper every day and then send them follow-up ideas for the stories. I'm not saying that's necessarily good advice. I'm sure there are editors who would just tell you to go away.

She did feel comfortable offering one piece of advice, though: a journalistic variation on the golden rule.

I think my only advice would be when you're interviewing, just to approach people the way you would want to be approached. Obviously there are different situations. If you're interviewing the chief coroner because you think he's running a bad service, you're going to be interviewing him slightly differently from a person on the street. But I just think if you treat people with respect, they're usually willing to open up. They're usually willing to talk, if you treat them kindly and you tell their story accurately.

# Commentary

The instructional points to be extracted from this story are many, but they must begin with an appreciation of the invisibility dilemma: how low social status of a victimized group can allow serialized horror to go unnoticed by police and press alike. Further lessons involve the kinds of skills needed to persevere in the investigation of unsolved crimes, especially when law-enforcement officials are apathetic or divided among themselves and you may be the only reporter on the case. The appropriate response to such situations is research, research, and more research. By the thoroughness of their research, these reporters were able to help advance a criminal case.

That three reporters were assigned for four months to the missing-women story highlights the need for management support at the highest level—a fact all three reporters were quick to acknowledge. But it underscores as well the seminal role that a single reporter's conscience and instinct can play in winning that newsroom commitment for a story and the mandating of required resources to cover it. Ultimately, this series owed its being to one reporter's initially lonely conviction that there was a story here worth pursuing.

The lucky break in the story, by the reporters' own accounting, was Lindsay Kines's breakthrough interview with Vancouver police. But for this series, as for most investigative work, the lucky break had more skill and knowledge in it than luck (although another way to look at it would be to say the skill and knowledge made the luck possible). Kines had spent years developing his sources on the police beat and his reputation for fairness and accuracy as a reporter who could be trusted.

Investigative reporting is expensive, especially since there's no guarantee at the outset that the story will work out or in the end be worth the expense. The *Sun* put three reporters on the story for four months—that's a year of reporter-power invested. Even so, the reporters tried to strategize the timing of the work in order to avoid as much as possible any untoward interference with the story's progress and eventual publication.

The *Vancouver Sun* is a major player in the daily newspaper industry in Canada, but what about smaller papers serving smaller communities? Can they really engage in this sort of in-depth work, as Kim Bolan suggested? The Canadian Association of Journalists (CAJ) gives out annual reporting awards in various categories including that of community newspaper. It has yet to fail to find deserving candidates. In 2004, for example, the CAJ gave the award in the community newspaper category to the *Independent* of Brighton, Ontario, for a series about rail safety. The series was sparked by a CP freight train derailment that had made the front pages of the big Toronto papers. John Miller, then working at the *Independent* during his sabbatical break from teaching at Ryerson University, followed up this front-page news for a day with an in-depth series called Keeping Track: An Independent Investigation on How We Can Live with Rail.[18]

Even more importantly, without smaller papers embracing investigative work, the work of investigative reporting *per se* cannot achieve its full potential. Most journalists on the leading edge of investigative reporting in the public interest agree that viable reportorial techniques, including computer-assisted reporting (CAR), do not represent a true advance unless they are undertaken widely, by all kinds of reporters, regardless of the size of the papers or stations the reporters work for.

One aspect of the missing-women story that the reader may not have noted is its partial origin in rumour. Of course, newspapers are in the business of reporting verifiable fact, not rumour. That's what is supposed to distinguish journalism from fiction, from gossip for intellectuals, from idle chatter, and from rumour mongering. On the other hand, in this case, a particular rumour that had circulated for years before a reporter decided to check it out turned out to contain a rather large grain of truth: a pig farmer would visit the Downtown Eastside and pick up a sex trade worker who would subsequently never be seen again.

The reportorial moral is as old as the hills, as simple as it is basic to all news reporting, not just investigative work: when in doubt, check it out. (There's a fallback position too, for when checking it out fails to reveal verifiable truth: when in doubt, leave it out.) The one thing a good reporter doesn't do when in doubt is to 'fudge it', meaning to write the story so as to 'disappear' (to bury or ignore) the disputed facts along with the reporter's role in the disappearing: that may protect the reporter and the paper from readers' scrutiny, but it won't finally fool anyone, and certainly doesn't qualify as journalism in the public interest. In other words, good reporting is transparent, meaning that the reader never has to wonder how the reporter knows what he claims to know; readers could, if they so desired, follow the story and delve into its background on their own.

The missing-women series illustrates the power of press scrutiny. What the reporters revealed made the public care; it raised awareness of the despairing plight of women working the city's red-light district. As the stories ran, police made up for lost time, committing to prompt release of information in the case, setting up a tip line, and making overtures to the victims' families in meetings arranged for the purpose. The series thus alerted the public, pressured authorities to strengthen the investigation, and helped lead to an arrest in the case. It pointed up deficiencies in crime-fighting technology (for example, the lack of a provincial DNA database for storing crime-related DNA samples), and in the longer term led to changes in the way the city's police department handled unsolved crimes.

But the series also illustrates the limits of investigative reporting. As Lori Culbert notes, the signs for the missing are back up in the Downtown Eastside. A culprit has been apprehended, but the underlying social problem remains. Thus the critical importance of following up investigative work is not to be underestimated; often, such follow-up is the burden of individual reporters, requiring them to take extra responsibility for, as Kim Bolan puts it, 'keeping the story alive'.

Clearly, investigative reporting can expose problems but cannot single-handedly solve them (a fact that may explain why some investigators lose heart). That women are still going missing from the Downtown Eastside also underscores the nature of the underlying problem, and the close relationship between investigative and issues reporting. Had Lindsay Kines caved to some sense of peer-group pressure or lack of confidence in his own independent judgment—instead of pursuing the case based on his solitary inkling of its importance—the secrets of the Pickton farm would still be secret, and no one would be discussing the plight of sex trade workers in the pages of the daily press or on the waves of the nation's broadcast outlets, or, for that matter, in households across the country.

That Pickton was charged with some but not nearly all of the reported disappearances underlines a curious aspect of the story behind the story. The initial and long-persisting idea among police that no single individual was responsible for all the disappearances constituted a conceptual blind spot that kept them from suspecting a serial killer, and that continued to mislead them, several years into the investigation, into failing to consider the possibility. For two apparently contradictory things were true: as it happened, there was a single individual connected to some of the missing-women cases; at the same time, the ubiquitous nature of violence against prostitutes made it easy for these cases to go undetected, to hide behind the nearly routine nature of violence against sex trade workers.

Among the other case studies in this book, the missing-women series is unique in that it arose from classic police beat work. Notice that working a beat allows a reporter to gain valuable expertise and contacts, but it also carries a risk—beat reporters can become jaded to the subject matter and come to identify with the sources they consult in order to cover the beat thoroughly. Maintaining reportorial independence on the beat requires awareness of this potential pitfall, and an ongoing commitment—beyond acuracy—to independent and critical thinking both on the beat and off.

# Endnotes

1.  Neal Hall, with files from Miro Cernetig, 'Judge orders two trials for Pickton to avoid mistrial', *Vancouver Sun* (10 August 2006). Pickton faced twenty-six counts of first-degree murder by the time trial proceedings began in the spring of 2006; these proceedings were covered by a sweeping publication ban. In August, the presiding judge decided to split the indictment into two trials. The first began in 2007 and is likely to last at least a year.

2.  Lindsay Kines, 'Police target big increase in missing women: Serial killer not behind missing-women cases, police official says', *Vancouver Sun* (3 July 1998), B1.

3.  Lindsay Kines, 'Missing women cases probed: Vancouver police will review forty unsolved cases dating from 1971, but they doubt a serial killer was involved in any disappearances', *Vancouver Sun* (18 September 1998), B1.

4.  David Hogben and Lindsay Kines, 'Twenty women missing; action demanded', *Vancouver Sun* (3 March 1999), A1.

5.  Lindsay Kines, 'Missing on the Mean Streets—Part 1: Privilege, despair and death', *Vancouver Sun* (3 March 1999), A12; and Kines, 'Missing on the Mean Streets–Part 2: Who we will not see tomorrow', *Vancouver Sun* (3 March 1999), A13.

6.  The numbers of women considered missing were variously calculated at different stages of the story, but they basically grew—to an eventual total of sixty-eight—as the story developed. Even harder to establish than the number of missing women was the time of the first disappearance. Some reports treat 1971 as the first incident; others say the first prostitutes disappeared in 1978; still others cite the year 1984. What can be verified is that an official police investigation was not launched until 1998 and that the deficiencies of that first investigation led to the striking of a new, joint police–RCMP task force in 2001.

7.  Kim Bolan, *Loss of Faith: How the Air-India Bombers Got Away with Murder* (McClelland & Stewart, 2005).

8.  Lori Culbert, Lindsay Kines, and Kim Bolan, 'Investigation turns up startling new numbers: Police to announce expanded probe', *Vancouver Sun* (21 September 2001), A1.

9.  In August 2007, as this book was being readied for press, the Pickton trial (which began in January of 2006) was about to begin hearing legal arguments in preparation for the calling of the first defence witness. For more on the case, see *The Pickton File* (Knopf Canada, 2007), by pre-eminent investigative journalist Stevie Cameron. Her new book on the subject, *The Pig Farm*, is due to be released by Knopf Canada in 2008.

10. Pronounced 'ledge', this is reporter-speak for *legislature*.

11. Lori Culbert, Kim Bolan, and Lindsay Kines, 'Police build a "bridge" to victims' families: Relatives of women missing from the Downtown Eastside invited to discuss case', *Vancouver Sun* (4 October 2001), B1.

12. The online story carries no byline and is dated 6 November 2002: www.missingpeople.net/how_lindsay_kines_and_sun_reporters.htm.

13. The *Hughes Report on British Columbia*'s child-protection system was released in the spring of 2006 following an inquiry led by retired judge Ted Hughes. It blamed the system's virtual breakdown on constantly shifting leadership and policy, and on deep budget cuts administered by the Liberal government of Gordon Campbell when it took power in 2001 and cut most ministry budgets by an average of 25 per cent. See Dirk Meissner, 'BC child system blamed in tragedy', Canadian Press (10 April 2006).

14. The independent review of British Columbia's child-protection system was sparked by the tragic case of Sherry Charlie, a toddler who in 2002 was beaten to death by her uncle while in the care of a welfare agency working with the BC government.

15. That's Eeyore, the laconic donkey of Winnie-the-Pooh fame, whose response to 'Good day' in one of the Pooh stories runs something like this: 'If it IS a good day . . . which I doubt.'

16. Lori Culbert, 'Story of a shattered life. Part One: A single childhood incident pushed Dawn Crey into a downward spiral from which she would never completely escape', *Vancouver Sun* (24 November 2001), D3; and Culbert, 'Story of a shattered life. Part Two', *Vancouver Sun* (24 November 2001), D03.

17. Lori Culbert, 'It's time "to support families": $100 million set aside to protect children', *Vancouver Sun* (22 February 2006), A4.

18. The first story ran on 19 March 2003, and was headlined 'The time bomb that missed Brighton by minutes'. You can read Miller's *Independent* series online: www.eastnorthumberland.com/news/news2003/march_2003/keeping_track.html. For Miller's commentary on the story behind the story, including tips for aspiring investigators, see *Media* magazine's 2004 online awards issue at the following URL: www.caj.ca/mediamag/awards2004/cajAwards/theAwards/02_commNewspaper/index.html#top.

# Chapter 2

# Reinventing Our Wheels

In the comprehensive and unusual newspaper series, Reinventing Our Wheels, journalist Paul McKay took apart the cultural icon of the car, returning to its origins to show the central role the automobile engine has played in today's crisis-level air pollution.

McKay took six months to research and write the twenty-one-part series. It ran over the summer of 2001 (19 May to 8 June) in both the *Ottawa Citizen* and the *Vancouver Sun*. He conducted more than sixty interviews (talking to everyone from medical experts and carmakers to city transit planners and progressive 'green fuel' companies) and examined the incurred costs in air pollution and human health from Canada's eighteen million automobiles. The series delivered some unwelcome facts, including that Canada's major oil refineries supply some of the dirtiest gas in the Western world and that the federal government's vehicle fleet fails to meet its own 'green laws'. McKay's study of the issues took him back half a century to the roots of the problem, and forward to the forefront of current environmental expertise. It concluded with some of the most innovative solutions being attempted in North America.

Comprising thirty stories that ran over twenty-one days, the series would ironically turn out to be of particular relevance to the readers of the *Citizen* and the *Sun*: In Eastern Canada, people were suffering through one of the worst ever summers for smog; in Vancouver, a lengthy transit strike meant more cars on the road spewing toxins into the air. The series revealed that the health-care costs associated with air pollution were continuing to rise while transit systems across the country operated on principles established in the 1950s and the big carmakers promoted sales of gas guzzlers for the highest profit margins.

But in focusing on analysis and the best advances in addressing the problem—including reducing vehicle pollution by better city planning and public transit, superior technologies, and community endeavours like vehicle-pooling—McKay did more than identify the bad guys. He spoke with some of the world's leaders in the production of green cars and gas and investigated a radically successful public transit system in Boulder, Colorado, that enjoyed the continent's highest ridership.

In fact, roughly one-third of the stories dealt with possible solutions. McKay reported on an oil company that sold the cleanest gas in Canada (a blend of high-oxygen ethanol and low-sulphur gasoline)[1] and an Ottawa biotech firm with a plan to use farm fuel to power engines—the latter firm was building a $30 million cellulose-to-ethanol plant.[2]

At a total of nearly fifty thousand words, the series constituted a small book. It garnered lavish praise from various quarters and the project went on display at a Vancouver science museum.

Think about how unusual this series was, what it meant for the sponsoring newspapers, which, like all dailies, feature lucrative automotive sections that bring in substantial advertising dollars. In a business that relies on revenue from sponsors, including automobile ads, a critical series on the car was unlikely indeed. But, then, Paul McKay is not your average investigator.

He began with two stories that revealed the extent of automotive pollution and its related health effects, noting that summer smog alerts, which had become routine in most of the country's cities, were on the increase. With more and more cars on the roads every year, experts estimated the pollution-related health costs in the billions of dollars and put the yearly national death toll as high as 16,000 (1,900 in Ontario alone).

Later stories revealed that Canadian refineries were selling stations gas so dirty that it could interfere with emission-control devices. The oil companies, which for a decade had fought pollution-control regulations aimed at reducing the amount of sulphur in gas, came in for special criticism. Turning to the situation south of the border, McKay exposed one scheme that involved the oil companies' tampering with more than a million big-rig engines to help their drivers evade anti-pollution regulations.[3]

McKay's investigation went beyond analyzing the problem to propose solutions, including using fuel-cell technology to design 'electric' cars and end the auto industry's reliance on fossil fuels.[4] McKay wrote of cars that would run not on gas but on an electric grid, and of their secret costs;[5] of cars that would be powered by nickel-cadmium batteries, purportedly making them emission-free;[6] and of advanced technology that would bring to the marketplace so-called 'smart' cars.[7] One story detailed the decade-long rise of fuel-guzzling SUVs, minivans, and so-called 'light' trucks, and charged the automobile and oil companies with ignoring environmental costs in favour of maximizing private profits.[8]

Throughout the series, McKay dealt in specifics, naming not only particular companies, but also particular cars. For instance, one story told how Chrysler got its PT Cruiser rated as a 'fuel-efficient truck.'[9] Another profiled the great-grandson of Henry Ford, who was leading the big three automakers in environmental awareness and action.[10] Still another praised the Volkswagen Jetta TDI as 'amazingly fuel-efficient'.[11]

The series included stories of individuals who were making a difference, and showed what drivers, as individuals, could do to become part of the solution.[12] It ended with a string of articles pinpointing the ills of the public transit system and holding the federal government to account for its inaction, its counterproductive policies, and its own failure to go green.[13]

Along with the analyses came success stories, including a feature on the American town of Boulder, Colorado, where a radical rethinking of the issues had resulted in North America's most successful public transit program.[14] McKay's series ended with a summary piece that put the problems in a nutshell and the challenge on the table, asking, 'Do we want to invest billions more [dollars] to make our cities fit for even more cars? Or do we want lung-friendly cities where the car doesn't define our civic culture but serves it?'[15]


# The Interview
(26 April 2006)

The series began as one of Paul McKay's big ideas. Immediately upon hatching the notion, McKay took it to Neil Reynolds, at the time his managing editor at the *Ottawa Citizen*, and a man McKay, among many other Canadian reporters, holds in high esteem.

> It was one of those ones that I took to Neil. And I said, 'What do you think about this?' And he said, 'Do it.' He said, 'I love it, let's do it.'

Reynolds left the *Citizen* for the *Vancouver Sun* before McKay finished writing the series, but Scott Anderson, who succeeded Reynolds at the *Citizen*, was also supportive. That's how the series ended up running simultaneously in both papers.

McKay came up with the idea the same way he does a lot of his major undertakings—with a piercing and wide-ranging intelligence, and a reflective awareness utterly devoid of arrogance. He'd been reading up on automotive pollution and had a tip from one of his Ottawa contacts, Bee Olivastri of Friends of the Earth, about Canadian refineries selling dirty gas. Through a freedom-of-information request, Olivastri had succeeded in getting 'the actual numbers on the amount of pollutants in the gas of each of the major refiners'. McKay recognized the proverbial tip of a major investigative series.

One of the things that really intrigued me about the project: nobody had done this story, really, because you couldn't see the forest for the trees. And I thought, Neil is going to love this because cars are around us everywhere. We see this story here about pollution and congestion, and we see a story here about low ridership of public transit, and we see this story here about smog, and we see this story here about GM in financial straits—but they are all separate stories.

Nobody had really put them together because virtually everybody who writes about cars in the newspaper industry loves them. There are auto sections in every daily newspaper, and those sections are profit centres. The amount of money that the Wheels section in the *Ottawa Citizen* or the *Toronto Star* or the *Vancouver Sun* spends on the contributing journalists, compared to the ad revenue they get, is fractional.

I'm not saying that the automotive journalists aren't good reporters or are inaccurate or anything like that. But they're put in an environment, they live in an environment, where most of them review cars all the time, and they can give cars good and bad reviews on their merits. But they never question the car itself, and what it's doing to the environment.

Occasionally, there would be stories about this car's good fuel emissions, rah, rah, rah. . . . But there was a kind of bubble or culture within the car-writing segment of daily newspapers that either never thought about writing a series in this way, or thought about it, and decided, Nah, let's just keep doing what we're doing.

Wasn't there flack from the automotive section over running your series?

Well this is the beauty of working with Neil Reynolds. Because he immediately said yes, I love this. I remember the look on his face. . . . I sort of mapped out where I would go and I said right at the beginning to the editors, this is not going to be just a slam against cars. This is going to be a look at innovation and what can be done. Where are the thinkers out there? Where are the people who are asking where are we going to be twenty years from now? Where *should* we be twenty years from now? And not just on cars, but on public transit and city design and that kind of thing.

So the *Citizen*—bless them—sent me to Colorado to look at the best-run public bus service on the continent, in Boulder, Colorado. And just up the highway, in Aspen, Colorado, was this guy named Amory Lovins.

McKay already knew of Amory Lovins (an environmental critic whom he calls 'a very, very radical thinker'). In 1983, McKay published a book called *Electric Empire: The Inside Story of Ontario Hydro*, in which he cited Lovins, one of many critics who warned of environmental problems associated with the utility's heavy reliance on nuclear reactors.[16]

> I knew [Lovins] because he'd made the same argument earlier about the electric utility industry.
>
> He basically said, Look at what you have here with the automotive industry. . . . General Motors is a company that every year bets billions that their car, their model, is going to sell well, and they pump all kinds of advertising into trying to make sure that happens. But they never ask people what they want. So if it turns out that people go, Ah, no thanks, they pull up entire plants and punch out a twenty-, thirty-, or forty-thousand-dollar vehicle on complete speculation that they're going to be able to sell it. He said nobody else in the world would ever run a business like this.
>
> He had some great ideas [about how to analyze the industry]. . . . [He] did a calculation of how much of the energy in the gasoline that's put in a car actually gets translated into motive power, and it's 12 per cent. By the time you figure all the heat that's dissipated, and the fact that you've got a one-and-a-half-ton vehicle that's carrying a 150-pound passenger, or two 150-pound passengers and two kids, the whole thing, from an engineering/physics point of view, is ludicrous. You're getting almost nothing. He also pointed out that cars are the second biggest investment in most people's lives, after their houses. And they sit 97 per cent of the day.
>
> He was saying this is a textbook case of bad utility: It's like borrowing and spending all this money, borrowing all this money and making these payments every month, to use the car 3 per cent of the day. Now that is nuts. And to boot, it uses 12 per cent of the potential energy in the gasoline.

Despite the merits of McKay's series, the editor of the *Citizen*'s automotive section was not amused. He was in fact, 'pretty ticked off'.

> This was challenging the whole unspoken modus operandi, and this is kind of typical of Neil: he didn't do the diplomatic thing. . . . The other interesting thing is it never got mentioned, to my knowledge. It certainly never got nominated for an automotive journalism award.[17]
>
> The automotive journalists never said, Finally, somebody broke through, or, Finally, somebody did something innovative, or, Finally, boy, why don't I get that at my newspaper. It was exactly the opposite: it was like it never happened. It was like it *n-e-e-e-v-e-r* should have happened.

McKay chuckles when he remembers this reaction, or non-reaction, of peers to the story. Perhaps he can chuckle because, on the upside, readers expressed their unreserved appreciation.

> It was like a taboo had been broken—some crazy editor at the *Ottawa Citizen* had done this incredibly dangerous and . . . loony thing: He'd actually allowed this critical series of stories about the car to run. But the readers loved it. And much to my surprise, the car companies didn't complain. Because it was a bit of an issue at the beginning. I anticipated it—I mean Neil would have run it anyway, I'm sure—but I did say to the editors, Look, this is not going to be just an anti-car slam. It's going to be factual; it's going to be documented; it's going to involve looking at the problems.
>
> It's kind of a bleak irony, but that was the summer—we started it deliberately on the May 24 weekend, which is the first weekend that everybody in Ontario gets in their cars and goes to the cottage and starts putting in the miles for the summer. Of course, the traffic was jammed. And people were in their cars, on the 417 in Ottawa, heading out of the city with their *Ottawa Citizen*, stuck in traffic, and looking around and looking at all these SUVs . . . and that summer Ottawa got its first smog alerts ever at that time of year.
>
> That summer was the worst smog summer in Ontario history. We've had two worse since then. But in the year that the series ran, smog really hit home. They had [something like] several dozen smog days in Ottawa. And in a way—I hate to say it—but the timing couldn't have been more perfect, because people read this stuff and they were choking . . . they were taking their kids in [to hospital], and elderly people were being ordered to stay inside.
>
> When he [Neil Reynolds] went to Vancouver, I was starting to write this . . . so I pitched the idea that we run it jointly in the *Vancouver Sun* and the *Citizen*. I ended up spending about a third of my time in Vancouver, doing stories about smog problems and traffic problems and public transit in the Greater Vancouver Area. So, there are some stories in there about the Vancouver transit system, what they were planning for—and what they were failing to plan for.
>
> I did a story about this marvellous guy named Jack Bell, who invented and funded, as a philanthropist, a van program for his employees. Instead of driving their cars to work, they would get this van service he set up. Just a brilliant, beautiful idea.[18]
>
> So guess what happens? Vancouver Transit goes on strike, so people in Vancouver are hot about transit. And the series appeared at the same time. Plus the gas stuff that ran in the *Vancouver Sun*. We got stories from all across Canada, reaction from that. It was very popular, and it won a national award.

The impact spread further than reader response. In fact, in good measure, the series accomplished precisely what McKay had intended, and what he had told his editors he intended: to provoke serious thought on the iconic status and environmental cost of the car and to get people thinking about alternatives and solutions.

One thing about that in terms of after-effects. Now again, I wouldn't say that [the series] was the only reason, but I think three of the stories in that series dealt with gas taxes and the fact that the federal government was collecting this gas-tax money—billions every year—and none of it was going back into dedicated public transit. Up until that point, the federal government . . . was adamant that the gas taxes would go into general revenue and be spent how the government saw fit.

But the series looked at this issue and made arguments that the gas-tax money collected by the federal government could be sent back to the provinces in the form of specialized, stipulated, dedicated payments for public transit, to reduce smog and congestion problems.

I calculated the amount of gas sold every year in the Greater Vancouver Area, and then how much went to the federal government, whether that money was put back into Greater Vancouver . . . in the form of public transit assistance. Then people's taxes would be deployed to alleviate the problem.

After that series, the following budget year, guess what? [Former Liberal prime minister] Paul Martin announces to the Canadian Federation of Municipalities that this is what they're going to do. Of course his number was low—how much they were going to do it for—and the mayor's number was way up there. They sawed it off and eventually came to this agreement where now it's the law of the land that the cities are going to get these transfer payments based on the gas tax. And that will never be taken away; now that the cities are getting this, and now that this precedent has been set, all the major cities in Canada are going to benefit from that because they're going to get more federal money returned to them for dedicated transportation infrastructure expenditures.

McKay's stories typically go beneath the surface (and beyond pointing the finger of blame) to proffer solutions, perhaps a tendency honed in the days that he worked for an advocacy organization.[19] In one series on crooked lawyers, he included a piece on how to recognize and avoid bad lawyers; another article in the series offered suggestions on how to change the system itself.[20] In a third story, McKay told readers how paralegals could sometimes be consulted in place of much more expensive lawyers. He said the lawyers were 'furious' about it. But 'I didn't put that in the story,' he laughed. 'I thought, that's really an issue of market share.'

Having developed his various areas of expertise on his own, not as a beat reporter on staff with a major newspaper, McKay believes that in some respects the beat system is antithetical to investigative reporting, because reporters on a beat must cultivate their inside sources. Being an investigative rather than a beat reporter allowed McKay to 'hit and run', since he knew he wouldn't need to go back to those sources again. Another potential peril of beat reporting is journalists' own tendency to begin to identify with their sources, thus compromising their ability to cast a critical eye on events.

I did a series on the Export Development Corporation—another one of those stories that nobody had really ever put together—on what this government Crown agency was up to. But I knew when I was writing the series and when it was running that I'd never get another EDC story again. Basically, I was the enemy. And the same thing with the nuclear industry: I burned my bridges as a reporter; I could never go back there again.

The nursing home industry was another one.[21] After the series came out, nobody who owned a nursing home, and the Ontario Nursing Home Association, would want to deal with me. And in fact in some cases, like the nuclear industry, every time I wrote a story, they called up the publisher and said, you know, McKay can't be writing this stuff. So basically, I figured, well, I'll just move on to the next vector.

McKay's instincts told him the more unpredictable his intellectual peregrinations, the better.

Nobody would know where I was going to show up next, or what I was going to be doing. And one of the interesting things was even in Ottawa, I'm sure that there are people at the Export Development Corporation who read the series on crooked lawyers or on the nursing home, and said, 'Good reporting! About time!' And nobody reads who the reporter is, almost never.

So when a Paul McKay starts asking for material from the Export Development Corporation, of course they didn't suspect anything. They didn't say, 'Uh-oh, watch out.' So I had unrestricted entry. But by the time I was finished, there was no more entry again. Then the alert would be out and there might as well have been an all-points bulletin.

I just moved on to the next one. That's basically how I got away with it. But if I had been a beat reporter, or a political reporter doing that kind of stuff, I would have been finished. It's not like somebody's going to take you out and shoot you, or that there's going to be a published edict somewhere. It's just that they won't talk to you. It's a matter of being snuffed out rather than being overtly targeted.

McKay's work highlights an uncomfortable reality about investigative reporting: the reporter's occasional need for a thick skin. It isn't easy to be infamous or to have to withstand people's anger and even fury. It takes a kind of courage. McKay agrees but says that kind of courage is quintessentially different from the courage of the reporter on organized crime or of the war correspondent.

When I look at the crime reporter in Montreal [Michel Auger], when I look at people who do that regularly—now that's guts. That's a whole other level of personal courage and dedication. And people who do foreign reporting, war correspondents, like Hilary McKenzie. She was the Southam correspondent in Washington for a long time and then she went over when the US invaded Afghanistan. She did superb reporting from Afghanistan. Stories appeared in the *Ottawa Citizen* that were gutsy, courageous, just fantastic field reporting. Gripping, the way it was written, the subject matter, daring, dedicated—all those adjectives that you apply to the best reporters.

When McKay won a National Newspaper Award for the 2001 Reinventing Our Wheels series, his response was typically idealistic and grounded in social conscience.

I was stunned, because I thought that the *Vancouver Sun* series on the missing women was going to win. And a friend of mine, Noreen Rasbach, was the editor on that stuff, and she was and is the protege of Neil Reynolds. She started at the *Whig-Standard* and when he went to the *Sun*, Noreen followed. She's at the *Globe* now as the national editor.

When my name was announced, I went up on the stage, and I don't want to make too much of this, but I said I've got one of the best journalism jobs in the country and I'm treated very well by the *Citizen*, paid very well. So I'd like to suggest that the National Newspaper Association create a new category of winners for the National Newspaper Awards for stories written and published in the daily papers by freelancers, and I will donate this first $1,000 cheque toward creating that new category.

Noreen and Neil came up to me afterwards, because they were with the *Sun* group [nominated for the missing-women series]. We were friends and colleagues so it was kind of a bittersweet moment in a way. And they said, 'Right on for proposing that.' Russ Mills[22] was there and he said, 'Well I'm on the NNA committee this year and I'm going to bring it up tomorrow. I think it's a damned good idea.' My argument was that all the daily newspapers print superb stuff by freelancers and they never get nominated. There's no way their stuff can get recognized.

The National Newspaper Awards don't exclude freelance contributions from being nominated for the prestigious awards—in 2003, for example, freelancer Sarah Gibb was nominated for a superb series she wrote for the *StarPhoenix* (Saskatoon) about a family wrongly accused of child abuse—but McKay is right that no category yet exists to honour freelancers exclusively. And when Russell Mills raised the issue as promised at a meeting of the NNA committee, McKay learned, the committee members balked.

They hated it. Russ Mills came out of the meeting the day after and he said, 'I brought it up and I promoted it and there was absolutely no support for this.' And I said, 'Why ever not?' And he said, 'Unions.' The editors were worried that if they had a category for freelancers, that was a signal they were contracting out and relations with unions would tense up and it wouldn't do. The unions knew nothing about it. It was the editors, really, anticipating a problem with the unions.

It's an example of the fact that journalists as a group in Canada also have a kind of a clubby, in-group attitude. Years ago, I was on the board of the Centre for Investigative Journalism. It was created partly to inculcate and honour and bring a focus to the people who were interested in investigative reporting. Well, it doesn't exist any more; it got kind of morphed into the Canadian Association of Journalists. There are good people in the CAJ;, they do good things. But it's taken on more of a middle-aged, go-along-to-get-along [attitude].[23] That had happened along with the whole change in the ownership of the newspaper business in Canada, and who the owners are and what their expectations are and what they hope to accomplish. It has very little to do with news and value to the reader. In general, that's unfortunately the trend.

# The Kirschbaum File

Back in 1988, McKay wrote a long series for the *Kingston Whig-Standard* called The Kirschbaum File, about a suspected Nazi collaborator from Slovakia, Joseph Kirschbaum, who had become a Canadian citizen. The series ran in a forty-eight-page tabloid-size supplement to the once-family-owned and highly regarded *Whig-Standard*.[24] Even in 1988, it was a bold move. Today, McKay says, it would be unthinkable.

To look at what the *Whig-Standard* did back then—for a tiny newspaper, a circulation of about 33,000, and all the awards it won—and what it is now . . . that would be a perfect way of explaining what's happened to Canadian journalism in the past twenty-five years.

There's an old joke, you know. [At the time of the 1980] Royal Commission on Newspapers . . . the *Peterborough Examiner* and the *Kingston Whig-Standard* were owned by the Davies family. [Famed Canadian author] Robertson Davies, as a matter of fact, was the editor and publisher of the *Examiner* during the late 1950s and '60s,[25] and his nephew was Michael Davies, who owned the *Whig-Standard* when I was there. . . . The *Whig-Standard* continued to be a very good paper until recently; but the *Examiner* was just a terrible paper in the 1970s when Thomson took it over, and in the 1980s and '90s it continued to be a terrible paper. Someone came to the Royal Commission and said if the Thomson papers are the basement of Canadian journalism, the *Peterborough Examiner* is the sub-pump.

They had described the demise of the *Examiner*, from a fabulous newspaper in the 1960s (under—imagine—Robertson Davies!) and very literate, that had won all kinds of awards. The *Kingston Whig-Standard* was its companion, book-end, sister paper, owned by the same family. And, of course, it won lots of awards. The editor-in-chief while I was there was Neil Reynolds, who went on to win awards for his paper in Fredericton. He went on to do terrific work at the *Ottawa Citizen* and then at the *Vancouver Sun*—the last major project while he was the *Sun* editor was the missing-women story.

Well, he's out of the business now [though he still writes a column for the *Globe and Mail*], and I'm not sure if he would put it quite this way, but he did tell me that he saw no future in the Canadian newspaper world for projects like this, like the *Vancouver Sun* series on the missing women, and the stuff that I'd done at the *Citizen*. And I think that's why he left. He just thought the screws were tightening further and further and further, and there was less space, less money, less staff, less freedom, less respect—the whole bit.

He was my boss on this Kirschbaum story. This is extraordinary for a paper that has a circulation of about thirty-three thousand—I mean almost everybody in the newspaper business would say today that this is impossible, it can't be done. You might as well be living in a different universe. But the newspaper [the *Whig-Standard*] hasn't got that much worse in the last fifteen years. It's that the whole set of expectations about what a newspaper is and what it should be have changed. And they've largely changed from within, because of who owns them.

Concentration of ownership in the Canadian newspaper industry grew so severe that the problem has been addressed by two royal commissions. The commissions' recommendations were largely ignored, however, and the situation deteriorated just as the dire warnings had predicted it would. Obsession with the bottom line of the business tended to reduce the journalistic base and the quality of journalism practised in one-newspaper towns—a situation so ubiquitous that the very phrase 'one-newspaper town' now sounds nostalgic, almost quaint. It isn't that a conspiracy was afoot, for no conspiracy was required to conduct business as usual. As McKay noted, for all the hand-wringing, the sea change in the newspaper business occurred slowly, over decades.

One thing that hasn't changed in the decades since McKay wrote The Kirschbaum File, is the possibility that powerful interests may try to use libel law to intimidate publishers and stifle investigative reports.

The Kirschbaum story is interesting because when we were about to publish this, of course we contacted Kirschbaum. And we actually physically handed him a list of questions, because he told us through his lawyers that he wouldn't speak to us. So we did a stakeout of his house, and then we actually went to his church on a Sunday morning. We followed him in his Cadillac down to the church, with a *Whig* photographer, another reporter, and me, and when he came out of church we handed him [the list of questions] and took a photograph of us handing him the questions that we wanted to ask him before we published.

He took it, and then the next thing, about three days later, three McMillan-Binch lawyers got in a [Stephen] Roman plane, a jet, and flew to Kingston and had a meeting with our publisher, Michael Davies. They basically said if you publish that story you might lose the family newspaper that you've had since I think 1928, because we'll sue you for libel and you'll lose, so don't.

Our publisher—the blood drained from his face as the lawyers went away—and he called Neil Reynolds in and said, I'm paraphrasing here, but he said, the stakes are pretty big and this is what they're saying. So we had a very tense week . . . we had to go over all the materials again, and they were vetted by the lawyer again. And publication did get delayed, but finally, Neil and the publisher decided that everything was nailed down. So we published. And we never heard another word.

McKay had learned about Kirschbaum earlier in 1988, when he wrote what he called 'a kind of anti-obituary' about Stephen Roman for the *Globe and Mail*. McKay would eventually write a book about Roman,[26] but he had done much of the research for the *Globe and Mail* anti-obit years before, when he was working on his book about Ontario Hydro,[27] in which the story of the uranium magnate played large.

Roman figured in that story because of the sweetheart uranium contracts he signed with the premier at the time, Bill Davis. And, so, I'd gone up to Elliot Lake and I'd done some stories on the uranium, environmental part of it, and also the worker health and safety part of it.

When Roman died, there had been this big press barrage lauding all the things he'd done—you know, rags-to-riches story—and the *Globe* printed a piece I wrote that detailed all the abhorrent things that he had done. But nothing about Kirschbaum, because I didn't know anything about him yet. So I wrote that story, and Roman's family threatened a libel suit.

A process server arrived at my rural door one night, threatening a libel suit. But Roman was dead. Dead men can't sue. They also sent libel notices to the *Globe and Mail*. The editor at the time, Patrick Martin, called me up and said, 'We've got these libel notices.' I said, 'The story's accurate and the guy's dead.' And Martin said, 'Well they're threatening to take us to court. Can you send me a detailed itemization of every point in the story?'

And this is an obituary, right? So I said, 'Well you're going to have to pay me to do that because this is ridiculous and it's not going to go anywhere.' And he said, 'I know, I know, but just do it and we'll pay you for your time.' So I did, and sent it to him, and he phoned me back and said we just told them [the Roman family] to piss up a rope.

That was in 1988. Eighteen years later, McKay found out what had happened to some of the copies of his book on Stephen Roman.

This weekend, I was out for a walk—I live way out in the woods in eastern Ontario—and I came across my neighbour, who was just finishing cutting his wood. It was a nice sunny day and we stopped to chat. It turns out that he had worked in this small paper company here that had once been part of the Roman corporate empire, called Strathcona Paper.

I said, 'Oh, I wrote a book about Stephen Roman one time.' And he said, 'You wrote that book?' And I said, 'You know about it?' And he said, 'Yeah, I was a middle manager there and one day in the mid-'90s, a big semi-truck pulled up to the back doors and there were skids full of your book that had been bought directly from the publisher by the Roman family, and they were still wrapped in their plastic—skids full of books and they went into the pulp machine, the paper pulp machine.'

Roman had bought the books in order to destroy them.

It was the writing of Roman's anti-obit for the *Globe and Mail* that led McKay to the brilliant work of The Kirschbaum File. For the task, he 'had collected a whole bunch of material on his [Roman's] past, all kinds of royal commissions because of his past'.

Roman ran the biggest uranium mines in the world in northern Ontario. And he'd poisoned all kinds of workers because he hadn't ventilated the mines and they suffered radiation and silica dust poisoning . . . the mines had contaminated an entire 55-mile watershed with radioactive tailings. The story goes on and on.

After the obit ran in the *Globe and Mail*, this guy called me up. He was a researcher with the Canadian Jewish Congress in Toronto. He said, 'I just read your Stephen Roman story. I love it—finally, somebody told the story about Roman. But you forgot one thing.' And I said, 'Oh yeah, what's that?' Because I didn't think I'd forgotten anything.

'Well,' he said, 'he brought over a whole bunch of convicted Nazi collaborators from Europe after the war and set them up in his businesses.' He said, 'If you ever want to see the file, come on down and I'll show it to you.' I said, 'I'll be down in a week.' So, that's how the whole Kirschbaum story got started.

Among the things that McKay learned from the files of the Canadian Jewish Congress was that in the 1960s, Joseph Kirschbaum had brought a libel suit against a little Canadian Czech-language newspaper for an editorial about him. At this point, McKay was on leave from the *Whig-Standard*; he nevertheless gathered his arguments and went straight to see Neil Reynolds, who didn't take much convincing.

I said, 'The fiftieth anniversary of the start of World War II is coming up and I think this would make an excellent investigative piece.' He loved the idea and said, 'Okay, we'll put you back on staff. Go to Czechoslovakia.'

Reynolds supported the story idea from beginning to end, and there 'was never a single question about the cost', which was considerable given the complexity of the assignment, the travel expenses, and the need to hire a full-time interpreter.

> I was utterly thrilled, because this was Kingston, Ontario, not Toronto or New York or Washington. I was thrilled as a journalist to be able to go and do this. There's a bit of responsibility, because you feel like you've got to come back with something pretty valuable. But he also gave me a couple of months to work on the story, to do all the research and the writing.

It was while he was in the archives in Czechoslovakia that McKay found his defining moment. The country was still behind the Iron Curtain—a phrase used during the Cold War era to refer to barriers, physical and psychological, that prevented free passage between the Soviet-controlled Eastern Bloc countries and the West. Getting into the archives, even with an interpreter, wasn't easy. But McKay persevered, and it paid off.

> When I got into the archives . . . and I saw the overwhelming wealth of material about what Kirschbaum and his cronies had done, I knew that we were going to have a very important story.
>
> This is what's extraordinary about this story: the *Whig-Standard* sent me to Czechoslovakia—and it was an Iron Curtain country at the time. I was over there for almost two weeks. I had to hire an interpreter to get around. I went to the archives there and got the original photographs, prints from the original newspapers of the day. I got them all signed and stamped—that was part of our backup. I interviewed survivors, the prosecutor who had filed the formal case against Kirschbaum, and all the others, including a journalist who had covered Kirschbaum and was Jewish.

How did McKay manage to get hold of the files in an Eastern Bloc country?

> I think the only reason that I got in was that it was a communist country, and Roman was a fervent anti-communist. He had used a lot of his money to promote and publish anti-communist material. So I think the communist government was . . . amenable to writing a story about this Nazi era in Slovakia and Roman's association with it.

Such a venture by a newspaper would be nearly unthinkable today. Even back then, hard-hitting investigative journalism was rare enough.

> That was part of Reynolds's definition of what makes a real newspaper. He understood very well that that's not all of what newspapers are; but it's a com-

ponent. His idea of a paper was to have all these components, but you always
had to have six or seven of these major projects a year, and that was his model.
It was his model when he went to the East Coast, when he was at the *Citizen*,
and also when he was at the *Vancouver Sun*.

For the Kirschbaum story, McKay also travelled with another reporter to Vermont to
interview noted Holocaust historian Raul Hilberg, and to Ottawa to interview Justice
Department officials and sources on the Deschênes Commission. (The Deschênes
Commission had been established in 1985 to investigate the presence of Nazi war
criminals and collaborators in Canada. Kirschbaum was one of thirteen people the
commission had identified as war criminal suspects or those meriting further investigation.)

> Having that material in front of us when we met these various people, they basi-
> cally verified a lot of it as well. I'd say that was the key point, right there.

McKay hoped the series would provoke Canadians to think about the wider issue—
the presence in Canada of Nazi war criminals.

> I wanted to have an impact. I wanted [the Kirschbaum series] to go someplace.
> I wanted the public to read it and be motivated, and the Justice Department, in
> this case, to be motivated.

He believes the major impact of The Kirschbaum File was that it led to more stories,
generating interest and further work on several fronts.

> First of all, it convinced the publisher to do more stories like this because of the
> response from readers. Kingston is a very literate community. Queens University
> is there—the city has a very high percentage of civil servants and the like. And
> someone came up to him [the publisher] the day after it was published, and said,
> you know, this is what a newspaper should be. This could have been something
> that the *New York Times* did.
>      It helped a lot when Neil Reynolds came up with the next project, not nec-
> essarily mine, but other projects. It partly built or reinforced the culture of the
> paper at the time that said excellence counts. And when it won an award, that
> helped as well.

If the Kirschbaum series didn't lead to prosecution, the story's impact in the wider
community was indisputable.

> It exposed Kirschbaum in his own community, and as far as I know, he was fin-
> ished as a spokesperson for Slovaks in Canada. He basically just disappeared.

> In the Deschênes Commission follow-up, the Justice Department never, to my
> knowledge, ended up charging him or taking him to trial. In fact, I think it was
> someone from the Justice Department who told me that they decided not to,
> because they figured that Kirschbaum had been punished by this series of sto-
> ries more than they could ever punish him.

McKay isn't easily impressed, and the government's failure to prosecute left him cold
despite the commission members' praise for the Kirschbaum series. He believes the
series may even have given the government a convenient excuse *not* to prosecute. On
the other hand, McKay figures that Kirschbaum's wealth and connections were likely
enough on their own to discourage the Justice Department from pursuing the case.

> I kind of suspect they wouldn't have [charged Kirschbaum], because he had a lot
> of money and a lot friends, and he would have fought it tooth and nail. And they
> were making judgments partly on that basis. I wish I'd known about Rudolf Vrba
> at the time, because if I had, that would have added another dimension to the
> story. A very, very important dimension.

It would be seventeen years before McKay was to meet and interview Rudolf Vrba, a
man who captured his heart and imagination. Vrba immigrated to Canada after
World War II and taught pharmacology at the University of British Columbia
Medical School. But in 1942, he was a Slovakian teenager imprisoned in the Nazi
death camp at Auschwitz, Poland. He had been sent there, McKay would learn, by
Joseph Kirschbaum. In April 1944, Vrba and a fellow prisoner, Alfred Wetzler, made
a daring escape from Auschwitz and brought the first news of the Nazi death camps
to the outside world.[28]

   The occasion of McKay's meeting with Vrba was preparation for a feature article
that he was writing for the *Ottawa Citizen* in May 2005, for the sixtieth anniversary
of the end of World War II.[29]

> Everybody else was doing stories about the Allied troops and the various battles
> and that kind of thing. I ended up doing a profile of Rudolf Vrba, because nobody
> else was dealing with the Holocaust, as a commemorative piece.
>    Vrba was the bravest man I ever met, and what was extraordinary, despite
> all that he went through, was that he was a very ebullient man. It was so moving
> and inspiring to be with him. I spent a couple of hours with him in his Vancouver
> office the year before he died [in March 2006].[30] He talked with utter candour
> about what happened to him, and how it happened, and who was involved,
> including Kirschbaum.
>    He had transcended the horrible things that had happened to him, even
> though he didn't forget, and he was still relentless about calling those to account

who hadn't been called yet. He was a radiantly happy man, and very, very inspiring.

When I interviewed McKay on 10 April 2006, he had just left the *Ottawa Citizen* to work independently and was completing a screenplay trying to tell the interrelated stories of Rudolf Vrba, Joseph Kirschbaum, and Stephen Roman. He had also recently learned of the death of Rudolf Vrba.

> I was so sad to hear that he had passed away. This screenplay ties the story of the three characters together. A lot of it takes place in Canada, and it's really the story of whether justice catches up to people.

Does it?

> Well, sometimes it does, and sometimes it doesn't, but the essential goal for me in writing this screenplay is to make justice catch up with Kirschbaum and Roman. They spent most of their lives—and made lots and lots of money—whitewashing history.

McKay's outraged sense of justice denied drives his work, and he came by that sense of outrage early on. He knew when he was a child that he wanted to be a journalist. Pierre Berton's columns sparked his avid interest, and one story in particular inspired him. After reading it, the young McKay announced his journalistic intentions to his parents.

> When Steven Truscott was on trial, Pierre Berton was a columnist for the *Toronto Star*. In his column one day—and I was 12 or 13 at the time—he wrote this poem about a 14-year-old boy on death row. I read that and my world stopped. Partly because it was a poem, though not a particularly good one. Last summer, I was the Pierre Berton writer-in-residence. I lived in his home. So I dug up that poem from his material and read it again. It's also in Julian Sher's book [*Until You Are Dead: Steven Truscott's Long Ride into History*].
>
> Here I am, at 12 or 13 years old, and I'm reading the *Toronto Star* mostly for the sports section, to find out about the Maple Leafs. But I did read Berton's poem, and I thought, wow, there's a kid who's about a year older than I am who could be hanged, and I just learned the story from this guy, Pierre Berton.
>
> Berton's column [on the case]—it basically stopped Canadians for a while because he was an enormously popular and influential writer and his *Toronto Star* column was read by everyone. And when he put this poem in there, it galvanized a part of Canada. I think it might have saved [Truscott], and been the galvanizing point that led to the argument for clemency. So that's how I got started.

He had fallen for 'just this idea of digging into things and righting wrongs and the pen is mightier than the sword—that kind of thing.'

After graduating from university, McKay went to work for the Ontario Public Interest Research Group, and in 1983 moved to his first newspaper job at the *Kingston Whig-Standard*. He stayed at the *Whig-Standard* until 1990, when he took a break from the newspaper business to do other things. (Among his other ventures were stints as a senior policy analyst to the Ontario energy minister and as a case manager for an environmental group called Northwatch.)

When McKay resumed his newspaper career in 1997, it was as an investigative reporter with the *Ottawa Citizen*, where he remained, steadily winning the *Citizen* honours with his flare for the in-depth story and his characteristically independent thinking, until he left the paper in the spring of 2006.

When we met, McKay made some harsh criticisms of what he described as a newspaper business transformed almost beyond recognition, and certainly beyond the kind of ideals that had always driven his own work. Yet the work is still worth it, he says, if you don't mind not being rich.

> Decide what you want to do, and if money's a fairly big factor, forget it. Because really, I hate to say it, but in a digital kind of way, in an Internet-based, digital kind of way, the real investigative journalists are going to have to go back to being like [legendary US journalist] I.F. Stone was in the 1950s.[31]
>
> Here was this gnome-like little man who published this little newsletter almost exclusively based on public records that nobody else knew about because they were buried in the departments of defence or justice in Washington. And he spent decades, every day, burrowing into these records and searching the congressional record and tapping out this newsletter with the help of his wife. It set the standard for accuracy and effectiveness in investigative reporting. He was an investigative reporter bar none. And then in the evenings, when he'd take any time off, if he did, he would teach himself how to read ancient Greek.[32]
>
> Now of course, the world is completely different because we have the Internet and Google. But I think this is the face of investigative reporting in the future. It's going to be done by I.F. Stone types, who probably won't be on staff at a newspaper.

McKay's assessment is of critical importance. If he's right about a fractured future (and he's certainly not alone in predicting it), then investigative journalism, indeed all kinds of in-depth journalism, will rely more on typically independent individuals like Paul McKay. This future will be driven by those with an altruistic bent.

Well, first of all, there's your individual role and your individual reward, but the larger reward is if you can change things for the better. For instance, I did a series about nursing homes, and it led to some modest reforms in Ontario. Some of the reforms were elementary—and cheap.[33]

A lot of seniors move to Florida for their retirement years and live in nursing homes there, so that per capita they have more seniors than anywhere else in the United States. They've also had more problems with bad nursing homes than anywhere else in the States. But they've gone through this problem decades before most other states and Canadians have, and in a worse way. They finally decided that one of the things they were going to have to do was post the inspection reports on a publicly accessible website, so that people who had parents in a nursing home, or people who were looking for a nursing home for their parents, could read the government-inspection results of every nursing home in Florida.

Well that's cheap, because the inspectors are already typing up the reports for the government, so it's virtually no extra expense for the government to put these reports on a website. And that, of course, creates an incentive for bad owners to either get out of the business or clean up their act. They're exposed. And they know that people are going [to check them out]. If you've got a five-star rating, then there are going to be lineups to get into your nursing home. And if you've got a below-the-sub-pump rating, nobody is going to come near you; you're going to be out of business.

That can be rewarding. The most important thing is taking a reward from the benefit that you can help bring about. And the other is esteem from your colleagues. If you do good work and your colleagues know it, that is a big reward in itself. It's not necessarily winning big national awards, or anything like that. It's the respect of your peers. And that can lead to other stories, collaborations, opportunities—even writing books, working for non-governmental groups or other groups in a particular field that you're interested in. Excellence does have its own reward; it can be individual, but it's also a community benefit, a social benefit.

The effort is also collective, in a sense, even in the case of a lone reporter working the big investigative scoop. For every reporter on a big story, there are dozens holding down the newsroom, looking after the daily stuff. The support of those colleagues can come only to reporters doing good work, reporters who earn the respect of their peers. If that's the case, there won't be any grumbling about the investigative reporter's unavailability for city hall or spot news duty. And at the end of the day, there will be the pat on back and the 'Hey, great story!' from valued colleagues. This is more than nicety; it's part of what keeps reporters going.

If I were to sum it up for your students, I'd say these are your priorities: Number one, you want to correct social ills or expose where people are being injured or put at risk, whether it's airbags in cars, bad inspections at airlines, or dirty gas—whatever. If that's your number-one priority, that's good.

If number two is the respect of colleagues for excellence in your field, and number three is making a living, in that order, then you're a good candidate for investigative reporting—assuming that the reporting skills are equal. But if it's the reverse—you want to have fame and fortune as an investigative reporter—that's the first wrong step.

The curious thing is that you rarely meet an egotistical investigative reporter; the work seems to require a more passionate interest in the world than in oneself, and so mitigates against the long-term involvement of reporters with overarching egos.

The other thing I'd say, and this is partly based on my own career, is that there really are a million stories in the naked city. There's a story behind almost every door. Keep your ears open and an eagle eye, because there are stories everywhere.

# Commentary

One lesson to be learned from McKay's work is never to stint on research. Sometimes it takes a critical mass of information before you begin to see the real issues emerge. If McKay had limited his research geographically or historically, he would never have been able to reach some of the Reinventing Our Wheels series' most compelling conclusions—including that there are solutions. This is crucial: Good investigative reporting reveals problems, but also places them in a larger context and asks how the wrongs detailed arose, and how they may be made right. It isn't squeamish (it faces facts and names names), but it also goes beyond pointing the finger of blame to articulating possible solutions.

Reinventing Our Wheels shows the radical difference between beat reporting—especially political reporting—and true investigative journalism. McKay himself noted that he could never return to the sources on some of his investigative stories, that his technique was basically a one-time 'hit and run' affair. On the other hand, the investigative reporter still must cultivate non-hostile sources, such as activists and other people who want the truth to come out or at least are not invested in keeping it hidden. Thus the hit-and-run strategy, despite its occasional necessity, is meant only for hostile sources, those who have something to lose if the truth is told. Remember that McKay began considering the question of air pollution from cars after getting a tip from an activist. Aspiring reporters need to learn to really listen to rather than subtly prejudge source information. Don't swallow it whole, but do check it out.

McKay's tip was important, but it would not have led to a full-blown series without the reporter's ability to think outside the box. Investigative stories aren't generally derivative, or don't have to be—they can arise seemingly out of the 'thin air' of a reporter's reflections. As McKay noted, there had been plenty of stories about the damage the automobile engine does to our lungs, but no one had yet addressed the issues in such cohesive fashion.

The series emphasizes again the need for management support to get good investigative work to print. Expecting a newspaper, whose revenue lifeblood is advertising dollars, to criticize an economic and cultural icon such as the car in bold print is asking a lot. It takes an independent mind, like McKay's, to even conceive of the notion, and a pioneering spirit, like Neil Reynolds's, to see it to the finish line.

Such reporters and editors exist across this country, and not just at major big-city dailies. Trudy Beyak, an investigative reporter with the *Abbotsford News* for more than fifteen years, is credited as the driving force behind the termination of SE-2 (Sumas Energy 2), the plan by a US company to build a $400 million power plant in Sumas, Washington, just across the border from Abbotsford, a small city (population 114,000) in British Columbia's Fraser Valley. Beyak broke the story in the *Abbotsford News* on 3 June 2000. She continued to report on developments as the story unfolded and in March 2006 the company officially terminated its SE-2 project.[34]

Notice that the Reinventing Our Wheels series doesn't try to soften the impact of its revelations by mincing words or taking refuge in generalities—a common tendency in cub reporters. Instead, it names the individuals and the cars and the companies at issue and relies for 'safety' (from legal action) on the techniques of verification, on making certain that what is stated can be proved. What the investigative reporter writes may anger some of those involved in a story, but as long as the story is accurate and verifiably so, there is nothing untoward about that displeasure. Remember that your first loyalty must be to the truth, to finding it and telling it to your readers.

Literariness has a place in newspaper journalism. Many reporters get into the business because they want to write (and many fine reporters entered journalism for other reasons, too). But if there's poetry in you, bring it to the story. If you have a particular knack for narrative, let it roll: It isn't misplaced and won't make the story less investigative or hard-hitting. McKay certainly employed his literary talent in writing Reinventing Our Wheels. He used a technique sometimes referred to as *the circle technique* to make a long and wide-ranging series hang together, beginning with an evolutionary view of the human lung as 'nature's most elegantly efficient machine,' and returning in the final story of the series to compare the air pollution and health hazard represented by the horse-powered transportation of a century ago to those afflicting today's exhaust-soaked cities.[35]

About The Kirschbaum File, McKay is right, I think, that it underlines the sea change in the newspaper industry in the last couple of decades. The story behind the story of The Kirschbaum File reads like something from another century. It is hard to even imagine the story getting into print in today's newsroom, where the most common editorial cry is not 'Get thee to Czechoslovakia,' but 'Can you do it on the phone?' And yet, great editors, though perhaps not as well known as Neil Reynolds, still exist at Canadian newspapers. The proof is in the first-rate investigative journalism still being done at newspapers across the country.

For the aspiring reporter, then, another lesson: You've got to fight for the story, beginning with pitching the idea. Like people in other kinds of endeavours, you're bound to miss 100 per cent of the 'shots' you never take. The reporter who assumes the worst instead of going for the best ends by failing even to notice story ideas worth pursuing. I've heard many journalism students pre-rule on the chances for publication of a pet idea ('But no one will ever publish it!' they say.) That kind of thinking is a thinly disguised cop-out. Paul McKay's unlikely series on the car would never have seen print if he'd allowed himself to engage in such thinking.

Last lesson: Think about the work itself and how to get it done, not about the many obstacles to be faced on the road to completion. You can handle those one at a time, the way they come.

# Endnotes

1.  'The greenest gas in Canada', *Ottawa Citizen* (23 May 2001), A11.

2.  'The green, green gas of home', *Ottawa Citizen* (23 May 2001), A1.

3.  'Big rigs: Dirty by design: Big-rig engines are among the dirtiest on wheels', *Ottawa Citizen* (22 May 2001), A1.

4.  'Canada's fuel-cell revolution', *Ottawa Citizen* (24 May 2001), A1.

5.  'The hidden costs of plug-in cars', *Ottawa Citizen* (25 May 2001), A1.

6.  'Ford Thinks it has "a bright idea"', *Ottawa Citizen* (25 May 2001), A13.

7.  'The plot against big, dumb cars: An unlikely David is poised to topple the Goliath of the auto industry, pitting his smart, light cars against the lumbering fuel-guzzlers', *Ottawa Citizen* (26 May 2001), B3.

8.  'The trouble with light trucks: A decade-long surge in sales of gas-guzzling SUVs, pickup trucks and minivans has cost Canadians cleaner air. It's the auto and oil companies that are profiting', *Ottawa Citizen* (27 May 2001), A1.

9.  'How rules were bent for the PT Cruiser', *Ottawa Citizen* (27 May 2001), A10.

10. 'Ford leads Big Three in green makeover', *Ottawa Citizen*. (28 May 2001), A1.

11. 'Jetta beats the hybrids for clean driving', *Ottawa Citizen* (29 May 2001), A11.

12. See the following series stories in the *Ottawa Citizen*: 'The communal commute' (30 May 2001), A15; 'Pay only for what you need: The car-sharing co-op option' (30 May 2001), A1; and 'Athlete walks the walk in clean-air campaign: Olympian swears off private automobiles' (6 June 2001), A1.

13. See the following: 'How our transit lost its way' (2 June 2001), A1; 'Federal government favours car commutes' (4 June 2001), A1; and 'Canada fails to green own fleet' (5 June 2001), A1.

14. 'How the continent's best transit works', *Ottawa Citizen* (31 May 2001), A1. See also in the *Citizen*, 'Tele-commuting: fast, cheap, smog-free' (7 June 2001), A9; and 'A radical's ultimate mobility solution' (7 June 2001), A8.

15. 'Smarter fuels, vehicles, cities', *Ottawa Citizen* (8 June 2001), A14.

16. See *Electric Empire: The Inside Story of Ontario Hydro* (Toronto: Between the Lines, 1983).

17. The series wasn't nominated for any automotive awards but it did get nominated for, and won, a National Newspaper Award in 2002.

18. 'The communal commute: Jack Bell spent $600,000 of his own money to help clear Vancouver's roads of congestion and reduce the city's smog problem', *Ottawa Citizen* (30 May 2001), A15.

19. After graduating in 1978 from Trent University in Peterborough, Ontario, with a bachelor's degree in English literature and philosophy, McKay went to work as staff director for the Ontario Public Interest Research Group. He started writing for newspapers when he left that job in 1983, and in 1985 won his first National Newspaper Award for a series on the Ontario Workers Compensation Board, published in the *Kingston Whig-Standard*.

20. McKay's five-month investigation into the Law Society of Ontario produced a series called 'Lowering the Bar' that ran in November 1998. For the first piece in the series, see 'How crooked lawyers dodge justice: Law Society watchdog fails to protect clients from shady members', *Ottawa Citizen* (7 November 1998), A1.

21. This series ran in six parts in the *Ottawa Citizen* beginning 26 April 2003.

22. On 17 June 2002, after thirty-one years with the *Ottawa Citizen*, editor Russell Mills was fired by CanWest for failing to submit to his employer a story and an editorial on a scandal involving the prime minister. The firing raised a media storm of protest. See Joel Ruimy's article in *Media Magazine* online: 'Fired: If former *Ottawa Citizen* publisher Russell Mills can get sacked, then all journalists should watch their backs', *Media Magazine* (1 July 2002): www.caj.ca/mediamag/summer2002/pov.html.

23. I largely agree with McKay about the meaning of the transition from Centre for Investigative Journalism to Canadian Association of Journalists. On the other hand, with people like the CBC's David McKie at the helm of the CAJ's publication *Media* magazine, the situation appears to be changing again. McKie is an expert in computer-assisted reporting and thoroughly supports investigative work. See his article on the subject in the spring 2004 edition of *Media* magazine: 'Read all about it: *Media* magazine will resume doing its part to support investigative journalism' (1 April 2004), 4.

24. Paul McKay, 'The Kirschbaum File', *Kingston Whig-Standard* (10 December 1988), 1–47.

25. Davies was editor of the paper from 1942 to 1955, and publisher from 1955 to 1965.

26. Paul McKay, *The Roman Empire: The Unauthorized Life and Times of Stephen Roman* (Toronto: Key Porter, 1991).

27. *Electric Empire: The Inside Story of Ontario Hydro*, op. cit.

28. Rudolf Vrba, *I Escaped From Auschwitz* (Barricade Books, 2002). First published in London in 1963 under the title *I Cannot Forgive*, the book originated in a sixty-page report (known as the Vrba-Wetzler Report) on the Nazi-era Auschwitz death camp in Poland. Complete with diagrams of the camp layout, the report is considered one of the most critical documents of the era and is generally credited with saving the lives of 200,000 Hungarian Jews whose planned death train to Auschwitz was halted only by the report's revelations. The record indicates that the report was read by Western leaders (including Franklin Roosevelt and Winston Churchill and the Pope).

    In the original 1963 memoir *I Cannot Forgive*, Vrba criticized the role of Jewish councils in Europe during the war, accusing them of complicity in the final deportations of Slovak and Hungarian Jews to Nazi death camps. He wrote also of having been appalled at the West's sluggish political response to his wartime report. The book made him controversial among Holocaust historians and unpopular with some Jewish communities (it wasn't translated into Hebrew until 1998). Eventually, Vrba got some of the recognition he deserved: Israel's University of Haifa bestowed an honorary doctorate, and the One World International Human Rights Film Festival established an award in his name. The Vrba-Wetzler Report formed part of the documentation of the Nuremberg trials, and thus part of the annals of Holocaust literature. After the war, at a trial in Frankfurt, Vrba's testimony helped convict several SS guards. In Canada, where Vrba immigrated after earning a doctorate in Prague, he served as chief witness for the prosecution in the trial of Holocaust denier Ernst Zundel in 1985.

29. Paul McKay, 'Escape from Auschwitz', *Ottawa Citizen* (6 May 2005), A6.

30. The article appeared about a year before Vrba's death on 27 March 2006.

31. Stone, who died in 1989, published *I.F. Stone's Weekly*. His journalistic prowess was based on his technique of in-depth document research, presaging the advent of modern database analysis and computer assisted reporting.

32. McKay is referring here to a book I.F. Stone wrote late in his career, and for which he prepared by teaching himself to read ancient Greek. See *The Trial of Socrates* (Boston: Little, Brown and Company, 1988).

33. See McKay's six-part series, 'Ontario's Nursing Home Crisis', which ran in the *Ottawa Citizen* beginning 26 April 2003.

34. See www.siwc.ca/awards/chambercommerce_winners.php.

35. Paul McKay, 'Smarter fuels, vehicles, cities', *Ottawa Citizen* (8 June 2001), A14.

# Chapter 3

# Death Wish

In 2001, the *Globe and Mail* sent its earth sciences reporter around the world to investigate the state of the planet and its worst environmental hot spots. The resulting four-part series by Alanna Mitchell, called Death Wish, ran in the summer of that year and won instant accolades. A gifted writer, Mitchell had earned the earth sciences beat and the series assignment during her stint running the Calgary bureau for the *Globe* from 1994 to 2000.

It was then that Mitchell became fascinated with the complex and intertwined issues of environment, evolution, and extinction theory. Her fascination and her independent studies culminated in an article she wrote about Madagascar and its disappearing forests. In the spring of 2000, Mitchell's story won the prize for best environmental reporting from the International Union for the Conservation of Nature (IUCN).[1] With the prize came a term of study at Oxford University, so Mitchell headed to England with her two young children in tow. There, she wrote a thesis about the evolutionary history of the world's environmental crisis, a thesis she would later explore in even greater depth and with superb literary flourish in her first book, *Dancing at the Dead Sea: Tracking the World's Environmental Hotspots.*[2]

When Mitchell returned to the *Globe and Mail*'s main Toronto office after her Calgary stint, she made a bid for the earth sciences beat. A sympathetic editor gave her the job. In the Death Wish series, Mitchell used all she had learned in the previous years—all the scientific background, vocabulary, and insight—to bring readers a scathing account of the damage wreaked by human activity around the globe. Travelling to Alberta, the Middle East, the Canadian Arctic, and South America, she interviewed experts, activists, and officials to tell readers about the state of the planet.

In addressing several complex issues, Mitchell wove science with legend, and, in an unusually complete newspaper narrative that drew on cutting-edge research, sounded the alarm: Earth's very life-support systems are being compromised by human activities and threatening the species with extinction.

The Death Wish series exemplifies that variety of investigative journalism known as *issues reporting*. It requires that the reporter be especially determined, persistent, and thorough. Issues reporting involves finding the right new pieces of information to hang the old issues on, and of course persuading editors, cautious by nature, that the resulting stories will be worth the expense of time and resources required. The great potential of issues reporting is its power to educate and engage the public.

Does the human species have a death wish? Is it bound for extinction? These are the questions that drove Mitchell's 2001 series; over the course of a year, she visited four environmental trouble spots to try to answer them.

The investigation took her first to the Canadian West (where she covered the extinction of the dinosaurs and the newest theories of their demise); then to the Middle East (to document the ravages of desertification and the coming water crisis); after that, to the Arctic (to report on the climate change effects of global warming that threaten an ancient way of life and, ultimately, human survival); and, finally, to South America (to study the disappearance of the tropical rainforests and introduce readers to a noted environmental activist, 'a man with a plan to save the planet').

The series dealt with evolution and the so-called sixth extinction—the contention that humans will follow the dinosaurs and disappear from Earth in a sixth extinction 'spasm'—as well as with the idea of the human species as a kind of fifth element because of its global reach and apparent supremacy. The stories carried a common theme: having upset the world's ecological balance, humans are blithely doing irreparable harm to the planet and ensuring their own disappearance.

The layout team at the *Globe and Mail*, a paper well known for comprehensive coverage and superior design acumen, outdid itself on Death Wish. The exceptional spreads—featuring dramatic photographs and illustrations along with numerous sidebars that provided snapshots of the major issues—seemed to emphasize and mirror the scope of the investigation. And like the book after it, the newspaper series ended on a note of hope, showing what had been accomplished as well as destroyed, and what might yet avert disaster.

Publication of Death Wish in 2001 was timed to coincide with the beginning of Canada Environment Week, the ninth anniversary of the 1992 Earth Summit in Rio de Janeiro, and the UN's annual World Environment Day. Response was extraordinary, from the public as well as from the scientific community.

The opening piece[3] on the front of the Focus section put the crisis summarily: As water loss becomes critical and forest cover vanishes, temperatures rise and ice caps melt. The result is massive climate change that upsets the balance of the ecosystem. Species are compromised and begin to go extinct. The opening page jumped to an interior centre spread, where Mitchell cited the figures for species at risk (nearly a quarter of all mammal species) and quoted experts who said that unless the situation could be reversed, the extinction of the human species would occur even more rapidly than had that of the dinosaurs, the last creatures to rule the planet before humans inherited the earth.

But while the dinosaurs disappeared after succumbing to natural forces beyond their control, Mitchell wrote, humans are authoring their own demise. Taking readers to a dinosaur park in Alberta's badlands, the article told a cautionary tale, launching into the drafts of pre-history with an irresistible eight-word sentence: 'They call it the day the dinosaurs died.'[4]

This first story introduced a Canadian dinosaur expert, noted palaeontologist Philip Currie, who had a new theory—one with chilling implications—about how the dinosaurs had disappeared from the planet. Headlined 'At least the dinosaurs had an excuse', Mitchell's story turned complex science into gripping narrative as she introduced the idea that the human species constitutes a kind of fifth element, as powerful as earth, air, water, and fire, and that the ubiquity of humans and their failure to heed environmental warning signs will engender their extinction.

The piece reads like a detective novel as the reporter accompanies Currie on a tour of the badlands, home to more complete dinosaur skeletons than any other place in the world. But the article is no dry recitation of species-incriminating science. Mitchell used her incisive intellect, abundant literary gifts, and writer's eye for detail to reveal, in few words, something of the man behind the theory: 'Moments later, Currie crouches again, folding his long legs beneath him like a cricket. Triumphantly, he pries loose something that looks just like a square bit of mosaic. "Tendon!" he announces, smiling.'[5]

The established wisdom on dinosaurs held that an asteroid hit Earth some sixty-five million years ago and destroyed them. But according to Currie's new theory, Mitchell explained, the dinosaurs' demise was more complex. Eons before the final catastrophe, the dinosaurs had fallen victim to changing weather systems they could not adapt to. This weakened the species and presaged its disappearance even before the asteroid struck. In fact, had the asteroid hit ten million years earlier, the new theory posited, the dinosaurs would likely have survived, mammals would never have arisen, and humans would not have had the chance to advance to the top of the food chain. Then the kicker, as Mitchell noted the difference between the dinosaurs' situation and our own: 'Dinosaurs were the victims of fate. *Homo sapiens* is orchestrating its own downfall. Humans have become a force of nature—and a malignant one.'[6]

The damage humans are doing to the Earth has put the whole human species at risk, the series showed, as water sources are poisoned and/or exhausted, air is polluted, and the Earth itself is over-tilled and over-cleared to the point of interference with its carbon cycle. The behavioural habits of humans all added up to rapid climate change and a roster of associated environmental degradations dire enough to threaten the survival of animal species in general and humans in particular.[7]

Delivering several mini-lessons in earth sciences and evolutionary theory, the story's end had palaeontologist Currie drawing the connections between the demise of the dinosaurs and the possibility of humanity's own. 'Right now,' he said, 'we're blindly going along and destroying things and that could ultimately contribute to our own destruction.'[8] Mitchell ended with an implicit question, but one that science alone can't answer: Have we reached the point of no return?

The series' second instalment took Mitchell to the Middle East, to the deserts of Jordan, to investigate the state of the world's water and the single biggest environmental threat of desertification, the parching of the planet.[9] We learn that in the first ninety-five years of the twentieth century, water consumption rose sixfold, depleting groundwater reserves at crisis proportions in some places, like Azraq—the Eden of human civilization—where water consumption had outpaced the replenishing role of natural precipitation and turned a once-cool oasis into searing desert. Startling photographs of the parched ground of Azraq accompanied the text, which explained how the once-legendary oasis at Azraq was transformed—sucked dry of its water—in only thirteen years.

It was a phenomenon replicated around the globe, leaving some areas wanting, while in others water was so abundant that consumption rose as if no crisis threatened. From 1900 to 1995, world water consumption had increased at more than double the rate of the population. In some places, including Azraq, usage rates were so high that surface supplies literally shrank and groundwater reserves were depleted faster than they could be filled. Mitchell's story told how the Jordanians had begun pumping water from Azraq's ancient springs in 1980 and, by 1993, the area was declared an ecological disaster. In 1994, efforts were launched to reclaim the oasis from the encroaching desert, and while this effort was justly lauded internationally by environmentalists (in four years, the reclamation work succeeded in coaxing back a small part of the wetlands), the project's continuation was subject to the caprice of political expediency.

The story quoted an expert who cited the world's water shortages as the most serious single source of an environmental crisis. The water problem, along with the erosion of forest cover and rapid climate change, boded ill for the very near future. Here, Mitchell delivered more mini-lessons on how water, which 'should be the ultimate renewable resource', is supposed to work, and in so doing brought the story home to Canada, the country with the world's largest stores of freshwater: 'But humans are bungling their stewardship of freshwater stores all over the world—even, as Canadians well know, in places blessed with abundance.'[10]

For the third story, Mitchell travelled to Canada's Arctic to investigate the global warming that threatens a way of life thousands of years old, and ultimately the Earth itself.[11] She took readers to the hamlet of Sachs Harbour on Banks Island to 'see' the effects of 'the big melt'—the thinning of the sea ice from the ravages of global warming—on the land and on the way of life of the people who have lived there generation after generation. The Inuvialuit know that the Arctic sea ice should be thick and solid, that it shouldn't look like 'a sheet of frosted glass that has been dropped on a concrete floor'. And they had been reporting the changes in the sea ice and their polar environment to the International Institute for Sustainable Development, based in Winnipeg.

This penultimate story of the Death Wish series introduced Rosemarie Kuptana, who was born in the Arctic and had devoted most of her life to fighting for her people. President of the Inuit Tapirisat of Canada in the 1990s, Kuptana had been aware of the environmental threats to the Far North and her way of life; her grandfather had 'prophesied years ago that the sea would grow warm'. In November 2000, Kuptana presented a video that documented dramatic evidence of pollution's global warming on the land and life of the Inuvialuit. 'Polluters may not get the point,' Mitchell wrote, 'but the residents of Sachs Harbour can't avoid it.'[12]

Mitchell's fourth and final story took her to the equatorial rainforests of Suriname in South America and to US primatologist Russell Mittermeier, president of Conservation International, and the 'man with a plan to save the planet'.[13] Formed in 1987, Conservation International promoted investor-friendly solutions that would see conservationists and companies working together. A 1999 *Time* magazine article had lauded Mittermeier for his unorthodox but effective campaigns, including one that averted a planned logging operation and established instead 1.6 million hectares of untouched rainforest as the Central Suriname Nature Reserve.

In the manner of intrepid reporters everywhere, Mitchell braved many of the dangers the rainforest had to offer, including harpies, piranhas, vipers, and jaguars, to follow Mittermeier around and get the story. Mittermeier was, after all, 'considered by many to be the world's mightiest environmentalist'. In fact, Mitchell couldn't have invented a better hero around which to build the narrative had she been writing a novel. For over a quarter of a century, Mittermeier had been returning to the wilds of Suriname, where he first visited as a young 'monkey researcher' working on field studies for his doctorate.

Devoid of sanctimony, the final *Globe* story bristled with excitement and adventure, with Mitchell showing readers something of the exotic culture behind the ecology. She relayed, for example, the legend of Werehpai, 'a member of the Akijo tribe, [who] the cannibals said . . . lived in the caves for thousands of years'. As the final story drew to an end, Mitchell brought her readers close, managing to slip in the first-person pronoun, normally excised from newspaper copy: 'Finally, I realize that the piranhas have become a metaphor. Fear of them—just like the fear of challenging the forces that injure the planet—is strongest when imagined and never faced.'[14]

# The Interview
(6 March 2006)

The idea for Death Wish began to hatch several years before the series actually ran. It was 1994, and Mitchell was posted to Alberta to open a Calgary bureau for the *Globe and Mail*. She would end up staying until 2000 and developing the background knowledge that would lead to the series that changed her career path and her life.

> The *Globe* already had a business bureau there, but they wanted to bump up the quotient of news from Alberta. They had somebody in Edmonton doing the political stuff, but they wanted somebody based in Calgary. It was very much a [then publisher] William Thorsell thing. He had come from Alberta, and he believed trends would be set in Alberta, and he wanted somebody to cover them. It was very controversial at the time within the paper, because nobody but Thorsell wanted a reporter in Calgary.
>
> I was sent there on sufferance . . . but once I got there I had a lot of range. I started to look around to see what I wanted to write about and one of the things that fascinated me at the time was what was happening with the natural parks. Because at that time nobody knew that the national parks were in ecological trouble. It was just barely on the radar screen.

The impetus for the first story she wrote about the national parks was a phone call from a local activist.

> One of the environmentalists in Calgary called me up and said, 'You know there's a real problem with Banff National Park.' And I said, 'You've got to be kidding.' He said, 'No, just call any biologist you want to. And if you want, I'll show you all the documents. I'll take you out there and show you.' So I thought, 'Well, this is a great story, if it's true.' And it turned out to be true.

I was just fascinated with these issues, with the policy issues. If we have a policy that says we're supposed to have a national park that's ecologically sound and we don't have a park that's ecologically sound, what's happening? What's missing? That fascinated me.

So, I became interested in the national parks, and then I just got reading. I got on this learning curve and I was absolutely fascinated with all these issues.

Mitchell's reading jag and learning curve began with a 1998 article by David Quammen in *Harper's Magazine*.[15] She can still remember that very first piece and the circumstances of the reading.

I had gone to cover something and one of the environmentalists I was interviewing said, 'I read this really interesting piece, by David Quammen. It's on the sixth extinction.' I read it coming back on the plane [to the Toronto bureau of the *Globe and Mail*] and I was just immersed in it. I had already done a whole lot of work on a bunch of other things. I'd done a lot of work in the field—scientists are so generous with their time, they just explain things to you. I received an amazing education from Canadian and US scientists. And whenever I had a really huge question, I would phone my dad—secret weapon!—and he'd explain it all to me.

The daughter of esteemed field biologist George Mitchell, Alanna grew up in the Prairies and early on acquired an interest in environmental policy issues, honed by dinner table conversations with her father. She never lost that interest. From the time of the first parks story, she was hooked on its wider ecological implications. Mitchell's correspondence with her father was a pleasure for both—dinnertime conversation paying off—and the journalist continues to consult her secret weapon regularly in the course of her work.

Mitchell wrote the inaugural piece about the national parks in 1994, the first year of her Western sojourn. But afterwards, she said, 'I got a hell of a lot of grief from the *Globe* and was not allowed to write about parks for quite a while.' Grief aside, she was still thinking about the issues when she returned to the Toronto bureau of the paper in 2000, after her marriage 'disintegrated abruptly'.

For ages, I'd thought about trying to write something about the sixth extinction spasm. And I thought and thought and thought and thought and thought, because, you know, it's hard to pitch something very abstract to newspaper editors. And finally I found a project in Madagascar that I thought would combine different things: there was a business angle, there was this really great environmental angle, and there was a Canadian angle.

The Madagascar story[16] would win a prestigious award from the International Union for the Conservation of Nature (IUCN) in 2000 (a prize that included a term of study at Oxford University) and lead the following year to her writing the Death Wish series. Note that the Madagascar story was not assigned to her by the paper's editors. It arose from Mitchell's own initiative, and, moreover, she had to fight hard to get to write it.

> I pulled in every favour I had at the paper—I mean every favour I had. I just went over there for like twenty cents, and came back with this story, and it won this big award from the IUCN. That looked good on the paper, and by that time we had an editor who was a Brit, Richard Addis, who could see the sense in writing about these issues. It wasn't all foreign territory to him; he could see the value in that. It coincided with me coming back to Toronto. I said to him, 'I want to be the earth sciences reporter.' And he said, 'Okay.'

The IUCN is also known widely as the World Conservation Union. Based in Switzerland, it set up, with the Reuters Foundation, the prize for environmental reporting that Mitchell won in 2000 for the Madagascar story. When she submitted the Death Wish series the following year, World Conservation Union officials told her they didn't want her to win the award two years in a row, and finally they asked Mitchell 'not to apply any more', although she served subsequently as a judge for the annual competition.

The battle for the Madagascar story turned out to be worth the burnout. On the basis of that story, the sympathetic editor (Addis) suggested she go ahead and write a series.

> I was just supposed to be doing news and feature writing on earth sciences. I really wanted it to have a strong sciences bent. . . . I argued strongly against doing a '70s paradigm of the good guys and the bad guys—you know, the valiant little environmentalist against the big bad companies—because I think it's so much more complex, more global than that. And he could see that, so after I won the award, Addis said, 'Well we're really interested in a series. Why don't you think about doing a series?' And that's how Death Wish came about.

Strangely, Mitchell attributes her coming up with the ideas for Death Wish to blind serendipity, and not to her long hours of learning or her persistent arguments for the story. It's interesting how frequently gifted reporters will credit luck for their story ideas. I think that may be their word for inspiration. Mitchell is no exception. 'I just came up with these ideas—it was just absolute luck,' she said. I have a theory about that too: When you're doing what you're supposed to be doing, the universe kicks in.

Think about all those old adages that get at basically the same point: 'God helps those who help themselves,' for instance, or 'The harder I work the luckier I get.'

The research for Death Wish took Mitchell around the world, but it also took her far afield in terms of original expectations. She began with the usual, and required, reporter's skepticism, and ended by sounding the environmental alarm. All that takes a good deal of work. But the real feat, she maintains (and virtually all investigative reporters will tell you the same thing), is making sure the piece gets in the newspaper.

> The trick is always to get it *into* the paper. You can do all this research and do all this thinking and develop stories like I did for this oceans book [*The Deeps: The Secret Ecological Crisis*, released in 2007]. I mean, a lot of the thinking for this oceans book I did at the *Globe*, and tried to pitch the stories. They just said, 'Forget it, we're not interested. We've already written about the end of the universe. What else have you got?' So I replied, 'You don't say that about hockey stories.' But it didn't work.

To ensure that the Death Wish stories would run, Mitchell thought strategically.

> The way I got that one into the paper was to develop a little catch phrase for it, which was not Death Wish at all. It was about the fifth element, humans as the fifth element. Originally, those four stories were supposed to be one for each element, and I wrote them originally in that way.

But that's not how it worked out for the series (and neither would this architectural idea make it into the book she would write several years later).

> In the end, it all fell out. We didn't do it that way in the paper and by the time I wrote the book, I just didn't feel like I wanted to talk about that. I wanted to talk about something different.

One of the most satisfying aspects of the series (reminiscent of Paul McKay's series on the car discussed in Chapter 2) was its ending on a note of hope. After the third piece, the reader could be forgiven for feeling overloaded. But the fourth piece, the last, redeemed reader interest by offering solutions under an irresistible headline: 'The man with a plan to save the planet'.

Brilliantly executed, Mitchell's final Death Wish article is like insurance against reader doldrums, a savvy piece of writing that pre-empts a 'What's the use?' response. At the same time, Mitchell's voice pervades the article and provokes an equally personal response in the reader. Like a whispered call to redemption, it elicits caring. And it was no mistake. Mitchell said she realized fully that people would need 'some big Tarzan hero' to be able to consider the issues without getting so discouraged that they would give up thinking about them altogether. That part, she said, 'was very strategic'. Also, Mitchell herself 'wanted to have a solution'.

Of Death Wish, Mitchell said she wishes she had 'written it better', but in fact the series was beautifully written—stark, evocative, compelling. And reader response was over the top, fully evident in the stream of phone calls, letters, and emails it provoked.

> I remember the absolute flood of letters and emails I got for months after the series ran. People wrote to say that their lives had changed as a result of it and other wonderful things like that. I had never received such a response to anything I'd written.

The major obstacle for Mitchell on Death Wish, aside from the massive amount of time required to research and write the series, was to convince the *Globe*'s editors that the project was worthy of the space. Reporters working on investigative pieces know they cannot afford to get it wrong, even in minor ways. Because what is being proposed is new, critical, and often countercultural, publication is bound at the very least to ruffle some feathers. The reporter must burn the midnight oil and leave no trace of smoke, making sure every last detail is corroborated.

Getting the go-ahead to write can also prove elusive. That Mitchell had to fight for the series should be a lesson to students and young reporters. Just because a story idea doesn't get support immediately from editors (or teachers), doesn't necessarily mean it's not viable. In fact, Mitchell thinks it's probably a *good* sign to get initial resistance from the top.

> It probably means it's a *great* story. You're always pushing boundaries. In some ways, I wish that I had pushed harder, because the first part of the series went on a Saturday and the other three Monday, Tuesday, Wednesday, in much less space. I wish we had had—they were originally thinking a separate section. I wish I had been able to convince them to think bigger on that.

Immediately after the series ran, she continued to write earth sciences stories and was able to report scientific findings on climate change and extinction, mostly because the field was burgeoning across disciplines.

> You know how science and medicine sometimes just coalesce around an issue? For a while, it was the human genome project, and I think right now it's climate change. And that was becoming more and more clear even back then, when I wrote the piece. I could envision myself with pieces of the puzzle. So the way I tried to follow it up was to really keep track of a lot of the journals and to try to

do it on a strictly scientific basis, because I felt that that was considered to be a harder, a more palatable way to write about it. In the end, it wasn't; it was just dismissed as a social beat.

But soon after Death Wish, things began to change for Mitchell. Her job at the *Globe and Mail* became difficult, in ways first subtle and finally intolerable. She realized in a kind of aftershock that the series had altered her career trajectory, and in fact 'changed my whole life'. She took an unpaid leave from the paper to write her first book, the stunning *Dancing at the Dead Sea*. It was then that the editors decided she should be removed from the earth sciences beat.

> The editor phoned me up and said, 'Well, I'm taking you off the beat. I don't want you to write about this any more. I want you to write about education.' I said, 'But I'm not interested in education,' and he said, 'But you're a mother, you'll do it well.' I eventually did write a little more about science, near the end when all the other science reporters left and they allowed me to do some very basic stuff—they said they would have to rein me in tightly. But they allowed me to do a little bit of reporting on science.

Why did the paper's management want to take such hard-won expertise and throw it out the window? Mitchell believes 'they didn't like the conclusions I came to.' This despite the fact that reader response showed many had been moved to tears by the stories, at once provocative and satisfying.

The initial friction worsened steadily after the series ran, and ultimately resulted in her leaving the newspaper. The editor in Mitchell's corner, Richard Addis, had left the *Globe* and his replacement wasn't interested in earth sciences.

> Eventually, when I was writing *Dancing at the Dead Sea*, he told me I was no longer allowed to write about those issues. After I'd won three international awards, and gone to Oxford, and written a book. That was the main reason I quit.

Leaving the *Globe and Mail* took courage, and getting to that point took some time. Mitchell found that the job had become untenable—not all at once, but over a period of several years after her return to Toronto from the Calgary posting, and especially after Death Wish ran.

After Mitchell won the prestigious IUCN environmental journalism award for her story on Madagascar, she got the chance to spend a year studying at Oxford. But to be able to take advantage of the opportunity required her to make more sacrifices. Unable to secure a leave of absence from the paper, she banked overtime hours, working extra days, holidays, and weekends, to facilitate the year's study. Thus she managed to make good on the Oxford fellowship, and spent 2002 in England with her two children.

The next year, Mitchell took four months of unpaid leave to do more research for *Dancing at the Dead Sea*. Then health problems interfered with her plans and she was forced to take a medical leave. Senior management was not pleased.

When she got back to the newsroom, Mitchell was 'in the doghouse'. Her absences, it turned out, had upset some people in high places. After wondering for a while whence the cold shoulder, she consulted with a senior editor about the situation, and learned that she had indeed displeased the paper's management.

> I was absolutely in the doghouse. And I finally went up to one of the most senior editors I worked with there and asked, 'What is going on here? It's suddenly like I've murdered someone.' And she said, 'Well, it's strike three.' And I said, 'What do you mean?' She replied, 'Well, you know, you went to Oxford, you took a book leave, and then you took a medical leave. Strike three. You haven't been here.'
>
> I thought if this had been a man who'd gone off to have heart surgery, would they ever in a million years have said that? No way.

Mitchell heard that if she worked 'very, very hard,' she might be considered rehabilitated and manage her way back into the paper's good books. Instead, she quit two weeks later, in December 2004.

Since remarried, Mitchell was a single mother at the time she made the 'crushing' decision to leave the paper where she had so distinguished herself. It wasn't an easy or obvious choice.

> I didn't have a lot of flex, but I finally got to the point where if I had to sell my house, I had to sell my house, because I just could not work there any more. It was just absolutely not possible for me. There you are—you're at the top of the profession that you've been working at for a long time. Where do you go after all that?

In terms of policy change, the influence of *Death Wish* is 'hard to pinpoint'. Despite its impact on individual readers, the series did little to reverse the phenomena Mitchell had documented. Recent figures show the planet continues to teeter toward disaster with melting ice caps, dying deserts, and emptying oceans. On 2 May 2006, the IUCN released its Red List of threatened species (up to 16,119) and revealed a continuing decline in biodiversity, with more plant and animal species facing extinction than ever before.[17] There can be little doubt, nevertheless, that Mitchell's series made a difference in terms of educating and alerting a Canadian public already sympathetic to proactive measures for environmental health.

For Mitchell as a writer, the impact was personal and couldn't have been greater. After leaving the *Globe*, she joined the International Institute for Sustainable Development and set her authorial sights on a more independent path.

Death Wish was a series of boundary-crossing significance, and, of course, it required (and requires) follow-up. But because Mitchell left the paper some years after the series ran, and even though she'd initially conceived of the project while at the *Globe*, she ended up following the story in her book *Dancing at the Dead Sea*.

Though the decision to leave the *Globe* was hard, in retrospect, Mitchell understands something of its inevitability. In fact, she left the paper uncertain whether she could commit any longer to journalism.

> I wasn't sure I could believe in it any more. And I think now I do—it's been a year and a bit—and I've done a lot of thinking about it. But I decided to do it in a different way, which is to write books and magazine pieces.

In this, she may represent the crest of a wave, one of a vanguard of professional reporters dissatisfied with the current environment in the newspaper business, and rankled enough by that dissatisfaction to seek alternatives.

Mitchell is another example of a top reporter who didn't consider herself an investigative journalist.

> I never considered myself an investigative reporter, and the *Globe* didn't either. And when you asked me, when I got your email about doing this interview, I was flabbergasted. . . . But you know what? In truth, I used to do this before. I did it with social statistics as well—that was the first thing I did at the *Globe*. And I even did it with my financial reporting when I was at the *Financial Post*. For three years, before I went to the *Globe*, I was doing a lot of fairly heavy duty investigative reporting on financial stories.

She concedes, however, that a kind of contrarian or countercultural brand of thinking did characterize her time at the *Globe and Mail*. When she left, people commented that she 'used to write all these totally unlikely stories that nobody else would have written.' Her advice to aspiring reporters is terse. The edge is still on the leaving, but for that, still useful: 'Develop a thick skin. Go to charm school.'

When you talk to journalists who have been through hell and back for the story, it's almost as if you can hear them thinking, 'Don't be an investigative reporter; be an accountant.' But usually the passion and the idealism will poke holes through the thin sheath (in Mitchell's case, gossamer thin) of self-protective cynicism. In the end, for her at least, there wasn't really much choice but to honour her strongest inclinations and strike out on her own. When Mitchell looks back at her decision to leave the *Globe and Mail,* she realizes that despite the agonizing and the hardship, she made the right choice. Passion in reporters can appear suspect to hard-nosed newspaper people, and so it was for Mitchell at the *Globe.* But she insists that same 'suspect' quality of passion is essential to the work.

> If you've really got something you think is important to say, and you're passionate about it, you need to say it. That was always a knock against me at the *Globe*—that I was too passionate. I was *way* too passionate. You know you're not supposed to be passionate if you're a newspaper reporter. Except that, as one of the senior editors pointed out to me, if you're writing about people dying of AIDS in Africa, it's okay to be passionate, because it doesn't threaten the economic system of our country. But if you're talking as I was—trying to position yourself as a science reporter—I could not be passionate. It was seen as my great fault.

At the time of our spring 2006 interview, Mitchell was at work on her second book, about the oceans (*The Deeps: The Secret Ecological Crisis*). She enjoys occasional teaching and gives university guest lectures 'with some regularity'.

> Last week, I gave a lecture at the University of Toronto's School of Continuing Studies as part of a series. So, I do that kind of stuff whenever I can. I absolutely love to teach. I get a lot out of it. Purely selfish.

She believes that if young journalists just entering the business don't understand its current challenges when they go into it, they will be likely to forfeit or forsake their idealism as they undergo the enculturation of the newsroom.

That 'gendered' attitudes also played a role in her experience at the paper is something most female reporters could likely confirm from personal experience.

> I was fighting everything, because I was a single mother, and that was seen to be a weakness. They put up with it but it seemed to be a weakness because occasionally there were things I couldn't do. Not very much, actually. I was pretty disciplined about pulling through all that stuff, because I had to be. I was the only earner in my family. So not only was I a single mother—I think they thought they kind of had me over a barrel—but there was also the fact that I was writing about science, which was really supposed to be a guy's gig.
>
> So there I was writing about science, a single mother, and—I was ambitious—I wanted to write a book and I went off to Oxford. I didn't clue in to that, but a few people told me that was part of what was going on. I don't know.

Recent studies tend to contradict the popular wisdom that says women in media have come a long way and now enjoy a greater measure of equality in their work lives than ever before. For while female journalists may be more visible in today's newspaper newsrooms than they were in decades past, they are still far from competing on equal terms. According to figures from the Canadian Newspaper Association released in 2002, although 43 per cent of all newspaper employees in Canada are female, women account for only 12 per cent of publishers and 8 per cent of editors-in-chief. And most of the women employed in newspapers are confined to 'pink-collar ghettos' (comprising 70 per cent of employees in advertising departments and 80 per cent in accounting and finance).[18]

According to MediaWatch, a Toronto-based, non-profit organization that monitors and addresses sexism in the media, while more than half of Canadian journalism graduates are female, only 30 per cent of the country's newspaper articles are written by women. Still other studies suggest that female journalists are under-represented in certain areas of major coverage considered seriously important, such as politics and the economy. Worldwide, 38 per cent of professional journalists are women and 28 per cent of newspaper editors are female; women represent only 5 per cent of managing editors and editors-in-chief.[19]

Researchers have also tackled the question of whether it matters if women hold positions of power, and answered in the affirmative:

> In 2000, women editors and journalists took over the newsroom for one day at a newspaper in Wichita Falls, Texas. For the day's top story a choice had to be made between a crime-stopper's story about a peeping tom and an item about local women fighting for equal rights. When the women opted for the latter story, a heated argument erupted. Journalist Laurence Pantin reports that 'the women finally won, but only because they held the key positions on that day. All other times, the peeping tom and stories like it would have prevailed.'[20]

Matters of intellect and gender form a subtheme in Mitchell's new book, *The Deeps*. She believes women have a distinct take on science, and that their presence in the journalistic field means stories may go in some interesting directions that might otherwise never be taken.

> The people who are looking at the oceans are women. Not all of them, but many of the really high-profile scientists in this stuff are women, because when they went into science the oceans were not the sexy topic. They went into something that was less sexy but had more scope, and now it's turning into this incredible topic. And they are asking different questions. It's possible because you have men *and* women asking questions that you're getting different answers altogether. It's really fascinating—a subtext of this book I'm writing.

Mitchell had never intended to become a journalist. Her first love was the visual arts. Still, her literary proclivities announced themselves early.

> I got into journalism because I love language, research, and writing. I took my first degree in English literature and Latin literature so I could figure out more about how the English language works and how great writers have used it over time. Then, a few years later, after I had finished paying off my student loans, I went to J-school at Ryerson.
>
> I hadn't intended to be a writer or a journalist. I originally wanted to be a visual artist and had planned to go to the Ontario College of Art after finishing high school in Regina. But I got a scholarship to go to university and ended up there. When I look back on it, I think I always wanted to show society to itself in some way. I've always had a burning curiosity and an urge to explain.

# Commentary

In the newspaper series Death Wish, Mitchell's voice is characteristically restrained. In *Dancing at the Dead Sea*, it is much more passionate. For the series, she undertook a classic journalistic investigation; for the book, she underwent a personal journey that surpassed the ordinary avenues of research and led to a transformation of her own thinking as well as to a radically altered career trajectory. In fact, although much of the material in *Dancing at the Dead Sea* originated from the *Globe* series, it's transformed in the book, where Mitchell was able to deepen the issues and give full play to the subtleties of voice. Where, for example, the newspaper series focused on environmental science, the book encompassed essentially literary forays into the personal and cultural meanings of environmental destruction.

Comparing the book to the series can be instructive in this regard. For example, while the newspaper series asks whether humans have a death wish, the book goes much further to take seriously and explore that question. And, of course, the book allows the writer to use personal pronouns, including the first-person pronoun, absolutely *verboten* in newspapers save for exceptions like columnists, guest contributors, reviewers, and letter writers. In the Death Wish series, Mitchell managed to bring personality to the newspaper page; in the book, she was much freer to use the first person liberally. For example, at one point Mitchell asks, 'Are humans incapable of seeing the big picture? I wonder'; and speculates (also generally off limits in newspaper writing), 'As a species, it's not our strong suit to think long term.'[21]

What would have been out of place in the newspaper series was carefully expanded upon in the book. Not only personal observations, but also myth and legend found a home in *Dancing at the Dead Sea*. For example, in one of the book's philosophical asides on the nature of truth, Mitchell referred to the Greek legend of the Trojan horse. She synopsized the story of Cassandra, the daughter of King Priam of Troy, and the only inhabitant who understood the imminent danger.

> She cried out her prophecy. Everyone ignored her. The next day, the Greeks, lodged in the horse's belly, broke out and turned their fury on their Trojan foes. Cassandra's fate was to be raped and then commit suicide as she was handed over to yet another Greek leader for violation.
>
> But those too blind to believe her were cursed too. Unwilling to be inconvenienced by the truth, mired in denial, they told Cassandra she talked too much. Troy fell. The Trojans were slaughtered.[22]

Where a newspaper article typically contains (or feigns) in-depth knowledge as background information or in sidebars, a book allows a writer to go beyond the facts and entertain more personal truths, while simultaneously inviting the reader to bear witness. For example, while the sixth extinction is discussed briefly in the Death Wish series, the mention is quite dry in its impersonal authority. In the book, Mitchell expresses her own deepest thinking, and misgivings, about what all the science might finally mean and why humans generally weren't paying attention to it. For instance, this:

> Why is it that we are so fixated on keeping the death of individual *Homo sapiens* at bay—with vaccination programs and anti-cancer research and intricate cardiac operations and famine relief—but we don't spend nearly as much time and money making sure the species as a whole can survive?[23]

Having posed the big question (a question that would surely have been edited out of the newspaper copy for its unabashed reference to self), Mitchell in the book attempts to answer it: '. . . No matter how capable humans are of understanding science, science will never have the emotional force of legend. Humans respond reliably not to information, but to meaning.'[24]

Mitchell had to persist in her attempts to push the envelope of the earth sciences beat, and finally, she had to follow the story in a book. Her experience exemplifies two apparently contradictory lessons to be had: First that a story may well be worth pursuing even if editors don't initially see the point of a reporter's proposal. And second, that some stories won't 'fit' in a newspaper format, which suggests that newspapers of the future may opt to widen the newspaper model, and that reporters may turn to magazines and books to tell their true stories.

Recall how after Death Wish had run, Mitchell's proposals for further stories of the same ilk struck editors as smacking of old news. It just didn't compute as news.

Consider the response of editors, as Mitchell sarcastically put it: We've already done the end of the universe. What else have you got?

Is this a trend? Will investigative and in-depth journalism move out of newspapers, to magazines, books, and as some claim, online venues? As newspapers continue to cleave to traditional formats and a focus on the so-called bottom line at the expense of the press's purported mission, will they abandon difficult, time-consuming, and expensive investigative reports?

# Endnotes

1.  Alanna Mitchell, 'A special report on the vanishing forests of Madagascar', *Globe and Mail* (15 April 2000), A13.

2.  Alanna Mitchell, *Dancing at the Dead Sea: Tracking the World's Environmental Hotspots* (Toronto: Key Porter Books, 2004).

3.  Alanna Mitchell, 'At least the dinosaurs had an excuse', *Globe and Mail* (2 June 2001), F1.

4.  Ibid., F4–F5.

5.  Ibid., F4.

6.  Ibid., F4.

7.  Ibid., F4.

8.  Ibid., F5.

9.  Alanna Mitchell, 'The world's "single biggest threat"', *Globe and Mail* (4 June 2001), A8–A9.

10. Ibid., A8.

11. Alanna Mitchell, 'How the North is getting burned', *Globe and Mail* (5 June 2001), A10–A11.

12. Ibid., A11.

13. Alanna Mitchell, 'The man with a plan to save the planet', *Globe and Mail* (6 June 2001), A10–A11.

14. Ibid., A11.

15. David Quammen, 'Planet of the Weeds', *Harper's Magazine* (October 1998, Vol. 297, Issue 1781), 57–70.

16. Alanna Mitchell, 'A special report on the vanishing forests of Madagascar', op. cit.

17. See www.iucn.org/themes/ssc/redlist2006/redlist2006.htm. 'The 2006 IUCN Red List shows a clear trend: biodiversity loss is increasing, not slowing down,' said Achim Steiner, director general of the World Conservation Union (IUCN). 'The implications of this trend for the productivity and resilience of ecosystems and the lives and livelihoods of billions of people who depend on them are far-reaching.'

18. See the article 'Women working in the media', under the category, Media Issues: Stereotyping, at the following website: www.media-awareness.ca.

19. Ibid.

20. Ibid.

21. Mitchell, *Dancing at the Dead Sea*, op. cit., 161.

22. Ibid.

23. Mitchell, *Dancing*, 57.

24. Ibid., 219.

# Chapter 4

# Asbestos, Again

In November 2003, *Toronto Star* feature writer Peter Gorrie received an information sheet from the Asbestos Institute (a Montreal-based pro-asbestos lobby group founded in 1984) that proudly proclaimed itself printed on chrysotile paper. Gorrie had requested the information sheet after learning of its existence at a conference. A lot of reporters and readers might have filed that information in the round cabinet, or turned the page and gone back to sleep.

But Gorrie knew that chrysotile is asbestos, what his subsequent article called 'a convicted mass-killer, one of the most feared substances on Earth'.

The article told the story of a highly orchestrated campaign on the part of the Quebec provincial government, the federal government, and the asbestos industry to 'rehabilitate' asbestos—the mineral known to have caused millions of deaths over the last century—on the grounds that it can be 'safely used'. Entitled 'Asbestos makeover reignites old battle', Gorrie's 2003 article managed to recap the history of the debate over asbestos, while detailing the reasons for the apparently last-ditch attempt by a desperate industry to save itself, and the economics and politics behind government support for the effort. It revealed that Canada—the third-largest producer of asbestos in the world, second only to Russia and China—and its support for 'the myth of safe use' stood in the way of the worldwide ban on asbestos urged by the mineral's many critics.

This story provides a model for investigating and explicating environmental controversy. Without taking sides, or telling the reader what to think or believe, it provided a detailed accounting of the history of asbestos and clearly set out the parameters of the (revived) debate. It shows what an alert reporter can accomplish with a single story. Instead of assuming he was dealing with a dead issue, Gorrie checked it out and was able to tell readers something they needed to know.

The idea for this story had arisen from a two-day conference sponsored by the group Ban Asbestos International. Gorrie remembered when asbestos was a hot news topic back in the 1980s, after horror stories about its health effects began to spread. But the asbestos story was supposed to be a done deal. Hadn't dozens of articles decades ago exposed asbestos as deadly? Hadn't stories in the 1960s and '70s made commonplace its status as one of the world's deadliest poisons? Didn't asbestos cause fatal lung disease? And didn't everyone agree on this?

Not quite everyone.

Though responsible for millions of deaths in the preceding century and banned in twenty other countries, asbestos is perfectly legal in Canada. In fact, the government supported the asbestos industry in the latter's attempt to rehabilitate asbestos in the public mind, to somehow make it appear safe. Both Ottawa and Quebec had contributed substantial funds to the attempt since the 1984 founding of the Asbestos Institute. While the institute spearheaded a campaign to rehabilitate asbestos, opponents lobbied for a global ban on the heat-resistant mineral.

Before its toxicity was understood, asbestos was called the 'magic mineral' and since the 1960s used in everything from car brake linings to home insulation. But it turned out that over time, tiny asbestos fibres would break away, and when these fibres were inhaled they caused a virulent and incurable form of lung cancer. Many countries banned asbestos as the horror stories of its health effects began to mount and circulate. But in Canada, asbestos is still legal and produced at three mines in Quebec's Eastern Townships.

Part of the campaign to 'prove' asbestos safe involved calling it 'chrysotile' and implying that it was somehow different from the asbestos of old. In fact, chrysotile is just another name for most of the asbestos ever used, the same asbestos that caused disease and that experts had ruled had no safe level.

Here's an important story that might not have seen print but for a reporter with a track record and a sense of responsibility. Gorrie was the only newspaper journalist to report on the conference held by Ban Asbestos International. Fortunately for readers, he had the background knowledge to see that there was a story, and the talent and experience to get it into print. This is exactly what is meant by the ability to think critically and independently that is so core to the investigative reporter.

The single story ran on the front page of the *Toronto Star* on 22 November 2003.[1]

# The Interview
(28 March 2006)

The story arose from a routine assignment to cover a two-day conference of Ban Asbestos International. Gorrie had little time to do advance research, but he did have 'some background on the issue from doing stories about fifteen years ago'. He approached the assignment 'without any preconceptions or, to be honest, great expectations about what would come of it'.

> Asbestos had been around for a long time, and I thought it was pretty much a dead issue. So I went just with that level of curiosity to see what they were about without any particular expectations of what the stories would be, whether it would be one story or a lot of stories or none. I wanted to see what was up.

Without the background on asbestos, of course, it would never have occurred to Gorrie to be interested (after all, no one else was) or to check it out (again, no one else covered the conference or the issue).

> It piqued my curiosity because I thought based on what I'd done before that it had been banned or was in the process of being banned. So why were they [Ban Asbestos International] concerned about it?

When Gorrie learned that the concern revolved around the industry's effort to reha-bilitate asbestos, he started investigating.

> It surprised me, it shocked me, because I thought there was no safe way of using it and I thought that had been agreed upon, and that nobody was using it any more. The worst part of it to me was they were selling most of it in the Third World and trying to say—it was ludicrous—that you could actually send it over there and have it handled in a way that's safe. The idea that if you've got to recut a couple of inches off an asbestos board, you're going to send it to some Third World city, to a plant where it can be cut safely, and then ship it back again: it's nonsense.

From the conference, Gorrie got only the one story on the attempted rehabilitation of asbestos. But he didn't write the story immediately after the event. His experience told him it was more politic to wait.

> I realized it was the sort of thing that wouldn't get much space in the paper. So I thought, well, I'll just delve into it and see what I can find and do a proper fea-ture out of it. And since I'm a feature writer, it's what I do anyway.

The conference had provided background information and contacts, but the bulk of the research came afterward. He spread the digging over several weeks, working, as is usual at newspapers, on other stories at the same time.

Waiting paid off. At the conference, Gorrie had learned one thing that intrigued him and provided a linchpin and a lead for the story: the Asbestos Institute was sending out materials on paper made with chrysotile, the common form of asbestos, as part of the industry's campaign to rehabilitate the stuff. Gorrie wrote to the Asbestos Institute and asked them to send him a copy of this promotional letter on chrysotile paper, mostly because he couldn't believe such paper existed.

> It was a long drawn-out process over several months. At some point, I heard about the things they were trying to do with asbestos. They were using it in poles, and one of the other things was this paper. So I got intrigued by this; I didn't actually think it would exist. That was why, although I knew about it, I was actually surprised to get it, because you can see the asbestos—what looks like asbestos fibres—in it. And actually, after I wrote the story, I had it analyzed and it had a pretty high asbestos content.

You would need some background on asbestos to wade without drowning in the industry's promotional materials. For example, the industry campaign contended that asbestos was safe if you used the right kind and handled it properly. It claimed that chrysotile, unlike the asbestos of earlier decades, wasn't harmful. The industry also claimed that because the asbestos fibres don't persist for long in the body, asbestos is safe to use. In fact, as Gorrie's article noted, chrysotile accounts for most of the asbestos ever used, and toxins do not have to persist for long in the body to gestate a cancer.

The research did not involve any computer-assisted analysis or other expert techniques; it consisted entirely of 'talking to people and reading documents, either on paper or on the Internet'. Gorrie conducted telephone interviews with people across Canada and as far away as India.

> The journey was the constant unfolding of evidence. I was, in fact, somewhat skeptical at the start. It seemed like flogging a dead issue, since my limited advance research hadn't revealed the extent to which asbestos was still being used, and promoted. On top of that, the conference participants had a kind of 'true believer' quality that generally makes me back off. Many of the conference presentations were also on PowerPoint, which I tend to blank out on.
>
> So I came away not knowing quite what to make of it. But I had learned enough to decide it was worth pursuing. It didn't take much pursuit to make me realize that the 'dead' issue was alive and important.

Though the story clearly required the famous dogged persistence of the reporter, Gorrie doesn't consider it investigative. And he experienced not a defining moment, but rather a dawning awareness.

> Because information was unfolding as I did the research, there wasn't really a 'gotcha' moment. The more I got into it, the more I knew it was a good story. This wasn't investigative in the sense that I was ferreting out hidden documents or information. There wasn't even much off-the-record material. All of it was available, although sometimes it was either hard to find or, more often, [hidden in] a great mass of verbiage that contained a tiny gem or two of information.
>
> What I did was to go deeper and deeper into it, and then put it together. It was entered, and nominated, in the National Newspaper Awards' 'explanatory' category, not 'investigative', and that reflects how I see it.[2]
>
> There wasn't the arrival of a brown envelope or late-night phone call that made the story. However, I did struggle with many different leads before the heaven-sent arrival of the press release written on asbestos paper. As soon as I saw it, the lead [the first sentence or sentences of a newspaper story] was in my head and the structure of the article finally started to emerge.

The greatest difficulties were dealing with information overload and deciding how to frame the piece.

> The major obstacle was simply the great mass of information and persevering to find the salient bits, then condense and sort them into a coherent article with a compelling storyline. There was a lot of technical detail to explain. I wanted to make it simple and dramatic without losing accuracy or perspective. All the information was on the public record. Some took a bit of time and trouble to find, once I was aware of it. But nobody I encountered was trying to hide anything from me, and nobody I wanted to talk to refused. The Asbestos Institute even sent me the paper. But then, they were trying to make asbestos appear safe and normal.

Gorrie's writing is highly crafted; he said he revises drafts 'over and over'. Sometimes, he says, the broad outline of a narrative seems to present itself straight away. But the asbestos story gave him trouble.

> This one drove me nuts, because before I got the paper and that became the lead, I started it several different ways and I wasn't happy with any of them. It was either obvious or dull or it got convoluted.

Once he 'got' the lead in the form of the Asbestos Institute's chrysotile paper, he started drafting in earnest.

> That first section was reworked and reworked; I took stuff out and put stuff in and moved it around. Unless I'm on a tight deadline, I spend a lot of time writing and rewriting. That's actually one of my favourite parts of the job.

It shows. The piece is seamless, delivering the main points of the story in a narrative just understated enough to make the points without belabouring them. It accumulates detail and tells the story without introducing what Gorrie calls 'lumps'—hard-to-digest passages. His technique involves whittling down, and he practises this without necessarily thinking about it or being able to explain it.

> They usually begin being a lot longer than they end up. I like that whole process of whittling down. And as I do that, the whole structure becomes a lot more coherent. As I said, I move great chunks around and take some out. It's kind of an unconscious process. I don't have any theory of it.
>
> I was the Insight editor here [at the *Star*] for a while, so I edited a lot of features, worked with reporters on them, and one thing I tried to instill was that it's actually fun to do it: if it's not right the first time, it's not a big deal. In fact, the reshaping and working at it can be as much fun as doing the research.
>
> The research is all somebody else's material coming at you. This [drafting] is where you [the writer] come in. Otherwise, you're just recycling words or chopping down somebody else's report. My main thing is I want people to read it, respond to it, and get something out of it. And you only do that if the thing's well written.

If he had it to do over again, Gorrie would have considered putting together a series instead of trying to cover the whole issue in one story. A series would have afforded the chance to go even more in-depth (by, for example, allowing the reporter to visit the overseas places where asbestos was being used). Gorrie believes that such additions would have fortified the impact of an already strong article. He would also have interviewed asbestos miners and those suffering from asbestos-induced disease, even though the earliest stories on asbestos had already done this.

> It might have been better to have done the story as a series, including visits to the asbestos towns and mines in Quebec, to the home of at least one person suffering from an asbestos-related disease and, budget permitting, to India or another developing country where it's being used. . . . To actually go to a site where it's being used would have really improved the story. It would have required a separate article, but that would have been cost-prohibitive.
>
> At the time, though, there wasn't a lot of interest among *Star* editors: It took a long time to find a space for it in the paper. As it was, because I worked on it for a long time, and had the opportunity to go back to it, I was able to correct or improve on previous flaws. So, for what it is, I'm happy with it.

The campaign to ban asbestos never succeeded in Canada. Gorrie's 2003 story didn't end the industry's campaign to rehabilitate asbestos, or to 'outsource' its mining in developing countries.

> It's still being flogged in Canada, and as far as I know, the current situation is pretty much the same as it was.

But at least his story put the issues back on the map.

> The story does require follow-up. I have been in ongoing contact with some of the anti-asbestos advocates and, by coincidence, I was planning to revisit the issue when your first email arrived [three years after the story ran]. Apart from an analysis of the chrysotile paper I received—which, not surprisingly, revealed a high asbestos content—I didn't do anything immediately after the story ran. I wanted to wait long enough to see if the campaign to promote and develop new products would succeed, whether Canadian policy would change, the industry shrink or expand, and other countries take action either for or against asbestos products. The interval got longer than I'd intended, and the recent [January 2006] election has put federal government matters on hold for a while. My aim is to have another story done this spring.
>
> One thing I haven't determined yet is whether the new [Conservative] federal government is going to change the policy. Because the policy is based on protecting a couple of ridings in eastern Quebec, and I think the Conservatives did quite well there, so I assume they will maintain the policy. The lobby groups don't have a sense of it either.

The asbestos story nevertheless got a lot of reader response, and Gorrie wasn't surprised.

> Generally, when I first started doing features, I would be surprised sometimes by the response I would get to fairly technical stories. I did some pieces on alternative energy sources. . . . I did a centre spread and I got tons and tons of responses for that. I was surprised. Occasionally, I'm surprised when I do something I think is a lot more significant and I don't get as much feedback as I would have thought.
>
> But I've been doing it long enough now that I kind of know what's going to produce a response and what won't. Sometimes there are big stories, or important stories, but they're beyond people's ability to deal with it. Items that people can deal with in their homes or locally or have some control over themselves: these are the things they're going to respond to.

The substantial reader response indicates that some individuals have been made more aware of the issue. But has the story influenced at all the policies of government or industry? By and large, no. Gorrie's story ran in 2003. At the time of this writing in the spring and summer of 2007, the institute was still promoting 'safe' asbestos. By May 2006, support for chrysotile had become official policy: Member of Parliament Christian Paradis, then parliamentary secretary to the minister of natural resources, in delivering the opening address to a conference on chrysotile, noted that the government 'through the Chrysotile Institute, supports the safe use of chrysotile, both domestically and internationally. It does NOT promote the sale of this fibre.' According to the speech, chrysotile 'is the only mineral fibre that Canada produces and exports', and the industry 'is important to the prosperity of key communities in Quebec'.[3]

Gorrie believes the government saw the industry battle for asbestos as a kind of test case: 'They were afraid that if they gave up on asbestos they would be under attack on a lot of other ones [toxic substances] as well.'

Money thus trumped public health in the asbestos file. Health effects were well documented in the asbestos mining communities in Quebec's Eastern Townships that had the most to lose economically from an end to asbestos mining. But people didn't seem to worry as much about the health effects of asbestos as they did about the lost jobs that an international ban would mean.

> It's no different from the coal mines where sons follow fathers into the mines even though the father dies of black lung disease. They don't see any way out, and nobody's encouraging them to find another way. To me, the horrible thing is what happened with the families when the guys came home with their clothes covered with asbestos. It happened in Sarnia as well, 1,000 kilometres away from the mine, but they [miners] were using it.
>
> In terms of pickup on the story, the only time it's been dealt with much at all since then was when [Conservative cabinet minister] Chuck Strahl announced that he'd got mesothelioma from using asbestos in their family logging operation. They used a lot of asbestos in the forestry equipment, so twenty, twenty-five years ago, he used it without any protection. It was just lying all over the place.

Is it discouraging as a reporter to come across the asbestos story again, fifteen years later, and see that it's still not resolved, that despite all the ink already spilt on the controversy and the supposed agreement on the toxicity status of asbestos, opposing parties continue to argue over whether or not it's safe to use?[4] Yes and no.

> The fact of being able to write about it reduces some of the discouragement, because I think I might have a small bit of impact in changing it, which is most likely an illusion, but at least it creates the illusion.

Like many of the reporters interviewed for this book, Gorrie contested the meaning of the term *investigative*.

> I don't consider myself an investigative reporter in the now-accepted use of that term, and I don't have that job description. I am a reporter and a feature writer. That second title simply means I write longer stories that offer scope for greater depth, description, and analysis. If my work is investigative, it is in the same way that I believe all reporting is investigative—or should be: even doing a short daily news piece, we collect information, assess and check it, add a little background and context, and then present it all in a way that's useful and meaningful.
>
> Except in the worst stenographic kind of reporting, in which we basically retype something we've been handed, we investigate. Asking a question is investigative. Good reporters always think about what they're presented with and make sure they can write what's really going on. My work involves a lot of asking, thinking, reading, assessing, observing, and analyzing—over and over. Often, I attempt to get people to say things that they don't intend to say. Occasionally, I obtain material that's not meant to be public, or calculate numbers to look for discrepancies.

Neither does he consider the asbestos piece itself investigative—at least not investigative proper.

> There's your upper case *IR* investigative reporting, where you've got your teams and they look to uncover things and do some cloak-and-dagger stuff. . . . I guess the distinction I'd make about the kind of investigation I do in a lot of my stories, is I tend to get into a lot of detail, so it inevitably involves a lot of research and investigation in that sense. But the capital *IR* investigative reporting involves trying to get something that's not in the public domain, and people are trying to hold back. I know it's a cliché, but it's kind of a Watergate holdover. The *Star* has an investigative team and they tend to do that kind of stuff . . . they search for documents that aren't on the public record, or they get people to say things that haven't been on the record, or they come to conclusions based on computer-generated research—that kind of stuff.

The difference, then, involves resistance to the investigative story: someone somewhere simply doesn't want the story told and the truth exposed. In the case of Gorrie's asbestos story, the element of resistance from sources was lacking.

> Nobody was refusing to provide information; they might have provided some BS along the way, but they were willing to talk, and the Asbestos Institute sent me the paper. So everything was on the record in some form. It was just a matter of finding it.

In Gorrie's definition of investigative reporting, there's even an element of 'sneaki-ness' that rubs him the wrong way.

> I've been to a couple of workshops [on investigative reporting] and people tell great stories about how they sneaked into here and there or fooled somebody, and I just don't think it's a very productive way to operate. . . . If you go after things straightforwardly, either they will tell you what you want them to tell you or they won't, and that's revealing enough anyway. You can always get things another way. . . . My general reaction to the workshops has been that they're more about the reporters than about what they're actually trying to convey.
>
> The kinds of stories I like—and this is why I write the way I do—are the ones that tell you something you didn't know about how things work, they get under the surface and surprise you that way, but it's always about the story. I rarely put anything in about me; it's always about what's going on in the world.

Gorrie would be more likely to describe his work as 'in-depth' journalism, the kind antithetical to stenographic reporting.

> I try to take nothing for granted and to be fair to all sides; and certainly to not take what anyone says as gospel. My aim is to explain the world and get read-ers interested in it, and, perhaps, riled up or excited. I'm ambitious and opinion-ated enough that I hope my in-depth work will alter readers' views or behaviour, or government policy. I do it through research, and more research, until I feel I know the subject inside out and could write the story without reference to any notes or documents.
>
> None of this is through formal training. I didn't attend J-school and have been at only a handful of workshops. It has been a matter of inclination and experience gained during thirty years of reporting. As for the route I took to where I am now, I began working on weeklies in the North and Western Canada, was legislature reporter and columnist at the *Edmonton Sun*, worked for UPC and CP in Toronto, then moved to the *Star*, where I have been a business and environ-ment reporter, news and features editor, and, for the past five years, feature writer. I have also written for *Maclean's* and *Canadian Geographic*.

His advice to aspiring reporters underlines the value he places on adherence to proper reportorial method and to a straightforward approach.

> I don't have a lot of specific tips about nuts-and-bolts investigative techniques, such as computer research or detective tactics. I have learned that it's better to go at things head-on rather than resort to subterfuge. It is obviously important to arrange interviews in the proper order, so that you have the information you need for each one—with the toughest coming at the end, when you have enough ammunition that you won't be cowed or snowed. The main advice is to keep

thinking about stories, look at situations from as many points of view as possible, double-check everything you're told, and ask questions again and again. Don't be afraid to pursue any information or person. Also, and very important, be interested in what you're doing and view the research as an adventure. Simply, I love to uncover the world, and share the discoveries.

I should also say to just check things; if somebody tells you something, you check it. And if somebody tells you something and it doesn't check out, you go back and say, Well, this is what I know now, and what do you say about that?

That happened with the asbestos story to a certain extent. I went back a couple of times as I learned more things. I didn't follow that bit of advice about leaving the most difficult [interview] to the end, although sometimes you don't know what the most difficult is going to be. But you can't be embarrassed about going back and saying this has come up and I need to ask you some more questions. Sometimes you get only one shot at it, if it's a particularly dicey investigative thing, because once you've got somebody they won't talk to you again. But most of the time that's not the case.

Gorrie knows that getting the time and space for in-depth work is difficult and getting more so at most papers. He considers himself lucky not to have that problem at the *Star*.

I know it's a general problem, a general issue, but in my case it hasn't been: I can take tons of time to do stories. The *Star* allows that. There are eight of us now who do features and sometimes we have short deadlines, but on something like this we can take whatever time is needed. I think the ones of us who are doing it here are in a pretty unusual position, in that the paper will allow it. If I'm working on something long term, I'm not under a lot of pressure to wrap it up in a week. If I need more time, I generally get it.

I did one this past year on the used-clothing industry and that one went on for months. I would go and talk to people or do some investigations and then come back and do something else, and then when something else with used clothing came up, I would do that. Eventually it got written; it was spread over four or five months, I think. But I could give priority to the clothing story when I needed to—we're in a pretty unique position here.

Fortunately for his readers, when Gorrie sees people being misled or ripped off, he also sees red. The story about used-clothing outfits revealed that some groups were bogusly posing as charities for the poor, but were actually raking in profits of which the poor never saw a cent. Those transgressions bothered Gorrie mightily, but his being able to write about them once again helped relieve the tension.

Like most reporters, he hopes his stories will have an immediate impact, informing citizens and thus empowering them to take direct action.

> I feel better about the ones where people feel they do have some control by changing their behaviour; for example, the used-clothing one. They could start putting them into bins where it's actually going to do some good—some of the charity bins are fake and some aren't. Some are just private companies that take the clothing and sell it and none of the money goes to a charity even though the bins appear to be supporting charities. So I know that story at least changed the behaviour of some people and caused problems for the guy who was running the fake charity bins.

One of Gorrie's favourites in terms of impact was the famed series on dirty restaurants in Toronto by the *Star*'s amazing Robert Cribb.[5] The series provoked a new mandatory system of labels or 'passes' that identified the status of the restaurant in terms of cleanliness.

> The 'Pass' signs you see on restaurants all over the city—that's a direct result of his work. So that's a case where he did a series of stories that have had a very direct and positive impact on the city passes, the law that requires restaurants to be examined. You go to any restaurant in the city now, and you will see one of three coloured signs: the green pass sign means it's passed the inspection; yellow is a caution, and means it's failed in some areas and needs to shape up; a red one means they close it down. That's a direct result of Rob Cribb's story.

Being bothered is how Gorrie comes by many of his story ideas, which tend to arise in the gap between an incipient social problem and the response (or lack thereof) on the part of citizens and public officials. A recent case in point:

> One of the ones that really disturbs me: They're making all of downtown Toronto a wireless Internet zone. I haven't delved into this yet, but there are people who say [it's a problem]. At Lakehead University in Thunder Bay, the president banned wireless from the campus because he said electromagnetic radiation is a health issue. But without any debate at all, they're making the entire downtown Toronto one of these zones.

Gorrie was taken aback by the dearth of opposition to the plan or even debate over its merits. No one is protesting, and the move is widely regarded as progressive. People either don't believe or don't care that there are health implications. Or perhaps they believe and they care, but they think there's nothing they can do about it.

> I was quite floored—from the mayor on down, everybody's touting it as this great thing that's going to bring more economic benefits to the city. I mean, in that way it's no different from the asbestos mining, except that it's totally unnecessary in terms of the economy.

The *Star* has, in addition to its ace investigative team, an official eight-person stable of feature writers, to which Gorrie belongs. Beat reporters often write long stories, too, but the feature writers tend to go longer both in research time and final copy. What about classic beat reporting, the traditional backbone of a newspaper's reportorial technique? Is the beat-reporting system getting weakened?

> At other places, I know it is. Even at the *Star*, it's not what it used to be, and some things aren't covered now. We do not have a labour-beat reporter; we don't have an environment reporter. But then we do have a couple of education reporters and three health reporters, so I guess some of the choices for beats I disagree with, but generally there's a pretty strong beat system here.

The beat system at many other newspapers appears to be in decline.

> Because there are so many cutbacks, everybody has to be a generalist. The *Globe* and the *Star* are still anomalies that way . . . and even at CP, Dennis Bueckert has to do environment and health—that's way more than anybody could hope to manage.

The apparent erosion of the traditional beat system raises troubling questions about the future of newspaper journalism. How does a newspaper develop stories or train cub reporters to be great reporters without establishing beats, which allow the reporters who cover them to gain invaluable background knowledge and contacts?

> It takes a while to know enough that you're not going to be snowed or you know what the story is, or you know where to look, or people come to you with things. I do most of the environment reporting at the *Star* and I get people coming to me with things as if I were the environment reporter.

For his part, Gorrie does the best he can, writing stories and adding constantly to the list of stories in waiting—a list that is perpetually lengthening. He says that the overall market for serious journalism, whether in newspapers or magazines, has narrowed. Even those magazines that used to publish investigative and in-depth work seem to be softening their commitment to the genre.

> I used to write for *Canadian Geographic* magazine, and it still does some, but it's gone away from the longer explanatory, investigative pieces. It's like the papers: they want graphic bits around stories; they want sidebars and lists and all that kind of stuff. The nuts and bolts of the story tend to shrink.

Writing something original amounts to creating knowledge, and newspapers do educate, albeit outside the peer-review system of academe. If for Gorrie the research is what you get from others, and the writing is what you do yourself, there's still no medium like print for learning. 'Nothing activates the mind more than reading.' And readers will go the distance on an in-depth story if it's properly handled.

> It's about perceived attention span. Television shows have more jolts, so newspapers figure everything has to be short. But if you write something well, it can be long—you know, people read books, if they're written well. I write pieces that are longer than most people think they want to read in a newspaper, so it has to be well enough written that people can make it through without feeling that it's a huge burden.

On the other hand, the technology of television, many critics would argue, serves not to educate but to pacify: TV lulls people into passivity, helping them to believe that they're not responsible and that, as individuals, they don't much matter. The academic literature on this subject is wide-ranging, but a good place to start would be Neil Postman's *Amusing Ourselves to Death: Public Discourse in the Age of Show Business.*[6]

> This happens in newspapers too, but it's even more jarring on TV where you get a really devastating story, and then you're on to something frothy, and then you're on to the commercial—so the devastating thing becomes trivialized. It's the same as in print, except the hard story doesn't just pass by, it's still there. So you can read about something important and something trivial but the thing is still there. It hasn't just gone into the ether.

Gorrie once ran his own small daily in Canada's North, and he thinks fear of advertiser displeasure is vastly overrated. The modern problem for large dailies is not so much the fear of ad revenues lost to advertiser displeasure as of ad revenues—especially classified ad revenues—lost to higher technologies like the Internet. Even in smaller cities, where angering local advertisers can be costly, newspaper editors tend to pride themselves on editorial integrity when faced with conflicts between the preference of a major advertiser and the public's right to know.

> I've worked for some small papers and I also ran my own for a couple of years, and the fear of advertisers—I discovered from experience that it's completely groundless. If you do a paper that people are reading, the advertisers will go in it because they can't afford not to. You may lose one from time to time, but if you're doing a good job generally, they're going to come back because they have

to. So the protests tend not to last very long. That was actually one of the great lessons of running my paper.

A most difficult problem for good journalism, Gorrie believes, is concentrated ownership and its attendant ills. Increasingly concentrated ownership has left the Canadian newspaper business with but a few dominant players, and this despite three federal government inquiries into the state of the press since the late 1960s, all of which made copious recommendations—all roundly ignored—to halt concentrated ownership.[7]

> One thing that really bothers me about that is there are a few big companies, including Torstar and Metroland, that are buying up almost all of Ontario as far north as Huntsville, and over towards Ottawa now—they're all owned by Metroland. So it's really, really hard for someone else to take them on. Metroland just bought out the Huntsville paper, so if you went into Huntsville and said the paper is now garbage and I want to start my own, Metroland has such huge resources—it would be really difficult to take them on. Metroland is up to, I think, sixty-five weeklies now.
>
> The other issue I can see is a more general cultural one, which is that people just don't want to take time to do anything. It's got to be something new all the time. You can reform how the newspaper is presented in all kinds of ways and still have roughly the same kind of content, but if the culture is changing and people just aren't interested in that kind of content, then that's much bigger. You can put newspapers online, have one of those little book boxes you can read on the subway . . . but if people just want their instant jolts, that's going to have a bigger impact than the form it's presented in.

What if we're getting what the advertisers want, not what the people want? If it were true that people want only the jolts, why would they be reading articles like Gorrie's asbestos piece, much less calling him in the newsroom about it?

> But I'm not sure what proportion of the paper's readers read that kind of [substantial or in-depth] stuff. And they're being conditioned to think that [short and superficial stories] are what they want, so that's what it appears they want, and that persuades the editors to do it that way, and then the conditioning goes round and round.

What about the conditioning effects of good in-depth stories? Even if they represent exceptions rather than the rule, don't they have a conditioning effect too, conditioning people to expect occasional exposés in the daily press, and a response from appropriate officials?

Well there may be some of that, but I just think the general culture is going in the other direction. Not just news; it's another cliché, but if you look at the jolts per minute in movies now compared to what they used to be and on TV, the speed at which things are presented—it's a different world. A lot of people now can't stand having only one thing on at once: they want the TV, they want music, they want to be on the Internet, they want to be sending emails on the Blackberry— they've got to be doing several things at once or it's not enough.

[In-depth reporting] is a whole different process, because you can't just punch a few keys and get what you're looking for. The whole process used to be a lot slower, so your mind was working in a different way. You knew when you had to go to the library and look something up.

Because of the industry's decline (one prevailing worldwide, not just in North America),[8] it's much harder now than in earlier decades for aspiring journalists to break into the daily newspaper business, despite their often impressive qualifications.

It's incredibly hard to get in here now. There are all sorts of people coming in on internships, and they usually have a couple of degrees, several languages, and all kinds of life experiences.

This erosion of the journalistic base is part of the downturn—and, some predict, the death—of the daily newspaper, or at least the death of 'a free press' as a public-interest institution intimately allied with democracy itself. Many journalism graduates appear to be turning to weekly newspapers for that first internship or job, and while editorial quality is generally higher at daily papers than at weekly ones, there are notable exceptions. Moreover, given the slide of the daily newspaper business and the advent of online communications, the weekly or community paper may yet survive to serve a distinctly local market.

Gorrie worked early in his career for a small paper in the North, and says the experience not only taught him the ropes but also certified his passion for the work. Sadly, given the current state of the newspaper industry, the experience of such an apprenticeship is largely unavailable to aspiring reporters today.

My first paying job was at the *Ottawa Citizen* and from there I went up to Yellowknife and worked at a paper called *News of the North*, which is a weekly, but it actually was a real paper, and that was an incredible experience. I had to do paste-up, but we also did some pretty good stories. The paper tried to cover the entire Northwest Territories—with a newsroom of four or five people and a few stringers.

It seems like it would be a lot harder to get in now because there are fewer places that are doing quality work, and then to get into those few, the bar is much, much higher. I think it would be great if there was somebody with some money who would start a chain of weeklies and take on the shoppers [paid-circulation newspapers].[9]

Gorrie is not alone among industry observers in believing that the future of newspapers may rest with the small community weeklies, nor in speculating about how such ventures might renew journalism and lead to papers that see themselves as more beholden to readers and the public interest than to profits and a corporate agenda. What the newspaper should really be paying attention to, he believes, is the reader.

> People in small communities do want news. If there was a good paper that had actual news in it, it would do really well. You'd just need some resources to be able to take on companies like Metroland and the shoppers.
>
> It's a wonderful kind of thing to work at, if it's doing the job, because you get to know everything that's going on in the town and you can make a difference and have an impact—and it can be a lot of fun. If I won the lottery, that's what I would do. Or, if I somehow got a lot more money than I have now, I would love to start a little weekly chain. I mean, it's not impossible.

Gorrie ought to know: years ago, when he was living in Yellowknife, he and a couple of friends decided to launch an upstart daily newspaper and take on the local competition. The first hurdle was finding a suitable location.

> There were two of us who wanted to start our own paper but there was no place in the Territories to do it. So a friend of ours said, 'Well, come down to Fort McMurray.' We did and it worked out fine. The second year, we were a half-a-million-dollar operation, which isn't bad.

The three young newspapermen launched their first issue in 1979. The paper took 'a horrendous amount of work', but showed every sign of succeeding over the long haul. Gorrie remembers that the dismal state of the existing daily made winning readers almost as easy as taking candy from babies.

> It was a Bowes paper and it was awful, and we took it on. They were treating the advertisers badly, so the advertisers were happy to have an alternative, and their news coverage was abominable. So we treated the advertisers well, and we did news a lot better. It lasted quite a while. I sold out after a couple of years because I didn't want to stay in Fort McMurray, but it was kind of odd because we went through a horrendous first year, basically non-stop work, and it was just getting easier and financially a lot better when two of us sold to the third.
>
> It went for quite a while. Bowes got bought out by the Sun Corporation and then the Sun Corporation bought our paper and folded it because it didn't want

the two papers. But if the three of us had stayed at it—if I'd liked living in Fort McMurray—we would have kept it going for a long time.

It may be that as the business keeps changing, people will get frustrated to the point of action. Perhaps disaffected journalists will start their own independent ventures, their own community papers, their own online publications, perhaps even on a non-profit basis. Gorrie, for one, sees potential for public interest journalism in the rise of the community paper.

I know it's happening in Toronto, and elsewhere. There are community papers and some of them here aren't too bad at all. Some are junk, but some are good. So, I think there's some scope there as well.

# Commentary

Gorrie's status as virtually the only reporter for a major Canadian daily dogging the asbestos issue underlines one of the most important morals of this story: Decide for yourself what's news. Don't allow anyone else, no matter how exalted, to do your thinking for you, and don't expect to discover what's important for your readers by always following safely behind the news pack. Insist on thinking for yourself and through the issues.

Follow your own hunches and misgivings where they lead. Don't assume just because no one else is writing about it or is interested in the subject, that there isn't a story there worth pursuing.

When elucidating complex issues such as this one, provide the background information (including historical information) that readers will need to understand the story. Ask yourself what the reader needs to know every step of the way to make full sense of the piece, and then provide it.

Honour the tip. Not all in-depth or investigative stories begin with a tip, but all rely on tips at some point before the article is completed. When someone calls you with what seems a tall tale, don't assume the caller is mistaken or misguided, or the story baseless or improbable. Take the time to check it out—truth really can be stranger than fiction. Moreover, as an aspiring reporter, you want to train yourself to assume nothing, to understand as if by second nature that until you check something out for yourself, you simply can't know or assess its reality or worth.

Look for the significant detail or element that can bring the story together. Remember that the lead of a story doesn't just present the first paragraph—it encapsulates the story and tells readers why they should bother or continue to read it. In the asbestos story, the promotional chrysotile paper gave Gorrie the lead and helped to establish a frame that had previously eluded him.

Be thorough, not shy. You owe your readers the fullest accounting possible. Take Gorrie's advice and don't be afraid to return to sources as your understanding of the story evolves, even if this means having to confront a source with unwelcome facts. Continue to return to your sources as often as necessary to get the story straight. (Of course, this is not to advise conducting half-baked interviews on the basis of bad or spotty research, and then returning needlessly to sources expecting them to fill in the holes you could have pre-empted with proper background research and sound strategy.)

In the short term, Gorrie's asbestos story alerted readers to a failing industry's attempt to rehabilitate asbestos, despite the threat such rehabilitation presented to public health, whether in Canada or abroad. High reader response to the story shows that some readers at least took note.

It would seem in regard to long-term impact, however, that the story failed to effect change. The Chrysotile Institute continued with its campaign, evidently barely touched by Gorrie's exposé on the front page of the country's largest circulation daily. Many have written long and well about the changes in the daily newspaper business over the last few decades. I believe there are much less obvious but closely related 'metacultural' changes also under way. A gap appears to have opened up between the press with its traditional watchdog role and the very powers (including government) that the press is supposed to hold to account.

Recall Gorrie's preference for stories that readers can use, altering their behaviour to rule. The asbestos story was different. It exposed a problem that could not be solved by grassroots action (as the failed efforts of anti-asbestos activists suggest). Neither could any amount of individual behavioural change address or solve the problem. For one thing, most of the asbestos mined in Quebec was being exported to developing countries, not used domestically. As long as asbestos could be exported to developing nations, the Quebec mines could continue to operate regardless of the potential health threats to overseas workers. But if an international ban on asbestos were instituted, the Quebec mines would be closed; the Quebec workers would lose their jobs; and the Quebec economy, along with federal–provincial relations, would suffer.

The problem, then, requires a politically negotiated solution. Reporters have always understood their role vis-à-vis government as that of exposing problems and wrongdoing in order to shame or otherwise force the powers under scrutiny to do the right rather than the expedient thing. But somewhere along the way, the democratic chain that is supposed to link the newspaper exposé to political change at appropriate levels has broken down.

Now, it seems that, at best, the press can tweak the noses of the powerful and the powerful in turn can simply wait for the pain to pass and the 'story' to fade. These days, government officials routinely try to divert reporters to official websites, and to deny interviews with those in control (often, ironically, on the basis that the website can answer all questions).

But even more chilling, the aforementioned gap seems to be further entrenched now to protect the government from the people and from the press that by traditional wisdom represents them and their right to know. For example, the first fracas in 2006 between the media and Stephen Harper's recently installed government focused on the new prime minister's attempts to manage the press by restricting its access to him and his government.[10]

Because this emerging problem is a political one, solutions will also be political. The press has a responsibility to play a decisive role in explicating the problem and ultimately in helping return to the governed their democratic right to oversee those public officials who serve them. Not since the 1835 criminal libel trial of Nova Scotia newspaper publisher Joseph Howe has the press faced such a challenge or opportunity to redeem its very purpose.

# Endnotes

1.  Peter Gorrie, 'Asbestos makeover reignites old battle', *Toronto Star* (22 November 2003), A1.

2.  For the 2001 National Newspaper Awards, the category 'explanatory' existed in place of 'investigative'.

3.  See www.nrcan.gc.ca/media/speeches/2006/200607_e.htm.

4.  In the spring of 2006, the asbestos industry (the renamed Chrysotile Institute and International Chrysotile Association) held in Montreal an international conference on chrysotile, 'Chrysotile at a Turning Point: Results and Scientific Perspectives'. In response the anti-asbestos opposition took out an ad in the *Hill Times* for the opening day of the conference (Tuesday, 23 May 2006). The ad was headlined, 'Refuting Industry Claims that Chrysotile Asbestos Is Safe'.

5.  You can read Robert Cribb's own account of the year-long *Toronto Star* series Dirty Dining in *Media* magazine 8.2 (Summer 2001), 12–13. See also Chapter 6 of this text for the case study on Cribb's series, Dialling for Dollars, about telemarketing fraud.

6.  Neil Postman, *Amusing Ourselves to Death: Public Discourse in the Age of Show Business* (New York: Penguin), 1985.

7.  'The news business is now dominated by large corporations. By 2003, two media giants—CanWest Global Communications and Quebecor—owned one out of every two daily newspapers sold in Canada, accounting for 16 million papers every week. . . . This concentration of ownership and the media's power to mould and influence public opinion has been the subject of three federal inquiries since 1969.' Dean Jobb, *Media Law for Canadian Journalists* (Emond Montgomery, 2006), 71–72.

For more on the issue, see the studies themselves: *Report of the Special Senate Committee on Mass Media*, vol. 1 *The Uncertain Mirror* (Ottawa: Queen's Printer, 1970); *Royal Commission on Newspapers* (Ottawa: Supply and Services Canada, 1981). For the most recent study, see the report of the Standing Senate Committee on Transport and Communications, which began its work in 2003 and released its final report in June 2006. See 'Part II A: Causes for Concern: The Impacts of Concentration of Ownership on Diversity in Canadian News Media' in *Final Report on the Canadian News Media*, volume 1 of 2 (Ottawa: Queen's Printer, 2006). You can also read the report online at www.parl.gc.ca/39/1/parlbus/commbus/senate/com-e/tran-e/repe/repfinjun06vol1-e.htm.

8.   For more on the widely predicted demise of the hard-copy daily newspaper, see the following: Philip Meyer's *The Vanishing Newspaper* (Columbia, MO: University of Missouri Press, 2004); and 'Who Killed the Newspaper?' *The Economist* 380:8492 (26 August 2006), 9–10. For a Canadian perspective on the issue, particularly on the rise of the so-called free dailies, see Ken Alexander's editorial in *The Walrus* 3.5 (June 2006), 18, 20.

9.   The term *shopper* indicates a newspaper that is free to the consumer, its costs covered by advertising revenues. The term, however, is apparently not universally applied. I learned this when I moved in 1999 from Montreal (my hometown, and where I worked for the city's Canadian Press bureau), to Kamloops, BC, to teach journalism at the Thompson Rivers University Journalism School. I unwittingly raised quite a ruckus by using *shopper* during my lectures to refer to a local paid-circulation paper that came out several times a week. The paper (at which, to make matters worse, a faculty member's spouse was employed) objected strenuously to the use of the term, which it deemed synonymous with *advertiser* (essentially, an advertising sheet). Perhaps these differences in the terminology reflect cultural differences dictated by Canada's East–West divide; perhaps they are more locally rooted. In any case, while the terms may well be up for debate and renewal, for the sake of clarity here, I use *shopper* as Gorrie did, to indicate a paid-circulation paper, whatever the frequency of its publication. I use the term *community papers* to describe those that while small are still paid for by readers rather than distributed to them for free.

10.  See, among a slew of other media responses to the government's attempted shutout of media, Campbell Clark's 'Harper restricts ministers' message', *Globe and Mail* (17 March 2006), A1 and www.theglobeandmail.com/servlet/story/RTGAM.20060317.wxpmo17/BNStory/National.

# Chapter 5

# Criminalizing Dissent

While working their respective beats, two senior reporters uncovered a federal government program that used covert means, including domestic spying, to control public protest. Jim Bronskill (then of Southam News and now with the Canadian Press in Ottawa) and David Pugliese (of the *Ottawa Citizen*) told the story in the summer of 2001, in a five-part series entitled Criminalizing Dissent. Both reporters had noticed something untoward: Canadian police and intelligence agencies were spending a lot of time 'monitoring' people who disagreed with government policies on a range of issues and engaged in public demonstrations to make their views known. Using classified reports obtained through repeated access-to-information requests and numerous interviews with police, intelligence officials, and protesters, the reporters showed that such surveillance by various federal agencies, including CSIS and the RCMP, was not only real—it was routine. Civil liberties lawyers and other critics deemed such surveillance an undeclared campaign to criminalize dissent.

The package of stories told how the federal government spied on Vancouver Island peace activists and other presumably suspect 'counter-thinkers' (including Ed Broadbent, Svend Robinson, the Canadian Labour Congress, the Council of Canadians, the Anglican Church, and Amnesty International).

This kind of reporting involves naming an issue and attempting to put it on the public agenda, but it requires substantial background knowledge, the kind usually acquired on the beat. Bronskill (who covers security and intelligence issues) and Pugliese (who writes about defence and the military) had been seeking to work together on a project ever since the 1997 Asia-Pacific Economic Cooperation (APEC) Conference in Vancouver, where police, on orders from then prime minister Jean

Chrétien, pepper-sprayed demonstrators. The so-called APEC affair brought heavy criticism, sparked a commission of inquiry, and ignited controversy in the journalistic community.[1] You can read Bronskill and Pugliese's own account in *Media Magazine*, published by the Canadian Association of Journalists.[2]

The series revealed that the RCMP had created a special unit in advance of the 1997 conference to deal with the expected demonstrations. This secret Public Order Program co-operated with police forces across the country, sharing information and crowd-control techniques. The plot thickened with revelations of the unit's unsavoury tactics, which included monitoring those engaged in protest, infiltrating their meetings, and intercepting their private emails. The special unit kept tabs on those who expressed anti-corporate views, questioning and sometimes detaining protesters and organizers before their planned events took place. Critics called the business a frontal attack on democratic rights and an unmitigated threat to democracy itself.[3]

One story delved into the Mounties' spying on the Nanoose Conversion Campaign, a group that had taken the federal government to court to stop US ships from dumping poisons into Canadian water.[4] The piece showed that the Mounties, in a threat assessment conducted before the 1997 APEC Conference, had listed the Nanoose Conversion Campaign (among thousands of other groups and individuals) as a terrorist threat. A woman who had once led the Green Party also made the list. Subsequent stories showed that while the Public Order Program was a recent initiative, the federal government had in fact been keeping extensive files on 'suspect' figures for decades.[5] Among those considered suspect in the 1960s was the revered US civil rights leader Martin Luther King, Jr.

Some of the stories read like satire, almost comical in their detailing of the people and groups that the country's intelligence agencies saw fit to spend their time monitoring.[6] The Rhinoceros Party, for instance, had drawn intense scrutiny for its political pranks and performances over a thirteen-year period (from 1971 to 1984). But a newer kind of troublemaker was identified in police and security operations leading up to the 1997 conference: Canadians, as the reporters put it, 'who advocated free speech and assembly but opposed government policies'. These included a protest group of singing seniors called the Raging Grannies, the BC Teachers Federation, and the International Centre for Human Rights and Democratic Renewal.

One story told of police spying on a student who had protested cuts to education funding when her university awarded an honorary degree to the prime minister who had ordered them. Police officials interviewed for the story said they routinely questioned protesters and organizers, including union organizers, hoping to arrest them before their planned events could proceed. Police added they saw nothing wrong in the practice.[7]

As if to leave no doubt about the absurdity of these practices, the final story of the series related the so-called Halloween Episode, when RCMP officers dressed up in costumes and masks to infiltrate and disrupt a protest on 31 October.[8]

The humour tends to pale, however, when the episode is taken for what it was: an interlude of comic relief in an otherwise deadly serious campaign of widespread RCMP activities, sometimes conducted with city police, to monitor and infiltrate protest groups, especially those with the potential to embarrass the government or visiting foreign officials. Six stories ran over five days between 18 and 22 August 2001.

# The Interview: **David Pugliese**
(10 April 2006)

The story arose from informal conversations between Pugliese, from the perspective of his security-and-defence beat, and Bronskill, who covered mainly the Canadian Security Intelligence Service (CSIS) and the Royal Canadian Mounted Police (RCMP). The reporters had discerned a heavy-handed increase in security forces at demonstrations.

> We noticed that there was this presence both in Canada and the US of a large security apparatus any time anybody or any group would start protesting. Not only did you have the big security fences and security areas to keep protesters away, but you were also starting to see pre-emptive arrests of people before they could even hit the streets, and roundups of protest organizers and the usual suspects.

Pugliese has an idiosyncratic way of working; he calls it being a pack rat. Whenever something catches his interest, he starts building a file on it. Clippings from newspaper and magazine articles, notes from books, items found on the Internet—anything that has to do with the newly stoked interest goes in the file.

> You'd see a two-paragraph story saying [something like], Mr X arrested in advance of a protest. And no one was actually saying much. That was the other disturbing thing: there wasn't a lot of discussion. It was the typical Canadian attitude: Well, I guess they're troublemakers, so throw away the key, right?

Pugliese and Bronskill are mutually appreciative colleagues; each praised the other's professional acumen. They had tried before to work together on a story about access to information, but it 'never got off the ground'. The idea for Criminalizing Dissent took shape over successive conversations. 'It was topical,' Pugliese said. 'And it was something we figured we could sell our bosses on.'

When the reporters got the go-ahead, Pugliese already had an access request filed that turned out to be relevant to the series. In fact, when that request came back 'with some related information', Pugliese originally thought it must have been included by mistake. He was surprised to find that police kept files on protest groups as apparently non-threatening as the Raging Grannies.

> They had a synopsis of each group, and what they might do, and what threat they posed. There were some emails back and forth, where they were talking about stuff coming in advance from these individuals. That was strange, because to me that showed there was pre-surveillance going on and it was almost—just the tone of the emails suggested that they knew what was going on, because they were describing what was happening at these meetings. It was almost like they had someone there who had infiltrated or intercepted it somehow.

With the ATI reports in hand, the reporters began analyzing the documents. But when Pugliese started talking to the protest groups targeted for secret surveillance, he was in for another surprise, Canadian style.

> I started phoning these groups and they were very suspicious of me. They had to check out my credentials before they would talk. In one case—the Raging Grannies—they said, 'So what?' They didn't have a problem with it, which surprised me, because I had a problem with it.

At that point, Bronskill had also filed an access-to-information request with the RCMP, one that would yield a critical element of the series: the discovery of the Public Order Program that had been created to keep tabs on demonstrators and other vocal critics of government. The timing, says Pugliese, was sheer serendipity:

> It was amazing timing. They released it as we were writing. So we incorporated it into one of our main stories, which was almost a fluke. It looked like we knew what we were doing, but just the timing of it was great.

The files also revealed that the police spying was not a reaction or overreaction to 9/11 (the 11 September 2001 terrorist attacks on the World Trade Center in New York and the Pentagon in Arlington, Virginia) or to the rise of terrorism around the globe. In fact, police had been spying on people engaged in peaceful political protest for decades and all across the country.

We were tracking people in Newfoundland, Saskatchewan, and other places that protesters had been arrested. Again, this is where these little clippings come into play. There would be this one paragraph about some union organizer in Newfoundland getting a call from the RCMP, about a comment she had made about the prime minister. That type of thing was valuable—then you're able to track people down.

The series had to cope with a problem specific to Canada: the fact that government information is much less readily available here than in the United States and that Canadian citizens, unlike many of their US counterparts, don't seem to mind or at least don't make a lot of noise about it.

There was a lot of material in the United States and in Europe because in those countries, they seemed to have a real concern about this—a concern we didn't seem to have in Canada. It's the same, I find, in getting just day-to-day stuff. I cover this JTF-2 stuff a lot—Joint Task Force 2, the special forces unit. And here they will tell us *nothing*. But if you go to the US, there's the American commander that JTF-2 served under, and he's before Congress saying, 'Well, we captured one hundred prisoners, and we killed five hundred insurgents.' . . . So you were able to gather information. I mean, the DND [Department of National Defence] will try to do a closed shop on their own—but it's hard when these security things spread around the world, to keep a lot of these details secret or as secret as they would like.

Canada's DND is nevertheless 'pretty good at it'.

I can guarantee that if I made access requests today on those same documents, they would come back blank.

Since the series ran, the screws have tightened at Access to Information. Speaking in April 2006, Pugliese said press relations with federal ATI officials were at an all-time low.

Right now, Access to Information is almost shut down in the federal government. Stuff that I have got, that I have here in files—I see it now released in another package, totally blank. They're just cracking down. I've never seen it this bad. Someone mentioned to me that it's just as bad as in the Somalia days.[9]

I'll give you an example: The DND put in this communications system to the Americans—to certain commands, mainly NORAD. I put in a request and all I got was the name of the system, and everything else was blank, for security reasons. So I went on the Internet. On the Pentagon's website, I got the full details. So I

> thought this was ridiculous, and I did a story on it. But don't forget, [in Canada, access officials] do identify journalists when they get the request, so you're treated differently, and it takes longer.

At the time of our interview, Pugliese said the clampdown on information through the government's offices had 'been ramping up for the last year'.

> A lot of this stuff is being shut down. And again, it's not just the sensitive stuff. It's the mundane as well.

Pugliese fought a pitched battle with Access to Information trying to secure data about JTF-2 when he submitted a request for the force's equipment lists. He 'didn't expect the kitchen sink', but when everything came back almost blank, he filed a complaint with the information commissioner. A second release was ordered, with the explanation that certain information had been censored the first time 'for national security reasons' under section 15(1).

> It's a section of the Access to Information Act that they can use to justify their censorship. It's a wide-ranging one that they hit me with on a regular basis, because it's so difficult to fight. It's too broad, and the information commissioner of Canada tends to side with the government. This time, I had a decent investigator who said they were going to release a few more of the items that they had censored for national security reasons. And what came back that they had censored for national security reasons? A coffee maker, silverware, and some items from Canadian Tire. So I wrote a story on that—top secret coffee maker. They just hate my guts for that.
>     I think that shows you how you can abuse secrecy. I guess they figure that everything they do is secret. And unfortunately, if Jim and I went back and tried to do this series now, I think a lot of the documentation would be much more heavily censored than it was, which is discouraging.

Especially since there are not a lot of reporters working on these kinds of stories.

> No, and everyone seems to think that the access-to-information process is just drop your five dollars in the mail and then a month later someone delivers a big package with arrows pointing where to go.

What actually happens is a lot more time-consuming, and frustrating.

> You put your five dollars in and usually it takes about six or seven months for something to come back, and then usually you have to complain because it's typically heavily censored. That process now takes up to a year, because the

information commissioner is so jammed up with complaints. It was pretty fast in the old days, in the days when Jim and I did this. Now, I've got twenty complaints in, some of them a year old, easily. So that's what I mean: the whole system is being shut down.

Section 15(1) of the federal Access to Information Act, the section that gives Pugliese the most trouble, is routinely cited to justify the government's refusal to release information. (The original Access to Information Act was ratified in 1985, but certain provisions of the Anti-Terrorism Act, which came into force on 24 December 2001, amend the access law.)

Section 15(1) is the one that I run into the most. And if you have an access investigator that doesn't really know the file—they're generalists—then that person will take the institution's word over yours. Easy. So I think using Access to Information for investigative stories is becoming more difficult, because they're making it so. I think they've seen the power of this Act, and they don't like it, and they're shutting it down.

Pugliese doesn't have much faith that a spirit of public outrage will help turn the situation around, either. Too many Canadians, he believes, would rather not know.

I think there's a natural tendency in the public to get outraged when they see stories—and then go back to sleep. There's this natural tendency to defer to institutions, particularly when the government plays the patriotic card and the national security card.

Even the most innocent query looks suspicious if you gaze through a certain lens, with a certain focus or predisposition. 'The applicant becomes the bad guy.'

You should see the stuff people say on the Internet about me. You see a parallel in the US, with Fox News and the blogs: they target your personality as a way to undermine you. But I guess that's part of the deal. Well, you know you've hit a chord when you get that type of thing.

The reporters knew they had a story to tell right from the beginning—they just didn't know how big a story. There were two defining moments, according to Pugliese: first, the intelligence that alerted him to the possibility the RCMP had been infiltrating the groups it monitored; and second, Bronskill's findings on the Public Order Program. With these, the reporters realized the series would have some punch. 'Then we had two news hooks to move forward with.'

The major obstacles included teasing information out of the Access to Information Act and its enforcers, winning the support of editors at the two news agencies, and trying to pierce Canadians' complacent attitude toward authority. The subtext of such an attitude has always read that if the bigwigs of officialdom are engaging in secret surveillance of citizens, they must have their reasons, and the targeted people must have done something wrong. Thus, navigating the rocky road of access-to-information requests presented the most persistent difficulty.

> You get frustrated with some of the nuts-and-bolts obstacles that occur using Access to Information. If the information commissioner decides against you, that your complaint isn't worthy, there's always this line: Well, if you don't like it, you can always take departments and the government to court. It's this throwaway line. It ticks me off whenever I see it.

The line has always angered Pugliese because ATI officials, including the commissioner, know full well what a drawn-out and expensive process taking the government to court can be.

> We're involved in a court case about one of my access requests on Eggleton [Art Eggleton, the former Toronto mayor and federal Liberal cabinet minister]—that's how long these things can last. It's regarding the M5 documents—M5 referred to these secret meetings that Eggleton [as a cabinet minister] would have with all the top bureaucrats. I had seen this M5 appearing in references in some other document. I thought, 'Oh, that's interesting.' I had originally thought it had something to do with neo-Nazis. So I thought, 'Well, I'm going to ask for what this is and see what happens.'
>     The response came back saying no—they didn't have any documents. I said, 'That's weird, because I see a reference in other places, so how can you say you don't have anything?' I complained, and at this point they produced [about] three thousand documents, three thousand pages of something that originally 'never existed'. We're in court to fight for the rest, and this has been going for years.
>     My employer [CanWest Global] . . . good for them! I'm glad they're doing it. It's the principle—you can go to court, but it costs tens of thousands of dollars. And I think they know that when they refuse you. It's almost insulting in a way. Unfortunately, this country, unlike the United States, doesn't have these groups that go to court, like the American Civil Liberties Union [ACLU], which went to court to get all the Guantanamo Bay lists of who's held there. And it's all there for journalists to use. Unfortunately we don't have anything like that.

Even the Canadian Civil Liberties Association (CCLA) isn't actively involved the way the ACLU is in the States. (Though, ironically, it was a Canadian civil liberties lawyer who coined the phrase *criminalizing dissent* that became the title of the series.) Cost is a major prohibiting factor.

> Guys like Ken Rubin[10] . . . he has done some of these court cases on his own. I've talked to him about that possibility, but you're always running the risk that if you lose they'll hit you with costs. So all you need is a vindictive government department, of which there's potentially many.

The reporters worked for a couple of months on the series, while working on other files at the same time. Despite the prominent play the series received and the reader response it elicited, the secret spying by Canadian police forces continues.

> It still goes on. I just saw another article. I clipped it, because I'm a pack rat and I find that attribute is very helpful with these kinds of things. It was about some people who were arrested or talked to before a demonstration in Calgary, just this past weekend. So it hasn't gone away; it's still happening, though maybe not as much. Stories like the ones we did—it's the publicity thing. These agencies don't want the publicity. They don't want to be seen. . . . They're still doing it. You can be sure before the [Vancouver 2010] Olympics or other large international gatherings, you're going to see that.

Pugliese doesn't pretend to know what it would take to pierce public apathy. Comical errors on the part of security officials (such as the listing of infants as security threats) may provoke attention, but they don't effect change.

> There are no-fly lists, and when you get a baby who's been on a no-fly list as a terrorist, those types of stories get people talking. You need that extreme aspect to get people to talk now. Whether they remember it or not is another matter. Whether they want to do anything about it is another matter.
>
> I think the times that I've seen changes from stories that I've done are more when it's the little guy, the so-called little guy, being targeted or jerked around. I did a series of stories in the mid-'90s on soldiers who were wounded overseas and not given wheelchairs. So you do that and that gets people really upset and asking, How come this is happening? The bureaucracy tends to react on those, because it's easy to remedy. Just give the guy a wheelchair.

Pugliese remembered another recent article (he clipped it, of course) about an upcoming meeting of international finance ministers in a Canadian city.

> I think it was Winnipeg, and the police department said, No, we've got to say no to this meeting; we can't afford the budget because we would have to put all this security in place and we'd have to monitor the groups that are going to protest.

> It was part of their planning. They didn't have the resources, and they had to monitor these groups that might show up. City hall didn't want to kick over the $30 million they would have had to pay not only for spying but also for additional police. That's starting to become a problem for some of these cities. These meetings have to happen. But does the level of security that takes place have to happen? I guess that's the question.

Despite the attendant expense, Pugliese predicts, 'you'll still have the G-8 meeting out in Kananaskis, and anti-aircraft missiles set up in fields, and parts of the Trans-Canada shut down and that type of thing.' He believes that in the absence of concerted protest, Canada's police and security personnel will persist in domestic spying, despite the costs and the outside possibility of a public outcry.

> But I think we did our job, in that at least we informed people who wanted to be informed that this is taking place.

Pugliese's reading habits (he reads multiple newspapers daily, for starters) would tire all but the most valiant. He says he's 'like a vacuum cleaner' but approaches the Net with high skepticism because 'a lot of stuff on there is very unreliable'.

> Areas I'm interested in for potential projects or stories, I'll start collecting on, and that's what I mean when I say I'm a pack rat. Even the littlest report, from small agencies or newspapers—you never know when you might see a nugget of information that you can use or expand on.

Other than honing that famous reporter's instinct, it helps to develop areas of expertise and 'concentrate on one area'.

> Then you learn the acronyms and the lingo that are in these documents that you're looking at. Because you can hand a document on defence to another reporter, and he may not see the same things that I would see.

Once a reporter has gained substantial background knowledge over time, he or she is likely to notice connections that would escape a cub reporter or even a veteran reporter without the requisite history on the issues. 'It goes beyond instinct—it's knowledge too.'

> I tend not to throw anything out. I have reports going back to the '80s, the '90s. Sometimes you'll see the same trends or a new trend coming up, and everyone goes, Ah, we've never seen that. But you think, 'Wait a minute! That reminds me of something. We *have* seen that.' And that brings extra material to a story or a project.

It's that kind of background knowledge that can make a good story exceptional. Pugliese has tried to branch out into other areas but ended by reconsidering the wisdom of such an expansion.

> It's just so time-consuming that I've had to kind of rein myself back in to the security area. I've tried to help other reporters at our place to maybe get things [through Access to Information] on transit and light transit rail, and so on. [Some of these] things that are happening, the *Ottawa Citizen* would be interested in, and I get the reports back, but I just don't know what I'm reading, because I haven't been brought up to speed, and some of the stuff is so technical. I don't have that base of knowledge.

Pugliese counts himself among the ranks of those who don't consider themselves investigative reporters. 'I'm just doing my job,' he said. But he does admit to receiving hostile communications from members of the public who don't like what he writes. Some of the least articulate critics resort to character assassination online. It happens all the time, he said, that 'if you're hitting a chord too much', disgruntled readers will try to damage your credibility with online postings.

> They try to do that, the idea being that if they can discredit you, your professionalism, then people will think, Gee, is what this character is writing real?

The *Ottawa Citizen* did once threaten to take legal action against three people responsible for an Internet posting that attacked Pugliese's professional reputation. It was a military website and the offending comments were posted by a military public affairs officer.

> So I sent it to the *Citizen*, and said, 'Do you want to do something about this or what?' They couldn't believe the libel. They served the three people involved, and everyone folded like a deck of cards. I got emails from these guys complaining that journalists censor free speech and I said, 'Look, you're entitled to free speech, and you can say this stuff about me, but, as well, we have the right to go to a civil court. And then you've got to prove what you said.'

The cyber-attacks often come from people who don't understand much about the subjects they're addressing, and apparently care less. The much-vaunted potential of the blogosphere as an exciting, new venue for journalism is real enough, but bloggers themselves may also be engaging in nothing better than age-old mudslinging delivered by high-tech means. For some, blogging becomes a way to attack journalists and others who express views the blogger dislikes. Such bloggers assume (wrongly) that they are immune from defamation suits when their barbs are published online.

Despite the headaches, Pugliese still thinks reporting is the best work in the world. He moved aggressively in his career, coming to the *Ottawa Citizen* from humbler origins. He began by taking a radio and television broadcasting course at a college, and got his professional start working for weekly newspapers in small-town Ontario. Then he did another educational stint at Carleton University to acquire a bachelor's degree in journalism.

> I was in Thunder Bay working at a weekly, and I applied to Carleton, because I was working at a weekly, and I didn't really know if I was doing it right. I wanted formal training. And quite frankly, the main reason was the summer jobs and the placements were so important to make the leap into full-time daily newspapers. I didn't find that I got a lot out of Carleton, except for two one-week placements at the *Citizen*, which I did for free. Then I got a summer job, through that Carleton process, at *The London Free Press*. I did well at the *Free Press*, but still didn't get a job—they didn't have any job to offer me.
>
> So I went back to Thunder Bay, where [this time] I worked for the daily paper there, and then three months later, the *Free Press* said, 'We have a one-year contract, are you interested?' And I said, 'Yes, I'll be there tomorrow.' And so I was able to get into the system. There are other ways, too. Now that I've been around for a while, I realize . . . you see some people who will go overseas and just set themselves up in a country, say somewhere in Africa, and just start filing [and after several years are able to establish themselves as freelance foreign correspondents].[11]

Pugliese's pack-rat technique evolved over time. Occasional freelancing for newspapers, magazines, and military publications also helped him hone his method.

> I really noticed it in 1995, '96. I did a couple of pieces for *Saturday Night* magazine; one was on the Zaire mission—that would have been '96—and the other one was on police SWAT teams mistakenly killing people. There have been ten or fifteen of these incidents. Because those were two areas I was interested in, I had files on them, and I really saw the benefit of being a pack rat, of keeping files.
>
> I had a coroner's inquest, a report, from 1989 on this SWAT guy killing by mistake another police officer. And you would have thought, How would you ever use it? Well, it really played a key role when I was doing a six-thousand-word feature on that very topic seven years later.
>
> And at the same time, I was going through the stuff from the Somalia inquiry. And I thought, 'Well, that's interesting, that may be useful,' and it gelled with filing more access-to-information requests. That was a process . . . learning that and fighting through that system—and I mean fighting—to get stuff from institutions. So when I was getting this stuff, I thought it took so long and so much effort to get some of it, I'm not just going to throw it in the paper shredder; I'm going to keep this, I'm going to put it into boxes and organize it.

> For instance, helicopters—this whole maritime helicopter program, the mess from the Chrétien era: I've got two filing boxes on that, and any time I get a report or there's a news story about that, it just goes in there. It's not filed intricately, because that would take me forever. However, when I've had to do helicopter stories, I go to the box and pull what's relevant.

Pugliese is the author of the best-selling *Canada's Secret Commandos: The Unauthorized Story of Joint Task Force Two* (Esprit de Corps, 2002). The first Canadian journalist to write the story of the task force, he plans to write more books, 'eventually'.

> There are a couple of topics I haven't gotten to yet. You kind of need a rest, because it takes so much out of you, with all the other stuff that's been happening on the beat.

His minor obsession with the unit's historical record began in earnest in 1992 with his reporting on the first task force (JTF-1).

> JTF-1 wasn't even a special forces unit. It was just the task force that went to the Persian Gulf War in 1991. They used [the term] because it hides the facts about what they do. 'Joint Task Force': it could be anything. This secrecy thing, it started in 1992—that really put a burr under my saddle. When the RCMP had the role of counterterrorism, we had been out to Dwyer Hill, the installation there. They toured us around and showed us what they did. Everyone had masks on. You could take photos. But as soon as the DND took over, forget it.
>
> So that started that whole thing [his abiding interest in the joint task forces specifically, and in keeping historical records, generally]. You open that file box and you start pumping stuff in and then along comes 2001, and you're ready to write a book.

Keeping his memory stoked, and on perpetual alert, is also part of Pugliese's technique.

> I find that [memory] is the most important part of an investigative process. Because information is everything, keeping information over time. You'll see trends and things that you've forgotten, and that you may not find on the Internet because it exists only in paper form.

A major investigation can start anywhere—a stray but striking remark, a random thought, a single line in a book. It was in fact one line in John Bryden's book *Deadly Allies: Canada's Secret War 1937–1947*[2] that got Pugliese going on a 1999 investigation into Canada's chemical and biological warfare activities. In response to an access request, he received 'just a page that said, "San José project, 1945", with everything else blanked out.'

> So I started looking around. I looked at Bryden's book and it had a one-sentence mention of a San José project being done in Panama. So you start digging. And eventually, I hooked up with a US non-governmental peace agency that was working with Panamanians trying to get rid of the chemical weapons that were dumped there by the Americans. San José is an island off Panama that was used by Canada and the US as a testing ground for chemical weapons.
>
> But the DND wouldn't give me any information. I filed a complaint. They said, 'No, it's all 15(1), national security.' I said, 'The time frame is 1945. What are you talking about?' They said, 'No, we're not going to release anything.' And that pissed me off, so I started digging more and more, and sure enough, I find out about the island. I found a guy who said, 'Well, you know what, we've still got bombs there, and by the way, there's a new resort that just opened up.'
>
> So I booked a flight, went to the resort, and checked in. There were three tourists there—the place wasn't doing a whole lot of business. I put on a back-pack and went for a hike and I found my first bomb about 200 metres away from the hotel. It was a chemical, mustard-gas spray canister. This place was great. It was like *The X-Files*. Outside the hotel, the resort—which is very isolated, the island was privately owned—was littered with World War II bombs and debris. I love that stuff.
>
> These canisters that I found, there's the potential that the ingredient is still in there. So I kept my distance, took my pictures, went back to my hotel room. They said, 'Do you want to go for an eco-tour?' So I paid for that and went into the jungle, and for part of the tour they take you to where the US army used to have its base, to the labs, which are all falling apart, and to this thing the US navy had built, like a huge dock, to unload all the chemical weapons.

Back in Canada, Pugliese phoned the DND and asked about chemical weapons in Panama and what the department intended to do about them. Department officials stonewalled.

> The answer came back: 'We've never been to Panama, there are no chemical weapons'—end of comment. I was put into a tough situation because the public affairs guy I was dealing with obviously had been given this line to say. We had a pretty good relationship. Normally I would have said okay, just taken it away and used that line. But I said to him, 'Look, you've treated me properly, you're a good guy. I've just come back from Panama, and I've got a hundred photos of chemical weapons. I've been to the National Archives. I've got all the railcar numbers, the dates they left Suffield [Defence Research Establishment Suffield, in Suffield, Alberta], how many pounds of mustard gas were sent from Cornwall [in Ontario].'

What happened to the material from Suffield?

> It went down to Florida first; they put it on a barge, and then it went to Panama. Suffield was their big site, their big chem-testing place. Eventually they came clean. Then I just hit them with as many access requests as I could. I was so angry at being lied to. I've said to JTF-2 folks and the DND that one way you can really assure yourself that someone is going to continue writing about an issue you don't want discussed is to put a blanket of secrecy down. Talk about putting the red flag to the bull. And that's my personality. I said to them, 'You could have saved yourself a lot of grief if you had been more open.' That's an ongoing issue.

Aspiring journalists should develop specialties and areas of expertise, Pugliese believes, and then stay current in those areas and be prepared to follow the issues over the long term.

> When you're starting out, focus on a couple of areas of interest—you've got to have an interest. For example, Dave McKie of the CBC has an interest in health and prescription drugs.[13] He's a good example. Same with Jim [Bronskill]—he's into CSIS and spies. It helps when the area that you decide to look at is something you have an interest in, because you're going to be doing a lot of research on it. If it's not interesting to you, that can slow you down a bit.
>
> And I would encourage this pack-rat mentality. I think that's extremely important once you've targeted your area of interest. I've got a shed here that's full of paper—the floor is starting to sag—and I like paper, quite frankly. A lot of these government agencies want to give you disks now. I refuse them because when I get a load of reports I sometimes divvy them up into subject matter, and if it's just sitting on a DVD, you can't actually see it.
>
> The other thing, even though I crapped on Access to Information: Learn it, use it, and keep on using it, and if you have to file a complaint, do it. Just keep at it. It's like these giant iron doors: You just keep banging on them, and trying to kick them, and sometimes you get lucky. Sometimes as well, different departments will go through different phases, and these people change jobs frequently. I've seen people who honestly believe in government openness, and they'll say, You know what, I'm working for you—it's very rare—or whisper, You should ask for this, because they're frustrated by the system as well. Now, you don't get that a lot, but sometimes there's an honest person like that and if you keep at it, sometimes it will pay dividends.
>
> It's a process, and the more you learn, the more you're able to get around roadblocks that the bureaucracy will put up. I'll give you an example. A month ago, I phoned Public Works. I'd put in this request last year, and I had forgotten about it, and they sent me a letter saying if I didn't respond within a month, they'd abandon my request. I phoned; it had been four or five months, I had just been so busy. I knew what the ATI person was going to say but I thought, 'What the hell, I've got a few minutes and I'm not going to put up with this.' So I called,

and said, 'Hey how you doing, I'm ready for my request now.' 'Oh well,' they said, 'we abandoned that. You abandoned it by not writing to us.' So I said, 'Well I've got the Access to Information Act here. What page is that on, that you can do that?'

'Oh just a minute,' he said, 'I'm going to go talk to my boss,' and he put me on hold. Comes back and says, 'Well no, we can't do that. We're going to release it to you. But it's a $70 photocopying fee.' So I said, 'Well no, I'm not going to pay that. Under the Act, you have to send it to me via a government office, and I'll go in.' . . . I wasn't backing down. I said, 'Look, we can do it the hard way, and I can file a complaint, or we can do it another way.' So he relented.

I guess the point that I'm making is that by knowing the Act, I'm able to use it. They're going to throw up every roadblock they can. They do not want you to get information. That's the bottom line. They do not help you, no matter what, when it comes to customer relations, openness, or transparency. If you're not armed with that knowledge, they will blow you off. I've had people say to me, 'Oh I put in a request—it was a $500 search fee, so I abandoned it.' I say, 'No, you don't abandon anything. You fight all the way.' If they know that you're a person who's going to file complaints and not give up, sometimes they work a little bit better with you.

Pugliese said he 'stumbled' into the newspaper business. He'd always been interested in military and defence matters and initially liked 'that you got to ride in helicopters and do interesting things'. He wasn't driven to journalism by a desire to write, or to correct wrongs.

No, no. Unfortunately, I was never one of those. I kind of envy people like that, who say they knew what they wanted to be when they were 16. I guess I could have done more, got into the business faster, and had more time, even though I've been doing it for twenty-five years.

He began in his mid-twenties working for weeklies, but Pugliese's career started to take off with the transition to daily papers. He still loves reporting, and concedes 'there's been some good work'.

Trouble is sometimes I think it gets lost in all the rest of the infotainment.

# The Interview: **Jim Bronskill**
(13 April 2006)

Like Pugliese, Jim Bronskill remembers noticing an upsurge in the presence of security forces at certain events.

> Whenever there was a demonstration or protest, the security would be massive. David and I had been talking; we wanted to do something together, and I remember thinking that we could team up on something about the communications security establishment, which is the electronic eavesdropping agency. It falls under national defence; it's a spy agency and it's supposed to be directed at foreign individuals. I thought that would be a good subject for us because it overlaps our beats.

Bronskill credited Pugliese with broadening the focus of the series to look at the overall trend toward greater surveillance of Canadians with anti-government views.

> As I recall, it was David who suggested something broader, to do something on surveillance writ large. I was looking at the trees; he was looking more at the forest. I think maybe because he wasn't covering this stuff in a daily way, he could see a bit of the broader picture. Maybe I was caught up in the mix of it too much.
>
> I was thinking of something that we could do that would draw on inside knowledge and documents, which it did in the end. But David cast a broader net, and proposed the idea of surveillance in general, not only in Canada but also in Europe and other places. There were a lot of threads out there, but we weren't aware of anyone who had really pulled them all together. So that clicked with me, and I said, 'Yeah, it will be more appealing to the general reader and a better sweep of stories.'

The reporters had roughly seven weeks to write the series (although they had been engaging in preliminary and related research for about six months before that).

> We did it pretty quickly. All told, we had seven weeks, and I remember having to do daily stories during the first part. I didn't have seven clear weeks, definitely not. We kind of tag-teamed, but David did a lot of the work at the front in the first half of the seven weeks, and I kind of picked up the ball on the second half. It worked well, because he handed stuff off to me and we compared notes. The other thing is we were in different cities, which didn't seem to matter that much. We communicated by email and phone, and we mapped out the five parts.

Bronskill distinguishes investigative work from daily reportage but doesn't like the term *investigative reporting* because 'it suggests there are some reporters who are non-investigative. Every reporter should be investigative.'

> I recognize that there is an animal that is investigative reporting, and very few people practise it, most days, including me. All of us do run-of-the mill reporting, and we do some stuff that approaches investigative. Then there's true investigative reporting, which maybe only a handful of people in Canada actually do regularly. I would set the bar pretty high for that kind of reporting. It does involve a fair bit of time. If daily reporting is a quick trip to the cafeteria, then investigative reporting is like a fine seven-course meal.
>
> And I think that's what you need—you need time, to get specific, probably at least five or six weeks minimum; you would need at least some travel or money to buy documents and materials. You would need the support of editors and their guidance in helping to shape a series. And you would need some patience as you ran into roadblocks. So all of those elements have to be there for it to be true blue investigative reporting.
>
> All that to say that it's not tied to the medium or the outlet. Anyone can do it—it's just you have to be freed up and given the time and resources and maybe money to do it. But the *Orillia Packet & Times* can do it. The question is do they want to do it, not are they able to.

The reporters initially debated whether the series should have five parts or three, and Bronskill held out for five.

> That may be another element of what constitutes investigative reporting, in that you map out a clear agenda of the stories you want to tell and you pick very distinct chapters so it's more like a little book or a little magazine. I think one of the strengths was that the pieces were well conceived and they had a theme, they stuck to their topic. They ranged from maybe 900 to 1,700 words. So they were of a length that people could digest. Without being onerous, they had enough heft. We gave that a lot of thought. I think that was my major contribution, mapping it out with David, figuring out what it would look like, and designing each piece. So it worked out well that way, partly through luck and circumstance.

Criminalizing Dissent did constitute investigative reporting in some respects, but not in others. For one thing, the series grew out of the reporters' respective beats.

> Again, it did flow naturally out of what we'd done and a lot of the material was sitting in our files, stuff that didn't make a story on its own or we hadn't got around to writing. It was like pieces of a jigsaw puzzle. We were able to do it in a fairly short time period, because a lot of the stuff was already there and we had that beat knowledge and background to be able to do it fairly readily. It was more

of an exercise in saying, Okay, let's step back—here's what we've learned over the last X number of years and this is the trend. If daily reporting is throwing out some dots, here we are connecting some of the dots for you, and for ourselves.

Pugliese and Bronskill went through none of the cloak-and-dagger goings-on often associated with investigative reporting. It was 'really a summary exercise'.

The remarkable thing about this was we were just looking at what was in our files and on our desks and we did some new research, and then we did some new access requests.

The information uncovered by ATI requests formed the backbone of the series and also provided news hooks for the stories.

We wanted to have some news in this. We didn't want it to be eye glazing. It was a summary kind of series but we wanted it to have a bit of juice and something new and interesting in each story. The access stuff helped provide some of the latest inside knowledge.

When he first learned of the Public Order Program, Bronskill was stunned.

That jumped out of the documents. It was a new concept and it was almost comical. It sounded Orwellian. I remember talking about it with my editor and David. We think of the crackdown now in terms of 9/11, but at the time, it was more about the anti-globalization protesters. The focus for me was looking at the techniques and interplay among the police, citizens, and protesters. The APEC protest in Vancouver in 1997 and then the Quebec City summit . . . those things had resulted in complaints and hearings. The dynamic between the police and protesters was more the focus at the time. That was really our jumping-off point.

Timing was an issue. As the reporters were writing the series, they were also awaiting the release of the APEC inquiry report on police behaviour. They worried that the report's revelations might upstage the series. In the end, it was mute on the issues raised in Criminalizing Dissent, a fact that underscored some of the insights unearthed by the series, and one that, as the reporters wrote in *Media* magazine, 'confirmed our initial sense the series would shine a light on some largely overlooked issues'.[14] Another issue of timing could have adversely affected the series:

It's almost eerie that about two and a half weeks later, 9/11 happened. My initial thought was, I'm glad we got it done, because if we had been in midstream we would have had to drop it or we would have been asked [by editors] if this was germane to 9/11. We would perhaps have had to rush it or do something with it and recast it in those terms. It would have probably got lost in a flood of copy. After September 11, there was a very strong initial call, or even a consensus, for stronger measures against protesters and against 'suspect' people.

So I kind of rolled my eyes and said, 'Oh well, that series was a waste of time because no one is going to have any time for those thoughts or arguments now.' But interestingly, a few months later, the argument came very much into play because people started thinking, Why are we passing all these anti-terrorism laws and why are we arresting all these people with dark skin when they haven't done anything wrong?

So it was interesting, and the story, I think, almost gained a new life. It did seem prescient, by sheer coincidence, because of those events. It was weird cosmic timing. I was just glad we got it done before September 11. And it became even more germane in some ways after, because all of these debates came up in Parliament and Congress and the whole question of civil rights and dissent and security was right on everyone's map.

Bronskill was aware when he began covering these issues—necessary security measures vis-à-vis free-expression rights—that he'd be living with them for a while. In the aftermath of 9/11, the issues gained public prominence.

I knew this would be a preoccupation for the next several years because these issues would be around and evolve, and there would be all sorts of new measures and debate about security on the one hand, and privacy and civil liberties on the other hand—the balance and the tussle between those two. And sure enough, that's been true.

Before 9/11, David and I were among maybe ten reporters in the country who followed this stuff; then overnight there were ten thousand suddenly writing about it. It was very strange to see. In a way, it was oddly gratifying—I don't know if that's the word. But it was also disturbing, in that these events had happened and it was a pretty grisly affair and a pretty depressing subject in a lot of ways.

If Bronskill had it all to do over again, he would take advantage of the advent of online publishing and supplement the hard copy with a website 'featuring scans of some of the documents we uncovered, additional photographs, and other supporting material'.

The *Citizen* in particular laid out the series nicely, and I was happy with that. But I think for these kinds of projects, so much work goes into them, it's kind of a shame that we don't go the next step now that we have the Internet. But it was never very well used, and it still isn't. CP has started to do some of this, and the *Globe*, but I think we can do much better. The CBC is the only one that comes to mind that does this really well, where they have stuff on *The Current* [radio], and then they'll have something on *The National* [television] that night, and then the same item will appear on the website. You can go and look at the documents that they found or listen to audio streams of interviews. I think we should all be doing that, all the media, but especially print media. And why not? It's kind of fun to be able to go online and read that public order memo from the RCMP. That's cool.

He believes that if the press were to embrace such online enhancements, it would increase transparency and might even help to restore public trust in the media.

People can see that something has been reported accurately. It's like extending an olive branch to the reader. You are giving up a bit of control in doing that, over future stories you want to mine out of those documents, but you can control that. And so what?

Sure, you have to guard your turf, and you have to be competitive, but you know, most other media don't follow up stories by their competitors, and we're probably as guilty as anyone. I think we need to do that more. *The Globe and Mail* could probably put online its whole sponsorship affair archive. Would people actually mine through it to find stories? Probably not. But it would be a great boon to the public.

Bronskill agreed with Pugliese on the increasing difficulty that reporters face when they try to get information through access requests. In fact, he had begun writing about problems obtaining such documents years before the Criminalizing Dissent series.[15]

In the security area, and because of 9/11, I still make a lot of requests to the same agencies: CSIS, the RCMP, and now more to Transport Canada, to some of the lesser known agencies—any that deal with security. Some are okay. I think they all do their best to answer the questions. But generally, it's become harder to get security-related information. After 9/11, the Privy Council Office [PCO] for a time vetted certain security-related requests and gave them a double read before they went out because of the concern centrally of disclosure of such information.

I read that the PCO was concerned about the wrong things getting out and certainly that overall concern has coloured—it's anecdotal, but I think it's coloured—the way these requests are answered now. I've heard people say, 'That's sensitive; that's security.' You hear it from the people processing the requests. It takes longer, and they go over it with a fine-tooth comb. I have one in to Transport Canada on the no-fly list [the list of people considered terrorists, and hence flight risks] right now, and the Access guy told me it's been flagged as a sensitive request. So it's getting the double look, extra scrutiny from the minister's office.

It's taking longer to get responses and you get less. There are some quantitative examples. In fact, I wrote a paper in connection with my work at Carleton.[16] It's on airport infiltration tests. Before 9/11, they would, and still do, have these

Transport Canada inspectors who try to sneak through airport security with knives and guns and bombs, to test the system. We used to be able to apply under Access, or even informally, and get the results. We wouldn't get the actual results always . . . but they would at least give you aggregates—say, 6.3 per cent of Transport Canada inspectors got through. They wouldn't necessarily tell you which airport or which time of day, but they would give you some results. After 9/11, they shut it down. They just said in bold terms in the letter that because of the events of September 11, they would not release this stuff anymore. So there's a concrete example.

David McKie is helping do some teaching at UBC, too, and one of the students there did a study of Transport Canada—a master's research project, in which she got a database of security-related information. The gist of it was they are applying more security-related exemptions to releases than before September 11. So there's a quantitative study, one of the first ones to look at that.[17]

Bronskill also mentioned the work of Syracuse University academic Alasdair Roberts on government secrecy.

He's recently published a book called *Blacked Out: Government Secrecy in the Information Age*. He articulates the same thing better than I can about the scope of the problem in the US, Canada, and elsewhere, about how the security imperative has meant less information for journalists.

On the one hand, we weren't asking for quite as much stuff as before 9/11, but on the other hand, I just found I used to get more, and more quickly. I think part of the problem is a syndrome where there's a heightened interest in security issues, and more reporters and members of the public are asking for this stuff, and as a result they're swamped with requests. So they have more requests to answer than they used to and that makes it harder too, probably. It's no easier, let's put it that way.

Ironically, about five months after our interview, Bronskill himself became the target of the government's domestic spying routines, when one of his requests for documents through the Access to Information Act came up for special mention. The identities of those seeking documents under the Act are supposed to be protected (partly to protect the requesters from reprisals); revealing them violates the Privacy Act.

But in a 20 September 2006 article, the *Gazette* (Montreal) revealed that Bronskill's right to confidentiality had been violated by the federal government during a 15 March 2006 telephone conference call involving at least eight departments. His identity was divulged and the 'minutes of the call were distributed to an additional nineteen people in the Privy Council Office and the Prime Minister's Office.' Citing the deputy information commissioner, the story, by the *Gazette*'s Elizabeth

Thompson, said that the confidentiality rights of requesters were routinely flouted by the government's ministerial staff. The story said that 'officials freely discuss media requests for information their departments have received. They also exchange information on who intends to submit a request and who is about to receive documents under the access law.'[18]

Bronskill, described as 'one of Canada's foremost experts on access to information', was also quoted: 'This seems to be another indication that federal departments do not always respect the law,' he told Thompson. 'It is disturbing that the rights of a requester can be trumped by the desire to manage the flow of information.'[19]

Bronskill completed both his bachelor's and master's degrees at Carleton University's School of Journalism. Together with David McKie, Bronskill now teaches a graduate course in research methods at his alma mater. On teaching journalism, he believes the most important thing is to keep it relevant.

> It helps to peg some of the teaching to the news. So when Juliet O'Neill's house was raided, we happened to be planning a segment on search warrants, and we emphasized it because of that.[20] If I hadn't been doing a story about what warrants were available, I wouldn't have had the up-to-date knowledge. So it does mesh nicely and we do bring in examples from our colleagues. We get a data projector and put databases up that David gets, and we do scanned documents that I get and decode them. David will play radio stories and explain what went into them. We take a story and say, 'Let's deconstruct it. How was that done? Where did the idea come from? What documents are involved?'

Outside the classroom, he believes, journalists 'all learn from each other'.

> Journalism, from the top down, is not very good at professional development. I'm always marvelling at how government people I know say things like, I was on a one-week training course; or, I have a month off to study French; or, We have another retreat next week. And it's all paid for and it's part of their job. And that's great. But that doesn't happen a lot in journalism.

To compensate, he advises aspiring journalists to attend conferences and workshops held by the Canadian Association of Journalists and take courses to learn on their own time. Though described by others as an expert in prying information from government strongholds, Bronskill sees himself as a perpetual learner (which goes a long way to explaining his keen intelligence).

> I'm learning stuff—from David, from the students, from just thinking about it. They say to teach is to relearn, to learn again. You have to remind yourself: 'Okay, well, how do I get a search warrant?' Because you forget. There are ways to fur-

ther your knowledge, but not everyone in journalism has understanding bosses or the budget for training. That's why we learn from each other.

I've learned so much from David McKie and Andrew McIntosh [the former *National Post* reporter who broke the so-called Shawinigate story] who is now at *The Sacramento Bee* in California.[21] He's still doing his thing but in a different country, which is fine. Maybe he'll come back and bring some of that knowledge here, but for the moment, he's lost to Canadian readers. And that's too bad.

He agreed with Paul McKay and other reporters who believe one sustaining factor that keeps good reporters in the business is the respect of their peers.

That's true, there is a kind of fraternity—and sometimes it's the only [recognition]. No one has read your story, but your colleague at least saw it and says, 'Hey, good story,' and I think that means as much as anything. And it's inspiring to read something by David Pugliese or any of these guys. I go, 'Wow, a lot of work went into that.' It makes you set your sights a bit higher. So it's competition of the best sort, and it makes you want to do something worthwhile, or at least try. I think that's what you need: a real story that demands to be told.

Born in Ottawa, Bronskill grew up 'mostly in Toronto'. His association with the Canadian Press had begun before he graduated from Carleton.

I was interested in CP and had worked summers in Toronto on the sports desk, the Ontario desk, and then weekend nights in Ottawa, and then became an editorial assistant. As someone once cleverly said, the master's degree is the snooze button on the alarm clock of life. There was nothing else for me to do. I was working summers at CP and I was in the master's by that point. I had to do this thesis, which took me three years, part-time. It was on culture and free trade and the sound recording industry, and it was a journalistic, book-length piece. So that took a while, and during that time I was working at CP as an editorial assistant just so I could live and finish my thesis. Then they kept giving me more things to do, like editing and working weekends and nights. Before I'd finished my thesis, I had a full-time job at CP [Ottawa], which was nice.

He went to work for Southam News in 1996. He was laid off after Southam 'morphed into CanWest,' and returned to CP Ottawa in 2003.

I wasn't alone. It's kind of a shame, although they've hired a bunch of new people, gradually, which is nice, at least at CanWest News. But the *Post* has gradually shed people, which is too bad, because it was a very good paper and it did a lot of good work. I think the *Globe* is slipping back to its old ways a little bit. It's too bad. It was kind of fun there for a while to be in newspapers.

He was never at the *Post*, but after it launched in October 1998, Bronskill saw a lot of wire stories—his own and colleagues'—run in the paper.

> I was at Southam News and we were not part of the *Post*, but they relied pretty heavily on us in the first year to provide stories, so we would have a lot of stories in the paper. Gradually, they found their own feet and started building more of a wall between the *Post* and Southam. And then Southam became CanWest.

With the erosion of the journalistic base that has accompanied increasingly concentrated ownership of Canadian newspapers, it also seems to be getting harder to break into the business of daily newspaper reporting. Thus it becomes more important than ever for journalists and journalism teachers to pass on to aspirants not only the techniques and skills of journalism, but also, and perhaps even more importantly, the inherent values of the craft.

> I think that's excellent advice, because you can build a career on such advice. The only thing I would add, really drive home, is you've got to get your style down, you've got to get your basics. You've got to understand. We try to encourage students to do something a little different. We say, 'Look, we know this is weird and a bit hard, filing these requests and playing with computer databases. It's like alchemy or something, and you might wonder what this has to do with journalism. It's not better, or a substitute for the basics, but it can give you a little bit more of a skill set with which to do interesting stuff. We know it's not much fun sometimes to have to fill out these silly [access request] forms, but it's worth it. Work away at longer-term projects in your spare time, bit by bit. Over a period of weeks or months, you'll acquire enough information to begin preparing a story or series.'

He advises his students, whether or not they see themselves as investigative reporters, to plan ahead and stay organized, keep and update special files such as ATI requests, schedule background research, and 'ask for something every day'. Bronskill also advises them to observe closely, follow up their own stories, and wander widely outside the familiar.

Though Bronskill doesn't consider himself a specialist in computer-assisted reporting (CAR), he lauded its potential for in-depth reportage.

> I think it's extremely powerful for the right projects. Like material from Access, it's not a universal tool for every project, but it has a definite place, and I think we're only scratching the surface on what it can do. It's a mindset: You have to think, 'How can I apply it to this story?' Sometimes it's not the right tool, but when it is, it's amazingly powerful. We're doing one now where we got six hundred forms from the RCMP describing how they've used tasers,[22] the stun guns. They gave it

to us on CD-ROM, but it's just scans of pages—1,800 pages, 600 three-page forms. So what we've had to do is print them out—they're sitting on the floor here in a pile—and staple them, and now we have to punch it all in. But we're going to do that, and I think it will be exciting.

We did a series on it last year, Sue Bailey and I—it was a good little series. It didn't come to any definite conclusions, but it raised some questions. [The taser] is a polarizing issue. Some say it's perfectly safe and it saves lives; others that it's akin to torture. We don't pretend to have the answers, but it certainly raises those questions. The great thing about [CAR] is now you can analyze how the taser was used over a period of a couple of years by one police force. On these forms it tells you whether the person was armed or not, where the victim was hit on the body, what the officer did before firing the taser. So you punch all that in and then come statistically to a solid statement about it. That can be a powerful thing.

I think [CAR] is underutilized. A lot of people go into journalism because they have a math phobia, an aversion to numbers. I think it's changing a bit, because some of the ones we see at Carleton have science backgrounds, they know what Microsoft Excel is. They're a lot more computer literate in that sense than I was, that's for sure.

But I think again it's going the next step and saying, 'Okay well how can you apply this to the story process?' That's something I'm still learning to do. We're trying to urge [students] to think creatively. This year, they looked at a balance sheet, the back of an annual report. They have to figure out what all the terms mean and then they have to think creatively about analyzing that. Then we had them go the next step and look at the salaries for Ontario public servants. All the ones that make $100,000 are put on this sunshine list, are disclosed, and so we had them look at that and crunch some numbers and just find trends. We don't get too hung up on technique as much as using it as a tool.

It's the critical thinking—thinking like a good reporter—that matters and that produces results. In other words, it's the thinking that produces the method, not the other way around.

That's the mantra of our course: teaching people to think critically. My little pet phrase is 'the iceberg theory of journalism', especially with government. You have the government or the business or [other source that] will show you the tip of the iceberg. So in government terms, it could be the website that the justice department puts up. There's the tip of the iceberg. Your job is to look at the tip, explore it, and then try to find the rest of the iceberg, by using access, by using computer-assisted techniques, by being a good interviewer, by going down to the courthouse, by making lists of sources and connections.

It's critical thinking; it's not accepting the tip as the full iceberg. It could be a balance sheet, an Access document, it could be a really good interview you had with someone. All those are tip sheets to something bigger. And you have to take those and do the interviews to flush them out and use them as a wedge, a foot in the door, and to say, Hold it, there's something more here, and get who-ever to open the door. They're a wedge into the rest of the iceberg. So that's really in a nutshell what we've tried to focus on. All these things are the same, though. One happens to be a bunch of numbers; another happens to be an Access document; still another one happens to be a revealing interview. It's your job to decode that and try to take it further.

I think being a good listener is probably the most important thing. Again, we have a kind of top ten list for this, too: being organized; doing the research upfront, before you interview the person so you know who they are and what you want to ask; having a list of questions but not being wedded to it; structuring your inquiries properly so you don't ask the toughest question first. So all that to say reporters need to be orderly and methodical, listen to what interviewees do say, and then pick up on that—don't just blindly file your nails while you let your tape recorder take notes.

Listen, follow up, make sure it's a conversation, make sure you make it clear you're interested in what the person's saying—and hopefully you are. Get them to tell anecdotes if it's that kind of interview. Get them to describe things.

Sometimes you'll ask really odd questions; like they'll say, Oh yeah I remem-ber driving across the border to freedom when I escaped Czechoslovakia, and you might say, What was the first thing you did?; and, Oh, you had lunch. Then you might ask, What did you eat? What did you have for lunch? Really odd, bizarre kinds of questions that you might not ask your friend.

But if they said, I had a glass of wine, you might ask if it was red or white, which is a bizarre thing to ask, but you have to ask that because then when you sit down to write the story you can say, Doris sat on the patio and sipped her red wine as she looked out onto freedom.

So get detail. Learn those techniques of getting what you need in the story while you're interviewing the person. And if it's a tough interview, use techniques to elicit information. Don't ask close-ended questions, ones that will elicit yes or no answers. Ask open-ended questions. This is David's: The best question is, 'How do you know that?' Make them tell you exactly how they know that, and prove it. It draws them out into explaining things. At least it forces them to account for what they're saying. I mean, it's easy to just sit there and take notes.

# Commentary

Access-to-information requests and computer-assisted reporting are two of the strongest tools that reporters can use to get at the truth. But it's important to remem-ber what Bronskill was at pains to stress: These are tools, and the basic ingredient in successful investigations is not the latest tool but the age-old advantage of thinking independently and critically. Before there was an Internet, before information was instantly accessible via 'googling', reporters dug for the facts of the matter, and deeper, for the meaning of the facts. They used telephone books and reverse directories, police reports and government documents, sources and supposition to track down the facts and get at the truth. All of it begins with a real research question (or several), not with a summary of the existing literature and certainly not with an opinion masquerading as a question. Aside from a bona fide research question, the element that tends to make the difference between failure and success is often simple perseverance.

The Internet can make available vast amounts of information, but it is not after all a library, where material is vetted, overseen, and organized. Not only is much of the information found online difficult if not impossible to verify, but also virtually all of the information you can get from googling a word or phrase is by definition decontextualized and dehistoricized. Further, the ease with which information can be had by googling tends to discourage deeper investigation, especially among a generation of students who didn't grow up using libraries (unlike their elders who had no alternative), and who are consequently little disposed to question the validity of the information they're reading, nor to ask the primal question: How do you know that? Yet that transparency is part of what you as a journalist owe your readers.

Criminalizing Dissent is commendable for its victory over the potentially 'colonizing' perils of beat reporting—the danger that in becoming so identified with their subjects, beat reporters lose the ability to regard them critically. There was no way that Bronskill and Pugliese could have written such a thorough-going series without their respective beat expertise; just as certainly, there would have been no way to even conceive of the stories without the independent cast of mind both reporters exemplify. So here is another example of how beat reporting can lead to more in-depth and investigative work: the untaming or unchaining, if you will, of the beat reporter.

Finally, Bronskill and Pugliese's series underlines an issue raised in the previous chapter on the asbestos story: A gap—or chasm—appears to have grown up between the revelations of a good hard-hitting news story, and an appropriate response (or any response at all) from the responsible and/or implicated parties. For example, you might expect a concerted government effort to counteract the damning information in the *Gazette* (Montreal) story that revealed how the federal government routinely violates the privacy rights of those seeking government documents through the Access to Information Act. You might also expect these facts to concern the larger public and the politicians elected to represent them. But the immediate response to the *Gazette* story was more politics: The newly dethroned Liberals called for the establishment of still another formal investigation. Yet the Liberals themselves while in power had fought hard against more and easier access to government documents through information laws. They were not as blatantly caught in the act as were Stephen Harper's Conservatives on the matter of freedom-of-expression rights, but it would be, it seems to me, criminally naive to imagine that the Conservatives hold an attitude toward free-speech rights essentially different from that of the Liberals—or, for that matter, any other party forming the government. All governments (and aspiring governments) seek to manage information. That's why it is the job of journalists in a democracy to 'watchdog' governments, among other powers. To investigate in the public interest means to uphold the right of the people to know what their governments and other powerful entities are up to.

Of course, information overload helps to explain how important issues get lost in the daily shuffle. Nevertheless, the story clearly called for a substantive response from government—a response that never came—rather than one from the press.[23] It was the press, after all, that uncovered the unsavoury truth, not a whistle-blower from within the ranks of government. Elizabeth Thompson, like other fine reporters, was doing precisely what she was supposed to be doing, and her story clearly ranks in the public interest.

Consider too the immediate impact of Criminalizing Dissent: a flood of reader response, online and off, condemning the then Liberal government's bald-faced attempts to suppress free speech, to discourage demonstrations, and ultimately to squelch all forms of public dissent. A former Liberal cabinet minister wrote to the solicitor general blasting the police and their tactics. This would seem an appropriate response to the series' disclosures. But years later, the cache of secrets has grown exponentially, the access laws haven't been appropriately reformed, and it is the reporter seeking access who is now targeted for surveillance.

# Endnotes

1. Nick Russell, 'The APEC affair and Terry Milewski: If the journalist takes sides in a story, he damages his credibility, the credibility of his newsroom, and of the entire industry', *Media* 5.4 (Winter 1999), 7–8.

2. 'The criminalization of dissent: Jim Bronskill and David Pugliese reflect on their portrait of life under the spyglass', *Media* 9.1 (Summer 2002), n.p. www.caj.ca/mediamag/summer2002/index.html.

3. 'Keeping the public in check: Special Mountie team, police tactics threaten right to free speech and assembly, critics say', *Ottawa Citizen* (18 August 2001), A1.

4. 'Spying on the protest movement: Private emails find way into military hands', *Ottawa Citizen* (19 August 2001), A1.

5. 'Secret files chill foes of government', *Ottawa Citizen* (20 August 2001), A1.

6. 'Under the Canadian spyglass', *Ottawa Citizen* (20 August 2001), A4.

7. 'How police deter dissent: Government critics decry intimidation', *Ottawa Citizen* (21 August 2001), A1.

8.  'Mounties in masks: A spy story', *Ottawa Citizen* (22 August 2001), A1.

9.  Pugliese was referring to the Somalia affair. In 1992, Canadian Armed Forces soldiers were sent as peacekeepers to Somalia, a small African country torn by civil war and ravaged by famine. Scandal erupted when the soldiers were accused of torturing and murdering Somalis. The operation ended in 1993 and an inquiry into the allegations began in 1995. The inquiry itself was controversial; it proceeded amid widespread allegations of a cover-up at the highest levels of government and the military, allegations supported in the inquiry's final report ('Report of the Commission of Inquiry into the Deployment of Canadian Forces to Somalia', July 2, 1997). As well, the commission's work was cut short in January 1997 by then prime minister Jean Chrétien, and it never got to one of the most sensitive issues: the torture and murder of 16-year-old Somali civilian Shidane Arone. The commissioners publicly accused the government of political interference in the inquiry in a blatant attempt to whitewash the Somalia affair.

    For more on the Somalia affair, see the book written by one of the commissioners, former journalist and journalism educator, Peter Desbarats: *Somalia Cover-up: A Commissioner's Journal* (Toronto: McClelland & Stewart), 1997.

    See also David Pugliese's article 'Running for cover: There are signs that the Department of National Defence has learned little from the Somalia inquiry', *Media* 6.3 (Fall 1999), 6.

10. Ken Rubin is an Ottawa-based public interest researcher and freedom-of-information advocate who has filed thousands of access requests over the last few decades on a wide range of controversial issues including genetically modified foods, drug company practices, contaminated water, and government transparency (or more precisely lack thereof).

11. For more on freelance reporting from overseas, see Alan Goodman and John Pollack's *The World on a String: How to Become a Freelance Foreign Correspondent* (New York: Henry Holt, 1997).

12. John Bryden is a Canadian politician, journalist, and author. His book, *Deadly Allies: Canada's Secret War, 1937–1947*, traced the history of Canada's often pioneering role in the development of chemical and germ warfare during the war and in the immediate postwar period. From files buried in the National Archives, Bryden was able to piece together the wartime stories of work done on anthrax in Quebec and on mustard gas at Alberta's Defence Research Establishment Suffield.

13. Chapter 14 of this text, 'Talking Investigative Journalism', includes an interview with David McKie, a reporter with the CBC's investigative unit and one of the people responsible for the spectacular award-winning series 'Faint Warning', about the potential dangers of prescription drugs and Health Canada's failure to disclose information it had about drugs with serious side effects and drugs withdrawn from the market for safety reasons.

14. *Media* 9.1 (Summer 2002), op. cit.

15. See two of Bronskill's articles on access laws: 'Improved access: Lengthy delays. Blank pages. Shredded documents. No wonder it has been dubbed the Access to Obfuscation Act', *Media* 6.1 (Spring 1999), 27; and 'Biting back: Using access to information laws'. *Media* 3.3 (Fall 1996), 31. As well, Bronskill is quoted on the subject in the *Columbia Journalism Review*. See John Wicklein's 'How government foils investigative reporters', *Columbia Journalism Review* 2 (July/August 1998), 61–62.

16. Bronskill and David McKie teach a graduate reporting methods class at Carleton University's School of Journalism, Canada's oldest.

17. Darcy-Anne Wintonyk, 'Hide and Seek: The Relationship between National Security and Open Government at Transport Canada since September 11, 2001', master's thesis, University of British Columbia, 2006.

18. Elizabeth Thompson, 'Shroud of secrecy violated in Ottawa' (*Gazette* (Montreal), 20 September 2006), A1. See also the CP report out of the Ottawa bureau: 'Report says federal officials illegally discuss those applying for documents' (Canadian Press, 20 September 2006). The CBC reported the same day that the Opposition Liberals

were calling for the resignation of a senior member of the prime minister's staff over the incident. Several days later, on Saturday, 23 September, the *Gazette* ran a series of articles from various papers on the issue. See the following: 'What does the government have to hide?' (by the *Toronto Star*'s Robert Cribb); 'Montreal's record could be better, informal tests show' (by Brenda Branswell); 'Call for Harper aide to resign over secrecy leak' (by Elizabeth Thompson); and 'Changes to access law keep more public data secret' (by the *Ottawa Citizen*'s Don Butler).

19.  Elizabeth Thompson, 'Shroud of secrecy violated in Ottawa', op. cit.

20.  On 21 January 2004, the RCMP raided the home of *Ottawa Citizen* reporter Juliet O'Neill seeking sources for a story O'Neill had written the previous year about Maher Arar. A Canadian citizen, Arar had been arrested on 26 September 2002 in New York City by US officials acting on information from the RCMP. About ten days later, Arar was deported to Syria, where he was imprisoned and tortured, and where he remained for a full year before finally being released, despite the fact that allegations against him were baseless. On his return to Canada, Arar fought tirelessly to clear his name, finally succeeding in September 2006, when a commission of inquiry exonerated him. The commission blamed the RCMP for its part in the scandal, saying that instead of acting to correct the false information it had knowingly spread about Arar and working to secure his release from his Syrian hellhole, it had moved to close ranks and cover its own tracks.

O'Neill later spoke of the 2004 raid on her home to journalism students. See Mike Whitehouse and Linda Whitehouse, 'Fighting for free expression: Three of the country's top investigative journalists have an emotional encounter with journalism students'. *Media* 10.3 (Spring 2004), 30–31.

In another article in the same 2004 edition of *Media*, investigative reporter Andrew Mitrovica took issue with the majority view of the raid as evidence of the state's heavy-handed interference in the work of a heroic free press. Mitrovica suggested that reporters, including O'Neill, were complicit in the Maher Arar affair because they uncritically repeated information they received from police and intelligence officers. See 'RCMP follies: When the Mounties raided the home of *Ottawa Citizen* reporter Juliet O'Neill, there was indignation. Some people even wondered if Canada of all nations had become a police state. Investigative reporter Andrew Mitrovica weighs in with his assessment—and it may surprise you', *Media* 10.3 (Spring 2004), 6.

21.  McIntosh is known for exposing the Shawinigate scandal in a *National Post* story headlined 'PM lobbied for disputed loan'. The story appeared on the front page of the *National Post* on 16 November 2000, during a federal election campaign. The story detailed a conflict of interest by then prime minister Jean Chrétien in his lobbying of the government's Business Development Bank of Canada in 1996 and 1997 for a loan for an inn in his riding of St. Maurice. To find out about McIntosh's own account of that award-winning story, see his article, 'The story that Jean Chrétien can't seem to shake', *Media* 8.2 (Summer 2001), 10–11. See also Dean Jobb, 'Good news for journalists: The recent victory of the *National Post*'s Andrew McIntosh to protect his source will resonate across the country', in *Media* 10.3 (Spring 2004), 8–9.

22.  The taser is a hand-held, gun-like device that delivers a strong electric shock when fired at a suspect. The word taser is a trademark for weapons known generically as conductive energy devices, or CEDs.

23.  Shortly after the initial *Gazette* story ran, the paper tried to keep the heat on, following up with four articles. See pages A12 to A14 of the *Gazette*'s 23 September 2006 edition for the stories. One of the pieces was written by the *Toronto Star*'s Robert Cribb, who characteristically made a beeline for the heart of the issue in a story headlined 'What does the government have to hide?' The other stories, by Elizabeth Thompson, Brenda Branswell, and Don Butler dealt respectively with a call for the resignation of a top aide, Montreal's record in accessing government information, and changes to the access laws that enabled the government to keep secrets about presumably public data.

# Chapter 6

# Dialling for Dollars

The *Toronto Star*'s Robert Cribb and Christian Cotroneo went undercover for this 2002 investigation of telephone telemarketing fraud conducted daily by hundreds of scam artists operating with impunity in Toronto's downtown core. The reporters conducted their research from inside the downtown 'boiler rooms' (office spaces hastily arranged and meant to be just as hastily packed up) and revealed that judging from the situation in its largest city, Canada's reputation as an international haven for fraudulent telephone sales was only too well deserved.

Called Dialling for Dollars, Cribb and Cotroneo's series comprised just two front-page stories that in a total of about six thousand words tore the veil from the local face of a multi-billion dollar industry. The stories brought readers inside the boiler rooms and showed them the typical rip-off techniques employed by the scam artists, who plied their trade inside Canada—where laws were loose—but targeted their victims outside the country (mostly in the United States), thus making the whole gambit perfectly legal.

The boiler room marketers collected millions of dollars each month, through ruses such as offering to sell credit cards to people who would otherwise have had a hard time acquiring them, in return for a 'small' up-front payment. The credit cards, of course, never arrived, and the victims, most of them elderly and vulnerable Americans, were left worse off than ever.

To gain inside access to the boiler rooms, Cribb and Cotroneo posed as potential recruits. They took instruction from managers, worked the phones with prepared scripts, and gathered documents. In classic undercover fashion, they documented the fraud by bearing witness to it. At one point, the reporters even wore concealed mini-cameras to their boiler room 'jobs'. Then, having survived their stints on the inside as telemarketers, Cribb and Cotroneo were able to reveal the unscrupulous tactics and glib talk the scammers used to steal from their unsuspecting targets.

The Dialling for Dollars stories explained not only how the operators of these illegal marketing schemes were getting away with it—by taking advantage of lax laws in Canada to swindle customers in the United States—but also how 'normalized' the scamming had become.

After the stories ran in early November 2002, the illicit industry beat a retreat from its various stations in Toronto's downtown core. The boiler rooms shut down in a hurry; scripts were destroyed and doors were locked. An estimated two hundred operations in Toronto pulled up stakes after the first article ran. Local law-enforcement officials praised the series and urged the courts to impose harsher penalties for telemarketing fraud.

Robert Cribb[1] is one of Canada's most accomplished investigative reporters, a man noted for the impact of his work, and one who embraces the term *investigative reporter* with unconcealed passion. His stories are models of the investigative art; it was Cribb whose Dirty Dining series in the summer of 2001 provoked the creation of a pass system for Toronto's restaurants and eateries. The year after the series ran, Toronto became the first city in Canada to enforce mandatory training for food handlers.[2] Cribb's other major investigations include a series called Mystery Meat, another undercover operation that took readers inside unlicensed slaughterhouses; Medical Secrets, which exposed problems, including criminal negligence, under Ontario's self-regulation system for the province's doctors; and Broken Homes, a series that revealed slum conditions inside Toronto's low-income apartment units.

Cribb is also a past president of the Canadian Association of Journalists, a lecturer at Ryerson University's School of Journalism, and a co-author of *Digging Deeper: A Canadian Reporter's Research Guide*.[3]

## The Interview: **Robert Cribb**
(19 May 2006)

Robert Cribb got the idea for this story after reading a newspaper brief about telemarketing fraud in Toronto. The two-paragraph item revealed only that a man had been convicted of telemarketing fraud for running a boiler room:

And that's all it was. There was one quote from a police officer. It said something like Toronto has now surpassed Montreal as the telemarketing fraud capital of Canada, which I just thought was an extraordinary thing, buried in a news brief at the back of the newspaper.

Here we have this multi-billion dollar fraud industry; Toronto is effectively the centre of telemarketing fraud in the Western world. The reason they're all here is that the laws around this in Canada are so lax that they all move here from the States to do it. And how do we cover this story? We cover it in little news briefs every six months, when somebody gets convicted. It just seemed like an obvious story to throw our attention at.

The story involved the reporters in high-risk undercover work—a route not taken lightly, even at the country's largest-circulation daily.

It took us a while to get to that point. It's a sort of last-ditch strategy—you always try to figure out other ways to do a story. It's complicated, it's time consuming, it's dangerous. So we had long debates about how to do the story. And at the end of the day, you have to justify this ten ways to Sunday, to editors, before you can do undercover—it's very controversial. It has to be ethically justifiable. So it's not taken lightly. You have to sit before the senior editors and make a pretty compelling case that this is ethically defensible and that we'll be able to explain this to our readers, because, of course, the standard operating procedure in journalism is to present yourself as who you are and identify yourself and be up front and open and clear.

So when we take this step, at least at the *Star*, it's not taken lightly. You have to answer two basic questions: Is there a strong enough public interest in the story? In other words, is it important? And is there any other way to get the information? My argument on this was that the story that's never been told is how does [the scam] work. What's the nitty-gritty? How exactly do these little boiler rooms, which are filling the downtown core—how do they do it? How do they make all that money? How do they get people in Europe and the States, in such shocking numbers, to take out their wallets and give strangers on the telephone their credit card numbers?

Cribb and Cotroneo knew that telemarketing fraud was a massive, multi-billion-dollar industry, and also that the boiler rooms had been operating for years with virtual impunity. What they couldn't figure out was how the boiler rooms continued to rake in the big bucks and get away with it. Other than 'the occasional conviction, which often doesn't warrant particularly stiff fines in this country,' the telemarketing scams went largely unpunished.

Cribb figured there were basically two ways to go.

You can go out and interview a couple of people who worked in them and do a news feature. Or you can go in and do the definitive story that explains how they do it, and who does it. What are their names? What words do they use on the phone? How do they get their scripts? Where do they get the names of these people? Who do they call? All those are the unanswered questions.

His instincts told him the first approach was too soft for the issue. He pitched the second to his editors.

So that was the pitch I made: If we're going to do it right, there is no other way to approach it. I mean, if you're going to write a story that says these are the companies doing this, they're doing it illegally, they're lying, they're committing fraud, the only way to do that is to witness it. So long story short, we got permission to take that approach and we went about getting boiler room jobs.

Procuring those jobs in the boiler rooms allowed Cribb and Cotroneo to tell the story from the inside. Getting hired proved straightforward.

It's pretty easy to get jobs in that industry. First of all, there are hundreds of companies doing it. They advertise in a free employment newspaper in Toronto that you can pick up on the street. There are lots of ads for legitimate telemarketing companies too, but you quickly learn the code, the language of the ads that are placed by the illegitimate operators—they tend to be the ones that make amazing promises about income, which are not that amazing, because they're actually fairly true. You *can* make a lot of money.

So we identified a bunch that we worked together. I would go in at, let's say, 10:00 a.m. for an interview, and Chris would come behind me at 10:15 or 10:30. We stuck pretty closely together for obvious reasons. It's an industry that we knew from talking to police was completely controlled by organized crime, predictably. It was a bit dodgy. Once we got inside, the story just—it just took shape. Because there it is: it's a remarkable environment to find yourself in as a journalist.

Usually the first morning that you're there, you're trained, and training consists of sitting for a couple of hours with an experienced 'telemarketer'. So you're sitting there listening to people lie, hour after hour, with the most extraordinary claims, stuff like they're calling from a bank: 'I'm calling you from Chicago, and I see from the computer screen in front of me that you recently applied for a credit card'—well, there's no computer in the room. So, while these people are thinking they're talking to a pin-stripe-suited banker from Chicago, they're talking to a guy with tattoos up and down his arms, and a nose ring and a Mohawk sitting in a spartan office on the second floor of a Yonge Street building.

Once they were hired, Cribb and Cotroneo began to observe how the boiler rooms operated. Employees would get slips of paper bearing the names and phone numbers of potential marks. The slips of paper 'are actually purchased from companies that supply them.'

> We focused on a particular scam—there are lots of scams—but the one we focused on, which was huge at the time, was the credit-card scam. It targeted mainly Americans who had lost their credit, who for whatever reason had fallen on hard times. So they're quite desperate to re-establish credit, because without it you can't do anything. If you can't get a credit card, you can't get a mortgage— you can't do anything. So you get the names from the manager of the office, and then you sit down and make these phone calls. You're basically handed a list of victims. From a journalistic point of view, it's an extraordinary thing: you have in your possession a list of people who are being targeted.

The boiler rooms were equipped with but a single incoming telephone line.

> I would always sit next to that because it would be ringing all day and totally ignored. It would be all these people calling to complain, or to say they didn't receive [their credit cards], or they'd been ripped off. Nobody would answer it. They'd just let it ring, or they'd pick it up and say who is this, and somebody would start to complain, and they'd say, Just one second, let me put you on hold. And then they'd just hang up.
>
> But I'm the new guy, so I'm naive, I don't know. The phone's ringing, so I pick it up. I would talk to these people and they would tell me what was going on, and I would say, Well let me just get your name and number and I'll talk to my manager and pass it on. I'd get it and I would sock it away, because that was somebody who I'd need to eventually talk to when I was out of there. It was tremendous, tremendously valuable. You're literally having victims call you and getting their stories, getting their names and numbers.

As employees, the reporters also gained access to 'all the documentation, the scripts.' They soon learned that the key to success lay in the script and in learning to embellish on the script to win their targets' confidence.

> The whole industry runs on scripts; scripts are gold. It tells you exactly what to say, and the scripts, in combination with listening to what the telemarketers actually say, which goes much further than the scripts—the good ones eventually learn to do their own thing—you're getting all of that. Obviously, for ethical reasons, we couldn't actually sell anything.

That the reporters 'couldn't sell' presented a logistical problem: none of the jobs lasted very long.

> We'd get fired after a couple of days, in all these places. We'd just keep going. I'm not sure how many we went to in the end. They're not going to tie up a phone if you're not selling. We certainly could have. . . . There were lots of occasions where I had people ready to pull out their credit card, and I suck as a salesman. The way the scripts are written, the tricks that you learn from the others—you can see how easy it is to do. If I ever got to that point, I would just hang up.

Cribb and Cotroneo spent about a month working in the various boiler rooms, collecting evidence and gathering background information and leads. To maintain their cover, the reporters would 'go out on smoke breaks with the people that had been working there a long time and pick their brains about the operation, who's behind it.' That involved a bit of acting.

> You've got to be one of them, for sure. I mean, I never smoked before, but I took up smoking because smoking was essential for collecting [information], for talking. Because it's great to listen to them while they're working, but you really need to get them when they're not on the phone. And what they all do is smoke. So we smoked.

Stress levels skyrocketed as Cribb and Cotroneo, on top of having to maintain an act of being just part of the gang and practising the hard sell, also had to figure out how to stop just short of making fraudulent sales to their phone victims.

> Yeah, going undercover is absolutely the hardest thing. I've done it three times now—three different stories—and it's by far the most stressful and difficult technique. We did it for an illegal slaughterhouse operation, that was a couple of years before; and just recently, this year, we did a series on illegal holistic centres [that are actually] massage parlours. But it's really hard to do. There's so much preparation involved and it's just stressful. You have no idea what's going to happen. You're on their turf, and if you're found, you've got to have a lot of contingency plans for what you do.

Cribb used a false name for the undercover work. He had a bogus resumé and story concocted and at the ready in case he was asked for personal information such as his social insurance number (because 'you can never give your SIN to a bunch of thieves like this').

To complete the story on bawdy houses posing as holistic centres, the undercover reporter could simply end the negotiations at the critical moment and leave the establishment. For the telemarketing fraud story (as for the slaughterhouse story), Cribb found that maintaining a cover proved a dicier proposition.

For the slaughterhouse story—we were in the middle of nowhere on a farm with a guy who slaughters animals for a living, in a dilapidated barn filled with knives. I wasn't the one who went inside on that, because I'd already been identified by the slaughterhouse guy. So it was another reporter who went in. We were sitting right outside, but obviously if anything had happened, we were all in it.

On the telemarketing stories, as in undercover work generally, the evidence collected on the inside was the evidence that made the case.

It was the inside stuff that formed the basis, the foundation for the whole story. It went really well, because again, I've never been so blessed with such compelling characters and amazing information. It gave instant access to a story that no one had told before.

One of the biggest obstacles was identifying the major players: those who actually owned the companies.

We wanted to go after the people who really run the show, not the little fish. But all these companies are numbered companies, it's not like you can do a corporate search and find out who owns them, because they're not named. We had some trouble finding the big cheese, so to speak, behind a lot of them. In one case, there was a place we really wanted to write about and we could not find out who owned it, because these are pretty shadowy operations. The only thing to do is to find out what their corporate number is. So how do you get that, right?

We racked our brains. . . . Friday is payday, and when they get their cheques, the cheques include the corporate identity, the numbered company name. But the problem was we weren't getting paid, because we weren't selling anything. So we'd been there for a couple of days and the head guy liked us. We were hedging about whether we would keep going, because we weren't selling anything. We went back on Friday afternoon—we knew they were getting paid then—and it was one of those fortuitous moments where it just went right for us.

Serendipity came in the form of a practised scam artist pleased with himself on a Friday afternoon and eager to brag about his superior experience in 'the business' and the size of his cheque.

The guy was saying, 'You should come back, you guys are good, you can make a lot of money in this business . . . our good sales guys can make two thousand bucks in a week.' And I said, 'Come on, you don't make that much money.' And they said, 'Yeah, we do, we do.' I said, 'If you can prove to me you make that much money, then maybe we'll come back Monday. If you're telling me this is all about money, then I need to know that's right, because I frankly don't think that's true. We haven't had any luck selling anything.' He said, 'No, it's true.' I said, 'You just got paid. Let me see, show it, let me see what you've got.' And he hedged a bit but eventually he pulled his wallet out and said all right, because he was bragging. And it was a big cheque—it was like two thousand bucks. I couldn't believe that. But the point was it gave me about two seconds to look at that eight-digit number and memorize it, which I suck at doing.

The odds of that working were like one in a thousand, right? But it was just the right guy on the right day with an ego big enough to make him want to show me his cheque.

Cribb couldn't have 'sucked' that badly during the cheque-number caper, because he managed to 'bury the number in my skull'. Armed with the number, the reporters were able to do a corporate search on it and find out the names of the company principals.

Much about the story surprised Cribb, including how much money the boiler-room workers made and how polished and lucrative the operations proved.

When you read the ads, you immediately dismiss them as being flights of fancy. But you know what? They're actually making a ton of money. . . . And I was surprised by the sophistication of their techniques, their sales techniques. They're really good at it, and utterly shameless, without the slightest grain of guilt, which is a fascinating thing to witness day after day, to watch people say anything, absolutely anything, to the most vulnerable victims.

But most of all, he was moved by the 'tremendously sad stories' of the victims.

Some of the people that we featured in the story will always stay with me. One of the victims was this couple from Texas. Her husband had a chronic illness, I think it was cancer, and he was dying, and the hospital bills were piling up, and she was trying to keep working and trying to take care of him and they had lost their credit. They had spent everything they had on his medical bills. They bought this credit card package in a last-ditch effort to restore their credit so they could get back on their feet.

It's just a horrible story. And a lot of the people that I ended up talking to were people like this, either elderly people on fixed incomes or younger people who for whatever reason, because of illnesses or bad decisions or whatever, found themselves poor. You talk to them and then you listen to these people next to you and around you call after call making such utterly indefensible, immoral pitches to them, taking money from them that is so significant to them. If there's anything that really stuck with me, it was that. I guess I didn't quite understand the depth of human immorality.

Does Cribb think that the people who are doing this—ripping off defenceless others—started off as rip-off artists? There must have been some people who would work for a couple of days and then say, Hey, this isn't for me.

Absolutely. It's a highly transient business.

So the ones that stay—are they trained to this lack of conscience, or is it natural?

I don't know. That would take a much longer and deeper psychological study. But they do make a lot of money, there's no question about it. So whatever guilt they might have is soothed by their paycheque.

For the two *Star* stories, Cribb and Cotroneo did pose those sorts of questions to some of the people working in the boiler rooms. Their responses went something like this: If the victims are stupid enough to fall for the scam, they deserve to be ripped off.

Yeah, there's a cutthroat nature to it, the ones who are good at it, the ones who stay, the pros. There is a very cutthroat, better-him-than-me, I'll-do-what-it-takes, I'm-number-one kind of attitude. There's no doubt about that. Is it learned? Is it nature or nurture? I don't know—I think there has to be a predisposition. I think there has to be a sliver of DNA buried in your brain that allows you to engage in that day after day. I think there are many of us who couldn't do it.

So I do think that there is a genetic predisposition to it. There's no question in my mind that there's a huge percentage of the population that might go in there naively, quickly realize what they're doing, and just say, There's no way I can do this, there's no way I can get on the phone with grandmothers in Iowa who are living on soup and tell them to go get their credit card, knowing that they're about to make a huge investment in nothing, that they will get nothing from this.

Cribb was 'a little bit surprised' that no one from the community had ever called the paper to report on these boiler rooms. What about those people who had applied for boiler room jobs thinking they were applying to legitimate telemarketing businesses and then quit when they realized they were involved in an illegal scam?

We found such people for the story in the course of doing the research. But I am surprised that the scam hadn't really blown up until then. I'm not sure why that is; I think the vast majority of people who go in, see it, and leave, do so quickly. Because you know within a couple of days. You're picking up that incoming line and listening to it, and obviously you're listening to the people around you. So it doesn't take long to figure out what's going on. I think they are probably in and out fast and they just say to themselves—I don't know. They leave, and that's their act of moral outrage.

One of the deeper insights that Cribb and Cotroneo's stories afforded concerns the extent to which this kind of fraud had become normalized, how invisible these rip-offs appeared in commercial culture, how like isotopes they were of legitimate mercantile practices. Even those who recognized the immorality of the 'job' failed to report it to authorities or tip off a newspaper.

> It could be that they were complaining to the appropriate government authorities. In our case, that's the Ministry of Consumer and Corporate Affairs, but it's clear that not much happens when those complaints are lodged. And it's such a massive problem, to be fair to them. I don't know how you even begin to crack down on something that big.

For Cribb, the undercover adventure featured several defining moments. One occurred his first day on a job, sitting with an experienced employee, watching him lie to someone on the other end of the phone line. The salesman had a name, and the moment ushered in the lead for Cribb's story: 'Dale is lying.'

> I love that lead. In an entire career, once: A three-word factual statement that somebody is lying. The only way you can write that lead—it's not Dale is lying, comma, according to sources, or according to a study. It's just 'Dale is lying'— and there's a pristine beauty about that. The only way you can write those three words in the newspaper is to actually sit there and witness Dale lying. That's the power of undercover. You actually get to be the fly on the wall, and you get to say what happened, period. Not comma, according to, but just period. You know why? Because I saw it, I heard it, I was there. It's rare we get to do that.
>
> That was a defining moment, because there's all the anxiety and stress going in, and then finally you're in, and you sit down and there it is, this guy on the phone to a grandmother in Iowa. Lying. That is repeated dozens of times, and then you start to speak to some of these people calling in and you realize the scope. You're sitting in one boiler room, in Toronto, knowing that there are two hundred others, where rooms are filled with these same types of people doing the exact same thing. It becomes an incredibly compelling story: you have thousands of these people, just in the downtown core of this city alone, right now, who are lying to poor people, and with virtual impunity. I mean, the number of charges and convictions relative to the volume of activity is ridiculously low.

Of course the victims are never local; that's the part of the scam that makes it so lucrative.

That's the beauty of it. You cross the border, and suddenly how exercised are the Canadian police going to be about this? There are no victims here. How freaked out are you going to be? Are you going to pursue crimes affecting Canadians or crimes affecting people in another country? Where are your priorities? It's cunningly devised.

There were some dicey moments in addition to the cheque-number-memorizing session, and several major obstacles.

The basic obstacle was figuring out how to do it, how to go in. That took the most amount of time; we did a lot of prep work. Getting at the owners was a major obstacle—there were some delicate moments during the process. For example, we wanted to get documents, we wanted the scripts, and they were incredibly protective of the scripts. The scripts could not leave [the boiler room], because there's huge competition between all these places. If you were seen taking a script, immediately there would be suspicions that you were working for the competition.

You would be fired?

Or worse. Getting fired was the least of it.

Cribb and Cotroneo did manage to liberate some scripts, but the procedure was 'very, very touchy'.

You play naive and you say, I'm going out for a smoke, and you just pick it up and take it with you. And most of the time somebody would say, Hey wait, where are you going? You can't leave this room with the script.
      But a couple of times, well several times actually, it was a matter of either going to the bathroom, or naively wandering, staring at it, heading outside for a smoke, where you could get a script out and slip it into your sock or whatever. We also went in with audio recorders, so we taped, which is stressful, because that increases your odds [of getting caught] if somebody sees a light.

They used digital recorders and eventually, toward the end of the project, went in with hidden buttonhole cameras.

We shot some video inside, and that increases the stress dramatically because when you've got equipment on, there's always the chance it will beep, or fall off or whatever. All of those I would say were very difficult stresses.

Had Cribb and Cotroneo been discovered with their hidden cameras, the fallout would have been at least extremely uncomfortable.

> Depending on who was there at the time . . . there were definitely thugs that worked there. We were never sure exactly what they did. There were managers and there was muscle. Now, if the muscle was there—they weren't always there—but if muscle was there, I don't question that we would have faced a physical problem.

The danger of physical harm increased after the stories ran, and Cribb received threatening voice-mail messages.

> They never talked to me directly but they'd leave messages. And they were extremely threatening. They didn't threaten to kill me, but it was more 'We're watching you, we see you leaving, you'd better be careful, you'd better watch your back, we're going to break your arms and legs'—stuff like that.

Cribb decided to consult police; he called an officer he knew who worked in the fraud division.

> And I said, 'You know, I'm getting these calls, and here's what they're saying. I'm just wondering what your thoughts are on it. Is this a big deal? And he said, 'Oh yes, it's very serious because these are pretty nasty guys.' I said, 'Really, you think this is something I should be concerned about?' He said, 'Oh yeah, I'd be very concerned about it.' So I said, 'Well what's your advice then? What should I do?'
>
> He said, 'You might want to change your path to and from the office and keep an eye out from your house and on your rear-view mirror—just keep an eye on things.' I said, 'Well is that going to keep me safe?' He said, 'No, no.' His basic message was it's extremely serious, and good luck with that.

None of the threats was ever carried out, but Cribb's stress level surged.

> You do of course become paranoid after that and you start to see things every time you drive home. So I don't know. I thought I had seen particular cars driving by my house a lot, but I don't know, it's hard to say.

The undercover project was so well planned that Cribb, in retrospect, can't think of anything that he and Cotroneo might have done differently.

> I have to say that we were very, very careful, and we were closely guided. We consulted almost daily with editors and our lawyer and so we were . . . I would

say we were very careful and strategic. We did the inside work over the course
of a month and then wrote it; the stories were tight, and we got in and out without being found. So in all those ways, I think it worked.

The follow-up work showed the companies had pulled up stakes and left town in
response to the series.

In the week or two after, we went back to all these places, and they had all pulled
up stakes. Cops estimated that about two hundred had shut down, at least temporarily. It was a pretty rewarding result. The story ran on a Saturday/Sunday and
then we headed out on Monday and just went back to all these places. It was
funny—they were all empty, the phones had all been removed, and there was a
copy of the *Toronto Star* in the wastebasket.

   It was pretty cool, pretty satisfying. One of the things that you always want
to do in investigative journalism is go after the people that deserve to be
exposed, the bad guys. And these were really bad guys. There is a certain pleasure in exposing people that are profiting from the misery of others. If there is a
mission in investigative journalism, that's it.

Have the boiler rooms returned to Toronto in the years since the November 2002 stories first drove them out? Was it a temporary solution? If it was a permanent solution,
where are the boiler rooms operating now?

I have to tell you, we haven't really revisited it. I think [the stories] definitely made
a dent, but what it's like today—it would take another investigation to know.
Maybe that's what we need. I just haven't looked at it lately. But you certainly
don't hear about it the same way you used to.

   I teach at Ryerson, and when that series came out, a lot of students said to
me that they actually worked at one of those places for a while, and then quit.
There are a lot of students; they cater to students. I've talked to students over
the past two or three years, and this story comes up, and I always ask how many
of them have either worked for these places or at least gone for an interview. A
lot of them have said to me, No, we don't do that. Either it hadn't entered their
consciousness or they decided consciously not to do it. I think any time an issue
like that gets exposed and there's publicity around it, it creates a stigma, so there
is a certain percentage of the population after the running of such a story who I
think would no longer wish to be associated [with fraudulent telemarketers].

The stories performed a great public service by delving into the psychology of the
scam runners and lifting the veil of 'normalcy' from their practices. Once the scam
was exposed, people, especially prospective boiler-room employees, could no longer
shrug it off—they were forced to see such employment for the immoral behaviour

that it was. The stories thus brought the moral issue to the public's attention, putting it 'on the map'.

> Where I don't think it was before. Once, there were students who would say that they worked at such a place without shame. Now I don't think people would. You're always going to get a willing demographic, who are prepared to do it. But I think it's a lot smaller now than it was, just because, in this city anyway, those kinds of operations are now well known, on the record, to be fraudulent. It's just not cool to work there any more.

Unlike many of the reporters interviewed for this book, Cribb has no problem with the term *investigative reporter*. In fact, after jumping all kinds of professional hurdles to get there, he wears the title with unabashed pride.

> I always wanted to do it. It was the only reason I got into journalism, even when I was working my first job at the *Dalhousie Gazette*. It's the only thing I ever really wanted to do. I turned on to journalism I guess around high school, and then, in university, I worked for the paper—and that's when I started actually doing journalism. But, for me, the word itself was always associated with . . . I mean, I might not have articulated it that way, I might not have said I want to be an investigative journalist. But that's what I wanted to do, that's basically what it meant to me.
>
> So I spent the first half of my career doing the stuff I figured I needed to do to eventually be able to do this as a full-time job. And I'm blessed, because I ended up at the *Toronto Star*, a place that believes deeply in [investigative journalism] and commits resources to it. I did my years as a daily reporter. Most of my career I spent doing daily stuff. I started at the *London Free Press* and came here [to the *Star*] as a business reporter. You know, no editor will ever let a young guy do an investigative story. Nobody's ever going to say, 'Here, take a week.'

Becoming an investigative reporter almost always involves a period of apprenticeship, often lonely and generally unpaid. Most of Cribb's earliest projects were done on his own time. He would take holidays and use them to go after stories.

> My first investigation was on Mexican Mennonites who come up to southern Ontario every year to work as basically slave labour in the fields of southwestern Ontario. So I took my vacation time and travelled with one of them back down to Mexico and then looked at the housing conditions in Ontario and how they're basically exploited. But all that was on my own time. You've got to get a string of stories that convince somebody somewhere that you can be trusted with the time that's needed to do it on a more regular basis. And then gradually, you do two or three a year, and then five or six a year. It takes time.

As advice to aspiring investigative reporters, Cribb suggests that you ask yourself some searching questions, and make sure you're sufficiently motivated.

> Don't do this unless you're really passionate about it. Because it's way too hard. Unless you have that fire in the belly to do this kind of work, it just doesn't make sense. It's an indefensible career choice to make otherwise. Because it's just really hard, there are a lot of challenges. You get lawyered; you get people mad at you all the time; you become a professional finder of fault. Investigative reporters are a little like those annoying neighbours. You know, every time you meet them around the back hedge they're complaining about the yappy dog next door and the loud woman down the street. We're just constantly spending our days and nights thinking about bad stuff.
>
> And it's stressful. Having been a daily reporter for a long time, I sometimes long for the days you'd file your story at six o'clock, and hit send, and then you'd go home, you're done. When I was doing daily, I couldn't even remember what I wrote that day; within twenty-four hours I'd forgotten it, because the brain develops that twenty-four-hour pattern. I find with this stuff, you're just always thinking about it. You wake up at 3:00 a.m. thinking about it, and you're at home eating dinner and thinking about it. Because it takes place over a longer period of time, you start to live with stories, and they become part of your life and that's what you talk about and that's what you're thinking about all the time.

The work can't be compartmentalized or isolated from other aspects of daily life. 'You've got to live with it.'

> My other bit of advice is a long way of saying if you're going to do this kind of project work, you have to choose subjects that you really care about. It's not going to be very good if you don't care about it, because you're not going to give it what it needs to make it happen. You're not going to break ground; you're not going to go the extra step; you're not going to get the sudden flash of insight that brings it all together. You're just not. Because you're not going to care about it enough.
>
> I've done good stuff and I've done stuff that I'm not real proud of—and when I think about the difference between the two, it's the stories that I really cared about that I ultimately gave what was necessary to make them good. The ones that didn't work out so well were the ones I didn't care enough about from the get-go.

Investigative reporting requires a much larger and more long-term commitment from the reporter.

> It's unlike daily [reporting], where you're reactive, and you're responding to what's happening and you have very little choice in what that is. With investiga-

tive, you do. Any newspaper or broadcast outlet makes very distinct choices about what it's going to go after. And so you can find latitude there. The trick is to consider that very carefully and think about what story you're prepared to live with and breathe and care about for what may be weeks or months.

There's also frequently an element of surrender, as in the case of stories that take hold of a reporter's conscience and imagination: at some point, the only way to stop thinking about the story is to write it.

I have now a 'spidey' sense [that's spidey as in Spider-Man] that I might not have had early on, a spidey sense about a story—an instinct. It either rings a bell or it doesn't, and it's a pretty reliable thing.

Reporters have different names for this sixth sense about a story. But they all agree it is brought into being and then honed to a sharp edge by doing investigative work over a period of years. Cribb remembers that his early days at the craft were plagued by uncertainty.

I'd go home at night and work on these stories, and it sucked, because I didn't really know. When I work with my students, the hardest thing for them is to figure out what to do, what is the story. And I feel for them, because it's a tough thing to teach. I can't really teach them that.

He can, however, inspire them and show them what's possible, provide an example of someone who has done it and so can say, 'Yes, this can be done.' And yet, as meaningful as investigative journalism is for Cribb, he agrees it's not a line of work that suits everyone. In fact, it's a rather rare specimen of journalist who embodies the somewhat contradictory qualities that go into the making of an investigative reporter.

I think it's actually [a good fit] for very few people. We have maybe three or four people here who do investigative work as their main job, but I don't think there's any more than that who would even want to. There are very few people in my newsroom who do, and this is the biggest newsroom in the country. Nobody wants to do it here. It has this reputation of being very prestigious and what everyone aspires to do eventually—I think that's crap. I think the vast majority of journalists in this country have absolutely no interest in it. And it's because they're smart.

Daily reporters are in the paper a lot more than he is, Cribb said, and he finds that frustrating. On the other hand, he knows in his bones he was born to do investigative journalism and that despite the difficulties involved, he'd be miserable if he couldn't continue doing it. For the course he teaches with Fred Vallance-Jones at Ryerson, Cribb stresses the importance of understanding the true, unromanticized nature of the beast.

> It's an important point to make, because I think there's a real misconception around that. When I talk to my students, for example, they assume that everyone at the *Toronto Star* or the CBC is basically working their way up to being investigative reporters. Nothing could be further from the truth. I think if you put an email out today to this newsroom, and said anyone who wants to be an investigative reporter come forward and we'll grant you your wish, I don't think you would get more than a handful. Or you might get a bunch at first, and then you'd explain to them what it entails, and then they'd all drop out.

Investigative reporting requires a long-term commitment. The work encroaches on the life of the reporter. To withstand that kind of chronic pressure requires not just brains and courage, but also heart. You have to be driven by a certain passion for the work.

> You have to have a really strong sense of righteous indignation. You have to be somebody who gets pissed off. A lot of our stories are driven by just sheer outrage. And so there's probably a character sketch a psychologist could draw up: people who do this a lot tend to have certain characteristics in common. And it is pretty rare, I think.
>
> Going back to the telemarketing example, it was really hard. You're not going to do that unless you're really pissed off. When I was embroiled in the midst of that story, and I'm sure Christian [Cotroneo] would say the same thing, there was nothing I wouldn't have done to get that in the newspaper. I shouldn't say 'nothing'—there's a line to draw—but within reason, I was prepared to do anything. Especially once I got a taste of what was really going on.
>
> Going in, it's a bit of an intellectual exercise. You have your theories and your hypotheses about what's going on. Then you get in and you see it, and you talk to the victims, and you see the blatant lying and the wealth that's being generated and then you just get mad. And at that point, I turn into the bloodhound. I'm the pit bull on that.
>
> Is everyone like that? No, I don't think so, and I don't say that to suggest I'm such a great guy. You could make the argument that there's a mental imbalance required, because going around all the time getting pissed off about stuff is not necessarily a positive character trait. But you either get really engaged intellectually in something like that or you don't. And it does take engagement to go the distance on a story like that, which means you'll be having a pretty stressful life for months.

Cribb exemplifies an attribute often shared by investigative reporters. The common denominator in his investigative work—whether he's revealing unsafe handling practices in abattoirs, exposing dangerous doctors, or pricking the public's conscience over housing for the poor—is moral outrage.

What angered him most in the Medical Secrets series was a particular physician, the extent of the damage he caused, and how people in positions of authority had turned a blind eye to the doctor's transgressions.

> There was a very clear definitive moment on that story. It was a document. It was the Butcher Bradley story. It was about this Ontario doctor who was brought before the College of Physicians and Surgeons twice for negligence in the deaths of two people, and injuries to others. We subsequently found other victims. And then, we noticed in the documents that he had disappeared, he'd moved from Ontario before the college could issue a disciplinary decision on his second case. And the question came up: Where is he? Eventually we found him, in Virginia. And we obtained a document. I'll never forget when I first opened the document. It was a six-page disciplinary decision outlining unbelievable negligence that led to the deaths of four more people there and serious injuries to a bunch of other people. The college knew he had left and they knew where he was going and they didn't even call Virginia to let them know. They let him go.

It's the desire to hold wrongdoers accountable that drives reporters like Cribb, and a righteous indignation that fires their pursuit of the story. But the righting of wrongs is rarely a simple undertaking. To begin with, for every clear wrongdoer, there are dozens of bystanders, those who know of the wrongdoing but say and do nothing to stop or expose it. Like other investigative reporters, Cribb sets out to 'get the bad guys', but he doesn't kid himself about that other, less visible, more complex culprit, the one that in a sense we all harbour when we think or say, 'It's not my fault, not my responsibility, not my job.' For Cribb, then, one of the culprits in the Butcher Bradley story was the 'system that allowed it to happen'.

> There are two culprits in that story. There's the doctor for sure, but there's also the system that you and I trust to protect us that utterly failed. Again and again we showed it in that series. But that particular story crystallized it and, you know, you get there by talking to the children of people who died under his care, because of his reckless negligence. You see the human devastation of that and then realize that the watchdog, so-called, in place to protect us from those kinds of tragedies is asleep at the switch. It's easy to get pissed off about that.

# Commentary

The immediate impact of the Dialling for Dollars series was the shutdown of boiler rooms in Toronto's downtown core. About three and half years later, however, a massive effort called Operation Global Con resulted in hundreds of international arrests targeted at mass-marketing fraud schemes like the one Cribb and Cotroneo had exposed in Toronto.[4] Although neither reporter would claim credit for that, both deserve kudos for raising awareness of the issue among the public and law-enforcement agencies. The latter *could* act, and eventually did, to combat the illicit multibillion-dollar industry.

Just as impressive as the obvious impact of the stories were the insights they revealed into the human side of the tale, including, for example, the comments elicited by the reporters from their telemarketing co-workers about the morality of their jobs. The stories show how to engage in covert investigation while maintaining moral standards of behaviour; Cribb and Cotroneo worked out ways to stop short of actually selling the 'packages' to their assigned marks. And they provided a stunning reminder of how easily individual conscience can get buried in the context of a 'job'.

Cribb's work ought to be required reading in journalism schools. He understands—and articulates—the true nature of investigative work and the downsides of the long-romanticized craft. Yet despite the inherent difficulties, he couldn't imagine doing any other kind of work. You could say he's living proof of his own contention that the prerequisites for success in investigative reporting are a passion for the work and a capacity to be outraged by pernicious acts or individuals. As Cribb likes to put it, the undercover reporter needs to get 'really pissed off' about wrongdoing.

His comments about the 'system' as culprit, and about those who turn a blind eye to injustice—those who know but won't tell—point to profound insights far deeper than the ills of a single fraudulent industry or a single investigative story. Such insights urge a consideration of how wrongdoing, once exposed, tends to reveal the social context that permitted its progress under cover of business as usual. Dialling for Dollars revealed that Toronto's boiler rooms were abusing the law to operate with impunity in plain sight. The series also suggests that such organized wrongdoing can be 'disappeared' from public view, not by conspiracy, but by an ambient social apathy through whose lens the criminal act appears normal and inevitable.

Investigative reporters are often required to voice concerns that many would prefer not to hear. Aside from the satisfaction of getting the job done, and the encouragement of admiring peers, it is this conviction in the rightness of the task—so evident in Cribb's reflective commentary—that sustains reporters in their ongoing efforts. Such work thus begins with conscience and empathy, with the human capacity to 'only connect', and I believe it is strengthened, however subtle the evidence may be, by every story so motivated.

# Endnotes

1. Christian Cotroneo was, unfortunately, unavailable to be interviewed for this book. Robert Cribb's retelling will have to stand for both.

2. You can read Robert Cribb's own account of the year-long Dirty Dining series in *Media* 8.2 (Summer 2001), 12–13.

3. Robert Cribb, Dean Jobb, David McKie, and Fred Vallance-Jones, *Digging Deeper: A Canadian Reporter's Research Guide* (Don Mills, ON: Oxford University Press, 2006).

4. Operation Global Con involved co-ordination among various law-enforcement agencies in the US and Canada (including the RCMP and the Competition Bureau of Industry Canada), and revealed that the majority of victims were senior citizens around the globe. See Sarah Chapman's 'Massive fraud sting leads to 400 Canadian charges', CanWest News Service, 24 May 2006, online at http://www.canada.com/topics/news/national/ story.html?id=e1d5013c-5de3-4080-b778-b32fc8b0fce5&k=8711: 'An international sting cracking down on illicit mass marketers targeting victims in the United States has led to almost 400 charges nationwide, police said Tuesday. RCMP in Ottawa said Operation Global Con, which has been ongoing since Jan. 1 2005 and was conducted by law enforcement agencies across the globe, resulted in 372 charges and 96 arrests in Canada, where investigations were concentrated in and around Halifax, Montreal, Toronto, Winnipeg, Edmonton, Vancouver, and Calgary. The investigations have so far netted 19 convictions including 13 guilty pleas.'

# Chapter 7

# Under Siege in the Ivory Tower

*The Globe and Mail's* Anne McIlroy produced a provocative series of stories in 2001 about growing corporate influence on the work of academics. She had been writing about the power that drug companies wield at Canadian medical schools when she received an anonymous tip about Dr David Healy, a well-respected Welsh psychiatrist and researcher, and an expert on anti-depressant drugs like Prozac. The University of Toronto had courted Healy for more than a year and then offered him a prestigious job at the head of its Centre for Addiction and Mental Health. But the job offer was summarily rescinded after Healy gave a speech in Toronto in which he said that Prozac and similar drugs can cause a small number of patients to commit suicide or behave in other violent ways. He said the drug and others like it (part of a new class of anti-depressant drugs, the so-called serotonin-specific reuptake inhibitors, or SSRIs) should carry warnings of the risk. Eli Lilly, the company that manufactures Prozac, was a major donor to the university and provided substantial research funds.

We'll look mainly at three stories that McIlroy wrote over a period of several months, as she followed the unfolding of the initial tale about Dr Healy and the issues it raised. (The three stories were not conceived as a series; only the final story ran under the banner headline, 'Under Siege in the Ivory Tower'.) The first story, about David Healy and his withdrawn job offer, ran in April 2001.[1] The second article, published about three weeks later, confirmed that the university had rescinded the offer because of Healy's critical views on the pharmaceutical industry in general and on Prozac in particular. The final piece ran several months later and represented the culmination of McIlroy's work over the intervening months. It opened up onto the larger issues of how corporate funding by pharmaceutical companies stood in potential conflict of interest with the work of university-based drug researchers, and more broadly, with the much-touted academic freedom of the 'ivory tower'.

McIlroy first approached Healy months before the initial story ran in the *Globe*, but at that early stage the doctor was reluctant to speak to the media. As the situation evolved, McIlroy gathered information and gained Healy's trust. By the time he agreed to go public with the story, she had nailed down most of the facts.

In May 2000, Healy accepted the university's original offer of a combined faculty and clinical position. Later that year, on 30 November, Healy gave a lecture in which he tried to hold the pharmaceutical companies to account, criticizing them for being more concerned with profits than with the efficacy and, especially, the safety of the drugs they sold.[2] He reiterated his views on Prozac, saying studies confirmed the drug carries a small but clear risk of triggering suicide, and he urged the drug's manufacturer to put a warning to that effect on the label. Finally, he suggested that pharmaceutical companies were remiss generally in failing to warn potential users about possible side effects of the medications they marketed.

Barely a week after the speech, Healy received an email from university officials withdrawing their offer of employment. The email suggested that Healy's lecture indicated his approach would clash with the centre's 'development' goals. A copy of that email was sent to the *Globe and Mail* in an unmarked brown envelope. With that envelope, and a telephone tip from someone close to Healy, McIlroy's journey began.

## The Interview: **Anne McIlroy**
(15 May 2006)

McIlroy remembers the unmarked envelope and the first telephone tip. They introduced her to David Healy, the source at the heart of the story.

> He was one of the main players in this story—the British researcher who lost his job offer when he talked about the risks of Prozac. I did a number of stories about him. I broke those stories; no one else had written about that before then.

Soon after the first story ran in April 2001, McIlroy began to realize that Healy's story was not isolated. She was dealing not with a single case at a single institution, but with an entire syndrome that affected academic researchers across the board.

> I started getting emails from other researchers saying I should look into this, I should look into that. It seemed to be a much broader phenomenon out there about corporate pressure being brought to bear on researchers. So that's where this [final] piece came from, a piece to sort of pull it all together and paint a picture of the climate that was evolving at universities across the country.

McIlroy first contacted Healy shortly after receiving a telephone tip, in which the caller had suggested that the real reason for the university's withdrawal of its job offer to Healy—his public criticism of Prozac and the drug companies—was a matter that ought to be made public.

> Someone phoned me from the University of Toronto asking for anonymity and suggesting I look into this. A couple of days later, I got a package of documents, a sort of paper trail, from someone who was very close to David Healy.

The arrival of anonymous tips, however enticing, put the responding reporter in an awkward position: McIlroy would invest a substantial amount of time finding out whether the information revealed by the tip was valid and verifiable, but she knew it could be time easily wasted. And so, despite having in her possession documentary as well as anecdotal evidence, McIlroy proceeded with caution.

> My main fear was that I thought it was a great story, but I didn't know the person who had called me. And I didn't know Dr Healy. You've always got to make sure that they're not cranks, that you're not being used. So it took me a long time. I worked on it, and I was lucky. I had enough time to just pick away at it, and find out about his reputation, and verify the small things. It had to have everything in place before I went with it. I had to be satisfied that it was a legitimate story.

McIlroy confronted her first obstacle soon after conducting this preliminary research: Healy was reticent to involve the media in his woes.

> I spent a little time figuring out if it was true and trying to verify as much as I could, and then I phoned him. But he didn't want to talk. He thought it would maybe jeopardize things for him, that perhaps it [the job] was still going to happen.

She persisted and, eventually, Healy changed his mind and decided to go on the record with his story. This was the critical break in the process, because without Healy's co-operation the matter would have had to remain private. McIlroy believes that Healy's change of heart had to do with his gradual acceptance of the idea that the university was prepared to withdraw an offer of employment in order to avoid jeopardizing its financial relationship with a powerful pharmaceutical firm. He had, after all, publicly criticized the drug companies before—he'd put his views on the record—so he never expected his lecture to scuttle the job offer.

> I think he saw that this was really happening, that he had lost this job offer because of what he'd said about Prozac.

On 14 April 2001, McIlroy broke the story with an article headlined, 'Prozac critic sees U of T job revoked'. In the piece, Healy described how a week after his fateful lecture the university withdrew its job offer in a tersely worded email—the same email that had arrived in the *Globe and Mail* newsroom and jump-started McIlroy's investigation.

The first article relied heavily on Healy's own testimony, largely because university officials declined all but the most cursory comment, and individual professors who were bothered by the incident were at the same time afraid to be named and perhaps lose their own research dollars or their jobs.

But the head of the Canadian Association of University Teachers was under no such pressure to remain silent. James Turk suggested that the university's decision was based on its fear that appointing Healy would 'give them trouble raising money'.[3] Turk and others outside the university who were in a position to criticize argued further that because medical schools were so dependent on pharmaceutical industry funding, stifling criticism of drug companies and their products amounted to interfering with academic freedom.

For weeks, university officials had continued to deny any connection between Healy's lecture and his 'unhiring'. They maintained that corporate funding had nothing to do with their decision, but otherwise refused to comment on the case, citing confidentiality concerns.

By the time of her next story, about three weeks later, McIlroy was able to confirm that Healy had been fired for voicing his views.[4] University officials finally allowed that Healy's criticism of the drug companies had sparked their change of heart. A letter to Healy from the physician-in-chief of the Centre for Addiction and Mental Health called some of his comments 'scientifically irresponsible' and 'incompatible with published scientific evidence'. But the university continued to maintain that corporate funding played no part in the decision. The letter, dated 20 April, claimed a more defensible reason: 'What was jeopardized by your talk was not our relationship to Eli Lilly but your credibility with and relationship to your future colleagues at the centre.'[5]

This second story unleashed comment from other University of Toronto researchers who began to contact McIlroy at the *Globe* with similar horror stories of corporate influence in the academy and veiled attacks on academic freedom, issues that up to this point had not been addressed in the daily press. Many of the researchers believed that Healy was being punished for speaking out. None, however, was willing to say so publicly.

As the plot began to thicken and the evidence mounted, McIlroy became convinced that Healy's story was part of a much larger one.

> I was surprised, the more I dug into it, at how tight a world it is that they work in, and especially in psychiatry, how anyone who speaks out can really be put in a very difficult position. You think of science as being open, at least theoretically, to the idea that they may be wrong. Right?
>
> Things are always changing in science, and in psychiatry, perhaps because they're still muddling their way through in many senses—they don't really know why these drugs work—and because so much of it is funded by drug companies. But I really was surprised at how dark it was, and that David Healy, if anything, had underplayed [events]—he hadn't exaggerated. The more I found out, the worse the picture looked.

She discovered, for example, that Healy had voiced his critical views before in published work; the drug companies had acted before to silence such criticism; and the silencing generally involved blunt attempts to discredit the professional standing and personal character of the speaker.

> [For example, there was a] paper that Healy wrote for this other journal, and then the journal lost its funding from Eli Lilly. And the involvement of other researchers who got lots of money from the company—their role in it. It's a very tight-knit community, and a couple of carefully placed comments with the people who matter can ruin someone's reputation.[6]

It took McIlroy several months after the first two articles ran to gain the background for the third and main story, the one that tied the pieces together to show that Healy's ordeal was part of a pattern. There was a quilt of corporate power that operated 'undercover' to influence decisions made about drug trials and other university-based research projects. These decisions affected the public's right to know about the risks of the drugs they consumed and weighed on the academic researchers whose careers depended on corporate sponsorship. McIlroy's third and final piece began to reveal the corrosive effects of corporate funding on the academy's traditional core values, including the right to free speech (a right enshrined in the Canadian Charter of Rights and Freedoms for all, academics included).

McIlroy finished writing that last article in the summer of 2001, just before she went on maternity leave. But the *Globe* didn't run the 'think' piece until September.

It was long, and I guess they were waiting for space to run it.

Timing, as if by divine intervention, played a role in the story's impact: 'Under Siege in the Ivory Tower' ran just three days before the 9/11 attacks.

While the first two stories had run in the paper's front news pages, 'Under Siege in the Ivory Tower'—at nearly four thousand words, longer than the first two stories combined—formed the centre spread of the *Globe*'s Focus section.[7] And while the early stories concentrated on the case of David Healy, the final article spread out from there to consider whistle-blowers at other universities. The story's lead laid down the gauntlet: 'Some call them our kept universities.' And the subhead laid out the issue:

> Public issues—from genetic engineering to psychiatric illness—have become more complex than ever, requiring academic specialists to help sort them out. Yet Canadian universities get more and more of their funding from private, corporate interests. What happens when these facts collide—for example, when a scientist discovers that a funder's drug is dangerous? As one researcher put it, 'This place is a fortress.'

Perhaps University of Toronto officials were gun-shy. For this wasn't the first time the university had come under fire for a decision that seemed to place pleasing corporate sponsors ahead of academic freedom, or even public safety. In 1996, in a controversial and headline-making case, Dr Nancy Olivieri had also been targeted by the university after her published research, funded by a large pharmaceutical company, came to negative conclusions about the drug in question, an iron-chelating agent called Deferiprone.[8]

McIlroy's final article suggested that in the field of medical and pharmacological research, the fox was guarding the chicken coop. It revealed that pharmaceutical companies funded 42 per cent of the drug research being done in Canada's largest medical schools,[9] and quoted James Turk, who had edited an anthology of pieces about the dangers posed by commercialization to Canadian universities and researchers.

Turk's book, *The Corporate Campus: Commercialization and the Dangers to Canada's Colleges and Universities*, included an article by Olivieri about her research at the University of Toronto's Hospital for Sick Children on Deferiprone—an experimental drug developed to treat a rare blood disorder. The research was funded by the giant pharmaceutical company Apotex, a major corporate donor to the university.

When Dr Olivieri found potential problems with the drug and wanted to warn patients about it, she was threatened by Apotex with a lawsuit based on the confidentiality agreement she'd signed. Four of Olivieri's colleagues joined her in filing a grievance against the university. The Canadian Association of University Teachers launched its own probe into the affair, producing a report that eventually vindicated Olivieri.[10]

In 'Under Siege in the Ivory Tower', McIlroy compared Healy's story to Olivieri's, noting the role that character assassination had played in both. Rumours about both doctors spread throughout the university and beyond. She was a troublemaker; he was given to embracing half-baked theories. Healy, McIlroy said, was in the end 'comparatively lucky'.

> He was proven right. At the time, he was talking about a tiny study that he had done, but in the end he was right. And now there are warnings about these drugs, especially for children.
>
> But he could have been wrong. He wasn't saying he knew everything; he was just saying he was worried, people should be worried, and there should be warnings. But it did turn out that he was right, so he has been vindicated. He might not have been so lucky. He was very courageous for coming forward at that point to say what concerned him.

What really unnerved McIlroy was the fear that apparently prevented senior faculty from commenting on the issue. Her own academic background in science predisposed to her to regard that field as objective by definition. To learn that it was as vulnerable to political corruption as any other line of human endeavour was a rude—and rattling—wake-up call.

> It was disturbing. These are really smart people who have a lot of responsibility. And this is a community that we all depend on. Now, obviously, there are very good psychiatrists—I don't mean to tar them all with the same brush. I was just surprised at how scared those who supported Dr Healy were to speak out. I mean, these are tenured professors at the University of Toronto—and they will say only privately that there was wrong done?
>
> They were too scared to say openly that there was wrong done, for fear of losing everything they had worked for. That was quite shocking to me. And if it's like that at the U of T, imagine the situation at smaller institutions, [for researchers in] perhaps more precarious positions.

Yet the pharmaceutical industry also functions in the public interest, funding valuable research in the battle against disease. And if the fear of researchers to speak openly all comes down to the massive power of 'big pharma', saying so doesn't solve the problem.

They certainly have a lot of power; they fund a lot of research. But they also do a lot of good—we wouldn't want a world without them. It just seems there are a lot of signs that there must be the proper safety checks in place for this kind of thing not to happen.

While McIlroy wouldn't like to see a world without the pharmaceutical companies, she would appreciate one in which medical and scientific journals are free of corporate advertising.

I like these journals that don't have advertisements from the drug companies. It leaves me more confident that what they're telling you is not tainted by the fact that the people writing the papers get all their money from a drug company.

The defining moment, when the story grabbed McIlroy, didn't come until it was time to actually start drafting.

It was slowly building over time . . . and then when I wrote it and had it all laid out in front of me, I thought, 'This is really solid.' Afterwards, the reaction was quite interesting and also made me realize that it was as big a story as I had thought, or perhaps bigger.

Part of what made the story difficult to research and write was its cast of pharmaceutical executives. Because of its entanglement with drug company bigwigs, McIlroy's article ultimately involved powerful interests at the university as well. She would get advice from higher-ups at the *Globe* 'who aren't there any more but who were at dinners with senior people from the University of Toronto'—they would offer her contacts and tips.

My boss would phone me and say, I think you should phone this person and this person and this person about this Healy character. And so I would phone them and one of the guys ended up harassing me by email for years afterwards about the stories I had written. I wasn't under pressure to do it—they were just passing this on. And I got a number of emails saying this guy's a scientologist, which he's not. It was clear that there was this high-level campaign to discredit [Healy].

There was never any suggestion from McIlroy's bosses to back off the story, just to make sure she had her facts nailed down. The advice from superiors was never heavy-handed.

It wasn't done that way at all. It was more, Maybe you should check this out. And as a good reporter, yes, I would check that out. The paper played the stories extremely well, and stuck with them over quite a period of time. The *Globe* was definitely behind the stories.

McIlroy still regrets that she was unable to get more people to comment for the record.

> I think the story would have been much more compelling if I could have persuaded more people to talk. I got the staff list at the CAMH [Centre for Addiction and Mental Health] and I phoned everybody who worked there—I couldn't get a single person to go on the record. Many of them talked to me off the record, but they would not go on the record. Or they wouldn't talk at all. Or they were hostile.
>
> You want to give both sides of the story, [but] the university and the CAMH were quite difficult to deal with. They didn't want to talk. They said it breached Healy's confidentiality [even though] he was saying go ahead. I wanted to fully find out what happened, and it was really hard to get a clear picture because they wouldn't say. For example, there was this very respected psychiatrist who played a role. He wouldn't talk to me. So it took conversations with five or six people [whom she had to promise anonymity] to find out that he had had a word with someone senior about Healy. Every little piece of information took a lot of work to get.

The university's 'downright refusal to talk' presented the single biggest obstacle and perplexed McIlroy. If university and CAMH officials hadn't done anything wrong, and believed they had done nothing wrong, why would they not want to tell their side of the story? Surely they realized how suspect they made themselves appear by a stubborn refusal to enter the waters of the swelling debate.

> I was surprised. To me, it just looked like they weren't being forthcoming. I thought if they had something to say and they really had a reason for this, they should say so.

They never did. 'It just sort of slowly came out over time.'

McIlroy had several months to work on 'Under Siege', a luxury that was 'rare at that time at the paper'. If she had it all to do over again, she would spend more time following up.

> The only thing I wish is that I could have followed it more closely. I was pregnant and I left shortly after I wrote these. I wish I could have stayed on the story. I was off for an entire year, and then I came back and sort of picked up the odd thread, but I would have liked to have written this story the whole way. Because it did end up, Healy ended up, bringing about real change, at least for the warnings

that are given about these drugs. So I would have liked to be able to do that, and maybe have written a big piece at the end about it all.

I think there were a number of key developments around the same time, like with the journals saying, Hey, hold on a second here, you have to declare your conflict of interest or we're not running your study. I think maybe people are just getting more and more aware of it—the growing role—even in [fictional works] like John le Carré's book *The Constant Gardener*, that sort of thing.

In the popular mind, people are now more suspicious of drug companies than they were before. I think that's a good thing, because I don't think anybody should ever take a drug before researching it. You need to know yourself what's out there about it, and make an informed decision. Don't take anybody's word for it. There are risks and there are benefits. For you, maybe the risks are worth the benefits, but you should be informed.

McIlroy also compared Healy's case to that of Michelle Brill-Edwards, a senior doctor and researcher with the Canadian government's Health Protection Branch, who resigned from her long-time position with the regulatory body over irregularities in the drug-approval process.[11]

The same kind of thing happened to her. People painted her as being crazy: 'Oh, that woman!' There are these very subtle ways of undermining people, as well as very open ways. With Healy, they did it too: he's a scientologist—weird stuff like that.

And even if they [the scientists] are wrong, they're courageous. Because they're putting it all on the line. Maybe that's harder for people to understand, but if they have their suspicions and evidence to warrant concern, that's when it's most courageous—not after you wait fifteen years and you have it ironclad, and people have died. I remember with the plan to put hormones in milk—there were some other scientists who spoke up. And we definitely need people like that.

There are still others besides Healy, Olivieri, and Brill-Edwards who learned first-hand the power that pharmaceutical companies could wield over their careers. One of them was Ann Clark, a University of Guelph biologist who was nearly ostracized after she set up a public website on genetically modified foods. Ten other academics had agreed to participate in the online effort, but only anonymously. Critics willing to be named were generally those who had already retired from the academy and so were no longer at risk of repercussions that could hurt or halt their careers.[12]

The structural and formal limits of the first two 'news-page' stories frustrated McIlroy and fed her desire to write the third piece, where she could move away from showing the facts to examining some of the complexities researchers grappled with and some of the constraints within which they worked. The early stories had been 'hard to write.'

I did find it frustrating to write in five hundred words. That was one thing that was hard about those stories. They are he-said-she-said. It was like, 'Okay, he says this, and he says this might be bad.' And they say, 'No, that's not why.' And I think, 'Gosh, what does that mean?' And I wondered what people would come away with from the stories. But over time, I became confident that I had the picture, and that readers would get the picture.

McIlroy is grateful that she was given the time and space to do the final piece justice.

The contextual piece, I think, gave more of a sense of the environment that they [the scientists] were working in, which is what grabbed me about the story most of all. And this piece was able to convey that, so that was lucky.

While conceding that 'Under Siege in the Ivory Tower' helped provoke change, McIlroy credits Healy, not her story, for making the critical difference.

I think it would be fairer to say that Dr Healy provoked change. Because he was the one who kept up with it, and testified [later] at trials in the United States. But having it out in the open made a big difference, and I think he was grateful that it happened. It did get picked up—a lot of people wrote about it all over the place.

Although she doesn't regard herself as an investigative reporter, McIlroy does recall that she mapped out her entrance to the newspaper business.

I always wanted to be a writer, and this seemed like a way you could make a living at it. I have a science background—I studied science as well as journalism at university—and I think that gives me a good set of tools to write about things that are complicated but important. So I write about a lot of different things that are developments in the world of science and medicine, but these are the kind of stories that matter the most. And so I really like to do them.

Most journalism students have backgrounds in English or the humanities. Those rarer students who find their way to J-school through the sciences take quite a different approach. For starters, they're already used to the idea of proof and evidence. And, of course, for science stories, they already have the necessary background or at least the vocabulary. McIlroy gravitated toward the sciences early on, and went to a science-oriented high school in the Ottawa suburb of Kanata.

There was big growth in the computer industry, so a lot of the kids at the high school were very into computers and science. But I've always just thought it was

really interesting stuff, and important for people to know about. And challenging
and fun to translate it for them.

McIlroy did her bachelor's degree in journalism at Carleton, but she was hired at the
*Ottawa Citizen* in 1985, before she'd even completed her degree.

> I got hired at the *Ottawa Citizen* when I was in third year, so I finished my degree
> part-time and started there. And then I was a general assignment reporter, I think
> for a year. Yeah, at least a year—that year I worked nights and went to school in
> the day. And then I became the science reporter there. That was great. I spent
> most of my career covering science and the environment, and politics. I did pol-
> itics for about ten years. So it's been a combination of the two. I much prefer the
> science.

Common wisdom has it that it's harder these days to break into the newspaper business, but McIlroy says it's probably always been hard. One way to distinguish yourself from the competition is to develop expertise in a particular area, as she did.

> It was hard when I got in, too. I got my first job at the *Ottawa Citizen* in 1985, and
> I took it because I thought they might not have jobs the next year. I remember I
> did take science to differentiate myself, to do something different. I think it's
> important to find something you love to write about and to educate yourself in
> any way you can. You have to be willing to do stuff that doesn't particularly inter-
> est you at first, but you can always keep your eye on the ball for what you really
> want to do. You usually have to start [as a general assignment reporter], but it
> always helps to have a specialty or a language or something like that, that differ-
> entiates you.

# Commentary

A major obstacle in undertaking stories of undue or malign corporate influence is
persuading potential sources to go on the record when the possibility exists it could
cost them their careers. McIlroy attested to this difficulty when she discussed the
refusal of university officials and researchers to comment for her trio of articles. Even
David Healy, the critical source at the centre of the story, was initially unwilling to
go public. From this work, an aspiring investigative journalist should learn that often
the story demands the reporter's persistence and a refusal to take no for a final answer.

But such difficulty also points to a deeper obstacle: the human tendency to resist
'believing' in the facts. Healy's initial resistance came down to not wanting to believe
that his potential employers would repay his courage with a withdrawn job offer and

a smear campaign. McIlroy herself had a hard time believing that the picture of science in the academy was as dark as it indeed turned out to be. Recently, I watched an edition of CBC Newsworld's *The Big Picture with Avi Lewis* entitled 'Can We Save Planet Earth?' and learned that nearly half of Canadians don't 'believe in' global warming.[13] The old joke would seem to apply: denial, it says, isn't just a river in Egypt.

On the other hand, once McIlroy had done enough research to undo her own disbelief, she wrote an important series of stories that alerted the (still reading) public to the issue. David Healy, once he understood the depth of the opposition to making public what he himself was initially loath to believe, continued to speak out. In fact, he became an even more effective agent of change. In 2004, he published a groundbreaking book about psychiatry and the drug industry,[14] and he continued to work as a psychiatrist at the North Wales Department of Psychological Medicine at Cardiff University in Wales. His article on the controversy, published in the open-access journal *PLoS Med* (Public Library of Science) in 2006, and entitled 'The Latest Mania: Selling Bipolar Disorder', provided an indictment of the effects of corporate influence on the very practice of psychiatry.[15]

So the world that McIlroy hoped to see, where writers in scientific and academic journals are not beholden to corporate sponsors, and where all of the writer's corporate connections are stated up front as a condition of publication, is an emerging reality. The journal *PLoS Med* prefaces all its articles with a full listing of such corporate connections, including whether the author received funding to write the article.[16]

That McIlroy's third and more in-depth article grew from such humble beginnings offers another lesson in journalistic technique. The larger theme of the last story (corporate influence in academia and the loss of academic freedom for individual researchers) was arrived at through the assiduous collection of initially disparate facts. Such work requires a tolerance for intellectual uncertainty that, while perhaps inspired by a passion for the big picture, is balanced by adherence to reportorial method. Fledgling reporters, in their laudable desire to get at the meaning behind 'just the facts', tend to try to begin with a preconceived, essay-like presentation of the issue (or the reporter's take on the issue) 'reinforced' and sometimes merely adorned by related facts. Such a procedure may produce a satisfying rant but it won't make for good investigative journalism. Turn that around and do what McIlroy did: tolerate the uncertainty until the facts begin to convince you of a possible larger truth.

Of course, in a linguistic or literary sense, it would be naive to regard or try to present the facts as atoms of truth, as independent realities somehow radically different from opinions or claims or even controversy. All play into the mix of public debate, including commentary that appears in the form of newspaper articles.

What is a fact, if not a long-held belief established over time, a belief that is subject, in the best of all worlds, to perpetual contestation on the basis of new facts? The briefest survey of the history of science (which prides itself on establishing facts as clearly as the study of literature foregrounds the interpretation of meanings) shows the discipline advances precisely by continuous testing and con-testing of the purported facts. At the same time, it isn't established facts that motivate research into a subject, but a dispute or claim that has yet to attain the status of fact. Facts, moreover, are finally inseparable from their context. We call mere collections of established fact encyclopedias and look to them to settle only the most superficial disagreements.

Fortunately for journalists, the job is less philosophically confounded than all that: For the reporter, the difference between a fact and an opinion, for instance, is that the former can be verified. Some opinions, of course, appear better founded than others. But the validity or value of an opinion is still ultimately judged (in the court of public opinion or in a court of law) by its basis in, and reliance on, facts.

McIlroy began her research with an anonymous tip about an academic targeted for speaking out on a controversial issue. Her careful accumulation of detail resulted finally in a 'big picture' that at first she herself had barely glimpsed—a picture she came to see fully only in the final stages of drafting 'Under Siege in the Ivory Tower'. That big picture showed how drug-company funding for university researchers stood to compromise public health and academic integrity. It showed how the public at large stands to be affected by politics in high places when the same research institutions that decide what medications are approved begin to answer to a private firm's profit motive instead of to the public interest.

When the facts began to gel, McIlroy knew she had a 'big story, maybe even bigger' than she had thought. And she was right: Healy's continued (and publicized) efforts did finally result in the placement of warnings on Prozac labels. The University of Toronto did ultimately decide to tighten its ethical guidelines governing medical research. Other researchers did come forward for the record.

The inherent logic of McIlroy's third story extends to educational and research institutions generally, which cannot work as they ought to—in the public interest—if they are largely funded by private ones. 'Under Siege in the Ivory Tower' pointed to these implications by tracking similar cases and citing multiple sources. The more people who testify to a given situation, the less possible it becomes to target any one source or to keep the larger truth hidden.

By comparing various cases, McIlroy established the existence of a controversial pattern of external corporate influence on academic freedom. She wrote about other cases of academics targeted for exercising what they saw as their professional duty to inform and their democratic right to speak. She recapped the story of Nancy Olivieri and her battle to prevail against the combined displeasure of the University of Toronto and Apotex for her 'adverse' research findings. She mentioned Ann Clark, the University of Guelph biologist who weathered numerous attempts at character assassination after she set up a public website on genetically modified foods. (As mentioned above, ten other academics had agreed to participate in the online effort, but only under the veil of anonymity). In these and other cases of medical researchers restrained, critics willing to lend support and be named were generally retired academics, who were no longer vulnerable to career repercussions.

But corporate influence was not limited to medical research, the story revealed; it had spread throughout the academy.

A case in point was that of David Noble, a York University historian who waged his own battle for academic freedom about a month after Healy went public with his. Noble had been chosen to hold the J.S. Woodsworth chair at Simon Fraser University. The chair was created to promote free debate on public issues in honour of the labour activist and politician, but ironically the university then blocked Noble's appointment, apparently because it disliked some of his published views. Noble had studied the changing meaning of academic freedom since medieval times and been a vocal critic of university commercialization. He analyzed the kinds of conflicting interests inherent in the evolution of corporate funding for universities, with university presidents beginning to sit on to the boards of powerful multinational corporations and profiting financially from doing so.

In our interview, McIlroy pointed out how the Noble case differed from those of the medical researchers previously discussed. The speech of contrarian medical researchers could have clear consequences for the profits of the drug companies that were funding the work. In the case of Noble, free speech, with no obvious dollar value attached, came under direct attack.

The move away from government funding and toward corporate funding for universities had begun in the 1970s across North America and Europe. In Canada, the federal government played an important role, in effect greasing the corporate rails with legislative approvals.[17] As the federal government began to cut back on its funding for university research in the late 1980s, Canadian universities were forced to seek funding dollars from the corporate sector. What government funds were available were made dependent on the ability of university researchers to engage corporate partners for funding. It was this overall move to commercialize the academy that threatened its long-standing traditions of independence.[18]

Interestingly, McIlroy's earliest road maps for the initial story came not from other media reports (which didn't yet exist), but from books, especially *The Corporate Campus* anthology edited by James Turk, then head of the Canadian Association of

University of Teachers. In his introduction, Turk noted an 'unprecedented explosion' in recent decades of incidents where academic freedom had been violated, its dictates steamrolled in the new corporate environment. *The Corporate Campus* bulged with essays by academics, medical researchers, and other critics who had run afoul of their respective institutions over corporate sponsorship and academic freedom.

McIlroy read the book and called Turk, who proved a rich source of information about what he described as a sea change in university culture. She was duly offended by what she learned from her wide reading and research for the 'Under Siege' article. It seems to me that it ought to offend the sensibilities of anyone trying to make a living 'afflicting the comfortable and comforting the afflicted' to see moral courage punished and the scientific truth go begging.

# Endnotes

1. 'Prozac critic sees U of T job revoked', *Globe and Mail* (4 April 2001), A1.

2. Healy's speech was part of a colloquium called 'Looking Back, Looking Forward—Psychiatry in the 21st Century: Mental Health and Addiction'.

3. 'Prozac critic sees U of T job revoked', op. cit.

4. 'Hospital confirms MD's views cost him job', *Globe and Mail* (5 May 2001), A5.

5. Ibid.

6. In 2000, the Hastings Center think tank on ethical issues in New York City saw its annual donation from Eli Lilly cancelled after it published articles on Prozac, including a critical one by Healy entitled 'Good Science or Good Business?'

7. 'Under siege in the ivory tower', *Globe and Mail* (8 September 2001), F4–F5.

8. *The Olivieri Report: The Complete Text of the Report of the Independent Inquiry Commissioned by the Canadian Association of University Teachers* (Toronto: James Lorimer and Company Ltd., 2001). See also Olivieri's own account: 'When Money and Truth Collide', in James L. Turk, ed., *The Corporate Campus: Commercialization and the Dangers to Canada's Colleges and Universities* (Toronto: James Lorimer and Company Ltd., 2001), 53–62.

9. Ibid.

10. See *The Olivieri Report*, op. cit.

11. Michelle Brill-Edwards, 'Private Interest and Public Peril at the Health Protection Branch', in James L. Turk, ed., *The Corporate Campus: Commercialization and the Dangers to Canada's Colleges and Universities* (Toronto: Lorimer, 2001), 63–68.

12. E. Ann Clark, 'Academia in the Service of Industry: The Ag Biotech Model', in Turk, ed., *The Corporate Campus*, 69–86.

13. 'Can We Save Planet Earth?' *The Big Picture with Avi Lewis*. CBC Newsworld (27 September 2006).

14. David Healy, *Let Them Eat Prozac: The Unhealthy Relationship between the Pharmaceutical Industry and Depression* (NY: New York University Press, 2004).

15. David Healy, 'The Latest Mania: Selling Bipolar Disorder', *PLoS Med* 3.4 (11 April 2006). Online access at the following URL: http://medicine.plosjournals.org.

16. Healy's *PLoS* article, for example, is prefaced with the following information:
    'Funding: The author received no specific funding to write this article.
    'Competing Interests: DH has been a speaker, consultant, or clinical trialist for Lilly, Janssen, SmithKline Beecham, Pfizer, Astra-Zeneca, Lorex-Synthelabo, Lundbeck, Organon, Pierre-Fabre, Roche, and Sanofi. He has also been an expert witness in ten legal cases involving antidepressants and suicide or homicide and one case involving the patent on olanzapine (Zyprexa). None of these interests played any part in the submission or preparation of this paper. 'Copyright: © 2006 David Healy. This is an open-access article distributed under the terms of the Creative Commons Attribution License, which permits unrestricted use, distribution, and reproduction in any medium, provided the original author and source are credited.'

17. See my article about the meaning of corporate funding for journalism schools in particular: Maxine Ruvinsky, 'Media Convergence and the Canadian J-School: Social Conscience in the Age of Information', *International Journal of Learning*, Vol. 11, (2004), 1249–1255.

18. See Neil Tudiver's *Universities For Sale: Resisting Corporate Control over Canadian Higher Education* (Toronto: James Lorimer and Company Ltd., 1999).

# Chapter 8

# Blind Faith

In 2005, *Hamilton Spectator* reporters Steve Buist, Joan Walters, and Luma Muhtadie[1] exposed the local face of a national and international issue when they decided to investigate the relationship between medical researchers at Hamilton's McMaster University and the giant pharmaceutical companies that fund university research to bring to market sometimes life-saving and occasionally life-threatening medications. At McMaster University, researchers annually conduct hundreds of clinical trials on new prescription drugs. Such trials involve testing on human subjects and constitute a critical step in the road to getting the drugs approved for sale. The university researchers at McMaster represent a fraction of the thousands of academic researchers across the country involved in the development and testing of drugs before they hit the consumer market.

The series revealed that in 1994 Health Canada had begun offering a quicker approval process and charging the pharmaceutical companies fees for drug evaluations. Since that time, drugs were withdrawn from the market for safety reasons twice as often as in the previous thirty years. The stories raised questions about the safety of the prescription drugs we use, how they get approved, and how they are monitored once on the market. They also pointed to the potential for disastrous conflict-of-interest situations as drug companies, at the considerable expense involved in clinical trials and the approval process, sought to sell their products at a profit, while university researchers sought to maintain their labs and research funding (paid for in large part by the very same drug companies).

The sums involved merited attention. Canadian spending on prescription drugs had doubled in a less than a decade ($20 billion in 2004), and drug company funding to

McMaster University had increased nearly fourfold between 2002 and 2004 (from $34 million to $129 million), representing a jump from one quarter to one half in the proportion of industry funding that comprised the university's budget for drug research. At the University of Toronto, the series reported by way of comparison, the pharmaceutical industry accounted for less than 10 per cent of the university's drug research money.

After investigating for three months, the reporters were able to identify one hundred university researchers at McMaster's Faculty of Health Sciences (with a full-time faculty of 515) who had financial connections to drug and biotechnology companies (connections that ranged from consulting and speaking fees to clinical trials, research funding, and even stock options). But because no rules required professors to disclose their financial connections to the pharmaceutical industry—and because university officials by and large refused to comment on the matter—the number of faculty with such connections could have been (and could be) even higher.

The series concentrated on two drugs that had been removed from the market for safety reasons. The first was Vioxx, an effective arthritis drug developed by the US pharmaceutical giant Merck and Co., and introduced to the Canadian market in 1999 by the parent company's Canadian arm, Merck Frosst Canada. Vioxx had received numerous positive reviews in pre-approval tests (including one study done at McMaster). But it made headlines when it was withdrawn from the market in September 2004 after a study showed it caused heart attacks and strokes. The withdrawal was too late for many who had used the drug and suffered its ill effects. The opening story of the series told of one Canadian woman who suffered a stroke and lost an eye after taking the drug for a year to alleviate her severe osteoarthritis. Believing Vioxx was responsible, she joined a class-action lawsuit against the drug company. The suit alleged that the company had withheld information from doctors and patients about the drug's dangers.[2]

The reporters also addressed rising concern over the so-called 'off-label' (or unapproved) prescriptions for drugs originally intended for a different purpose (a practice that represented millions of prescriptions to Canadians and an estimated four to five billion dollars in sales). At the time the series was written, people who consulted Health Canada's drug product database were unable to get information on which drugs had been withdrawn for safety reasons.[3]

The second drug that Buist, Walters, and Muhtadie focused on was Neurontin, approved in 1993 as an anti-seizure drug for epileptics but prescribed widely for other off-label uses including muscle pain and mood disorders. The infamous tale of Neurontin's impact on users soiled the reputation of its sponsoring drug company Pfizer, the world's largest, when it was revealed that in order to boost sales worldwide (from $23 million in 1993 to $2.4 billion a decade later), the company had aggressively and illegally marketed the drug for a plethora of non-approved uses despite evidence it caused suicidal behaviour. Again, the revelations came too late for Joan Burgess, a Canadian woman who went from vivacious to morbidly depressed and finally suicidal after taking the prescription drug to relieve pain. Before she committed suicide, Burgess discovered what she believed to be the cause of her transformation. She watched a US television show about a class-action suit against the makers and marketers of the drug.[4]

The series made a stellar contribution to the burgeoning body of evidence suggesting that the whole process of drug approval and regulation required a systems overhaul. Called Blind Faith, it comprised ten main stories that ran over five days in June 2005.

## The Interview: **Steve Buist**
(6 August 2006)

Steve Buist's enthusiasm for this series arose from his science background, his interest in the scientific method, and his hunch that some scientists had strayed from the professional fold into the welcoming arms of the pharmaceutical industry.

> Ethics in science is a huge issue right now, and as you can see by recent developments at the *Journal of the American Medical Association*, having to confirm that they're taking articles from people who haven't fully revealed all their ties to pharmaceutical companies. Good scientists understand that they're no different from any other person—there's the potential to be influenced. And if somebody's giving you something, then you have the potential to be influenced. So it's a bit galling to find that a lot of scientists don't believe that; they think they are somewhat godlike and above influence.

Buist regards that attitude itself as anti-scientific, because in science, as in all bona fide research, the seeker is supposed to begin with a genuine question. Buist thought about this issue for a while, and then came up with a local angle.

> This project started from a very simple beginning: Let's look at McMaster's researchers and see who has ties to the pharmaceutical industry. I spent six weeks at a computer, basically just running from A to Z, every faculty of health-science member to see whose names I could come up with that had announced ties to pharmaceutical companies or biomedical companies. So we just started keeping a list, logging every one that came up. Eventually, we contacted all

hundred or so of the people we found and asked them to talk to us. Some did—
it was a hugely underwhelming number. I'm sure that it was difficult for some of
them.

Another trouble for the reporters was that they had no idea what proportion of all
McMaster's research their list of names represented.

You also need to keep in mind that we found a hundred but we may have missed
two hundred because there are no requirements for people to actually divulge
this information publicly. I don't think I'd call the issue a crisis [in scientific ethics],
but it's certainly a very important and emerging theme: the influence of pharmaceutical companies on research. And that's the fundamental issue here.

Buist began searching for the names of McMaster's health-sciences researchers by
scouring the scientific journals.

After a while, when you've done two hundred and you've got four hundred more
to go, you start to develop a rhythm, you start to have a sense for how you can
ask the questions to get the answers you're looking for. But yeah, it was nothing
more than tiresome detective work.

As Anne McIlroy noted in the previous chapter about her series four years earlier, the
failure by researchers to disclose information about their ties to the drug industry was
so routine that it wasn't even regarded as a problem. Those who did speak out found
their careers derailed for their trouble. Clearly, telling the truth didn't always work in
a given researcher's favour. Buist believes that the 'example' of previous whistle-blowers seems to have made most researchers overly cautious about what they will disclose.

They are in a precarious position sometimes in terms of their standing within their
own university environment. Although a lot of them weren't saying anything particularly outrageous.

There was a single researcher who spoke to the responsibility of scientists in the academy to address these issues. But Buist credited luck, and not the aroused conscience
of a possible whistle-blower, for the success of the series.

In the end, for us, there were some fortuitous circumstances. The whole Vioxx
situation kind of exploded right around the time we were doing this. And the trials against Vioxx were just really getting going. So it showed people concrete
evidence: Here's what we're talking about, folks. I mean Vioxx was the poster
child for what can happen when you don't have faith in the results of your trials
and there are such huge amounts of money at stake. The proportion of

McMaster's research budget that is bankrolled by the pharmaceutical companies is just staggering.

All we were trying to say with this series is that the fact that a doctor is receiving a nickel from a pharmaceutical company doesn't inherently mean that the doctor's tainted or that his or her work is tainted. All it means is that we need to be vigilant about what effect this can have on science. It doesn't mean that [the researcher] is evil. It just means that we need to build in safeguards just as you have experiments that are double-blind so that the scientists don't know who's getting the drug and who isn't. We need to build in these safeguards to the system so that everyone knows that everything's above board.

Blind Faith started with a single question: What is the relationship at McMaster University between medical researchers and the powerful pharmaceutical industry? The research led to the discovery of widespread off-label uses for some drugs and to specific medications with suspect safety records.

It really did all start with just an idea to look at McMaster and then look at their researchers. I had long wondered what pharmaceutical company connections there were, and that's really where it started. Then along the way some interesting side avenues opened up, like the use of off-label drugs. *Off label* is a fancy way of saying that it's not approved for that use [i.e., it was prescribed for another condition or purpose]. *Not approved*—that's not a phrase they like to use in the medical community. They prefer *off label* because it sounds a lot more benign.

And then of course the other main avenue we started going down was looking at who had done work on drugs that were eventually withdrawn from the market for safety reasons. The Vioxx people were saying, 'Great news, customers, we've found this other use for it.' And then ultimately the drug gets withdrawn. It starts to raise questions about whether there were problems with the research. If you worked on a drug and gave it a thumbs-up, and then the drug is withdrawn from the market because it's killing people, how do you feel about that?

And not just did you do work on the drug but were you getting paid by the drug company at the same time? The important thing we were trying to show that kind of got swept aside is that everyone would agree the number of scientists out there who are just flat out cooking the books, that's a very, very, very small minority of people. The bigger problem is how many people are being subtly influenced and not realizing it. So, for instance, even just the sorts of experiments that you might conduct, you might start tailoring your research to ask the questions that are important to the pharmaceutical company but not necessarily that you [as a researcher] find particularly important. But if you've got twenty-five grad students in your lab and you've got to feed the beast every year, maybe you start thinking, 'Okay, well I'm not particularly interested in this topic, but I know that if I do this experiment drug company XYZ will fund it. So that will keep five of my grad students happy for a year.'

And then a hundred of those decisions adds up to a system in disarray without any-body meaning to do anything wrong?

> That's right. So you're very subtly being influenced to follow somebody else's agenda, not your own. Why? Because money makes the world go round and you need that money to fund your lab.

Buist said the sheer complexity of the subject matter made the tale difficult to research and to tell, especially in the form of a series of newspaper articles (as opposed to, for example, in an academic journal or a book). And although the paper received substantial response from readers about the series, Buist isn't sure about its overall impact on the reading public.

> There were certainly a lot of people who grasped the significance of it. But in the newspaper business you can write one story about a dog that died in a fire and you get three hundred phone calls. What pushes people's buttons to contact a newspaper isn't necessarily proportionate to how important the story is.

The story took Buist down some unexpected paths and turned up newsworthy infor-mation, including that there had been an increase in the rate at which prescription drugs were withdrawn.

> Those side avenues that I talked about with respect to off-label uses of drugs and withdrawn drugs . . . we had some news stories come out about the grow-ing rate at which drugs were being withdrawn from the Canadian market in recent years. Those were bonuses that we didn't expect, so that was nice. And I think what pushed the series over the top for us was we were able to go out and find some actual people—I'll use the word, I don't like the word: victims. But these were people who at some point in the system were victims. So we were able to put some human faces on why these stories were so important.

Realizing the extent of the problem provided the reporters with a defining moment.

> I wasn't surprised at the number of people who had connections; that part didn't surprise me. I think what surprised us was when we started to get some sense of how much money this brings into the university. When you start connecting all the dots, that's the dot that was, 'Wow, this is an important part of McMaster's world.' I think one of the things—if I can use this term—the 'holy shit!' moment for Joan and me was when we realized that McMaster brings in something like three or four times more pharmaceutical company money than does the University of Toronto.

So you have to think, McMaster is not as large as U of T. You can't say that U of T doesn't have a qualified medical school—it's probably the most prestigious medical school in the country. And yet McMaster is attracting more pharmaceutical company dollars. So you have to ask yourself the question: Why is that? What is it about McMaster that makes it such an attractive place for pharmaceutical companies to come and conduct their research?

The reporters, and the series, never came to a single answer to that question. What the seminal query did spark was more questions, and these in turn fuelled their research.

Is it because one place is more receptive than the other? Maybe. Is it because one place is more aggressive in running clinical trials? Maybe that's it too. But it was one of those things: 'You're telling me that Mac gets three or four times the amount of drug company money that U of T does?' That just makes no sense.

To establish the number of the university's medical researchers involved in potentially compromising funding arrangements with the pharmaceuticals, the reporters had first to find out the total number of researchers with relationships to the drug companies. That ultimately proved an elusive goal.

To this day, I can't tell you whether the number of people we identified was even remotely close to being accurate, because there's no requirement for them to disclose this publicly. We could have missed huge numbers of people.

There was, of course, no central database to consult, no public directory of the connections between researchers at a public university and their sponsors in the high-stakes and decidedly private pharmaceutical industry.

Researchers are supposed to provide this information to the university, but as you'll see in one of the stories, we were able to show that the university may not have any record of people having interactions with drug companies. One person was quoted anonymously in our story saying that he was never required to divulge this information. And nobody ever asked him about it. The other obstacle was a huge one for us: many of the people at McMaster were not interested in speaking about this issue with us. That's about as charitably as I can put it.

The research that went into the series was so substantial that it's hard to imagine the reporters could have missed anything. In hindsight, Buist is fairly certain Blind Faith turned over the largest boulders, though he also knows much remains to be investigated.

> Believe it or not, there were actually some areas that we didn't explore that we probably could have. We could have made the series longer, but we felt that five days was enough to beat people over the head with. I thought it was a pretty thorough series—there aren't too many other things I would have done differently, I don't think.

The impact of the series was also difficult to assess.

> I'm not sure there were any direct impacts. There were no changes in legislation. It's not like the world changed overnight when we published the series. I guess the only impact we could hope to have had was maybe an increased awareness about an important issue, which seems to continue to rise in importance in the science world.

Accordingly, the reporters hope to do some follow-up work.

> There are still some areas that we didn't explore that we hope to. Joan and I have just been talking about maybe going back down some of these different avenues that we put aside. I don't really want to tell you too much about them because I don't know if it's going to work out. But certainly the whole issue of clinical trials is important and would be one area that we want to look at.

# The Interview: **Joan Walters**
(9 August 2006)

For Joan Walters, who came to love investigative work later on in her career, the Blind Faith series was quintessentially investigative, and then some.

> It was really something to do, I'm sure Steve told you. It didn't win us many fans [at McMaster], but it was certainly an interesting experience. No question.

She commended the paper's editors for their support of the series—for their commitment 'both in bravery and in resources'—especially given the medium-market circulation size of the *Hamilton Spectator*.

It is part of the *Spectator's* working philosophy on investigative projects to try to end with a forward-looking piece that turns to possible solutions, both to make the articles more useful to readers, and to keep the heat on the appropriate authorities.

If that's possible to do. Sometimes it isn't. We've done some that don't end that way. We did one, more local, on fitness chains, that actually ended with the government changing the legislation. So we didn't have to do remedial work, because they did it. That's not uncommon—that's the action, the impact. Or in some cases, somebody says I'm suing or somebody is charged. So it depends on how the story develops.

The last story in the Blind Faith series was 'kind of remedial'.

It talked about what other places are doing, what kinds of things that people can do, what should be required or might be required of public institutions, that kind of stuff.

Walters and Buist, who had worked together on several other major projects before undertaking the Blind Faith series, discussed the issues at length before pitching the idea to their editors. Both had been following the news on big pharma and especially related developments in the United States.

We had been talking about the rising concerns and about somehow corralling some of the things that were breaking, mostly in the United States. Just before we started our research for this story, the very first few stories came out of the States, in big papers like *The New York Times* and *The Washington Post* in particular, about links between scientists at the National Institutes of Health in the United States and the drug companies who had an interest in some of the work that was being done there. The revelations were that these people were taking fees or consulting for the pharma companies and getting free trips [or other freebies]. It was a breaking story in the States. We could see it building, because both of us separately had been watching this issue for, I'd say, about a year and a half, two years. I had been doing stories two years prior to this about individual cases of research that our newspaper felt were worthy of public attention, but that didn't really breach any rules.

Without knowing it, Walters had actually begun the base research for what would become Blind Faith several years before the series ran. Following the issue mostly out of personal interest, she stumbled on a gem of a story.

I discovered that a researcher at McMaster, whose specialty was anti-depressant drugs, had applied to the Catholic School Board and was about to distribute surveys on paper to girls who had started their periods. He had asked for permission to just collect information from [female high-school students] on how they experienced their periods. Did they make them sad? Did they get teased by the other kids? And he pitched it to the school board as a need to gather some basic information for both the board and himself to have for his broad general research into how girls feel when they have their periods.

In fact—and he hadn't even told the Research Ethics Board this—he was planning to use the surveys to collect the names, addresses, and phone numbers of girls who would be potential recruits as subjects in a study that would use Prozac on girls of that age. It's a true story. I was personally so blown away by how this system could have operated.

We wrote several stories about this [in November 2002]. So that ignited my interest in the area. I didn't understand anything before that really about how drug companies and researchers operated together. It turned out that he was getting mega dollars from Prozac, but he didn't have any subjects. He was having trouble finding subjects.

Walters was able to break the story when a nurse in the clinic where the McMaster researcher worked unwittingly gave up some key information.

She said, 'Well, he's getting just terrible response to this attempt to get girls on Prozac.' The school board cancelled [the project], and the Research Ethics Board called an inquiry into it [after the story ran]. We don't know what the results were.

Her interest in the issue ignited.

That is how I actually [started with the issue of ethics in science] ahead of time. And then I was watching all this, I was learning, I was reading endlessly, Steve and I were talking. He's told you he has a science background. He had a completely different level of interest. He had this broad global interest in stuff like how a system works at a place like Mac. What is it that they do? Do they get consulting fees? Are they allowed to? How do we find out?

We talked about this in the newsroom for a while before it came to fruition. Then suddenly he and I were both clear, and we had an editor who was quite intensely interested, I think probably because we storyboarded it properly. We went with an actual proposal of what we wanted to look at and the paper said okay, take the risk, start looking.

While Buist 'slogged through the computer strands, endless, endless computer searching', looking for ways to identify the links between McMaster researchers and the drug companies, Walters began conceptualizing the series.

I started producing concepts for how we could explain to the public why this matter should be of such high interest to them. And that led us to the idea of doing it from the point of view of the individual user of a drug.

Buist's interest veered toward the science itself and whether the system of drug development was working as it should (i.e., with built-in safeguards against potentially dangerous prescription drugs). Walters began with a kind of gut-level reaction to the story about the researcher seeking for Prozac a possible market (vulnerable teenage girls).

> Precisely. And it's one of the reasons the two of us work well together on investigative projects. I really believe in research and writing teams, especially coming from a collaborative background like a wire service.[5] I find that usually when you have two people with quite different orientations and in some ways at opposite ends of the spectrum, you end up with dynamite stuff that you don't get if you're on your own.

What sustains Walters through the twists and turns of difficult stories (issues and investigative reporting cannot be dispatched in a single news cycle) is the one quality that all great reporters seem to share: a fierce curiosity. Without that character trait, investigative work would be without inherent satisfaction, and altogether too difficult.

> And the other thing I think you have to have is the ability to connect, to follow something for a long time and then notice the anomalies or see the new questions, the why and the what.

Walters understands that important stories have history; they don't erupt full-blown from nothing. Uncovering those stories requires the reporter to see and appreciate events within the 'actual continuum' that is their context. The story about the researcher seeking a possible market for Prozac, for example, began with a single high-school student. And that first story led finally to the Blind Faith series.

> I just looked up this girl at Hamilton Catholic High School—it was in November 2002. That was the entry point for me . . . that was where the actual continuum began. Technically that's where it began, but the research for Blind Faith didn't begin until after we had put together a conceptual grid of how this might work and went to our editors and said, 'This is what we'd like to do.' And as I said, it was one of those points in the planning stage of a newsroom where we had a solid enough idea—we weren't just larking about any more—and they had an understanding of what might result. They had no idea that it would, but because it was us, they thought okay, it's worth the risk.

Both reporters had proven their mettle and earned their editors' confidence. In a newsroom, there's no better collateral than a track record—and no substitute for it either. Once the two senior reporters got the go-ahead, they began researching in earnest, following back tips or clues, as if pulling threads in a fraying sweater to see where each would lead. They started with the small stuff. Walters paused here to remember the sequence of events, and then suddenly, a eureka moment:

> I know exactly what we did! We did it with the minutiae; we did it with the names. We didn't know who was on faculty and who wasn't. We didn't know how we would have to narrow down our search to get that list. We got that list. That's what we did first. We said, 'Okay, is it going to be people who are just full professors, or assistant professors? Do they have to be on campus, or can they be associates?' So we sketched a profile.

They compiled that profile from information they garnered not from the university officials (whose reticence to comment presented the reporters with their first and most enduring major obstacle), but on their own—from the Internet. McMaster could have saved them a lot of time by simply giving them a list of the school's medical researchers.

> Which McMaster didn't do. And they were already pissed because in addition to the story I told you about, I had done several more, and so had Steve. They were less explosive [than the Blind Faith series], but the university just didn't like us. They wouldn't talk to us. Ever. So we couldn't exactly phone them up and say, 'Okay, so now we're going to come after you on this and we need your help.' We knew that they wouldn't help us. We did it on the Internet.

It was the journey (not the destination), and the questions (not the knowledge) that motivated Walters to keep digging and connecting the dots. She found inspiration in the questions that captured her interest, even if such questions also 'make you not sleep at night'. When university officials and researchers refused comment, the reporters turned the roadblock to their advantage.

> Interestingly, because that was a block for us, one of the first things we did was to draw the specs for the project. We identified what we needed to find, and it was pretty obvious that what we were going to need to do and what we had described to our editor was to relate this to McMaster. So we needed to find a drug that had been 'shamed'—that's pejorative—but we had to find a drug that was relevant to the public that had been partly or fully developed at McMaster and a person behind the drug who would talk to us about it, which we did accomplish.
>
> We also knew we had to find someone who had suffered [from taking the drug]. One of our editors said he didn't want the stories to run unless we found somebody who had died. And we said that maybe we should just go and find out

what happened before we put those kinds of restrictions on the project. Let us just report it. And he backed off right away.

He thought the story would be powerful and meaningful only if the full consequences of bad research and bad drugs were communicated to our readers, and he felt that that could be communicated only if we could find somebody who had died as a direct result of a drug. We didn't agree with him. We just thought that we needed to find people who had experienced bad medicine. And so that's what we set out to do. Now in the bargain, we did find a suicide, but that wasn't what we set out to do. That was just research.

The series focused on two drugs—Vioxx and Neurontin—that turned out to have 'very strong, very supportable links' to McMaster.

It wasn't like they were secrets, and it also wasn't like they were tenuous connections. These were primary researchers connected directly to drugs that had been withdrawn.

In the case of Neurontin, the drug was blamed for the suicide of a local woman.

We made it clear, I hope, in the story that there was a question about whether that drug caused this woman's suicide. But we told the story of how people around her thought it had, and how the lawsuits that have since been launched say it did. So we felt comfortable with that. But my point was that what we set out to do at the front end was write the specs for the researchers we meant to explore: Who would they be? How would they be described, and chosen? We had to find them, and their email addresses, and their phone numbers, and their mailing addresses for the registered letters, and so on. We also had to find other people who represented the issues as we saw them and as we wanted to develop them in the series.

So that was all front-end work. We had to get that done to make sure that there actually were these people and that we could find at least a sufficient number of researchers to look at their links. And then Steve . . . he had to make sure that those links were there. We were operating on a premise that they would be [because] one of the first things we did was we sat down and said, Okay, what is another university that's reasonably comparable to McMaster that has a medical school, that gets money from drug companies, and that might have rules. Where could we go?

Walters ended up talking to researchers at the University of Toronto, McGill University, and universities in Western Canada. She settled on the University of Toronto 'as a reasonable place for us to at least do some comparative leg work.'

[This was] so that I could understand—since Mac didn't seem to have any rules—what the rules might look like if you were in a university that took drug money and that had ethics guidelines and controls, however loose they might be, over the relationship between pharma and medical staff. I was astonished at how helpful the U of T was. They did not know what we were doing. We didn't tell them. I simply said to them, 'I need to understand your rules. I understand they are well set out, that you've done a lot of study on them. Can I get the studies? Can I see how they came to be? Can I talk to some of the people who developed them?'

I spent at least a couple of weeks talking to University of Toronto folks from the dean of medicine to the provost to the people who actually administered the ethics system, simply collecting information. Which they had no trouble giving, because it was fact. And that gave me an understanding of how it might be done. And then I spoke to people like Margaret Somerville.[6] And I spoke to a guy out in BC who was recommended to me as someone who had a particular knowledge of off-label drugs. I spent a whole Saturday on the phone with him, exploring how it works in BC. He's a neuropsychopharmacologist who works for the government trying to establish whether off-label drugs should be considered for inclusion in the medical plan out there. So I did a lot of talking to the people who actually work with the rules or the drugs.

Once the background research was complete and Walters understood the scope of the problem, it was time to 'get down to the specific details and data' the reporters would have to harvest and digest 'before we could even speak about this in the paper'. At first, they were awash in a sea of apparently unrelated facts.

We didn't have a clue what we were doing. Steve was just slogging, just racing. And then he began to develop an understanding; he's a very good researcher, to boot. He began to develop ways of finding some of the salient information about these people. Because you know, you plug in John Smith from McMaster and he's a researcher, but you get like eight million hits for him. Steve had to narrow that all down. So while he was doing that, I was collecting this other information, and after a period of time we came back together and firmed up the storyboard.

To get the story, the reporters interviewed people all over Canada and some places in the United States. In the process, they got an education in how relations between the academy and the pharmaceutical industry were supposed to work, and in at least one case, that of McMaster, how they actually did work. They began with questions and the questions became more and more focused as they learned more about the subject. Reporters—and their editors—know that when they take on investigative projects, they can't afford to overlook or be wrong about even the most minor details.

But the university's researchers, even those who disagreed strongly with the way things worked at McMaster, were loath to go on the record with their views. The reporters tried repeatedly to contact the researchers they had identified. They made overtures by phone and by email. They even sent out registered letters in the hope of finding someone who might speak to the issues. Virtually all the researchers, fearing for their own careers, maintained a wall of silence.

> And that's often a central point for people who do this kind of investigative reporting, especially at a newspaper. It's the understanding that the person at the other end of the line has: that if he opens his mouth and it somehow isn't honoured by you, or somehow is misconstrued, or it just appears in the newspaper, that he's dead.
>
> What surprised us in this case was we knew that there were people who disagreed with the fact that Mac had no brakes on this whole system. None. They felt very, very strongly about it, so I guess we had the expectation that some of them, when we sent them the registered letter, would at least confirm their involvement or their non-involvement, and perhaps say a sentence or two. But in the end, almost nobody did.

From their sources inside McMaster's medical school, the reporters learned why.

> The dean had sent out some kind of an email or letter that we never saw—that surprised us, too, that we never saw it. It just said don't talk to the reporters, we'll take care of it. And that was enough. They were so fearful for perhaps their offices or their research dollars or the approbation of the dean that he didn't have to send a big long letter. He just sent two sentences out and it shut down like a blackout. That shocked me.

Some sympathetic researchers helped them with background information (for example telling the reporters about the dean's letter). But despite their efforts, Walters and Buist found not a single researcher willing to go on the record about the way his work fit into the drug-approval process.

> Steve had a couple of phone calls from people explaining about the email, about the letter the dean wrote, which I guess was brave. But this is a small town; this is not Toronto. So there's a really heavy-duty, self-protective instinct.

When the reporters found out about the dean's missive, they knew they were onto something big.

> It was thrilling! It was, holy shit, this is really happening! And the other part of this was our lawyer, who is absolutely awesome. Every time we thought he'd stop us, he didn't. And that was because of the way that everybody [at McMaster] was reacting.

The *Spectator*'s lawyer and its senior management agreed the reporters could proceed with the story, that they hadn't broken any rules or flouted any journalistic standards. Most important, they had extended the right of reply to their would-be sources.

> It was like, 'You gave them a chance, you don't have to stop, this is perfectly fair. You're not drawing conclusions; they are reacting.'

Like Buist, Walters identified as the major obstacle in pursuing the story the reticence of university researchers and officials to go on the record or even be interviewed, and the attempt by the university's media relations arm to stonewall the reporters.

> I think it would be safe and fair to say that we do not agree with—and we have publicly said this—the attitude that if you just shut it down and say nothing, it's better than giving any information at all. So that was a huge decision that they made [to say nothing at all], which was the biggest blockage.

Reporters faced with stonewalling officials must find a way over or around the wall to get the story. That takes thinking like a detective—and time.

> It meant that we had to calculate—we spent a ton of time in the process of putting this whole thing together doing our own calculations—how much, what percentage of the money coming in for research came from pharma. It wasn't an obvious linchpin in our story, but for us that was a huge blockage, because without the financial statistics, how do you know? So we got the information from a variety of sources: old reports, new reports, growth of the industry, and we put together [something] like a financial thesis. We checked it with U of T. I don't mean we gave them information—we just checked about the growth and the size and the scope at a comparable university. And we talked to as many people as we could about that side of it. They wouldn't talk to us on the record, though.
>
> Mac made it harder and harder and harder for us, because this is an integrated university with many points of research, so some research money is calculated as coming only to one hospital, and some is calculated as coming only to Mac, and some is calculated as coming to the whole health-sciences department, which covers various groups.

The university had the financial information the reporters wanted but refused to release it, forcing them to try to elicit it from other sources and to piece together the bits into a whole by thinking in conditional terms. Once they had what they believed was a viable model, they confronted the university.

> We'd sort of come up with a thesis on how it might be occurring. We looked back at previous years, which was a huge help, and then in the end we had to

present that to them and say this is what we're publishing. If it's incorrect, you owe us the honour of telling us it's incorrect. And we will explain in the story if you don't answer us that you wouldn't tell us. So we did our best to calculate it and here's what we came up with. Well, strangely enough, it was pretty close, and they did cough up the figures in the very end, like maybe twenty-four hours before publication.

This is precisely what is meant by *hard-hitting* investigative reporting. The research was fuelled at least in part by the reporters' conviction that this was information the public had a right to know and that they as reporters had a responsibility to provide.

Especially when somebody's blocking you. So I would say that the biggest blockage was the lack of forthcoming financial information, which, after all, is public. But FOI [the Freedom of Information and Protection of Privacy Act] didn't apply [to the universities] in Ontario until this past June [2006]. Until two months ago . . . it just didn't apply to them. They were exempt. And then the exemption was lifted in June and rewritten to include the universities.

Trying to find people who had experienced the potentially devastating effects of the drugs the reporters were investigating presented another difficulty. And once again, the reporters ascribe to luck what their perseverance finally turned up.

We were kind of lucky there because there were lawsuits in the US for both the drugs we picked, Neurontin and Vioxx. But that doesn't help you because . . . Canadians aren't in the US classes.

Classes?

They create classes in the United States for class action [lawsuits]; they describe the class. They say, for example, you had to have been taking the drug between this year and this year, and you had to have had the following types of consequences. And if you didn't, then you can't join the class of people that is suing a company. So I went to all the lawyers in the United States that I could find who were involved—there must have been twenty for Vioxx and sixty for Neurontin.

When the reporters began researching, they believed there were no such suits under way or planned in Canada. First, they learned that a Canadian user of Vioxx had indeed initiated a lawsuit against the makers of the drug. Next, they made contact with a US lawyer intimately familiar with the progress of lawsuits against Neurontin.

On the Neurontin side, the US lawyer . . . it was amazing talking to him, because he's the one who gave us the transcripts of a previous case. We got some testimony from a former sales guy from the company that had been fined $400 million for promoting Neurontin for illegal purposes. The guy who had started that whole thing in the States had had his testimony sealed, and when I called the lawyer about the Neurontin lawsuits in the States and he heard what we were doing, he asked, 'Do you want a copy of the unsealed testimony?'

What do you think? The answer was yes! He sent me parts of the transcript, which I then had to double-check and make sure were legit. The sales guy had testified about how the people who manufactured Neurontin [were instructing sales staff] to get out there and sell this. You know, 'I don't care about safety. I don't care about what the doctors say. Just get out there.'

He was also the one who gave me the name of a lawyer he thought he'd met at a convention, who he believed was starting a lawsuit in Canada. It was tenuous stuff, but as it turns out, that's how we got the story of Joan, the woman who committed suicide [after being prescribed the drug].[7] We had at least six or seven possibilities at one point [of people to interview about the drugs' effects on their lives], but for various reasons—their discomfort or our discomfort—we needed to narrow it down. The people we settled on, we felt were the fairest representation of the circumstances.

Looking back, Walters believes she could have been more aggressive than she was in her attempts to get university researchers to speak. It's the one thing she would do differently if she had the chance.

I think I would have gone to some face-to-face meetings, because I think that might have sprung loose some of the obvious discomfort inside the university. That was the part that I regret we didn't get at.

It's a lot easier to blow off a reporter on the phone than it is face to face.

It is. And it's easy enough for us to say, 'You know, it's a great story, don't worry about it, we'll come back to it.' But I think, well I don't know, second sight is always great. But I think if I had the chance to do something more, I would have tried harder—though I believe we tried very hard, because we phoned them all. We sent them registered letters. I had a binder, and we were ticking them off as we reached them or their offices. Or we'd communicate by email.

But I really think that I would have done some face-to-face work—just show up at the offices or find them as they walked down the hall at the hospital, on the off chance that somebody might have said, 'You know what, you're absolutely right. This is something that shouldn't be happening.'

The immediate impact of the series was limited to raising public awareness of the issue, but Walters said she hopes that in time, and with follow-up, the series' revelations will lead to appropriate institutional and legislative change.

It sparked a huge public discussion in Hamilton, in the medical community and also outside it. We had people saying, 'Holy cow, I didn't know this was going on in Hamilton.' Obviously, that's what you want. But I don't think the immediate impact went beyond that. We do expect to find in time that changes have been made, but I don't know that for sure right now.

The public debate provoked by the series, however, did extend to other universities that receive money from pharmaceutical companies to engage in research on as-yet-unapproved prescription drugs.

I know that there was horror at other universities, except for U of T, which had already done it [made appropriate adjustments], maybe because they're big and they have the resources, I don't know. So what was the long-term impact? I think we fulfilled our responsibility as a newspaper to raise an issue that needed to be discussed both in professional and public circles. I know it's been discussed in parliamentary circles, but I don't think it would be correct to say that it's exclusively because of the story we did; we just contributed to the general discussion.

Investigative work helps to widen and deepen debate on an issue of public concern. In a sense, the enterprise is ultimately collective, even though it's lonely work a lot of the time. Even so, reporters who do this kind of work don't usually evince any possessiveness about the stories themselves. Instead, they measure success in how far the stories travel, how many other reporters pick up on the issue and begin their own investigations in their respective communities.

You know the number of awards [the series] was nominated for, which is not the reason anybody does this in the first place, but because of that the story travelled. It came to people's attention because of that. I think that was good, but I'm not suggesting that resulted [solely] from the story. I'm just saying that it contributed to the public understanding and the professional discussion about the issues that have come to the fore. We now see people quitting editorial boards at medical journals because they think the ethics are bad. So we felt very strongly that no matter what happened, it was part of informing the public, and newspapers have to do that.

Investigative reporters invariably share this sense of the import of their responsibility. They understand they must unearth and tell the truth, even when certain individuals or the public generally appears not to want to hear it. I believe it's this conviction, this belief in the value of a free press, and in its primacy for a democratic society, that keeps investigative reporters digging past midnight and against the odds.

There are breakthrough points in a story where you realize that you are lifting the curtain or shining the spotlight on something that other people want to stay dark. And I think of all the things that this accomplished, it was lifting the curtain, so that people understood and particularly because Hamilton has so many clinical trials and so many people dabbling in things that are funded by or related to big pharma. We never said big pharma is bad. We simply said you should know what happens.

Walters didn't see herself as an investigative reporter (although she concedes that the Pulitzer Prize–winning investigative journalist and author Seymour Hersh was always her hero) until after she started engaging in projects like Blind Faith. It was the work itself that transformed her attitude.

Although I had done investigative work at various times in my career, including when I was a political reporter for CP working in Ottawa, I never would have considered that my primary focus. I've been here at the *Spectator* for only five years. I was with Southam in Toronto before that. And even then, although I was doing some investigative work, I certainly wouldn't have described myself as [an investigative reporter]. But when I came here, this paper had a wish to begin doing harder-hitting, deeper stuff locally. And that's when I started to begin to realize that I was or was mostly an investigative reporter.

The *Hamilton Spectator* is now a 'sister paper' to the mighty *Toronto Star*, and deserves its growing reputation, but the paper wasn't always known for its investigative work.

Until the sell-off of the Southam papers, first to Hollinger and then to CanWest, the *Spectator* was a Southam paper. And then, before I got here, it got parcelled off in a period of two or three years. It was owned by three different groups—Sun Media, CanWest, and Hollinger. Then it was sold to the *Toronto Star*, and that's where it's stayed.

The commitment to investigative reporting came, not surprisingly, with this change in ownership, but it also coincided with a change in the *Spectator*'s leadership, when Dana Robbins became editor-in-chief. ('He is amazing; he is a really brave guy.') Robbins supported the work from the beginning, and his support never flagged. In a column he wrote at the launch of Blind Faith, Robbins made clear that the project had the solid support of senior management.[8]

How Walters herself got into the newspaper business constitutes 'a really quick story.'

I fell into it. I was in social work at the University of Waterloo and I walked into the twice-weekly campus newspaper—and that was it. I hardly went to any more classes. Then, when I finished my degree, I did social work [briefly] but I couldn't stay away from the newspapers. So I started as a classified ad clerk. I was *Miss Brown* and *Miss White*—Miss Brown was obits and Miss White was wedding announcements—in the classified section of the *Kitchener–Waterloo Record* [now known as *The Record*]. And I convinced the managing editor to let me write, volunteer write. Back then you could do that. He stuck me in the women's department and I wrote for a year and then he came to me and he said, 'You know what, you need some training.' At that time there wasn't much training in Canada so I went to the States and got my masters in journalism at Northwestern. Then I came back and worked for CP, and that's where I began.

Working for the national wire service Canadian Press is akin to trial by fire. Reporters for CP deal with stories of national rather than local interest and are generally expected to be able to pick up on events and issues with little or no previous background. In other words, if you can stand the heat and survive CP, you're probably going to make it as a journalist. Canadian Press was Walters's alma mater.

I absolutely loved it. Like many, many people. I shouldn't say this anywhere near an editor—but you know what? Sometimes you wouldn't have to pay me to do this.

This is a common thread among reporters. I can remember thinking the very same thing as a young reporter. I was spurred on by the thrill of being able to ask all those burning questions—and actually get answers from people in a position to know.

Yes, me too. And I like those moments where you go, 'Oh, I get it.' Whether it's a story or a bit of information or a source or whatever.

If she were advising journalism students, Walters would recommend they get some daily reporting experience and never stop reading.

I don't think you can do much in journalism until you've done daily reporting. I don't care where it is, it gives you the facility to recognize the information that is different. And until you have that skill, you're nowhere. The second part of the advice is you absolutely have to read. You have to read everything, all the time. It's not like you have to sit down with a stack of magazines or newspapers every night, that doesn't really help much. It's more that you have to exercise your curiosity constantly. And it doesn't matter if you're reading ads, or the Internet, or bus shelters, or the *New York Times*. You have to read constantly and figure out what it is that doesn't sit right with you while you're reading it.

> You have to read critically and you have to figure out what it is that would interest you. Well, I guess a third part is you have to have interests. I've always had interests. I'm sometimes amazed by how few interests some young journalists have. If you ask them what they're passionate about, they don't have a clue.

With these remarks, Walters hit on a central issue for journalism educators everywhere: how to communicate the radical individual responsibility involved in first 'getting' the story, and then getting it right. The hardest thing to get across, or past, is the notion that investigative work can be 'assigned'. The fact is that the investigative reporter almost always initiates a project through his or her own thinking. No one can give you an investigative story. You can't buy one like a new car, or earn one like a promotion, and it certainly doesn't just come to you. Reporters who actually work on investigative projects know full well what the process involves: first, you think it up, and then you chase it down. Those who persevere through these two stages (way more easily said than done) are those who 'get' the big stories. Walters agreed.

> I think that's the other thing you have to have: tenacity. You have to develop it, you have to swallow your fear, and you just have to do it. It's like learning to do pickups. The first few times you do that as a young reporter, you just feel like you're going to die because it's so awful to go to somebody's house and say can I have a picture of your dead daughter. But the fact is you have to do those things. You have to be brave enough to walk up to a door and knock on it, not come back and tell your editor that there was nobody home.

On the other hand, great reporters generally have had great mentors at the formative stages of their careers. Not necessarily 'teachers', these mentors pass on to their younger colleagues a respect for the craft and a passion for the work.

> I absolutely agree. And I like what we're doing here. We are considering young journalists as they are, people to be protected, people to be nurtured, and people to be moved through, by many means, including mentoring. And places like the *Ottawa Citizen*, with that internship program . . . that's an awesome program they have, with six interns a year, and they go all over the world and write for the front page. They sometimes make it and sometimes don't. But at least the *Citizen* is supporting them.

# Commentary

Steve Buist and Joan Walters were moved by different facets of the issues at hand. Buist was plumbing a long-time interest in scientific ethics and wanted to find out how the drug-approval system actually worked. Walters was driven by the lapse in ethics she'd already investigated in earlier stories and wanted to bring to account those who preyed for profit on the unsuspecting. Once their research was under way, both reporters were moved to even greater effort by the individual stories of pain and suffering endured by people who'd been on the receiving end of bad drugs. In other words, from the start, the Blind Faith project was 'motivated'—invested with the reporters' collective curiosity and their conviction that the secrets were worth every effort to reveal. It's unlikely they could have withstood the frustrations of the research and the hostility encountered along the way had they been only mildly impressed by what they were uncovering.

This series highlights again the importance of support from top management, not only in the sense of the time and money required to see the series through, but also in terms of moral support. Both Buist and Walters noted that they began the project with a question and a hunch, and precious little more. To launch a major investigative project with so little on which to proceed took courage on the part of the reporters, and integrity on the part of the newspaper management that backed an effort hardly guaranteed, as with all investigative work, to yield results. As Walters noted, the *Spectator* would surely have been less likely to give the go-ahead had less experienced and trusted reporters brought the story proposal to their attention.

The reporters, and Buist in particular, took pains during the interviews to concentrate discussion on the issues—the need for safeguards throughout the drug-approval and marketing processes, and for complete transparency over health concerns. It's easy for reporters to get into a 'good guys–bad guys' frame of mind and to adopt that format in their stories (conflict being the common frame of so many daily news reports). Instead, these reporters built a kind of tension that runs through the series, keeping the reader focused on the larger problem. They neither shied away from the hardest-to-hear personal stories, nor failed to explore who and what was responsible. And although it isn't quite as simple as the good versus the bad, the stories still flushed out both heroes and villains, and the reporters unflinchingly drew their portraits without sentimentality.

They knew the research had to be thorough and precise, in keeping with the hard facts that showed vulnerable people at risk in a situation that invited conflict of interest among powerful corporate entities—another example of where investigative reporters can't afford to get the details wrong.

Like Anne McIlroy covering the David Healy affair (see Chapter 7), the reporters were surprised to find university administrators and tenured faculty afraid to go on the record to speak to an issue that could hardly have been more a matter of the public interest. One story likened the relationship between the industry and the academy to a 'scrambled egg . . . unlikely to be unscrambled'. That the university needed the drug firm money and that the drug firms needed the university's researchers (and ultimately their seals of approval) justified scrutiny of both the academy and the industry. It called for transparency and accountability in their relationships.

The dramatic stories in Blind Faith of those victimized by bad drugs put a human face on the main issue, but the issue remained the focus: how to revise the system so as to prevent the drug disasters fomented by for-profit corporations operating with impunity behind the closed doors of the supposedly public academy. The series spelled out the separation between the disinterested pursuit of knowledge that is the academy's professed raison d'être and the maximization of profits for return on investment that is the corporation's.

The immediate impact of the Blind Faith series was ostensibly limited to local reaction and increased awareness of the possible dangers presented to consumers by prescription drugs. The longer-term impact of the series is more difficult to assess, and that's why in reportage the pursuit of truth, the defining goal of all investigative reporting, appears to proceed as if by relay race. Northrop Frye wrote years ago about how great literature (the so-called canon) comes from other great literature that preceded it in time (rather than from the minds of individual writers). And the idea that progress depends on our ability to 'stand on the shoulders' of those who went before is commonplace in every area of human endeavour, including the common law.

So it is in the literature of investigative reporting. Other journalists before Buist and Walters had approached the issue of drug safety, albeit from different perspectives. A great example is the Faint Warning series that was featured throughout the week of 16 February 2004 on CBC Radio, Television, Newsworld, and online at www.cbc.ca. The series had involved a five-year access-to-information battle to get the federal government to release the Canadian Adverse Drug Reaction Information System, a database of adverse drug reactions reported to Health Canada.

The issue of drug safety continues to make headlines. For instance, a little more than a year after the Blind Faith series ran in the *Spectator*, and almost exactly two years after the withdrawal of Vioxx from the North American market, the *New York Times* published a report about a widely used heart-surgery drug with potentially lethal side effects that its developer, Bayer AG, had failed to disclose to the US Food and Drug Administration (FDA).[9]

Investigative work, once it achieves a certain momentum, tends to cut across borders and categories. Yet the kind of 'turf' possessiveness that marks competitive professionals in so many other lines of work seems remarkably absent among investigative reporters. When reporters from one paper or broadcast station see colleagues from other papers and stations pick up on the issues they first explicated, they don't think, 'Hey, that's our story.' Instead, they applaud the new work as a sign of success, because success in investigative work is measured in impact—progress toward action to right the wrongs uncovered.

Reporters with integrity and passion for the world outside their own skins realize only too well that no single story can have the desired impact of many stories, continuing to report what some would rather keep hidden, following up on every lead, building on and making reference to each other. Operating in this fashion, journalists can serve a larger and greater purpose. They can help to further knowledge above and beyond disseminating 'the news'.

# Endnotes

1. The third of the three reporters, Luma Muhtadie, was unavailable for an interview. She left the *Spectator* shortly after the series ran to pursue an advanced degree in health sciences at a US university.

2. 'Risks, Rewards & Research', *Hamilton Spectator* (25 June 2005), A1. This first story of the series reported that the drug company was facing thirty-five lawsuits in Canada over Vioxx. It included a statement from the manager of public affairs for Merck Frosst Canada defending the company against allegations that it failed to properly monitor the drug and disclose its potential dangers.

3. 'Worry grows as MDs prescribe drugs for unapproved uses', the *Hamilton Spectator* (29 June 2005), A1.

4. 'A bitter pill', *Hamilton Spectator* (29 June 2005), A6. Neurontin was originally made by the drug firm Warner-Lambert, which was bought by Pfizer in 2002. The television program from which Joan Burgess learned about the side effects of the drug and the resulting lawsuits against the company revealed that Pfizer's Warner-Lambert division had pleaded guilty to charges of illegally and fraudulently marketing the drug for off-label uses and settled its various civil and criminal liabilities with $430 million US.

5. Walters worked for the Canadian Press before moving to the *Hamilton Spectator* and still speaks affectionately of the national wire service and the kind of team efforts and lack of 'star system' mentality that characterize the organization and its dedicated staffers.

6. Somerville is a professor of law and medicine at McGill University and the founding director of the university's Centre for Medicine, Ethics and Law.

7. 'A bitter pill', *Hamilton Spectator* (29 June 2005), A6.

8. Dana Robbins, 'Sometimes blind faith is a roll of the dice', *Hamilton Spectator* (25 June 2006), A2.

9.   Gardiner Harris, 'FDA Says Bayer Failed to Reveal Drug Risk Study', the *New York Times* (30 September 2006), A1. Harris reported that the giant German pharmaceutical company Bayer AG had failed to disclose to officials study results indicating that one of its heart surgery medications, a drug called Trasylol, could increase the risk of death and stroke. Harris wrote, 'The disclosure comes exactly two years after Merck announced it was withdrawing its arthritis drug, Vioxx, after a study showed that it doubled the risks of heart attacks. Since then [regulatory officials and top scientists] have concluded that the FDA lacks the regulatory authority and the money needed to detect and protect against drug dangers.'

Part Two

# Documenting the Truth:

# Computer-Assisted Reporting

# Chapter 9

# Nowhere to Go

In the fall of 2001, *Toronto Star* writer Kevin Donovan set out to write about the lives of Ontario's developmentally handicapped and ended with not one storyline, but two. The first showed how bad provincial government policy and planning had stranded a pioneering generation of parents who eschewed institutions to raise their special-needs children at home. The second uncovered widespread abuse in the group homes that had replaced the institutions of a previous era.

In the 1950s, Ontario's social services ministry began encouraging the parents of developmentally challenged children to raise those children at home and help them lead fuller lives in their communities. In earlier decades, parents had followed the advice of government and experts—they placed their infant children in the large institutions that then existed as caregiving centres for special-needs kids. In such institutions, the children would grow up, spend their lives, and die.

The Ontario government fully funded the large centres where children then labelled 'mentally retarded' were sent to live. What that simple fact belies is *how* they lived. One of Donovan's stories referred to a 1960 Ontario government film, *One on Every Street,* to show the kind of isolation in close quarters that characterized the lifestyle endured by the institutions' inhabitants, many of them children. In one infamous Orillia institution (once called the Asylum for Idiots), misbehaving youngsters were forced naked into bathtubs filled with ice—a common procedure unblinkingly dubbed 'ice-packing'. The institution also ran a farm where it worked selected children to exhaustion, burying two thousand of them in mass graves (only two hundred of the two thousand graves bore names) on the same farm.

It would have been hard to argue with the provincial government's seemingly enlightened change of attitude when it began advocating a new policy: instead of a system to 'warehouse' children with special needs in sterile institutions where they frequently suffered abuse, a home- and community-based effort to embrace and accommodate them. By the 1970s, the counter trend to deinstitutionalization was standing government policy; by the 1980s, all but three of the previous decades' institutions had been shut down. The move to deinstitutionalization saved billions of dollars for the provincial government, which in turn promised financial aid to the parents who had pioneered home care.

But Donovan found that financial hardship was commonplace for these parents—many of whom had given up careers to stay home and act as primary caregivers for their developmentally handicapped children. He found woefully inadequate provincial government funds overall, with thousands on waiting lists for aid, and glaring inequities in the distribution of the paltry sums available. Among those who cared for their developmentally handicapped children at home, a few families got lots of money, and some got a little, but most got next to nothing. Because people with developmental handicaps had no legal entitlement to government funds, and because only those who complained the loudest and longest got funding, the patchwork provisions and inherent inequity persisted.[1]

Decades later, the children raised at home were grown, and their now aging parents were seeking to make arrangements for them in the inevitable event of their own deaths. But they found hollow the earlier assurances of government that such supports would be available when the time came to make arrangements for their children. By then, most of the massive institutions in Ontario were closed and the group homes that were supposed to replace them were already overloaded, with long waiting lists for available spaces. An entire generation of courageous parents who had forged the home-care movement discovered just how empty were the government's promises of help. They would go to their own graves not knowing what was to become of their grown but still vulnerable offspring, forced to leave them with literally nowhere to go.

After the provincial government closed the big institutions, it created hundreds of group homes, but these could hardly accommodate the more than seventeen thousand developmentally challenged children in Ontario who had been raised at home. Whatever spaces there were in group homes generally went to those who had been displaced from the large institutions when the latter were closed. Thus Donovan had identified a crisis that was only getting started in 2001. 'For every adult with a developmental handicap,' he wrote, 'there is a child just entering the system.'

What Donovan discovered had further policy implications. He was able to show that even the money the government did spend to provide care and services to the developmentally handicapped didn't add up; that the ministry could do more for the developmentally handicapped if it stopped treating them as a homogeneous group and started paying attention to individual needs. Its $940 million budget for developmental services was inefficiently apportioned. The bulk of it (roughly two-thirds) paid for some thirteen thousand people in residential or institutional care, while the remaining third went to support those cared for at home, whose numbers were *five times* greater (roughly sixty-five thousand). That translated into little more than $4,000 a year per family.

When the caregiving parents died, the grown children were typically placed in government-sponsored group homes, at a cost of $55,000 to $65,000 yearly per person. The numbers indicated the looming crisis: Several *billion* dollars would be needed to finance group homes or alternative solutions for the thousands on waiting lists. The waiting lists themselves were a sad joke, since most people on them were waiting for spaces that didn't exist. That in turn often meant the developmentally challenged were being *misplaced*—in hospitals, nursing homes, and other institutions unequipped to address their needs, and, ironically, at much greater cost than that of a group home (had these been available).

Donovan knows how to target his readers' sense of justice and compassion. The lead story in the series delivered a direct hit, showing a 41-year-old developmentally handicapped man found beside the body of his dead mother in their Windsor, Ontario, home, waiting for her to wake up. He had been waiting for twelve days.[2] A postal worker who came to the door finally alerted authorities and the man, still uncomprehending, was taken to an emergency placement. He represented one of many such individuals displaced by the policy shift that had begun in the 1950s.

To tell this part of the story, Donovan talked to caregiving parents, government officials, social workers and activists, and of course to the handicapped themselves. Then he traced the problem back to its roots in government failure to honour or even understand its own policy directives and exposed some of the tragic results these had engineered.[3]

Donovan put this policy-inspired dilemma in a nutshell with a pithy two-liner: 'The plan that saw parents replacing institutions as primary caregivers was widely hailed as forward thinking. It relied on one key factor: parents who lived forever.'[4]

For the second storyline of the series, Donovan used computer-assisted reporting to analyze three years' worth of 'serious occurrence reports' obtained through Ontario's Freedom of Information and Protection of Privacy Act. It had taken the *Star* more than a year to get the documents released. The reports were supposed to be filed with the Social Services Ministry following allegations of abuse, or when residents died, were injured, or went missing. The ministry was then supposed to examine the cases and do its own investigation where warranted, but it rarely carried through on this part of its mandate. Even when abuse was confirmed, the workers responsible were not necessarily fired; the outcome was left to the discretion of individual agencies. There could be mild or even no repercussions for people shown to have abused their vulnerable charges. The records revealed that most of the reports were simply stamped 'received' and filed away, and that even when the allegations of abuse amounted to criminal activity, police were often not alerted.

The documents revealed 274 cases of abuse of people with developmental disabilities by workers in group, foster, and other home-care establishments from a sample of agencies that served about half of the thirteen thousand people in residential care across Ontario. Analysis showed that roughly 4 per cent of those in care had suffered abuse at the hands of their caregivers. Although only small numbers of paid caregivers were abusive, the reported cases themselves were severe. These individual stories of abuse defy apathy *and* understanding: for example, a young man beaten bloody by a drunken group home worker for wetting his bed;[5] another young man forced, by way of 'discipline', to spend a night in the freezing outdoors, after which seven of his frostbitten fingers had to be amputated.[6]

The stories of theft, beatings, and sexual abuse that Donovan uncovered didn't tell the whole story, since they represented only those cases that had been reported in a three-year period—the proverbial tip of the iceberg. Moreover, of the 274 incidents, only twelve had been investigated. Chronic underfunding in the developmental services sector and spotty oversight by Ontario's Social Services Ministry meant that no one knew how many other cases went unrecorded, uninvestigated, and unpunished. One critic suggested that such abuse by generally underpaid and overworked staff in the sector (the worst-paid 'bottom rung' of the Social Services Ministry) was becoming 'normalized'.[7]

In the 1999 case where a man was forced to spend the winter night outdoors and subsequently lost seven of his fingers, the incident wasn't reported until an outside social worker heard about it and alerted police (an act that eventually led to the conviction on criminal charges of the two workers responsible). In the case of the man beaten for wetting his bed, the truth began to come out only after the worker was summoned by the local Association for Community Living. Eventually arrested, he pleaded guilty to assault and was sentenced to a year in jail. These cases represented two of hundreds reported to the ministry over the period covered by the abuse reports.

It's fitting to introduce this book's section on computer-assisted reporting with a series by Kevin Donovan. Donovan leads the investigative team at the *Toronto Star*, itself not only the country's largest circulation daily, but also its undisputed leader in investigative reporting (though hot on the *Star*'s heels and gaining fast is its much smaller sister paper, the *Hamilton Spectator*). Donovan is also among the reporters who launched computer-assisted reporting in Canada, writing one of the earliest CAR stories in 1995. Considering twenty years of his award-winning reportage, he called Nowhere to Go 'probably my favourite'. It consisted of seven stories that ran over four days in late October 2001.

# The Interview: **Kevin Donovan**
(11 April 2006)

Nowhere to Go originated with a tip from a source on one of Donovan's earlier series about Ontario's child-welfare system.

> I had worked on a project on child abuse and the failure of Ontario's child-pro-tection laws, which are of course once again in the news.[8] I developed a contact out of that; it was a social worker, a professor actually, and she had emailed me and said, 'This is something you should really look into—you did a good job on the child-abuse series.'[9]
>
> This is someone who had helped us on that story. At the time, I didn't know anything about developmental challenges except for when I'd gone to school I had some kids that I was friends with that had Down's Syndrome and other issues. And I always remembered that, and one kid in particular that had a rough time at school. So I filed a bunch of freedom-of-information requests. It would take a long time to get the information I wanted.

Stories often find their way to Donovan in the *Star* newsroom: 'I'm sort of like the lightning rod around the *Star* for when tips come in.' That's partly because of his rep-utation among readers as a sympathetic reporter, and also because of his long-time link with investigative reporting at the *Star*. He was made an investigative reporter at the *Star* in 1989, only four years after starting at the paper, eventually becoming head of its investigative unit, which he reorganized in June 2005.

On the Nowhere to Go series, something about the plight of these families struck him hard and got lodged in his conscience.

> I had a tough time getting my head around it, but what really attracted me to the story, because I'm a parent of young kids, was the concept of parents who had these adult children. At the time, my kids were 1 and 3—what I call the heavy-lifting part of parenthood. I was imagining what that would be like, if my children, when they were 50 and I was 80, needed my care. So that's where I got the idea.

Then, once I started talking to all the parents and social workers and spending time in group homes, it was very compelling. I always knew going into the story that the main issue would be getting people to read the story, because statistically only about 1 per cent of the population has a connection to somebody with a developmental challenge. I don't do stories just so people will read them, but you do want people to read the story. And I was always trying to figure out ways—like the parent angle seemed to be a really good way—to explain the story to people, because unfortunately in our society we don't pay too much attention to these families.

The stories presented Donovan with a cast of characters whose roles represented some of the heights and depths of human behaviour.

On the abuse side, it was hard to imagine how anybody could abuse somebody who's so vulnerable; on the other side of the series, I was just trying to imagine how parents could devote so much love and attention to somebody for so long, and what really hard work it was. I remember one fellow, a young man named Robert. His dad would take him into the shower—he was about 30 and the dad was 50 or 60, and they were just amazing. I was struck by it.

After receiving the initial tip from his social worker source, Donovan started filing requests for information with the Ontario government.

One of the things I asked for was serious occurrence reports, which have to be filed in group homes if there's an incident of abuse or injury or death. I also filed for a lot of financial requests, and I got publicly available information from the Public Accountants of Ontario, which is what I call the government's chequebook—all provincial governments in Canada have them. That gave me the annual payouts to group homes.

So I filed a lot of those requests, and those actually took about a year and a half to get. They charged us $3,500, which we paid. At the *Star*, fortunately, unlike many other papers, we can afford these fees. What we always do is pay it, but we appeal at the same time. That was the first case where we did that and won, and actually got a cheque back from the government.[10] That fee is a drop in the bucket perhaps to the *Star*, but a lot of journalists use [information requests] now, including smaller papers, because it's an order that's out there that says government information should be available to the public. A lot of good things came out of that.

Many reporters say it's become much harder to file successfully, that access requests have become impossibly difficult. Before the province's freedom-of-information law came into effect, much information was routinely available. With the advent of the law, much of that once-routine information came under its 'protection'—now, reporters must file for it. Though he agrees that freedom-of-information requests have become more difficult to negotiate, Donovan believes there are still things reporters can do to increase the chances of success, such as streamlining the request.

> I think reporters have to be much wiser when they file their requests than they are. When I first started doing requests, I would always ask for everything, and that's actually quite unreasonable. You have to do a lot of reporting to find out what you're looking for. I remember in 1990, 1991, when the Freedom of Information Act came into being in Ontario, I was doing a series of stories on one of our local governments here which actually ended up with several councillors being charged and sent to jail.[11] Up until December of 1990, there was no Act, so I would just go into the council office and flip through everything—just tonnes of information, which you would never get today.

The story involved the city of York, one of six municipalities that comprise the Greater Toronto Area. The city councillors had 'hooked up with a bunch of the developers and there were a lot of shenanigans'.

> So I was able to look at phone records and expense records very easily, as soon as I wanted to. Then, when the Act came into being on January 1 [1991], I remember I was presented with a piece of paper that I had to fill out. I joke that it's been downhill since then in Ontario.

It's a commonplace complaint among reporters of investigative stripe: the various freedom-of-information acts have actually made it more difficult, not less, to pry loose information from government holdings. Despite the headaches, Donovan has no intention of backing off on access requests, because they can pay huge dividends.[12]

> On this request [for Nowhere to Go], the government really did drag its heels. But in the course of all the reporting, a lot of changes were made, even before we published, because they were so concerned that the *Star* was about to do this big story, so they did start putting a lot more money into the system.

One of the great things about journalism, and investigative journalism in particular, is its reliable unpredictability. The reporter never really knows what will turn up when the search begins; at the same time, it's a given that there will be surprises somewhere along the way. When Donovan was researching Nowhere to Go, he discovered that his subject had a long and rather distinguished history at the *Toronto Star*.

> Back in the 1940s and '50s, Beland Honderich, now dead, was our publisher. He wrote some stories about developmental challenges, and his stories were all

about how they needed to set up institutions. Then in 1960, Pierre Berton, who was a columnist at the *Star*, wrote stories about how the institutions should be closed and people should live with their families. And then I come along, twenty, thirty years later, and do a story [saying] that's great, but now they really have nowhere to go—again. I didn't write about that, but I found all this stuff out when I was researching the story.

With all its twists, turns, and frustrations, the series ultimately exceeded Donovan's original hopes for it.

I did not know that I was going to get anything on abuse. When you make one of these FOI requests, you shoot an arrow in the air. I asked for a specific type of record filed at a specific time. I remember I had gone down to Windsor to interview some families and was flying back, and I had just received the documents. I'm sure the people on the plane thought I was nuts, because I felt like I wanted to throw up when I was reading some of these reports.[13]

Donovan was also able to get 'plugged into' a group of social workers known as adult protective service workers, who acted as watchdogs in a system otherwise devoid of people mandated to oversee operations and intervene when necessary. These workers comprised a network of inside information for the burgeoning investigation.

These guys always seem to be about to lose their jobs in Ontario, but they deal with these small communities. In fact, it was an adult protective service worker who intervened on behalf of the fellow you mentioned who lost seven fingers. Well, the story was known to everybody in that community. And nobody was doing anything about it until she stepped in and went to the police with information and had charges laid.

The adult protective service workers were some of the heroes (unsung until Donovan's series) who helped the stories materialize by providing background information and tips, and securing access to families willing to share their stories. Donovan credits those families with helping bring the scandalous situation to light.

Quite often, they were really, really good about it, and they would also be good at getting me in to talk to social workers or executive directors at the various agencies that look after the individuals, and who were all, I must say—a generalization—but were actually really helpful to deal with. They were also completely unused to dealing with the media, because very few people write about these situations. There were some stories I've worked on where it's been really hard to get people to talk, but this was not one of them. The families were ready to talk . . . because, except for the social workers, they really felt that nobody [in the media] had paid any attention to them at all.

Many of the workers involved in the field were also aware of the problems, but had been frustrated at being unable to do much about it. They, too, needed to talk.

> I think it's hard for the people who work in these communities, who are quite poorly paid—in fact, they're the lowest paid of all the social services personnel in Ontario. It's hard for them, just on a day-to-day basis. 'What do I do all day? Well, I help a 50-year-old man get dressed and maybe go for a walk in the garden, and that's a really good day.'

Donovan was particularly taken with the story of Arlene Kennedy, a young woman who was placed in a psychiatric ward because no group-home openings were available.[14] Entering the world three weeks premature in a difficult birth, Kennedy was diagnosed with cerebral palsy at six months. She was cared for at home until she was 20, when a health crisis led to her placement in an unsuitable institution—the psychiatric ward of a hospital. 'Outside her door,' Donovan wrote, 'is a maelstrom— hard-to-manage psychiatric cases who lurch, shamble, and scream.' She spent ten years there before the unrelenting efforts of her father, a retired RCMP officer, netted her a spot in a group home. Ironically, the group home, where Arlene was happy and enjoyed a much higher quality of life, cost about a third of the $175,000 annually it did to keep her institutionalized.

Arlene's story provided a defining moment for Donovan, when he realized that in her case—and perhaps in many others—the problem wasn't the usual lack of funds, but rather the tendency in large, bureaucratic organizations for employees to proceed via automatic pilot, indiscriminately following rules and orders without grasping the true nature of each individual case. Instead, a single (supposed) solution was routinely offered for thousands of people treated as identical because they had developmental handicaps. Arlene, for example, was capable of living more independently and eager to move to a group home.[15]

> She was just in the wrong place. And her dad, this great guy, could not get the government to realize that there was a better and cheaper alternative. Because of our involvement in the story, they were able to help her out and do the right thing for her, and she's having a great life.

Arlene's story led Donovan to an important insight. The first stories in the series had concentrated on the need for more money in the system, but that, Donovan learned after considering Arlene's case, wasn't the root problem.[16]

> Something struck me. We don't actually need more money in the system; we really just need to spend it more wisely. It was when I interviewed the family and

met Arlene. I met with her on quite a few occasions. She's such a delightful person, and here she was in this psychiatric facility, just because that's where she ended up being. That was costing taxpayers—and yet this other great organization in London could look after her for a third of the amount.

Although Arlene's story had a happy ending, for most aging Ontario parents of children with disabilities, the situation was bleak and becoming intolerable.

There are some families out there who are quite good at lobbying for their child, but the majority are not. They are just scraping by.

Official intransigence—from stonewalling access requests to refusing interviews—presented the major obstacle in writing the series.

As far as difficulty, the government was really hard to deal with. They dragged their feet in giving us the records, and there were certainly some agencies [where] it was difficult to get them to talk and answer questions, particularly about the abuse. But they all did ultimately.

You'd think it would be fairly damning for government officials in this sector to refuse to respond to a reporter's questions. But in Ontario, as elsewhere in the country, reporters are more and more directed to public relations people, or worse, websites. Even senior reporters from large, prestigious media outlets find themselves less able to gain direct access to important sources. 'So often, we end up talking to the public relations person,' Donovan said. To write Nowhere to Go, he needed access to the executive directors of the group homes, especially those where abuse had been reported.

There was one—Onondaga—that had a number of cases, and some pretty brutal cases. We decided we wouldn't publish the story unless we got them to explain why something happened and what they were going to do about it. It took a bit of diligence with them. But with the families and social agencies, really, it was a bit like a tap opening up. They wanted to tell the story.

Aside from securing the reports through Freedom of Information and dealing with reluctant agency directors, Donovan found he had to educate himself, and then do some consciousness-raising work in his own newsroom. That he learned much in writing about a subject he previously knew almost nothing about partly explains why the series ranks as one of his favourites in a long career of hard-hitting investigations at the *Star*.

> I think there was a little bit of education I had to do, too, at my newspaper. I'm very fortunate to quite often get my stories on the front page—I've been around here a long time. But this was not the obvious story. I did a series on charities, and that's an easy story to sell. [Nowhere to Go] was one where I remember when I would be talking to senior editors, I'd have to say, 'Well, we used to call these people mentally retarded, but we now call them developmentally or intellectually challenged.' It really took a while, just as it had done for me, because I didn't know anything about this. Reporters should always learn on the job.

If he had it all to do over again, Donovan would wait to see the records he requested through the province's freedom-of-information laws before beginning the reporting phase. For Nowhere to Go, he began reporting before the access request netted results.

> What I try to do myself, and with other reporters now, is you file the request, you work hard on it, but you get other stuff done until you see the records. The reason I did it that way [started reporting before receiving the reports] was that I really didn't think I would get the information that I ended up getting through Freedom of Information.

He would also have tackled related aspects of the story and given them fuller treatment, whether in additional stories or in sidebars. 'There were some families that had special issues that were not general to the broader story—one can always think a little bit faster.' His only firm regret about the series is that he was not around to do the immediate follow-ups. The day the series started running, Donovan was on assignment in Afghanistan.

> The story resonated with a lot of people. We had a young reporter who did, I think, one follow-up. But I should have been there—I always follow my own stories. That was just difficult. In Toronto, reporters—and I'm probably one of them—are philosophically opposed to covering other reporters' stories. Really, I think it's important to follow your own stories. This one was kind of funny because a lot of the reaction was already in the story, and a lot of the Harris government, shockingly, ended up throughout the time of the investigation increasing supports.

Why shockingly?

> Shockingly, because you know, everyone thinks, 'Harris government: bad.' But [the increased supports were] because of [current federal environment minister] John Baird who was the social services minister. He had some family member who was affected. So this was his cause, and all the social groups loved this guy

and were sorry when he left, because he was really a champion. I remember just before we published, I interviewed him and showed him stuff to get his comments. And I was expecting him to say, 'There's no problem in the system.' But the first thing he said was, 'Yeah, we've got a problem, and we're trying to fix it.'

Though he would like to have done 'a better job of following up', Donovan's confident about the story's immediate impact. The longer-term impact of the series is more difficult to assess.

It's hard . . . you work on so many different projects. And you can make a career of following each story. Eventually you realize you've got to move on to other things. I've been working on a series of stories about some doctors and a methadone treatment program, and there have been some very easy follow-ups to that—a task force is being set up. There are some stories where there's an obvious follow-up and reaction, but in the case of Nowhere to Go I really do believe that the *Star*'s commitment to it caused [authorities] to make a lot of changes.

Donovan's own path to investigative reporting led from a summer internship at the *Star* in 1985 to becoming the editor for the paper's investigative team.

I always wanted to be a reporter, since I was about 15. I ran for student politics in my school in grade 9 and lost, and was able to get a job for no pay at my high-school paper. And then the grade 13s all quit and I got an office in a bathroom, and a darkroom—I never had a locker in high school. My buddies and I worked together on that. And then at university I ended up being the editor of *The Gazette* at Western [the University of Western Ontario]. So that was always what I wanted to do. When I came to the *Star*, the first four years were just solid general assignment reporting and going all over the place. Then I noticed—it was obvious—that I wanted to go deeper into stories and I wanted to be on the front page more. So I ended up working with a variety of reporters here on bigger stories. In 1989, I won a National Newspaper Award and the *Star* set me up as an investigative reporter with one other guy, long since gone. And that's what I've done ever since.

He did a brief stint in the mid-1990s in the dual roles of junior editor and investigative reporter.

That I found very difficult—to do both jobs at that time; I hadn't really thought it through. And then we had a lot of big stories . . . some I was editor of; others I was the reporter for. About 1998, I said, 'Look, I can't do this any more; I've got young kids. Give me one job.'

I don't want to give up being a writer. So we've got this arrangement now that's still in its infancy, where I don't have a dedicated group of reporters—which I'm trying to get. But we've decided to wait on that a bit. Instead, from different departments, if they have an idea, they report to me, although I keep their department head in the loop. I try to help them with the reporting and conceptualizing how to write the story, and then other people take over when it comes to putting it in the paper.

Donovan has spent his entire career at the *Star*, a paper with an unparalleled record of investigative reporting. That he still sees room for improvement tells you something about the kind of dedication that characterizes his work.

We could do a lot better. The best ideas, my best ideas, have always been my own. My mom had a great idea once, and my wife's had one, too. Friends come up with stuff; people call in with tips. Editors don't come up with great ideas; they're not in the field.

He often thinks 'about what makes a great investigative story or project' and believes the initial idea is 'the key thing'.

I think editors—I am one now—tend to sit around and go, 'Hey, let's look at child abuse,' or, 'Hey, let's look at the energy market in Ontario.' And that's totally the wrong way to do things. You need to have a guiding light, like we had on this methadone story—a person in the background who had put a lot of the story together and came to us with it. We had to do a pile of work, but we knew there was a story. The art in investigative reporting, and the way to really make it grow at the *Star* or the *Globe* or any place in Canada, is to come up with a great idea.

And it's not always a long, drawn-out affair. Some investigative pieces can be dispatched fairly quickly.

There are some, like the one I did last year, that I had always wanted to do. It didn't take very long; it was on lawyers in Ontario. I had always noticed that lawyers were convicted by their law societies of stealing, and I had a hunch that they were never being prosecuted. It was really easy to do. A lot of the records— probably all the records—were publicly available. We just had to analyze them and do the reporting on it. I love a story like that where going into it you quite quickly know that you've got a story.

Great ideas can erupt anywhere, provoked by anything from a chance encounter to a back-page news brief. The trick is to remember that there's almost always a story once you scratch beneath the surface and keep digging. 'A nice tip from a government source,' Donovan added, 'doesn't hurt either.'

On the other hand, investigative reporting isn't for everyone, and for those hoping to launch themselves as investigative reporters, Donovan's advice is a little counter-intuitive.

> One thing is don't go to a newspaper and say you want to be an investigative reporter—or a foreign correspondent. Because it sort of sets up all these [expectations]. Few people can do this job. In fact, most people around here don't want to do this; nobody's saying, 'Doesn't Kevin have this great job.' There's so much time you have to spend with one issue, and I think that most reporters by nature want to do the quick-hit, front-page stories, which are great, and obviously we need a lot of that.

Echoing Robert Cribb, his colleague on the *Star*'s investigative team, Donovan said aspirants must be prepared to burn the midnight oil, and pay for it to boot.

> The advice I would give if you are trying to move from general assignment to doing investigations is you basically have to do it on your own time. That's what I did, and it's often a young person's game, because you can't be doing your eight-hour shift, and then looking after your kids, and then trying to break into the field of investigative reporting. So I would do my general assignments at the *Star* and then totally on my own time, not paid for, I would go out and dig up stories.
>
> And as for general advice for getting into the business? Personally, I think it's the most fun job in the world. It exposes you to so many different issues and people. I would say don't go into it unless you're really inquisitive and imaginative—that's what makes a really good reporter. And I think the writing can come; I was a dreadful writer when I started, and I think I'm a good writer now.

To 'great writing', he does not even aspire. A desire to write was not the thing that led Donovan to the business in the first place.

> I enjoy the writing, but I think I enjoy the investigating, the interviewing, and trying to get people to admit stuff they don't want to, way more. I like the chase, the hunt. When you do get a job at a paper or radio or TV station, you have to pay your dues and do a lot of general assignment reporting, which is so important. In fact, it's a good idea to mix it up even once you do get that great job as an investigative reporter, to do shorter stories as well.
>
> When SARS hit [in 2003], the managing editor said, 'You're always doing these long projects. Do you want to do this investigative stuff but on a daily basis?' And I said, 'Yeah, I'd love to.' That was great—I am addicted to the daily newspaper even though I don't write for it very much. And so that's really

helpful. You remember; you get out there. When I'm working on a story now, I'm always in the same issues, but if you go back to daily reporting, you suddenly remember, there's the police beat and the health beat and the legal beat—it's just helpful.

When Donovan interned at the *Star*, he was up against some sixteen other interns for a permanent job. Four of the sixteen were hired.

It was like that for a number of years and now we have this one-year intern program, and then the summer program. We seem to have a lot of the intern jobs, but we unfortunately hire very few young people.

Some commentators believe that investigative and issues reporting, and in fact any kind of in-depth reporting, will move away from hard-copy newspapers to magazines, books, and online sites. Donovan noted a decline in investigative reporting at newspapers, but said he believes the decline is temporary or cyclical. For the foreseeable future, he's sticking with the press.

Well, I'm biased. I don't think it's dead. I do think that fewer and fewer people are doing it. My goal at the *Star* in the next few years is to try to get more people doing it and more people from different areas of the newsroom. Like any place, we have our usual suspects, and they're great, but my goal is to get a great business investigation, a great entertainment or sports investigation—I think readers would love to see that sort of stuff.

As an aside, talking about interns, I'm working with a reporter, a young reporter who's 24, whom I worked with on these methadone stories. We have this year-long program; she's on till August, and I'm trying hard to get her hired. Her goal is to be an investigative reporter, and she's really, really good at it. She went to the *Star* and said instead of the rotation being city, business, entertainment, sports, for my year, could I do a couple of months in this investigative unit I've heard about. That was her idea, so young people clearly do want to do it. And I like to work with young reporters. They don't necessarily think every story has been done, and that's great.

Investigative reporting is just asking another question. So I think we need better coaching in newsrooms to get reporters to push stories a little bit harder than they push them right now. But I don't think it's dead. You see it at awards time—everybody wants to submit and be nominated and win an award. It's really a matter of having people in positions like mine encourage people to do this.

The *Star* is clearly proactive in this respect. A case in point is the racial profiling series the paper ran in 2002 documenting unequal treatment for the city's blacks at the hands of police.[17] The stories, which involved a team of five reporters, won all kinds of awards. (The series also provoked the Toronto police to launch a $2.7 billion lawsuit against the paper—a suit eventually dismissed by the courts.)

> That was totally Jim's idea. [Jim Rankin is the reporter/photographer who led the five-reporter team assigned to the story.] It took him over two years to get that information and he fought tooth and nail for it. And he got it, and he got it in the paper. It's pretty amazing, and that's just Jim, sitting at his desk—you've talked to him, right?—he's very quiet.

It can be hard to keep up the idealism, though—a problem well known among veteran reporters.

> It's hard on a bad day. Reporters can get pretty down on themselves and their organization, I find. It's hard, but I know that when reporters do a story, a good story that strikes a chord, they can get a lot of respect from the public. Newsrooms are dysfunctional places. I'm pleased to hear that people came to the *Star* and thought it was a great place.[18] And I think it's a great place. But I'm like a Pollyanna. Many people get bitter. But, you know, there's nothing like a good story to raise them out of their bitterness and to cheer them up.

Generally speaking, Donovan worries about readers (not reporters). Are they reading these major investigative takeouts? In the case of Nowhere to Go, he's confident of audience interest.

> Everybody who could get to a newspaper and knew about developmental challenges read the story, because we got, I think in the first day, a thousand emails.

On the subject of computer-assisted reporting, the cutting edge in investigations, Donovan is the man to consult, his influence foundational. One of the earliest pioneers, he helped introduce CAR to Canadian newspapers. When he began learning CAR techniques, though, he was just as intimidated by the newness and the jargon as the next person. (A comma-delimited file? Say what?) But it didn't take him long to get rolling. In fact, Donovan's first big CAR project in 1995—on public housing in Ontario—was one of the first in the country.[19]

> What happened was that John Honderich, our publisher at the time, had gone to a conference in New York, and came back and sent me this email: 'What do you know about this computer-assisted reporting?' There were no PCs in the newsroom at the time. I didn't know anything about computers . . . except I had a word processor.
>
> My wife actually suggested the (story) idea. She said, 'There's something going on with social housing. The NDP government has put all this money into it,

and there don't seem to be any checks and balances on all these projects they're building.' So I went to the government and asked them for electronic data, which was a shock to them. They actually gave me the information, but I didn't know anything about relational databases or even the spreadsheet, so I got the *Star* to buy me a computer. I had the first PC in the newsroom.

Then I went to a course in the States—it was the NICAR [the National Institute for Computer-Assisted Reporting] spring conference. And I remember being so nervous because I didn't know really what to ask people. I am fairly technically astute now, but at the time, I didn't know even how to ask for what I needed.

When I came back, Jim Rankin, Carolyn Mallan (who's not here any more), Dale Brazao, and I did a series called The Money Pit, and that was such a great little CAR project. I remember Dale—he's Portuguese and a great all round investigative reporter—and I were talking about it. And I said, 'You know, it looks like the worst company that seems to be doing all these shenanigans, financial and otherwise [with housing units], is owned by a Portuguese priest.'

It turned out that Brazao was familiar with the priest, and had 'heard about him for years'. This background knowledge and Brazao's ability to speak Portuguese added a lot to the investigation and the package of stories that made up the series.

So the Saturday story, the first one we ran, was the omnibus story. And then the Sunday piece was all about [the priest Brazao interviewed]. It turned out he was abusing the seniors—he was getting lots of money from the government but treated them just awfully in their housing units.

There's no question in Donovan's mind that the power of computer-assisted reporting can do a lot to strengthen investigative efforts. When he was appointed to head the investigative team at the *Star*, he made beefing up the paper's CAR assets a priority.

When I got my job [leading the investigative unit in the early 1990s], I said I want to hire a CAR analyst just like the Americans do. And we ended up hiring this fabulous guy named Andrew Bailey from the *Buffalo News*—he sits just behind me right now. What had happened was that Jim [Rankin] and I over the years had developed some ability in CAR, and we ended up doing everybody's technical work for them. Most reporters, I think the world over, have a hard time with a spreadsheet, let alone anything more complicated.

That's a big plank of mine with my little group here—to do more of that. This fellow we've hired is just so beyond anything. He's so great. Andrew's not a reporter, he's just really, really good with data and understands newsrooms. He's a librarian/researcher. When I was interviewing people at the *Buffalo News*, to try to make the decision, they said he's a great guy, but he seems to be spending too much time on CAR projects, and not enough time in the library. Great! And so we're just getting started, but we did a series on train derailments across Canada in the last month or so. And he did the analysis for that.

The reporters come up with the ideas, and then Bailey helps figure out how to provide statistical and other analytical backup. Donovan said the addition of Bailey to the staff of the *Star* made the paper the only daily in Canada to have a CAR analyst on board.

> He's into all this other stuff where he's trying to figure out how to do it. His latest thing is what they call 'Web scraping'. The *New York Times* has about twelve CAR analysts now. A big thing for the future of CAR is where you have these programs that can actually link into the government websites that have all the bad water reports for the Ontario government, let's say. And instead of having a reporter go through all these PDFs and make an Access or Excel datasheet out of those, there's a program that can actually go and find those forms and then put it all into an analyzable format. We're trying to do some stuff on that right now.

## Commentary

The main lessons to be had from Nowhere to Go come not so much from the computer-assisted reporting skills that Donovan had honed over the previous six years, as they do from his tenacity in getting the necessary records released, his independent thinking on the policy issues, and, most importantly, his focus on the ideas at the heart of the story.

Of course, I do not mean to downplay the importance and potential of computer-assisted reporting. With its advent, journalists no longer need to rely on commentary from 'experts'. They can crunch their own numbers to do their own analyses, thereby helping to increase the transparency of the press and, thus, its credibility. The coming of CAR may also put an end to a certain anti-intellectualism in newsrooms (which seems to have faded over the years, in any case, probably as educational levels and salaries have risen for professional journalists and individual reporters have become frustrated with the often superficial nature of their work). If this strain of anti-intellectualism ever had a place in newsrooms, its days are now numbered and most reporters are glad of it.[20]

Donovan's series shows once again that the coils of access-to-information laws are worth navigating, despite the difficulties clearly entailed. Acquiring government records through access requests can be difficult—and by all accounts is becoming more difficult—but the battle is still worth the spoils. In the case of Nowhere to Go, the information requests helped bring to light the abuse reports themselves as well as the fact that the vast majority of incidents were not investigated. When trying to access government information, persistence is often the better part of valour. The first line of resistance for a government department unwilling to release the information you've requested is to just say no. If the reporter can be dissuaded by this initial refusal, and many can be, the government learns how well the strategy works and the information remains locked away. Thus the battle to pry loose government data that ought to be public is a battle for more than information—it represents the larger struggle for freedom of expression and the public's right to know.

Access requests may provide raw data, and CAR techniques may help reporters analyze those numbers to define the subject under study, especially when the numbers are large or unwieldy. But at the heart of the story are the reporter's ideas and, especially, questions. For example, the abuse reports that Donovan finally received from Ontario's Ministry of Social Services showed hundreds of incidents of abuse. Using computer analysis, he was able to show what percentage of the whole these represented. But no report and no computer came up with—or could have come up with—the questions that shaped the series: How could such horrific abuse of some of society's most vulnerable members be occurring daily in government-sponsored facilities? How did we get here? What's wrong with the current policies? What are the underlying issues?

Donovan's astute explication of those issues revealed how central bad public policy and planning were to the creation and persistence of the problem and its related injustices. These were pressing issues that if not for the series would likely have gone unidentified and unobserved, remaining invisible to all but a handful of experts and the beleaguered families of the developmentally delayed. Notice as well that before Donovan tried to explain to his readers the intricacies of poor government policy, he made them care. He showed readers real people suffering from the effects of the policy, and the utter failure of authorities to act. He confronted them with a publicly subsidized nightmare that elicited collective outrage, if not collective shame. He told them the horrifying and heartbreaking stories of vulnerable people abused with the help of public money.

But he also made sure that the stories revealed enough background and context to engage readers in a search for solutions, not just villains, and to provoke them to informed response rather than resigned passivity. He rewarded readers for caring by showing that solutions and happy endings are also possible. The young man found waiting beside the body of his dead mother was sent to live in a house with one other person, where the two were helped by a social worker for eight hours each day. He was learning some life skills and hoping to eventually land a job in a restaurant. The father of the young woman virtually imprisoned in a hospital's psychiatric ward finally won her release and a more suitable placement. 'I loved the picture that we used of Arlene on the front page,' Donovan said. 'Because it was not a depressing picture at all.' A couple whose son suffered from spina bifida, along with both developmental and physical handicaps, finally secured annual government funding that allowed them to continue caring for their son at home after they staged a news conference at Ontario's legislature with the help of their local MPP.[21]

We tend to think of investigative reporting as hard-hitting, as motivated by an avenging spirit bent on setting right what is wrong. And these qualities are certainly characteristic of the enterprise. But there's another deeper quality that doesn't generally receive as much attention or praise: compassion. Donovan's Nowhere to Go series exemplifies the kind of compassion that, along with courage and curiosity, goes into the making of an investigative reporter. The initial tip for the story came from a professor of social work who knew that Donovan cared and because he cared, could and would do an excellent job. To sell the series to his editors, Donovan engaged in educational efforts to combat some of the sleepy assumptions and biased terminology that threatened to downplay the newsworthiness of the story he wanted to tell. And before Donovan could hope to pierce such preconceived notions in his newsroom and among his reading public, he had to recognize and redress them in himself.

## Postscript: The Beginnings of CAR in Canadian Newspapers

Full management support is an undisputed boon to the investigative CAR project, but it was reporters, not managers or editors (no matter how sympathetic), who pioneered computer-assisted reporting in Canada. Bob Bergen, a University of Calgary–based scholar and former *Calgary Herald* reporter (who worked for the paper until 2000), was among the earliest practitioners.

In 1993, Bergen used CAR techniques that were then in their infancy to write a story for the *Calgary Herald* about financial land dealings and the planned expansion of the Calgary Stampede.[22] Bergen was then a veteran at the *Herald* but still a novice at CAR. He did, however, have a computer at home. 'It was an old IBM clone, with a drive A for the program and a drive B for the data—and that was it.' As well, he had some background in statistics, having begun to use statistical software in the late 1980s while completing a master's degree at the University of Calgary. The *Calgary Herald* newsroom of the early 1990s, meanwhile, 'had a mainframe' and was 'in the process of switching to Macintosh computers for pagination'.

> It was all mainframe. Reporters used to share terminal access. There would be a terminal between two reporters and you'd use that to write on . . . that was the state of the art.

Bergen was nevertheless able to convince his editors at the *Herald* to get him a site licence on his computer for Microsoft Excel, a spreadsheet program. He became the only reporter in the newsroom to avail himself of such 'high technology'.

> And then, in 1993, when the assessment data came out in the spring, and the [managers of the annual Calgary] Stampede were thinking about expansion and talking about it, I thought, 'Well, now is our opportunity to get a hold of the assessment records—but I'm going to have to do the data entry.'
>
> What you're supposed to do is compare your assessment to your neighbour's assessment. If your house is the same as his house and his [assessment] was lower, you could argue yours should be lower. But nobody had ever gone and taken the entire neighbourhood before, which is what I did—there were more than three hundred houses in it. We started finding that there were multiple numbered companies and they were registered to the same law firm, but I didn't know that at the time. All I was doing was entering the registered owner, the registered owner's address, [and] the value of the property assessed.

The newsroom as a whole had failed meanwhile to embrace CAR or even accept the inevitable intrusion into the newsroom of steadily advancing communications technologies. For example, reporters' Internet access was restricted. (At the time of this writing, many newspapers continue to restrict reporters' Internet access.)

> When I was there [at the *Calgary Herald*], there were two hundred Mac terminals and there were three connected to the Internet. The publisher believed that the Internet was the 'smoke break' of the 1990s, meaning that people would [use it as an excuse to] goof off. If you wanted to go on the Internet, you had to go to the librarians, who were now in the newsroom because they were computerizing the electronic records. So, out of two hundred, there were three terminals that were attached to the Internet—and that was as late as 2000.
>
> I left in 2000 after the strike at the *Herald*. And I went up to the University of Calgary—that's where I'm working. We've got an information commons here; there have to be 250 computers in the information commons, and each of them—Macs and pcs—is hooked up to the Internet. I'm thinking how foolish it is that a newspaper, which is supposed to be a knowledge industry, is not hooked up to the Internet—it doesn't make sense at all.
>
> I like the *Globe and Mail*'s philosophy. They hired about thirty-odd journalists and expanded their newsroom and coverage. And it's [motivated by] a belief, similar to the New York Times's, that people will read a newspaper if you give them a good one. In order to give them the best one, you need journalists—and lots of them.
>
> When I look at a front page of the *Calgary Herald* from 1980—I've got one in front of me here from 1982, and there are four stories. . . . Now, all you've got are headlines and graphics. It's a different mentality. They're just filling the white space around the ads in [some] papers now—I call them glorified shoppers.

Bergen believes that the most important thing about seizing and fulfilling the potential of computer-assisted reporting is stressing the journalistic aspects of the work.

This is not social science, this is reporting. I've always believed [in that distinction] and it's the philosophy I brought into journalism. The summer before I went to journalism school, I watched the Watergate hearings in their entirety, and I thought, 'That's what journalism is for.' It's not just a case of filling the white space around the ads, as we cynically used to say in the newsroom. No, we have a social purpose, and I think that computer-assisted journalism is a very powerful tool in meeting those social responsibilities.

# Endnotes

1. 'Parents cajole for dollars', *Toronto Star* (29 October 2001), A1. Donovan compared two families with similar special needs—one received $108,000 a year and the other $5,000.

2. 'Nowhere to go', *Toronto Star* (27 October 2001), A30.

3. 'Portraits of courage', *Toronto Star* (27 October 2001), B1. In this story, Donovan focused on seven families who had made the decision to care at home for their developmentally delayed children and who were seeking to arrange accommodations and care for those grown children following the deaths of the family caretakers. Except for one three-and-a-half-year-old boy, the age of the developmentally handicapped people profiled in Portraits of Courage ranged from 23 to 49. Time was running out for the brave and dedicated parents who had launched the first generation of deinstitutionalization.

4. Ibid.

5. 'Beaten bloody for bedwetting', *Toronto Star* (28 October 2001), A9. The article told the story of a developmentally delayed man of 32 who was badly beaten by a worker in a group home in Oshawa after he wet his bed. The man became agitated and woke the worker, who had arrived two hours late for his shift and then fallen into an apparently drunken stupor that was interrupted by the disabled man in the next room. The worker beat and bit the man, drawing blood, then went back to bed. In the morning, the worker took the man to a doctor, claiming his injuries had resulted from falling down stairs.

6. 'Adults beaten in group homes', *Toronto Star* (28 October 2001), A1. The incident occurred in 1999 at a group home in Geraldton, Ontario.

7. Ibid.

8. Donovan was referring to the trial in the tragic case of Jeffrey Baldwin, a 5-year-old boy who died of malnutrition on 30 November 2002 while in the care of his grandparents. Subsequent events showed there was ample reason to refuse the grandparents as proper custodians, but when they applied to the courts for custody, no one checked the records.

9. The series, co-authored by Moira Welsh, was titled Children at Risk, and ran in the *Star* in April 1997.

10. 'Public has right to abuse records: Ruling', *Toronto Star* (30 October 2001), A3. In this final piece of the series, Donovan told the story behind the story of how the paper had acquired the abuse records in the first place. The *Star* had secured the records—for which it had waited fourteen months and paid $2,587.40—in a landmark freedom-of-information case. The fee from the Ministry of Community and Social Services, which kept the records, was said to be required to cover the cost of photocopying and deleting personal information from the records to protect privacy rights. The *Star* paid the fee and then appealed to the Freedom of Information Commission, arguing that the public had a right to know what happened to people with developmental

challenges who were cared for in government-subsidized group homes and other residences. The commission agreed, finding in the *Star's* favour and ordering the records released.

11. The federal Access to Information Act took effect in 1983; Canada's provinces and territories also have freedom-of-information laws (which go by various names and were instituted at various times). Records are also available from municipalities, either under the provincial access laws or under separate municipal and regional legislation.

12. In his *Media Law for Canadian Journalists* (Emond Montgomery, 2006), Dean Jobb, who teaches journalism at the University of King's College in Halifax, makes a convincing case for why 'no journalist or researcher should doubt the value of such [freedom-of-information] legislation' (339).

13. 'Adults beaten in group homes', op. cit. These stories detailed incidents of abuse in residential care facilities (mostly group homes, foster families, and day programs) across the province, showing that residents suffered beatings, sexual abuse, and theft at the hands of their purported caretakers.

14. 'Trapped: For 10 years, Arlene Kennedy was forced to call a psychiatric ward her home', *Toronto Star* (27 October 2001), A31.

15. Developmental handicaps can result from a variety of ills including oxygen deprivation at birth, autism, Down's syndrome, and illnesses like meningitis in childhood. Many of the developmentally delayed suffer as well from physical problems. Still, individuals categorized as developmentally handicapped, just as so-called 'normal' people, vary widely in the range of their needs and abilities.

16. 'Trapped', op. cit.

17. See Chapter 13 of this text: 'Singled Out: An Investigation into Race and Crime'.

18. Donovan was responding here to comments I made about a contingent of students from the Thompson Rivers University School of Journalism, where I teach. The students visited the *Toronto Star* newsroom in the spring of 2006 and came back raving about the experience, with the sparkle of possibilities in their eyes and their idealism reinvigorated.

19. Kevin Donovan, 'Housing millions down drain', *Toronto Star* (20 May 1995), A1. This was the lead story in an award-winning series called The Money Pit, which investigated abuses in the province's non-profit housing program and found millions of dollars were involved. The reporters, Kevin Donovan, Dale Brazao, Caroline Mallan, and Jim Rankin, spent several months on the series, which ultimately exposed theft, conflict of interest, and gross mismanagement of funds.

20. I use the word *anti-intellectualism* in a prosaic rather than philosophical sense, to refer to that brand of reportage that holds thought and ideas in deep disrespect and assumes that a 'real' news story has no use for them. It occurs to me as I write this that a similar brand of anti-intellectualism remains where you might least expect to find it—in the academies of higher learning.

21. 'Parents cajole for dollars', op. cit.

22. See the following 1993 stories by Bob Bergen in the *Calgary Herald*: 'Hot Potato' (5 June 1993), B5; 'Land Grab? Absentee owners could curb Stampede expansion' (5 June 1993), B1; 'Stereotypes offend resident' (5 June 1993), B5; 'The Happy Hotelier' (5 June 1993), B5; 'Investors the real victims' (5 June 1993), B1; 'Decision time: Victoria Park residents say city must come up with a clear decision Monday on their neighbourhood's future' (16 October 1993), B6; 'Stampede's vision for Victoria Park: Expansion could cost city millions' (16 October 1993), B1.

# Chapter 10

# Nobody's Children

Picture this: Thousands of childless Canadians longing to adopt, thousands of Canadian children pining for permanent families—and a homegrown adoption system working hard to keep them apart.

That's what three *Toronto Star* reporters, Jim Rankin, Leslie Papp, and Tanya Talaga, found when they decided to investigate Canada's adoption practices in the series Nobody's Children. They told the gripping tales of homeless children and would-be parents passionately wanting to adopt, both unwittingly victimized by a deeply flawed system.

The piece that launched the series carried a photograph of a seventeen-month-old boy, cared for in a foster home where he had been awaiting adoption since he was three weeks old.[1] He represented thousands of children growing up in institutions or foster care, their chances of finding permanent homes diminishing with every passing day. The lead put the problem starkly: 'Bureaucracy is a poor parent, but thousands of Canadian children are raised by no other.'

In 2001, when the series was written, an estimated twenty thousand Canadian children were without permanent homes. Most of these children were wards of the state, and without changes in the system they would remain so. The various agencies across the country responsible for domestic adoptions found homes for only a fraction of these children (about 6 per cent).

The series concentrated on Ontario, which had once led the country in progressive adoption policies but by the start of the new millennium had fallen far behind. In their quest to find out why, the three *Star* reporters—writers Papp and Talaga, with writer/photographer Rankin—did their own undercover survey, built their own province-wide database, and used computer-assisted reporting to document an ongoing tragedy.

Posing as prospective parents, the reporters checked out all of the province's fifty-two children's aid societies. Then they compiled the results in a database, analyzed those results, and pinpointed where the societies were failing. They found a confused and fragmented system, a virtual 'crazy-quilt of practices', where each society—funded and mandated by government but run privately by a voluntary board of directors—ran its own show, handling adoptions as it saw fit. Some agencies simply sent people away; others discouraged would-be parents with long wait-lists and bad attitudes.[2]

Prospective parents in Ontario were moreover unable to shop around for the most proactive society. They had to deal with the one operating in the area where they lived. Each agency compiled its own list of parental candidates, precluding access to those outside its 'jurisdiction', and there was no electronic, province-wide database that could link children needing homes with families wanting to adopt them.[3] The system had been working at cross purposes, without even a complete paper list of potential adopters.[4]

The underfunded system lacked shared standards and was packed with disincentives, including that people had to wait for years just to find out whether they were eligible to adopt. Foster-care arrangements were emphasized over the more expensive process of seeking permanent adoptions. There was even a law that blocked adoption for the 75 per cent of Crown wards whose birth families enjoyed court-ordered access to them.[5] Ontario was spending heavily on child protection but had more children living as Crown wards than ever before. In fact, the Ontario societies were united only by a dismal success rate, finding homes for less than 10 per cent of the children in care.[6]

Most of these children got moved from one foster home to another—sometimes sent back to their birth families only to be removed again months later—until they turned 18 and 'aged out' of the system. A history of repeated foster placements, critics noted, was related to emotional problems found in the children thus shunted about.

Most prospective parents, meanwhile, wanted newborn babies. A few people procured infants, but largely from the for-profit, private firms that had entered the adoption field since 1980. One critic quoted in Nobody's Children claimed that the 'culture of the courts' was to blame—the system was serving parents and 'maybe even lawyers' at the expense of the children.[7]

The adoption system hadn't always been such a mess. Ontario was one of the first provinces to establish a child-welfare system, and in the 1960s and '70s its children's aid societies had found adoptive homes each year for thousands of the province's wards; by 2000, the number had fallen to five hundred. The children had changed, too. In earlier decades, most Crown wards were given up as infants by their unwed mothers; by 2000, the vast majority were children removed from troubled homes.

Meanwhile, Canadians wishing to adopt but frustrated by a lumbering bureaucracy at home took their searches private and overseas. Despite the high cost (a minimum of $35,000),[8] some two thousand Canadians a year travelled overseas seeking to adopt children from other countries, while Canadian children in desperate need of adoptive homes went largely overlooked. The lingering myth that younger and healthier children were available overseas contributed to the problem. One article of the series featured a doctor who specialized in making pre-adoption diagnoses of foreign children from photos and videotape.[9] Another told of a controversial plan being considered by Toronto's children's aid society (CAS) to venture into the thorny but high-profit business of international adoptions.[10]

The story in the series that revealed the dark side of foreign adoptions told of dozens of people who had adopted children from outside Canada, or at least tried.[11] For some would-be parents, the foreign adoptions went well, but other applicants were heartbroken by the process. A corresponding tragedy was unfolding in the foreign countries that saw children adopted out of often desperately poor homes, sometimes against the wishes of their birth families, in a profit-driven private system rife with corruption. In one such case, a Guatemalan family pleaded for the return of a 5-year-old girl who had been adopted by an American couple against the family's wishes. While one court had taken up the birth family's legal challenge, another had authorized the child's adoption to the couple.[12]

Nobody's Children took six months and more than two hundred interviews to complete. These tales of homeless children and prospective families unwittingly separated by a failed system elicited a swell of reader response, earned praise from all quarters, and sparked plans for institutional change. It consisted of eight articles that ran between 29 September and 2 October 2001.

# The Interview: **Jim Rankin**
(6 April 2006)

The idea for the series sprang from a conversation between Leslie Papp and Tanya Talaga. Jim Rankin came on board a little later.

> Les and Tanya were looking first at a wider series, in which adoption would be just one part, but quickly they decided to focus it more narrowly on the Ontario

children's aid societies and their lack of success matching children in their care with prospective adopting parents. From there, they wanted to concentrate on people who were going abroad to adopt babies, mostly from Third World countries. It began a bit broad but got pretty focused on the issue of what's wrong with our adoption system in Ontario. Why aren't children getting placed more often? And where are people getting the children if they are adopting?

The research began, by all accounts, with the reporters talking to the people involved, including the children's aid societies. Papp, Talaga, and Rankin were getting different information from different sources; in order to find out what was really going on, they posed as prospective parents and contacted all the children's aid societies. Then they compiled the responses in a database that allowed them to document and analyze the failings of the province's adoption system.

> That was a neat thing we did there. We devised a questionnaire that we would, undercover, pose to all the children's aid societies in Ontario. And that took a lot of doing, to finally get through to the right people. The thesis was that it's such a hodgepodge of children's aid societies out there and each had its own way of operating that there really wasn't any consistency in the adoption process from one jurisdiction to another. That ended up being a major thrust of the series. So the questionnaire yielded stuff we could actually put into a spreadsheet. It was a basic counting exercise; it wasn't anything too involved. But it did paint a picture of just how hodgepodge the system was.

The research started with Papp and Talaga interviewing people to get the big picture. The undercover questionnaire was a way to bypass the sanitized, public relations face of the issue and get closer to the truth. And the database work not only allowed the reporters to analyze the system but also provided a kind of documentary proof of its failings.

> The questionnaire came after Tanya and Leslie had begun. We came up with the idea sort of after the fact. We thought, 'Okay, we know there's a problem here. How do we document it, look for the extent of it?' I don't remember who came up with the idea—I think Les—but it was a good one.

It didn't take the team long to discover some of the reasons why so few Ontario wards were finding homes. One of the big problems was that the likelihood of adoption receded as the children got older. People wanted babies—infants if possible—who supposedly came without 'baggage'.

> A lot of the children that were up for adoption domestically weren't babies, they came with baggage, with various medical conditions such as attention deficit

disorder or fetal alcohol syndrome. And a lot of parents we found who were looking to adopt didn't want to deal with that. They wanted a brand new baby. Not a great analogy, but it's not unlike when people go to the humane society: 'Do you want to get a kitten, or do you want an old cat?' And that was the kind of situation the kids in Ontario were in—they had passed the 'best before' date. Very sad.

What took the reporters a little longer to ferret out was the link to international adoptions.

We went looking to see where people were going to adopt internationally and we looked at some horror stories that came our way through different adoption agencies. It gave us a different impression of what's happening abroad. When there's so much money involved, and you're kind of on your own as an adoptive parent, going into a Third World country and relying on a system that is prone to corruption, and when you're talking $30,000 to $40,000 in costs, and much of it is going into the hands of lawyers in foreign countries, it becomes a very shady business. In many cases—the United Nations has documented this—it is a business, and mothers were talked into giving up their babies to receive a little bit of money. There were a lot of horror stories out there.

The story took Rankin to Guatemala to look at adoption practices there. The trip 'served as an example of what bad can come of the whole international adoption business.' He talked to a woman named Irene Lopez de Rosales, whose granddaughter had been given up for adoption, apparently against her wishes. She had tried in vain to locate the granddaughter. Rankin ultimately tracked down the adoptive couple in Knoxville, Tennessee, but they refused to talk to him about the case.[13]

The defining moment for the series came early on in the investigation.

Right off the bat, we were pretty sure there was a story, because it was quite clear that you had this quilt work of CAS's across the province. And whenever you see that, you know that there's no consistency, and it means that there are probably deficiencies.

The reporters found that while the children's aid societies shared a common name, and in fact belonged to a common association, they didn't communicate with each other often or well. All funded by the province, the CAS's didn't follow a single set of procedural rules or meet a common standard.

It's a weird dynamic. The province is involved, but it's left to a large degree up to the individual CAS's how they run their shops. They do get funding through the province but there's no one set of 'this is how you do things'.

I think it became exciting when we were able to put a human face on the stories, find the people who had been through difficulties. And that really made the series stand out, as it usually does—the real people.

We'd actually gone down to Guatemala to look at the plight of that Canadian couple we featured, an older couple, that were trying to adopt their second child out of Guatemala and were having great difficulty. It was around the time that Guatemala was singled out as having some pretty dubious adoption practices. So they were kind of left in limbo, and they agreed to have me go down at the same time they were trying to firm up the adoption. As part of the trip, I hit an orphanage, a local agency that's actually a sister agency to Covenant House down there. It does a lot of work with street kids and mothers, and they go to bat for mothers whose children had been given up for adoption, in some cases unwillingly. That was the case with the little [Guatemalan] girl we ended up focusing on.

Eventually, the reporters were able to find the girl's adoptive parents, though all they knew to begin with was that she had been adopted by a US couple.

We managed to trace back who actually adopted the girl. With a bit of sleuthing, we found out it was a doctor and his wife, somewhere in the States. Just before we published, we managed to find out where they were, and I made the phone call.

That's when he ran up against the kind of resistance that had dogged the investigation all along: some potential sources were simply unwilling to discuss the issues with reporters.

It was clear when we made the phone call we had the right person on the other end of the line. He didn't want to talk about it—at all. He ended up hanging up the phone and didn't respond to FedExed letters or anything else.

The investigation itself nevertheless netted some far-reaching results.

In terms of international adoptions, I think just the process of making phone calls in our investigation into it resulted in some pretty major things. I think in part the closing of adoptions in Guatemala, which happened just after my trip down there, probably had something to do with the fact that we were digging around.

Rankin is a photographer as well as a writer—a 'two-way', as they say—and he took the photographs for the series, compelling photos of children awaiting adoption in various institutions and arrangements of foster care. There's no question it would have been a lesser story without the photographs, but while these visuals added another dimension to the series, getting permission to run the photos presented one of the investigation's most enduring obstacles.

> One of the big challenges was CAS policies regarding pictures of the children, and also the *Star*'s own policy when it came to privacy. Do we identify kids who are disadvantaged or awaiting adoption? It was a bit of a hurdle and it proved to be an issue right to the end, and even after publication. We got permissions along the way, but some of the CAS's were quite miffed after the photos ran in the paper. That was a bit of a hurdle for sure. But in the end we actually did okay and I don't think we did any harm to any of the children.

Timing was an issue, too. The series was supposed to run the weekend after the attacks of 11 September 2001.

> I do remember there was a fair reaction. But it was also post-9/11, like just after, so there was a lot of stuff competing for people's attention. We were actually supposed to go the weekend after 9/11, and it got bumped to a month or two after that.

When it did run, the series got lots of response from the public and praise—even from adoption officials.

> I think it's one of those things: Everyone who was involved, including stakeholders in the system, knew that it could be a lot better and that there were problems and the pieces exposed those shortcomings. And I think everyone involved wanted things to get better. It wasn't a matter of sticking your head in the sand and saying, 'We don't have any problems.' We're talking about children here and trying to find good homes for them. So it's an ongoing issue.

Rankin didn't spring onto the newspaper scene a fully formed investigative journalist. But he didn't waste much time either. He graduated from university with a degree in biology from King's College in Halifax (and says it served him well: 'I wouldn't claim to use much of that knowledge any more, but it's the discipline of thinking that way. It helps.'). He began his career in newspapers as a photographer, not a writer. At the time, jobs for newspaper photographers were scarce, but Rankin managed to work some summer internships after he finished school. Eventually, he found his way back to university—to journalism school.

> I looked around and thought how can I get my foot in the door and get a full-time job. The *Star* has a long history of keeping two-ways—reporter/photographers—on staff. I went back for a one-year J-school degree out at King's College. It was a lot of fun, and it worked. I got hired on as a two-way at the *Star*. Over the years,

the job changed from being a daily guy doing whatever came up that day, some of it pretty police- and crime-heavy, to gradually doing more features.

By about three or four years into my time at the *Star* [in the mid-1990s], I developed a taste for computer-assisted reporting, and it was a very early thing back then. We built our own databases and that takes time. . . . If you're doing that, you're doing an investigation.

# The Interview: **Leslie Papp**
(18 April 2006)

Leslie Papp, now on the *Star's* editorial board, was the paper's medical reporter for years and has worked with the investigative team as both a reporter and an editor. In fact, he was the lead editor on a story we'll examine later in this book, about racial profiling in the Toronto police force.

At the time of the adoption story, Papp was a reporter on the investigative team, and he brought a lot of his expertise from the medical beat with him to the group. He, too, remembers the idea for the series originating in conversation with Tanya Talaga, his successor on the health beat.

The two of us were talking about stories and projects and we both had an interest in reproductive technology like in vitro fertilization. It's one of those areas where there are all kinds of research going on and huge need and also some really ethically worrisome procedures and areas of research.

We thought maybe we could do a multi-part thing on the perils of reproductive technology. So we mapped out this series, and for the last part we figured we'd do something on adoption: This is where you go when the technology fails and you still want a kid. We floated that up the bureaucracy and got the green light to proceed. As we were doing interviews and exploring the various themes, we found out that the most interesting one, and the one that had the most potential for news, was the adoption component.

For a while, they planned to write the series in three parts, closing with adoption. On the advice of their editor, they decided to drop the reproductive technology angle and do the whole series on adoption exclusively.

We were just going to do the perils—the ins and outs and the flaws—of the adoption system, which were many. At that point, Tanya and I thought we could really use somebody else, somebody with some computer-assisted-reporting background. And the advantage of Jim is he's also an excellent photographer. He was kind of at loose ends; he'd just wrapped something up. So we said, 'Do you want to come aboard?' and he said, 'Sure.' The editors thought it was a good idea, so we were off on the adoption project.

It was Papp who came up with the plan to devise a questionnaire, visit the CAS's as prospective parents, and then compile the results of the questionnaire in a database.

> One of the problems was that what we were hearing anecdotally from people who were navigating the system, getting run-arounds and so on, tended to be different from what people would tell us officially, when we were calling from the *Star*. They would tend to downplay the problems and the challenges. So we thought if we really wanted to at least get what the public was being told, we would do this survey. There are over fifty children's aid societies and we just asked the same five standard questions of all of them and then charted that—it wasn't the backbone of the series or anything, but it was just an interesting dimension to it in terms of getting a handle on how the situation varied from one CAS to the next. Even neighbouring ones could have very different policies, very different expectations of how long you can wait, very different rules. Some would just tell you, 'We don't take names.' Others would be far more supportive, and so on. Essentially, it established the huge variance in adoption expectations from one part of the province to the next, and even from one CAS to the one just next door.

Like Rankin, Papp believes the survey work was a peripheral element. The story really began when they started talking to the people involved. While the database provided documentary evidence that helped the reporters analyze why the system wasn't working, the team conceived the idea of constructing a database only after hearing the stories of prospective parents who'd had crushing run-ins with the 'system' of domestic adoptions.

> We were doing the interviews first, before the questionnaire. And when we were doing the interviews, people were talking about shortcomings in the system and the huge number of kids out there. As the dimensions of the problem became clear, we decided to focus our energies on adoption. And once we decided to do that, we thought, 'Okay, how do we grapple with this topic? How do we plumb this topic?' And then we came up with the questionnaire. We got a lot of anecdotal stuff about where the problems were. So the database was a way of making it quantifiable, of documenting measurable information to back up the anecdotal.

In one of his first interviews for the story, Papp spoke to the head of the children's aid society in Toronto, 'which would obviously be a big resource for us and a key player in this whole thing.' The official mentioned that the CAS planned to enter the arena of foreign adoptions as a way to fulfill the domestic demand for babies. But Papp knew that foreign adoptions came with their own set of difficulties and ethical quandaries.

When would-be Canadian parents, frustrated by the Canadian adoption system, went looking outside the country, they entered a world, especially in countries like Vietnam and Guatemala, where bribery, corruption, and baby buying were common. Prospective parents sought babies in virtually 'any land where babies are deemed a burden, where poverty weakens parents' hold on their children, where adoption is quick and final. And always lucrative.' Commercial trade in children continued despite calls from international agencies that cautioned high adoption fees were fuelling the trade. In Guatemala, reports cited evidence of 'widespread child-trafficking rings, involving highly paid lawyers, middlemen who find the babies, and foster homes, referred to as "fattening houses".'[14]

The head of the Toronto CAS, however, seemed unperturbed by these glitches.

> In terms of explaining how the system works, he mentioned that the local Toronto children's aid society, which has a mandate to serve kids only in Toronto—they don't even have a mandate to serve anywhere else in Ontario—at the time was planning to go into the business of foreign adoption, partly as a way of making money and partly as a way [of addressing the demand for babies]. At that point, you realize, 'Okay, I've got a story here.' This is a pretty controversial step. The whole foreign adoption market is fraught with ethical problems. And our local agency with a local mandate is going to go there?

If the plan got the go-ahead, the society would be competing with some twenty private agencies licensed to handle the business of foreign adoptions. As a whole, the provincial CAS's had never done much anyway to dispel the idea that children in the public system were somehow inferior specimens, or 'damaged goods'. But now the Toronto society appeared poised to simply abandon its domestic responsibility and ostensible mandate to find homes for Ontario's wards. (The society did end up proceeding with its plan the following year.)[15]

Ontario's strict privacy rules presented the reporters with another of the investigation's biggest hurdles.

> Provincial legislation protects the identities of wards of the state, so you can't by law name or photograph a person who's a CAS ward without special permission from the guardian, which in this case is the agency itself. The CAS has to give you permission to publicize or reveal that child's name or show that child's picture. So that was a huge, huge barrier to overcome. And we tried. Of course, we'd

have to have the agencies' permission and as we were going along some of the agencies were quite worried about what we were doing and weren't going out of their way to help, and it was really, really difficult.

But Papp persisted, and his persistence, along with his track record, finally paid off.

> We got a lucky break. I knew a guy named Roy Walsh who was the executive director of a large children's aid society in a region. I knew him back when we were both working in a much smaller town called Brantford. I was the health and social services reporter for the paper there, and he was working his way up in the CAS ranks. We had a pretty good relationship then, and so now that he was the executive director of this children's aid society, I was able to reach out to him and convince him of the worthiness of getting kids' photos in the paper, because the main selling point for him was that it really enhances these kids' opportunities to be adopted, to find parents.
>
> So he signed off. And some of the front-page photos and all that became possible only because he was willing to do it. Out of virtually all the children's aid societies in Ontario, he was the only one who gave us that permission.

Papp remembers that the day before the first story ran, the city editor was meeting with the *Star's* lawyer. The two were unaware that the reporters had in fact obtained the permission required by law to publish the names, photos, and stories of the child wards.

> They said there was a big, big problem. The lawyer said, 'I don't know if you're aware of this, but provincial law means we can't use any of these identities and photos and we have to stop it.' And we said, 'Well, we do have permission from the agency.' And then it was, 'Well, okay, go ahead then, that's fine.' But internally, there was concern to the end.

Another challenge in doing the series was entirely internal and had nothing to do with the legal or ethical concerns of the project.

> It just so happened that in April 2001, the paper awarded the Atkinson fellowship to two *Globe and Mail* reporters who were working on adoption.[16] That's the series they had pitched, and it was a multi-part thing, exactly on our topic. We were unaware that they had applied for this, and then it was announced in April. Our city editor said, 'Well never mind, it's totally different, and that's going to run a year and a half from the announcement.' So we proceeded.
>
> The problem is that the Atkinson people were very upset when they heard about our project. They were worried that it would look like we were copying their idea. The publisher is on the Atkinson selection committee, and he was unaware of our project when they awarded this one. The two reporters at the *Globe* were

convinced that we stole their idea and they complained to the publisher and the Atkinson people endlessly, suggesting that ours shouldn't run. So we had to fight that off. There was a lot of gnashing of teeth and as a result, our ability to follow up was really constrained. Normally, when you do a big series like this, a big policy thing, you do follow up with government, keep the heat on. We weren't able to do that, because after this ran, the word came from above: Okay, you guys are off this, that's it.

At one point, Papp said, the frustration had the reporters, among themselves, referring to the beleaguered series as Nobody's Project instead of Nobody's Children. Ultimately, though, the series ran, was well played, and received positive response.

There was that whole internal stress that you have to deal with. But in the end, I can't complain too much: we got a hell of a lot of space, we got a lot of time, and we essentially did the project we wanted. We weren't able to do the follow-ups, but I can live with that.

The Atkinson winners' piece on adoption ran about a year later in the *Star*, but was unable to overcome the problem the *Star* reporters had encountered.

It wasn't bad. I mean, they did a lot of homework. The trouble was that earlier problem that we ran across, the privacy rules. They were not able to find a CAS that would approve photos or identities. It's always good to have the other side of the coin: working contacts. In a sense, it's of mutual benefit. They [the CAS's] got a lot of inquiries after the series ran about those kids that were pictured.

Papp harbours only one regret: the reporters didn't get a chance to follow up on the story of the Guatemalan woman seeking the return of her granddaughter from the Tennessee couple that had taken the girl home to the States after a contested adoption.

Knowing what I know now, it's one of the things that I always regretted subsequently. We went to Guatemala, and we talked to a family there, to this grandmother who was fighting to get her granddaughter back. This was an ongoing process. Originally, we had only the name of the family who had adopted her, and eventually we were able to track it down to a family in Knoxville, Tennessee. We phoned down there, and they refused to comment. And we sort of left it at that. My regret was always we should have been more—we didn't explore that road as far as we should have—obsessive.

But somehow at that time, we'd already been battered on all this other stuff on the Atkinson and [superiors saying,] 'You're going too far.' And somehow just this idea of going there and in person confronting these people and saying, 'We don't think you have a right to your child'—that's essentially what it would have amounted to, though it's not what we would have said. But it seemed like such an intimidating, invasive sort of thing that we backed off.

In retrospect, we shouldn't have backed off. There was a case involved, there was evidence indicating that this child was not properly adopted, and there were efforts being made to have that adoption declared void. We should have gone there . . . and just put them under pressure and made them squirm and made them explain. But somehow at that point we just backed away. We just said, 'Okay, we phoned, they refused to talk, that's enough.'

And to be fair to management, it's not like they said, 'Don't go.' We get a pretty free rein, and we could have gone if we had determined to. Internally, the three of us just decided that, none of us wanted to go. That's exactly the way it went. Nobody had the heart at that point to go that extra step. But afterwards, I was looking at the project, and I thought, 'You know what, that's really missing.' We should have had that; we should have followed the struggle right to the ultimate destination, and we pulled up just short.

Papp wasn't one of those newshound kids just waiting for his chance to be a hotshot reporter. He more or less fell into journalism in his late twenties.

I've got a master's degree in modern European history. And I got the history degree just because I liked the subject. I really didn't think what I would do with it as a job afterwards. After I graduated, I was bumming around Europe and met a couple of journalism students there and a guy who was a freelance magazine photographer. He was working on a book about the Greek islands. And just talking to those people about journalism, I thought I could probably do that. In history, we do a lot of essays, it's all writing. So when I came back, I started thinking seriously about journalism. I had never worked at the school paper or any of that stuff.

He held his first newspaper job at the age of 28.

It was a weekly newspaper in Thunder Bay, now gone, called *Lakehead Living*. And I worked there for about a year and a half and then I got a job at a little daily paper, the *Brantford Expositor*. From there, I came to the *Star*.

Papp is not much for giving advice, especially about investigative reporting, because 'I myself was never an aspiring investigative reporter.' But he has learned a thing or two about it over the years.

My sense is not to be afraid to offend people. I think that's a key thing. Don't be afraid to make enemies. Don't be afraid of the inevitable letters and complaints that are going to come in, because people don't like what you've done. Because often there's an inverse relationship between the outcry from the established people that you've offended and the importance and value of what you've done. So the more the outcry, often the greater the value.

That was certainly the case on the *Star*'s racial profiling story, which netted a nearly $3 billion lawsuit from the Toronto police department. At the time of that 2002 series, Papp was on the investigative team, and served as the lead editor on the controversial series, called Race and Crime.[17]

> It was very, very hectic. Because what often happens here—at the *Star* there are a number of big projects under way—is there's kind of a traffic jam in the fall, where we start running one after another after another. And we absolutely, positively had to have that one done on time. We'd arranged the schedule, I guess, two months in advance, so at this point we have to finish the interviews; at this point we have to do the organizing; at this point we have to have the writing done; at this point, the graphics and editing. And we have to absolutely, positively run on this date. Because there was the Atkinson of that year and all kinds of other stuff that was occupying the key weekend slots. Getting it done to that timetable was really, really stressful. But we did it.

There is a classic newsroom tension between the reporter and the editor. It's the reporter's job to go out there and get the story, and even to fight for the stories that editors may not think much of to begin with. And of course, it's the editor's job to make sure that the story is not libellous or offensive, that it's thoroughly substantiated, and that it reads well. Papp is in a position to see it from both sides, having worked as both a reporter and an editor on *Star* projects. He believes the tension is an integral part of the process.

> I do think it's necessary. I find that with investigative reporting, especially the computer-assisted-reporting stories. Because not every investigative story is a CAR story, but this one certainly was. I find that often investigative reporters, especially doing the CAR stuff, get so into the data and so into the numbers that what they end up producing is more like a statistical report than a news story. And that's when the editor comes in and says, 'Look, we have to translate this into plain English.' And there's some friction there. But you absolutely have to do it; if people can't wade through it, because it's too statistical, then you lose impact.
>
> So that's a tension, especially on CAR stories. And it was a tension on the race and crime series. But it's very common in other ones, where the initial versions, when you look at them, are literally using statisticians' jargon that you have to ruthlessly weed out. The reporter inevitably says, 'But that's the most accurate, that's the way they do it.' And the editor says, 'Yeah, but we aren't researchers first, we're reporters first.' That's always a bit of friction there.

Without this friction, one could argue, some of the greatest stories would never have happened or would not have appeared in quite as compelling form. Editors and reporters push each other, and as long as everyone's ego is subservient to the good of the story and the public interest, it all seems to work out.

> It's always a give and take. I wouldn't say that when these things come to a head, the editor always wins, even at the *Star*, or that the reporter always wins, but it's always a mix and somehow it gets worked out at least to some sort of equilibrium.

The *Toronto Star's* impressive record of investigative reporting makes it a leader in the field. Papp believes that's because it's part of the paper's mandate.

> I think the thing is an institutional commitment, a dedication to it. And there are various reasons for that. Part of it is the Atkinson tradition—public service and trying to make change for the better and all that. Part of it is also that big investigative projects tend to win awards and the newspaper likes to do that. That's another reason for the investment. And once you're committed to doing these things, it tends to attract people who like to do them. So you get a pool of talented people who are able to follow that track, and success breeds success.

There's a lot of talk these days about investigative reporting and literary journalism and other sorts of in-depth reportage moving out of newspapers because of the pressures, mostly financial, in the newspaper business. Some observers believe that because of these pressures, investigative reporting will move from newspapers to magazines and books.

> It's possible. But my sense is that it's a huge investment in terms of time and space, and the newspaper is in a better position to deal with those commitments than a magazine would be. I mean, the profit margins in magazines are far lower than in newspapers. And given that burden . . . certainly if we're talking about internationally highly regarded magazines like *The New Yorker*, then yeah, they can do a serious investigative commitment that's not just a once-in-a-decade deal. They can do a regular investigative component. But *Maclean's* can't, and the vast majority of magazines can't. In terms of books, yeah, there's a possibility there.
>
> But the other thing with investigative stories is that they're a gamble. You can sink a lot of time and effort; there have been stories here that people have worked on for literally months and, in the end, there's nothing there. And you walk away. Even as a writer, you need the security of a big organization for when the ideas don't work out, especially if you're doing really cutting-edge stuff—it's a gamble and sometimes it doesn't work.

One of the other investigative things I did was a look at herbal medicine, where we got a bunch of herbal medicines and submitted them to a lab for testing. It was very expensive. And someone said, 'Well, what if nothing's wrong, they're all good, what would you have done if the tests had come in and there was no scandal?' I said, 'Well, then there's no story and we've wasted a lot of money.' And that could have happened. If you're an author working on a book, where are you going to get your income? For those reasons, I think it's still going to be newspapers that carry the brunt of the investigative load. They're just in a better position to do it.

# The Interview: **Tanya Talaga**
(19 April 2006)

At about the time of the series, a pregnant Tanya Talaga took over from Papp as the *Star*'s health reporter. Talaga also had a personal interest in the story. I remember when reading the series for the first time, wondering if one of the reporters had been motivated by a more personal engagement with the issue. I could feel that personal interest fuelling and saturating the stories—Talaga later confirmed what I'd surmised.

I had a lot of experiences with adoption in my own family, so I think that's probably where my interest came from. My sister was adopted; I had a half sister who was. And I had three uncles that were adopted out as well—my mother's brothers. So it was something that always interested me, because my sister had recently come back into the family. It was in the mid-'90s when we reconnected with her. For me, it was probably quite personal that way. And I was pregnant, and it was my first child, and I knew many people around me who had been trying to get pregnant and couldn't, so they turned to adoption.

With Papp, she had originally envisioned a story on fertility problems, featuring adoption as the last-chance stop if fertility procedures failed.

I actually had thought about doing a big story on fertility problems and leading to adoption, on the trend of women now working a lot and waiting to have babies. It's all over the news now, but that was my thought, to do something on fertility and what happens when fertility fails.

I was the health writer too, and I was just getting into the health news at that point, working with Les. We had talked about doing a series on that. So we put a proposal together for our city editor at the time, John Ferguson. And he suggested just focusing on the adoption end.

Before you go into your city editor's office and propose a project, you look into things. We were looking into things and we were noticing so many people were doing adoptions from China or from elsewhere overseas. Since I'd had that background of adoptions in my own family, I was really curious to know how many children in Ontario were being adopted out.

The reporters knew there were problems in Ontario's domestic adoptions system, but they never suspected the extent of the problem until they started investigating.

We were just appalled and shocked to see that so few were adopted, especially at certain ages. You know that, but it's amazing to see the numbers and how all the different children's aid societies don't work together and it's to the detriment of these children. Of course, you start finding out more things.

We found out about how this law worked in Ontario. If one parent somewhere, or a grandparent I think as well, wanted to be in that child's life, [he or she had legal access]. Even if the person never came to see the child, that child could never be adopted out into a family.[18]

So that child could languish in foster care and never be adopted out because there was someone somewhere saying, 'You know what: No.' That legislation was just changed a few months ago.[19]

Critics had long urged the government to reverse the 'double-bind' policy that denied adopted wards any further contact with birth families. Adoption advocates argued for a third option: adoption with 'contact', a flexible concept that referred to a range of options for ongoing contact, from distance (i.e., not face-to-face) communications through to a kind of 'family' status for birth parents. If the adoptive parents were amenable, 'contact' could even allow for adopted children to be visited in their new homes by their birth families.

Talaga credited the sharp editorial acumen of city editor John Ferguson for a suggestion that provided the series with the focus it needed.

One thing always leads to another, right? I mean, we're health reporters sitting around talking about fertility and the trends and how people are going for all these treatments and how much money it costs. And then at the other end, adoption. It was by process of elimination that we got down to just saying, 'Okay, we don't have years to do this, we only have a limited time, let's just do the adoption.' Our city editor actually suggested that, and it was the just the best suggestion, because otherwise it would have been too big.

She also agreed that the undercover survey was critical.

That was great, because we had Jim on board then and he's really good with numbers and databases. We realized there was no central database matching children and prospective parents. When you start talking to some of the people that work in the field, you approach it like any other story. You ask yourself what are the issues and concerns, how many kids are being adopted out. Some of the advocates told us there is no central database . . . so we realized we had to call all over the place to figure out what was happening.

There was a law that I was talking about earlier, banning adoption when wards have court-ordered access to their families. And there were home inspections, and sometimes people were waiting a long time for home inspections. We started to meet people who wanted-to adopt in Ontario but ended up going to China or somewhere else. They said the system was such a mess that they couldn't access children here. . . . It's all coming back in a flood now.

They had been waiting for weeks or months for home inspections but there weren't enough social workers to go in and do the home inspections; they put them on a list to adopt children. We had no idea how long people were waiting, so we had to call each of the fifty-two children's aid societies, and we thought the best way to do it was pretend we were parents and then we would get honest answers from them instead of being shunted to public relations.

Talaga concedes that the series provoked some change, but she believes the worst problems remain.

There's still no central database matching children with prospective parents. You know how it is as a journalist doing stories on lots of things. But it's sad. It's really sad.

She said she knew the reporters had a story when, after doing the preliminary research, they walked into the city editor's office to pitch the idea.

We knew that there was a story there, and it was going to be good. I don't think there was one moment, like a eureka moment, at all. With something like this, you just mine away at it. You get information, you get to know, or try to get to know, the people that are running the children's aid societies. Some of them, some of the leaders and some of the children's aid workers, were just amazing. I mean some were just far more forthcoming and honest than others.

Aside from gaining permissions to identify and photograph the children, getting people to talk sometimes proved challenging. And while some of the officials were helpful, others took a dim view of the entire project, and made no attempt to hide it.

The Toronto CAS was not very helpful, I do remember. But they are looking at it from a different point of view. They were a little wary of us, being the *Toronto Star*.

But they came through in the end. There were some other great people. Like Judy Grove, head of the Adoption Council of Canada, she was amazing . . . just really interesting things to say. She really knew what she was doing, knew her file.[20] So she was a good resource for us. But getting the kids' pictures definitely was difficult and even getting in to talk to some foster parents—we could not do that in Toronto, we had to go outside [the city].

Like the other reporters, Talaga was disturbed by the lack of opportunity to follow up.

You know, it's difficult. The story came out right around 9/11 and I gave birth at the end of October, so I wasn't around to follow up. If there was some way we could have followed the children to see if they were adopted out after the series, I would have loved to have done that. But I was off for an entire year, and I never went back to it afterwards.

How reporters gauge the impact of their work can depend partly on their initial emotional investment in the issues at stake. Papp noted changes in the Ontario agencies responsible for domestic adoptions, and Rankin mentioned the stories' impact at an international level. But for Talaga, the local impact fell far short of her original hopes for the series. She was, in fact, singularly unimpressed.

Zippo happened, absolutely nothing. I was really pissed about that—that nothing happened, because these are kids and why aren't they being adopted out? And why aren't we paying more attention to them? It's a very sad story. Given all the time in the world, I would have liked to do a lot more on foster care, but we really didn't have the time to do it. And I think that maybe because we were publishing around 9/11 as well, that this really fell on deaf ears. Looking back on it now, yeah.

Although Talaga evinces all the important qualities of investigative reporters, she doesn't consider herself a member of that august company.

We have an investigative team here, and I've worked with them before. We've got a really great team of reporters—Kevin Donovan, Moira Welsh, Jim Rankin, and Les—all great reporters to work with. But no, I don't consider myself an investigative reporter, I just consider myself a journalist. I wanted to be a writer or a lawyer. Then I didn't want to be a lawyer any more after I got involved with the campus press. I went to the University of Toronto and I was the news editor of *The Varsity*. Then I started freelancing. I never went to journalism school; I'm probably one of the last ones hired on here who didn't go to J-school.

The news editor duties at *The Varsity* and her own freelance work provided Talaga with training in the business, which stood her in good stead when she applied at the *Toronto Star*.

> I was doing a bit of freelancing, and in my news editor position at *The Varsity*, I had a staff of students. You know students—they come and go—but at one point I had a staff of forty students. *The Varsity*'s a huge paper.

After editing *The Varsity*, she wrote a chapter in a book published by Key Porter, *The Real Guide to Canadian Universities*. But that 'wasn't really journalism'.

> Then I got on as an intern here and I have been here for ten years. I got hired on at the desk as a copy editor. I had a really good summer when I was an intern. . . . After the summer, I went on the desk, and after that I got hired to be a reporter, which is what I really wanted to do.

Though she doesn't see herself as an investigative reporter and got into the business not for the chase but because she wanted to write, Talaga offered one excellent piece of advice for aspiring reporters:

> Make another call. Always make that other call. That was told to me once, it was during a meeting here at the *Star* with our editor-in-chief at the time, Lou Clancy. I remember him saying that to us, 'When you think the story's done, make another call.' It's always the right thing to do. You always get something. Especially if you have that nagging feeling that maybe you *could have done* another call. Make the other call. That's the best piece of advice. And keep working hard, keep doing it, keep writing. Just get out there and do it. That's the only way to do it—just throw yourself in.

## Commentary

This story required a major commitment of resources that must have taxed even the country's largest circulation daily. It emphasizes the importance of teamwork and the need for support from supervisory and management staff for the investigative effort. At the same time, it underlines a singular and enduring fact about investigative reporting: it proceeds against some sort of opposition. In the case of Nobody's Children, resistance came from several quarters.

To get the truth from the children's aid societies, the reporters had to go undercover,[21] posing as prospective parents. They would have got only sanitized versions of the societies' practices had they simply identified themselves as reporters at the start.

They had to dig to be able to expose the deficiencies of the law (how court-ordered access to birth families prevented children from being adopted, for instance) amid the restrictions of the law itself (privacy rules that forbade publishing photos of children, despite the fact that such photo and ad campaigns had proven effective wherever they'd been tried). The decision to engage in this kind of undercover work is also less ethically demanding, since the reporters were seeking information routinely dispensed to prospective parents—in other words, information clearly in the public domain.

The reporters had further to try to address public ignorance and pierce public misperceptions. Except for the prospective parents who knew only too well of the system's inadequacies, the public at large remained in the dark, and the darkness helped perpetuate the destructive 'system'. The public was largely unaware that there were thousands of children in foster care needing adoptive homes; and among those who did know, misconceptions abounded such as that you had to be married or rich, for example, to be able to adopt a child.

Because investigative work proceeds against all sorts of resistance, it must be unstintingly accurate, thorough, and substantiated. The investigative report that lacks this rigour invites critics to try to invalidate the entire story or series, if not the authoring journalists and their newspaper. The reporters contacted every one of the agencies; they didn't settle for a sample. Understanding the importance of the lesson that Tanya Talaga learned from an editor-in-chief, they made the last calls. (They could have pursued the case of the Guatemalan child further, as Papp noted with regret, but they did locate the adoptive couple, and Jim Rankin himself made the call.)

In this story, as in the previous one, CAR techniques helped the reporters not only to analyze the systemic problems but also to document them. Computer-assisted techniques speak to this need for accuracy and verification in investigative work, where the more the facts are unwanted, the greater the need is for 'proof'. Social workers, adoption officials, and other critics who had taken up the gauntlet in relative obscurity could then use this documentation to lobby for funding and reform.[22]

Just as important to the investigation, however, were traditional reportorial techniques. In fact, the series originated with the anecdotal. Reporters listened to people who'd had run-ins with the system, and realized that the problems were not acts of nature, but acts (or omissions) of bureaucracy. In other words, the work relied in the first instance on 'merely' anecdotal evidence. Note that the idea to compile a database emerged only after the reporters had faced official stonewalling from the domestic adoption agencies and especially after their interviews with frustrated social workers and prospective adopters indicated the scope of the problem. Once again, the investigative series drew its impetus from the stories of real people, not from a computer crunching numbers. Once again, the anecdotal proved seminal.

Recognizing the importance of presenting solutions to the problems they had uncovered, the reporters turned for the final story of the series to British Columbia, where a half-million-dollar campaign had transformed what had been one of the country's worst records on adoption into one of its best.[23] The BC campaign employed, among other inducements, TV spots and newspaper ads seeking to recruit prospective parents, and the provincial government ran adoption services with (presumably enforceable) common standards and services.

And yet the question of ultimate impact is troublesome. The series certainly exposed a confused system and its vulnerable child victims. Just as clearly, it earned reader response and promises of institutional change. But promises of change are not always fulfilled. For example, although the law was eventually changed to remove barriers to adoption based on court-ordered access to birth families, there still exists in Ontario no central electronic database to link prospective parents with homeless kids.

Thus the series, hard-hitting as it was, also underlines the limits of journalistic investigation. Related issues of inadequate child-protection services had been raised before,[24] and the apparently intractable problems, complete with recurring horror stories of children abused and even murdered, went back decades.

Although reforms were promised as soon as the series ran, not much had changed five years later. In 2006, Ontario's newly appointed ombudsman André Marin complained that 'close to 80 per cent of taxpayers' revenue generated by the province [was spent] by private bodies that are unaccountable to the ombudsman.' As an example, Marin cited the 'all privately run' children's aid societies, urging the establishment of an independent watchdog agency to oversee their daily activities.

'We cut them $1.5 billion of provincial taxpayers' money every year,' he said, 'yet we have no accountability for the administrative decisions they make on a daily basis affecting the most vulnerable people in society.'[25]

When the tragic case of Jeffrey Baldwin[26] made headlines about a year after the series ran, calls for change were predictably renewed. But it wasn't until 2006 that the province finally amended its Child and Family Services Act. And even then, the changes addressed some of the problems (for example, the amendment removed the 'access' barrier to adoption) but left others untouched (the children's aid societies remained in business for themselves, without an overseeing investigative agency).[27] The problems of corruption in international adoptions had only worsened.[28]

Even British Columbia, the province the series had touted for its progressive policies in the adoption arena, was under attack for its child-protection services after the 2002 beating death of toddler Sherry Charlie while she was under government-subsidized care. The incident did spark an independent review. It also led in 2006 to a large increase in funds to the provincial child-protection system. But the increase was required largely because of massive cuts to the system inflicted several years earlier.[29]

Clearly, there isn't much that an investigative series, however hard-hitting, can do to address such recurring nightmares when these are institutionalized by governments concentrating on bottom lines, especially when those bottom lines have little or nothing to do with the needs of various populations no matter how pressing the needs or how vulnerable or deserving the populations.

The reporters were saddened by what they found out: Children didn't count for much in the Ontario adoption system, a fact that unfortunately reflected the deteriorating status of children around the world. According to a 2006 United Nations report on violence against children, the vast majority of children around the globe (80 to 99 per cent) suffer some sort of physical punishment at home; in about a third of the cases, the punishment is severe. Neither are children safe outside the home. 'Hundreds of millions of children around the world regularly face violence in their homes, schools and care facilities—in all areas and all countries,' the report advised.[30]

# Endnotes

1.  'Nobody's children: More than 20,000 await adoption, but most remain wards of the state', *Toronto Star* (29 September. 2001), A1.

2.  'Chaotic system discourages adoption; Would-be parents give up on Ontario', *Toronto Star* (30 September 2001), A1.

3.  'Matching system "archaic": Province-wide database could link children with families seeking to adopt', *Toronto Star* (30 September 2001), A9.

4.  In British Columbia, the government had already created such an electronic database, but in Ontario, attempts to centralize fell to lack of funds, lack of co-operation among the societies, and most of all, lack of adopters. In BC, by comparison, prospective parents were vigorously recruited throughout the province and their names entered into the common database. Thus individual agencies were not limited in how far afield they could seek that perfect match. See 'B.C. leads adoption challenge', *Toronto Star* (2 October 2001), A1.

5.  'Nobody's children', op. cit. For the children living as wards of the state in Ontario, the law was a big part of the problem. It said that children whose birth families had court-ordered access to them could not be adopted. As well, adoption and access ruled each other out: even if birth families didn't avail themselves of the right to visit their children in foster care (which happened in about a third of cases), the children still could not be put up for adoption. Because it forbade adoption and birth-parent contact, the provincial law robbed thousands of Crown wards of the chance to find permanent homes—they never even made it onto the waiting list for new families.

6.  'Chaotic system', op. cit.

7.  'Nobody's Children', and 'Chaotic system', op. cit.

8.  'Chaotic system', op. cit.

9.  Tanya Talaga, 'Baby sleuth eases parents' fears: MD specializes in diagnosing babies from videotape and photographs', *Toronto Star* (29 September 2001), B3. The story told of Dr Angelo Simone and his Canadian Clinic

for Adopted Children in suburban Mississauga, which did a brisk business offering pre- and post-adoptive consultations. The service was much in demand because many children adopted from abroad (nearly half) turned out to have medical problems—often infectious conditions like hepatitis B—that would go undetected until the children were in Canada. Also prominent among the children who had spent longer than a year in an orphanage were developmental delays and attachment disorders.

10. 'Toronto CAS eyes overseas adoption: Aid society sees "potential benefits" but plan sparks controversy', *Toronto Star* (1 October 2001), A1.

11. 'Wanted: Babies: Murky, lucrative, and fraught with uncertainty, foreign adoption can bring great happiness along with heartbreak and tears', *Toronto Star* (29 September 2001), B1.

12. 'Wanted: Babies', op. cit.

13. Ibid.

14. Ibid.

15. See Leslie Papp and Jim Rankin's article, 'CAS to run Chinese adoptions amid concerns over placing Canadian children', *Toronto Star* (12 January 2005), A2.

16. The Atkinson Fellowship in Public Policy is awarded each April, and the report is published in the *Star*. See Patti Gower and Margaret Philp, 'Moving foster children off the shelves', *Toronto Star* (29 November 2002), A21.

17. See Chapter 13 in this text, 'Singled Out: An Investigation into Race and Crime'.

18. 'The birth of adoption's new deal? Ontario urged to let adopted wards keep in touch with birth parents', *Toronto Star* (1 October 2001), A10.

19. Reform legislation, including steps to remove access barriers to adoption, was introduced to the provincial legislature in June 2005. The next year, Bill 210 was enacted as Chapter 5 of the Statutes of Ontario, 2006.

20. Judy Grove, 'Waiting for Parents: Canadian Kids Need Homes', *Transition Magazine* 2.3 (Summer 2001). The magazine is published by the Vanier Institute of the Family.

21. I distinguish this kind of undercover duty from the more dangerous type of undercover work often associated with the term. For example, when you compare this story to Robert Cribb's Dialling for Dollars series, the difference becomes clear. In the case of Nobody's Children, there was little likelihood that the reporters would have faced any physical danger had the CAS's learned their questions were orchestrated, and they themselves were *Toronto Star* reporters.

22. Of course, some agencies had already been lobbying for change for years. The Ottawa-based non-profit organization Adoption Council of Canada is an exemplary case in point. A major series in the country's largest circulation daily bolstered the council's efforts to draw attention to the problems and effect change.

23. 'B.C. takes lead in adoption challenge', *Toronto Star* (2 October 2001), A1. The BC government had launched an all-out campaign to sign up adoptive parents. Its record before the initiative had been one of the country's worst: it housed over 1,300 Crown wards awaiting adoption, but had placed only 149. A further 3,600 hadn't even made the adoption list.

24. The *Toronto Star* had investigated the inadequacies of the province's child-protection services in a 1997 series by Kevin Donovan and Moira Welsh called Children at Risk.

25. Don Butler, 'I'm where the buck stops: Ombudsman', *Ottawa Citizen* (2 April 2006), A7.

26. Jeffrey was 5 years old and weighed 21 pounds when he died of malnutrition on 30 November 2002. He had starved to death while in the custody of his grandparents, who were tried and convicted of first-degree murder in his death. At trial, the Toronto Catholic Children's Aid Society acknowledged it hadn't checked the records when the grandparents applied to the courts for custody of Jeffrey.

27. Richard Brennan, 'Province must do more to protect kids: Ombudsman', *Toronto Star* (15 February 2006), A5. André Marin had earlier issued a news release slamming the Liberal government's handling of Bill 210, which proposed amendments to the Child and Family Services Act. 'There is no ability for a citizen to complain to an outside, independent investigative agency about the administrative decisions the CAS make on a day-to-day basis that affect children,' he was quoted as saying. 'How many more cases like Jeffrey Baldwin will there be before the government wakes up and sees that we need stronger accountability, the kind that comes from having an independent watchdog with strong investigative powers?' Such a watchdog agency was not forthcoming. See also a letter to the editor from the director of an Ontario CAS: David Rivard, 'Re: Protecting our children', *Sudbury Star* (20 April 2006), A11. Rivard said he hoped 'new accountability measures' would create the needed safeguards in the child-welfare system and prevent what happened to Jeffrey Baldwin from happening again.

28. Olivia Ward, 'More and more children adopted: Russia tightens adoption rules; UNICEF reports abuse widespread', *Toronto Star* (18 June 2005), A18.

29. Lori Culbert, 'It's time "to support families": $100 million set aside to protect children', *Vancouver Sun* (22 February 2006). See also Chapter 1 in this text, 'The Case of the Disappearing Women'.

30. On 13 October 2006, CBC News Online carried an item on the *United Nations Report on Child Violence*. The study involved 130 countries and was led by an independent expert appointed by the UN's secretary general.

# Chapter 11

# Reservations: Recipe for Disaster

In the fall of 2001, the *Hamilton Spectator*'s Fred Vallance-Jones combined documents research and computer-assisted reporting with more traditional techniques to write a series of stories about unsafe food-handling practices in Hamilton's restaurants. Using the city's health department inspection records from 1995 to 2001, supplemented by more than fifty interviews and thousands of pages of hard copy from the health department, Vallance-Jones set out to identify the culprits. He went after the ugly truth to expose the offending restaurants and reveal that violations of safe food-handling practices were widespread.

The result was a groundbreaking series called Reservations. It gave readers the lowdown on local eateries, calling food poisoning the city's 'silent epidemic',[1] and showed a city-wide inspection system in dangerous disarray. A specialist in computer-assisted reporting and public documents research, Vallance-Jones used database management and spreadsheet programs to analyze the data and found that some area restaurants had not been inspected for years. In 2000, nearly half (44 per cent) of those inspected were found guilty of at least one 'critical food-handling violation'—errors or deficiencies serious enough to make diners sick. Some establishments had been cited for repeated violations.[2]

The work began with a struggle to obtain the electronic data of inspection records through Ontario's Municipal Freedom of Information and Protection of Privacy Act. The battle lasted a year and a half (the city first claimed that it could release only paper printouts), but the last of the records were finally released in September 2001, a couple of months before the series ran.

For a paper the size of the *Spectator* to take on such work (despite its status as the sister paper of the mighty *Toronto Star*) showed massive smarts, enterprise, and courage. After all, newspapers rely on advertising dollars from local businesses, and restaurant ads represented a tidy sum to the mid-market *Spectator*. The most aggressive reportage that the local eateries were accustomed to generally amounted to nothing more serious than a bad restaurant review for a given establishment. To confront a systemic problem of unsafe handling practices and to call to account individual offenders was an exercise in feistiness. Even to conceive of the idea took integrity and backbone. Substantial resources were required and committed: a senior reporter unavailable for regular beat duties for weeks, the close involvement of senior editors, and about $1,000 in fees for the access-to-information requests that eventually won the paper the database information and made the story possible.

Reservations led with the story of a local wedding reception where the catered food had sickened the bride and some thirty guests with food poisoning.[3] Vallance-Jones tracked the couple down on the basis of scant clues from freedom-of-information documents that had most of their information blacked out.

Twelve stories ran over four days, unleashing unprecedented reader response—including anger from local restaurateurs and advertisers. The stories spurred prompt action from city hall to address the problems revealed[4] and once again showed the *Spectator* 'punching', as Vallance-Jones put it, 'above its weight'.

As well as reporting for the *Spectator*, Vallance-Jones teaches investigative reporting at Ryerson University and writes a column on CAR for *Media* magazine. He is also a co-author of *Digging Deeper: A Canadian Reporter's Research Guide* and webmaster of a superb website on CAR for Canadian reporters: carincanada.ca.[5]

# The Interview: **Fred Vallance-Jones**
(8 April 2006)

Fred Vallance-Jones got his start in journalism with student radio at Carleton University, from which he graduated in the spring of 1984. His voice—a wonderfully rich baritone—was made for radio. And radio reporting is what he always wanted to do.

Oh yeah. I was one of those kids who grew up listening to CBC Radio, and I think it was about grade 10 when I decided I wanted to be a journalist, and then I ended up going into radio. I went to a little station in Cornwall [Ontario] for a summer and then did the usual working overnight at the local radio station thing and ended up setting up a bureau on Parliament Hill as a freelancer—before I even left Carleton. So I did that for three years before I joined the CBC.

Fifteen years later, in 1999, and after working for CBC Radio in Ottawa, Charlottetown, Brandon (Manitoba), and Winnipeg, Vallance-Jones went to work for the *Hamilton Spectator*. He didn't find the transition from radio to print difficult.

> Oddly enough, the reporting work wasn't all that different. The essence is really the same; it's the difference in presentation more than anything. In radio, you work with sound and voices—and your own voice, of course. Whereas in print you are writing it down directly and, of course, the style of writing is a little different as well.
>
> Well, it's funny, [but] I think it [radio reporting] actually helped. People often would be of the view that those writing for radio, because they write stories that are short most of the time, couldn't possibly write something longer. That it's really all they're capable of. And I think that's a common error. I'm sure there are some people out there who are like that, but that's not really what I'm talking about.
>
> A lot of people get into journalism because they want to write. But that's not why I got into this business. I got into it because I had this insatiable curiosity. It was more the reporter than the writer in me that got me into this. That served to go across platforms because it was never that I just wanted to be on the radio or I just wanted to see my byline in the paper. That stuff, that ego stuff, has never meant much to me. It's more getting the story and for the audience—whoever that is, whoever is listening or reading—it doesn't really matter.

He sees the business of reporting the news as a collective enterprise, and says it takes all kinds to make a newsroom work.

> I always tend to think that I can't really get anything done without all the people around me. At the newspaper for example, if it wasn't for all the people working daily, writing those daily stories, I wouldn't get to do what I do. Think about by the time a package gets in the paper, who's had their hands on it: the reporter, probably even more than one reporter, several editors, and you have as well the copy editors, photographers, graphic artists. There is a large number of people involved in a story.

While Vallance-Jones believes that the basics of good reporting are the same regardless of medium, he concedes he did struggle briefly with 'getting used to the syntax' while making the transition from radio to print.

> It took a while to not always think in terms of Source 1, Source 2, Source 3, Source 4, and you kind of dispose of each one, with scripting in between, and that's how you do it in radio, typically, just because it has to be linear. You have to lead people from A to B, so you don't lose them. Whereas in print, there's much more of an opportunity to move back and forth. You're often driven more thematically than you are by one source, then another source, and so on. My early print stories all read like radio pieces. You'd have the lead, and then there'd be the first quote, which would be like the first clip, and it would go on like that.

In other ways, though, radio reporting helped to prepare him for newspaper writing. It taught him how to use 'voice'—not only his own distinctive one but also those of story sources. And it was good practice, because radio work 'forces you to write tight'.

> So it helps you in terms of writing newspaper stories [where] you want to write tight. But also, working with sound and working with scenes in radio, I did a lot of documentary work, and that involves taking people to where something is happening and trying to get them to live it, ideally. And you do that with sound, you do that with voices, you do that with expression, and building scenes. That skill, having learned to do that at the CBC, was really useful in print, because I still do the same thing. I still think in terms of building scenes, using words. I don't know if other print people think that way—probably they do.

Print reporting has its advantages, and its drawbacks.

> In newspapers, there's more of an opportunity to go back to somebody. You may return to a source later in the story, whereas in radio it's much more sequential. So the hardest part was learning that. But after I did, I never really found it all that hard. I find probably one of my biggest frustrations sometimes is a push by some of the more traditional newspaper people to take writing back to a more antiseptic kind of bang-bang-bang style, with less room for expression, because that's more traditionally the way newspapers do it. Here are the facts: boom boom boom.

But aren't the facts always provisional in a sense? There really is no such thing as the 'just the facts' of newspaper credo. How can a fact exist without a context?

> Yeah. I think it depends on the story, too. Some stories, where the facts are so compelling, can be carried that way. On other stories, you really need to explain the facts.

Investigative and issues reporters do have to persist. But they also need management support for the projects they undertake. Vallance-Jones praised the *Spectator* for its encouragement of and support for investigative-reporting projects.

I think we live in a bit of a charmed world at the *Spectator*, in that management there has been tremendously supportive of this work, continues to be, and in fact wants to expand the work. [Editor Dana Robbins] is committed to having more investigative stories in the paper this year than ever.

The *Spectator* already does a lot of investigative work, especially for a paper its size.

We like to say we punch above our weight. Which I think is true. No question about it. I mean I think the *Spectator* is on par with the biggest papers in the country in terms of doing investigative work, even though we're really a B-market paper in terms of circulation size. We're 110,000, the average of weekdays and weekends—a little over 100,000 on weekdays; about 130,000 on Saturday.

Plenty of papers in that circulation range don't even dream about doing the kind of work the *Spectator* is doing.

No, and that's too bad. I think that's because sometimes—I've got to be careful how I choose my words here—it's a business, you know, where the guaranteed easiest way to do it in an economical way is to have an acceptable number of reporters writing every day, because that fills the paper. My field is also expensive. Having me work on something for four months or six months—if you think about the kinds of salaries being paid, that's a significant commitment of resources.

And that's before you get into any of the other costs associated with it. I'm aware of that all the time; I think that's one of the pressures of this business . . . you're always aware that every day, the clock ticks by and that's another pile of money for your paper. So you try to work as quickly as you can, but also get the story, which of course leads to one of the greatest battles between investigative reporters and editors. Because editors always believe that investigative stories can be completed more quickly. And reporters always believe it takes more time than the editors think. Somewhere in between probably lies the truth.

Editors and reporters do agree that investigative reporting requires more time and resources, while providing less certainty than, for example, a one-shot story from a 'newser' (a news conference).

It's organic, that's the thing. And so it's driven by the demands of each project. There's no way . . . you can't say one project is going to take a month; maybe it will, but the next one might take six, even though the results seem similar, and it might just be because there was more to understand, there were more blind alleys, the information was more difficult to obtain, the government departments were reluctant to hand information to you, and it took months to gather.

So each one is its own unique beast. The daily news story is more of a cookie cutter. You can be sure that if you go to somebody at nine o'clock in the morning and say, 'I want a story tonight on the mayor's salary increase. Get the other councillors, get a political scientist to comment on it, give some context,' there's a story in the paper tomorrow. That's a predictable beast. The investigative story on the other hand, you're trying to find out why that is, or, even more fundamentally, find out what is and then find out why. And that can take a long time. Because a lot of things you're doing in investigations are finding out things that people generally don't want you to know. So that takes a long time, because they aren't volunteering the information.

It also takes courage, on the part of both the reporters and the paper.

Especially on the part of the paper, in terms of doing investigations. We tend to like to indulge in our research fantasies a little bit, but you're still doing it on somebody else's coin. So there is an accountability factor.

Still, these kinds of stories pay off, not only in terms of prestige for the paper, but also in terms of the greater public good.

Presumably, yeah, if you're telling the truth. And that's the bottom line of what you're trying to do, is to tell the truth, however you define it. But if you define the truth as getting as close as you can to what is verifiable, that's very important for the community, for the reader, because then you're not giving people the he-said-she-said, argument-type story where readers then have to make up their minds whether to believe [the report].

While daily reports, however important, usually provide a simple relay of information, investigative reporting provokes readers to think the issues through for themselves.

Well, you're taking a position. Investigative stories take positions, unlike other stories; they're not opinionated, but they do take positions. They say, 'Here's our best judgment based on our research of what happened here, or what's going on here, and we're going to tell you.' So again, that's another thing that makes this work unique. And a little bit stomach-churning sometimes, because you're going to end up upsetting people in your community and certainly Reservations is a fabulous example of that.

The series was originally scheduled to run in September 2001 but was held back because of the 9/11 attacks in the United States. When it finally did run in late November, the local owners and operators of Hamilton's eateries were not amused.

> We were essentially running stories that were talking about an industry that advertises heavily in newspapers: local restaurants. Normally, restaurants are used to receiving a nice review every day or every second day. And the worst those restaurant reviews ever say is, 'You know, the pâté was a little passé.' But suddenly we were saying that the pâté was going to kill you. And so, yeah, the reaction from the restaurants was not wholeheartedly supportive; but on the other hand, the reaction from the community was unprecedented. I can't recall in all the years I've done this kind of work where I got so many calls. I mean, my voice mail on my desk filled up. There was no more room. And I remember spending one day, shortly after the series started to run, trying to write down all the names and numbers of everybody who had called, and I was so busy doing follow-ups that I gave up. It's unfortunate . . . there were a lot of people who never got called back.

Most of the callers had good things to say about the series. But not all.

> There were a few people who called who weren't so happy. And there was the odd person who said, 'You're muckraking. You're just digging up the dirt here.'

So what's wrong with muckraking? 'Well,' says Vallance-Jones, chuckling, 'there are some people who don't appreciate it.'

The *Spectator* posted a summary version of the restaurant data on its website; readers could go online and check details about their own favourite places to dine. Within days, the site was attracting locals in droves.

> Until we ran the Poison series—Jon Wells's narrative series on a murder that ran about three years ago—they'd never had so much traffic on the website. It really was amazing; it touched a nerve in the community that I've never experienced since. It was the only time I've ever worked on something where the follow-ups and the reactions and the action by city council started to run on the front page beside the series by the second day. After the second day, people were demanding a crackdown, and by the end of the week they'd taken action. It was quite remarkable.

In a departure from the common practice of reporter-initiated investigative projects, this one began with a suggestion from the *Spectator*'s editors.

> The editors had wanted to do something on restaurant safety for a long time. And it was one of things where I think they had even spoken to another reporter who had done a freedom-of-information request for some paper records, but had been somewhat stymied because it was one of those cases where the reporters almost had to ask the officials what was the best thing to request. Officials sort of guided the reporters, who ended up with a stack of useless paper. Since I was

fairly new to the paper and doing this computer-assisted reporting, I said, 'Well, why don't we ask for the database of the restaurant inspections?'

Once Vallance-Jones had acquired the data early in 2001, he started crunching it. Then he was assigned to other duties for a while and didn't return to work full-time on the series until the summer of that year.

He wasn't hired at the *Spectator* as an investigative reporter, but given his acquired CAR skills, advanced quickly to that kind of work and became an undisputed leader in the field.

> I spent a couple of years covering city hall before I started doing CAR on a full-time basis. From the earliest days of my career working at CJSS Radio in Cornwall, I loved to dig into stories. I guess I just have a primal urge to find out stuff that other people want to keep secret. Besides, I see the quest for the truth, such as it can be determined, as the highest calling in journalism. I didn't officially become an investigative reporter until 1996 at CBC Winnipeg. Aside from three years covering municipal affairs, both at CBC and at the *Spectator*, I have done CAR and investigations full-time since.

He acquired his skills in computer-assisted reporting by following his love of digging and his 'primal urge' to find out.

> That goes back to 1994; the Canadian Association of Journalists had a session in Ottawa where they brought in some people from the US, from NICAR [the National Institute for Computer-Assisted Reporting]. I went to that session, because I was just curious about CAR. And I was excited enough about this idea, what you could do with it as a reporting tool, that once I got back home to Manitoba, I went to a Future Shop in Winnipeg and bought myself a copy of a program called FoxPro, which is a database system. It's a little more useful than Access; it's not that much more powerful but certainly Access was in its infancy then, so I started using FoxPro. I took that back to Brandon, and I didn't really do that much with it because I hadn't learned enough in that particular session to really start to use it productively. Eventually, I got a hold of NICAR and then in early 1995, May of '95, I went down to the University of Missouri where they had the boot camps run by NICAR and I spent a week learning how to do this stuff. And that was really where the dam broke for me, because I then saw all the possibilities.

Once Vallance-Jones was able to see how CAR techniques could be used to break or advance stories, it was simply a matter of taking the time to master the technical skills involved. A week was enough to get him launched.

> There are technical skills involved, but computer-assisted reporting is really a way of thinking. It's being able to understand the relationship between data and the real world. That's what CAR is: understanding what databases are, what gets put into them, and what the potential is that you can get back out of them. And once you understand that—of course, you have to have the technical skills—but once you've got that, then you can start to see how to plan. In fact, I remember having a conversation with one of the people at NICAR and asking him what kinds of data people typically went after.

Computer-assisted reporting amplified a trend (launched by the publication of Philip Meyer's classic *Precision Journalism*) to the use of social-science research methods in journalism. In a preface to the fourth edition of *Precision Journalism*, Meyer noted that after the first edition was published in 1973, he was referred to (by *Newsweek*) as a 'computer reporter'. Then—in what the author calls 'the next phase'—the book became better known and journalists began to use it as a how-to guide for public opinion measurement tools such as survey research. But the book 'was never intended to be just about polls or computers,' Meyer wrote. 'My intent then, as it is now, was to encourage my colleagues in journalism to apply the principles of scientific method to their tasks of gathering and presenting the news.'[6]

Vallance-Jones 'got' that, and once he did, he was off and running. He undertook his first CAR project for CBC Radio in Manitoba.

> When I came back to Manitoba, we were hearing a lot about this infrastructure program, because remember when the federal Liberals were elected in 1993, they promised in their Red Book that they were going to spend six billion dollars . . . to rebuild infrastructure as a way to kick-start the economy. Because, remember, there was a depression in the early 1990s. And so I thought, 'Well, they're handing out all this money; they must have a database of all these projects.' So I asked for the data. It took a long time; they didn't want to give it to me. They ultimately gave it to me only in paper form. They wouldn't give it to me electronically.

In the early days of CAR, a routine and simple way to stymie reporters nosing out a story was to agree to provide records in paper format only. In order for reporters to be able to analyze the data, they would have to rekey all the information to make it available in an electronic format that would allow for extended sorting and mathematical manipulations. Only then could the data be subjected to computer-aided analysis. But in this case, Vallance-Jones was stalled at the gate because he was unable to procure the database. Never easily dissuaded, he proceeded to build his own.

I built a database of all the Manitoba projects, by hand, and then I compared. I put each project into its riding and then added in the parties. So I had a field with parties, and a field with the ridings, and I also had the population of the riding.[7] So I was able to work out the per capita amount of money that went to ridings held by the government. And it turned out, not surprisingly, that the government party ridings got a whole whack more money than the opposition ones.

In Manitoba, they divided the money up three ways, and one-third of the money was allocated to what they called a strategic fund, and the strategic fund was essentially controlled by cabinet. So they spent huge amounts of money on dubious projects, such as 'gas-ifying' rural southwestern Manitoba—putting in natural gas lines in tiny little dying communities in that region, which happened to be represented by a powerful Conservative cabinet member in the provincial government named Jim Downey. He came from a small town in southwestern Manitoba, which is very similar to southeastern Saskatchewan. It's small communities, many of them. There's some oil and gas industry, but lots of these small communities had seen better days. Some were drying up, disappearing; people were moving away, schools were closed. The idea was they would hook up natural gas to all these little places. And maybe it was a good idea—I don't know—but that was a very expensive project. And that was one of the ways that the money ended being skewed into provincial Conservative ridings. Eventually, I got another database of the whole country. That was my first big database fight, because the federal [Liberal] Treasury Board was taking the position that they didn't care whether reporters had the right to have it, they just weren't going to give it up. Really, that's what it was.

Vallance-Jones appealed to the federal information commissioner, got the data released, and proceeded to write more stories.

I did some lighter stories, about how the money was spent on wave pools. There was this one little community in Alberta called Bittern Lake. In Alberta, they divided up the money on a per capita basis. So you got a chunk of money depending on how large the community was, period. Bittern Lake was a very small place, so they bought a lawnmower with their infrastructure money. They probably bought some other things as well, but they didn't have very much. What would you call these ridiculous things? It varied by province depending on how the money was divided up, but it didn't all go to building roads.

Like other investigative reporters, Vallance-Jones seems to have an unerring instinct for the heart of the issue.

It was extraordinarily political without being considered political. There would be signs on every street corner about infrastructure money. You know, 'Your government working for you.' . . . In the end, in Manitoba, it was a little skewed to the governing party because each province decided how to split the money up within that province. Across the country it probably built a lot of infrastructure, a lot of sewage plants and roads and so on. In Manitoba, it was biased toward the provincial government, the Conservatives, and they found a way to make this supposedly non-political program political. Across the country, I think it was more a little bit of fun.

So, what does that turn into on radio? A series? A documentary?

Exactly. You had to go out and find people, and find things with sound [and commentators]—absolutely. Not really much different from writing a big feature for print.

The proverbial reporter's aversion to math is a potential hurdle in the future of investigative reporting of the computer-assisted, social-science variety, but it's a hurdle that can be addressed and overcome. And the future according to Vallance-Jones will favour reporters who are numerate.

A lot of people get into this because they want to get as far away from math class as they possibly can. And I think there's still room for that. But I think the window's closing. More and more newspapers and broadcast outlets are at least giving extra credit to people who come to them and say, 'I have CAR skills.' But you and I both know that for most of the journalism that's done in this country, you don't need these kinds of [highly developed mathematical] skills. Yes, numbers are involved, but normally they're numbers that are handed out.

But even numbers that are handed out can serve to trip up the reporter who cannot 'read' or analyze them.

Absolutely, get beyond the spin. What I tell students is that a budget is itself a spun document. Most think that there is nothing more sterile, more objective, than a government budget. In fact, it's not; it's full of tables and facts that are presented in order to make a certain picture appear to be true. You could easily pick a hundred other tables that would show how terrible all these policies are. I think a lot of reporters don't get past the seven press releases—the handout message. So that's the way budgets get reported.

When he teaches his course in investigative reporting at Ryerson University's School of Journalism, Vallance-Jones doesn't need to address mastering the fundamentals, including basic math. His students are already proficient.

Remember, I'm teaching investigative reporting. So by the time they get to me, I'm not teaching basic skills. I'm teaching them how to use computer-assisted techniques to work on investigative projects.

He completed his bachelor's degree in journalism at Carleton University, and believes an education, including one in J-school, should be broadly focused. If Vallance-Jones were advising somebody who wants to break into the newspaper business, he'd suggest not setting your sights too narrowly.

If you're going to get a university degree, get as broad an education as you can; learn some basics that you can use later. As you know, at Carleton they quite a long time ago adopted the idea of the broadly balanced degree between the practical and the liberal arts.

The debate over the proper mix of theoretical versus practical skills for students has continued for decades at journalism schools on both sides of the Canada–US border.

At Carleton, they have been long seeking to find that balance. And so, for example, I did a minor in political science. I did history, geography, French, and so on, along with the journalism courses. And that's what I recommend: if you're going to go to university, you might as well take advantage of the university environment, because you're not going to get to dip into that again once you leave.

There are all kinds of disciplines at university that can teach you things that will be useful to you, so you might as well learn about the political system in our country and the history of that system and why it exists and how it has developed. Learn a little bit if you can about law and about how to study cases, and use case studies in law to understand how decisions are made. And do a little bit of Canadian history, so you understand how your country came to be . . . a little civics. In other words, get yourself a broad education and combine that with your practical studies at your professional school.

And take a statistics course. More and more journalists should consider that. Statistics courses are offered at every university. Take introductory-level statistics and learn some basic concepts. Then when you come out, you're much more prepared to deal with a complex world than if you had spent your entire time learning how to write an inverted pyramid. So I think get a good education—that's one bit of advice. Another one is to stay curious. Always be curious and want to know what's behind things. Always ask why. Don't just go out looking for the what, and repeat the what. Ask why. What's going on here? And when things don't make sense, ask why they don't make sense. Remain inquiring and skeptical all the time.

Vallance-Jones attributes his own ability to remain skeptical and inquiring to his native curiosity and years of experience spent honing his craft. He believes these qualities that distinguish the best reporters are learned, not innate.

> I think it's just long practice. I don't think I would have been like that in high school. I wrote essays in high school just like every other kid did. I think it's just something you learn. You write a bunch of stories that aren't very critical and you're not very proud of them, and you say, 'Wait a minute, I didn't really get to the bottom of that, I have to dig a little bit deeper.' I just want to know. I think you learn it. I think I learned it. I don't think it was particularly inherent. In fact, if you go back to my earliest history, I was terrible in English. I hated English.

An inspired high-school teacher changed all that.

> I think it was grade 10. It was a particular teacher who taught me to get excited about language and so on, and then I guess that's how I stopped thinking of writing as anathema. Then as time went on I developed this taste for it.

Vallance-Jones is driven by his own curiosity, but also by his ideals about journalism and the role it plays, or can play or should play, in a democracy.

> I think the reader deserves to know. In the end, that's what it comes down to. Always be in this for the reader or the listener, never for yourself. So, yeah, I think that's the satisfaction at the end of the day. I've told people something they wouldn't have known otherwise and might actually be useful to them or make some change in their lives. That's the ultimate. That's the satisfaction at the end of the day: having some change occur for the better, as it did [in the case of Reservations]. There's also a lot of satisfaction, on the other hand, in going in to work in the morning at 9:00 and writing your story or working on the rim[8] or whatever it is you do, and going home at the end of the day, back to your family and other things in life.

Whether you take on big investigative projects as a reporter or spend your workday in the newsroom on other aspects of the craft, such as editing, Vallance-Jones regards you as part of the big picture. And although the investigative reporter never really works a classic nine-to-five shift, everyone in the newsroom contributes to the grander purpose of the press.

> One must never be judgmental of people because they make different choices. Some people choose another path, and they're perfectly good journeymen and they do a good job at what they do. But getting to the bottom of everything

maybe isn't their passion. They have a different passion, maybe it's golf or hiking, or . . .

I just happen to be very passionate about journalism, and about the role of journalism. A lot of journalism scholars have made the comment that journalism and democracy kind of equate; and I agree, they do, you can't have one without the other. You can't have a real democracy without a vibrant press in order to allow debate, to air different opinions and facts, and to hold people accountable. Certainly others have made this comment, but what's the first thing that most totalitarian regimes do? Shut down the free press. They control the press.

It's very difficult to have a vibrant press without democracy. They are essential to each other. So I love journalism for that reason; I think it's a very important thing in our society, an exciting thing to be part of, even if sometimes we're thought of as not much better than the slime at the bottom of the bucket.

Despite bottom-line pressures in the business of journalism, Vallance-Jones remains confident about its future in general and the prospects for investigative reporting in particular.

I think journalism is always going to be around; it may take different forms. Although I do believe that there needs to be organized journalism . . . that it takes resources and a certain degree of organization to allow for the highest quality of journalism to happen. And you need editors, and people to keep you on track and keep you sharp. So I think that journalism is always going to be around and there will always need to be an organized form of it. But forty, fifty, or sixty years from now, will it be the same as it is today? I'm not about to predict the death of newspapers, because that's been predicted many times and hasn't happened yet. But certainly we're in a different era.

What about concentrated ownership and, now, convergence?

Well, those can both be good and bad. Obviously it's not good in a democracy to have all the media controlled by one owner. But I think on the other side of the coin, yes you have concentrated ownership of newspapers—though I'm not convinced it's any more concentrated today than it was in the '70s, when the Kent Commission was launched after the *Ottawa Journal* and the *Winnipeg Tribune* closed.

But the counterforce, of course, is the Internet and the much more broadly available range—almost infinite range—of expression that's out there. I think the audience is much more skeptical today, too, and that's one of the challenges that newspapers have. It's not like it was in the '50s when everybody subscribed to the local paper and the paper controlled the news agenda. The reader today is not nearly as accepting, and so it's a lot tougher. That's why the paper I'm at has worked so hard to be innovative.

In the old days of the newspaper business, the *Spectator*'s kind of initiative would have paid off in increased circulation. But as other reporters have noted, the financial underpinnings of the press have undergone a sea change in recent decades.

> I don't think there are very many circulation rises left in this business. I'm not a newspaper manager, so I'd better be careful how much I really can say about this, but my sense of it is that the newspaper business these days, at least the mainstream newspaper business, seems to be about how to best manage circulation losses and readership losses over time. Right now, I don't see anybody being very successful at growing readership and circulation dramatically.

Another reporter interviewed for this book said you don't measure success in the newspaper business by how much circulation you've gained, but by how little you've lost.[9]

> Everybody is gradually losing those numbers and I think that's partly reflective of the diversity of competition we were talking about. Kids today—I won't say 'kids today,' I sound like my dad—younger people today don't ever pick up a newspaper. They don't even think to.
>
> What's the future? I don't know. I think it seems to be evolving too rapidly and it gets a little dangerous to get into prognosis mode and say blogs are the future. And if you go back to your civics, too, I think to a large degree we have to do a better job of educating our young people about the basics of being a citizen. Because I think an awful lot of people don't have a very good sense of that at all. We see that in dropping participation rates in elections, in dropping readerships for newspapers. In a lot of ways, many young people get a sense of their citizenship from their participation in this other world: on the Internet, MSN, blogs and various other such venues.

But are these participants in Internet 'communities' getting citizenship, or are they just getting a sense of individual belonging to a particular group?

> Who knows? You could get philosophical and say maybe we're evolving to a new kind of citizenship, a borderless citizenship. The trouble is there are all kinds of possible negative implications to that, too, about how functional your society is. That's a good example of the need for organized journalism, because you need it to achieve that accuracy.

He sees dangers as well as potential in online 'news' sites that accept the reports of random contributors with no common standards or procedures for verification. Such electronic ventures, it's true, avoid centralized controls of any sort, but they also avoid quality control because the contributors are generally untrained in professional journalism.

> It's supposed to be like Wikipedia; it's supposed to be self-correcting, so that if a thousand people report a mass murder today in London, Ontario, then the facts will be quickly corrected, because there are such large numbers of people involved. But I'm doubtful about these sorts of enterprises. . . . Then you can get into the debate about journalism schools, which we won't.[10]

My own take on that debate is that journalism schools are more necessary than ever. Because of the increased pressures in the newspaper business, and because the journalistic base has been eroded, individual reporters have to take more responsibility for the development of their skills. They cannot rely, as in a previous era, on the editors at their first papers to bring them along. Such editors still exist—and may their tribe increase. But the modern newsroom, with notable exceptions, doesn't do much to mentor newcomers. Young reporters can't rely on a desk of editors and senior editors any more.

> No, I tend to agree. We need journalism schools; we need to educate our journalists.

A former dean of the famed Columbia University School of Journalism said he believes that journalism schools are more necessary than ever because a smaller newspaper industry won't be providing the same kind of support and instruction to young reporters that it did in a previous era.[11] The days of the legendary city editors who influenced so many generations of reporters are fading into history.

> Yes, that's true. So, the better the journalist . . . I saw a recent survey that showed university-educated journalists had the lowest levels of job satisfaction in newsrooms, perhaps for that very reason. They want to think, and the first thing they're told is, 'Don't think, just go do.' There's a lot of that, you know. There is an anti-intellectual strain in newspapers.

Part of doing investigative reporting or even just good journalism generally has to do with fighting for stories. Sometimes you've got to 'sell' the story to editors, convince them it's worth doing.

> Sure. You have to fight for stories, and sometimes you lose. Sometimes you lose and a year later it's a story and you wish you'd fought harder. I've had that experience. You push for a story and you're not 100 per cent sure but you'd like to pursue it and the editor says no, and then later it's a story. Sometimes you fight

and win. Sometimes it's, 'That's a great idea, go ahead and do it.' I think the gritty, people-oriented stories aren't hard to sell. The ones that involve policy, the dysfunction of governments, and so on are harder to sell because editors may not understand them.

Even Vallance-Jones doesn't win them all. As persuasive as he is in print, he sometimes finds it difficult to communicate a story idea to editors. It's not always easy transmitting his sixth sense about a story when he feels there is one to pursue.

One of my biggest weaknesses always has been getting my understanding of the story across to editors. Because I know in my gut, it's a funny place that I can't describe, but you can feel the story, you know it's there and you try to explain that to the editor and you're getting that blank stare back sometimes.

At the same time, he understands and appreciates not only that the editor has a job to do, but also the necessary push and pull between the two roles.

I do it once a week. I'm on the desk once a week on Sundays, so I know what they're thinking of on the other side. They're thinking, 'Okay, what am I going to get in the paper tomorrow?' And that's understandable because that's *their* job. But you know what? It's the tension in the end between the editors' need for stories and the reporters' desire to tell the right stories that I think results in stories getting told. Because the editors will push the reporters to do better, and to make their stories more relevant, more understandable, more accessible, and the reporters on the other hand will push to get stories told that the editors might not understand in the first place. I think that tension in the end is what results in great stories happening. You can't avoid it, anyway. It's inherent in the job descriptions. Reporter, job description: Be curious. Editor, job description: Make sure the story's right and clear. And make sure there's something in the paper tomorrow.

Young reporters in Vallance-Jones's own newsroom seem to exhibit the classic enthusiasm of young reporters everywhere. They're also idealistic and obviously believe in the institution of the press. They aren't there only to earn a living.

They tend to be very good ones, that come to the *Spectator*—high standards of hiring. They tend to have very high expectations of their futures and their rapid rise in the business and they tend to be very aggressive. And, you know, most of them are [aggressive]. Let's push the rewind button and go back twenty years in my life, and I was probably exactly like them.

It isn't hard to find high ideals among those starting out in journalism. Maintaining that idealism is more difficult: it can be discouraged and eroded over time.

I think there are a lot of badly managed reporters out there, too, who lose their passion and their fire because they just get tired of the same old, same old, 'Well, that's really nice but I need this other for tomorrow.' And they hear that three hundred days a year or whatever it is, and they give up. They say, 'Okay, fine.' It can be tough to keep the idealism up, and to keep the joy for the business up, because for most workaday reporters often there is that push just to get the story for tomorrow. But how many times have I heard—have we all heard—that exact line [in response to a story pitch]. 'Well, that's good, that's a great story, but just for today, can you do this.' That happens at the best papers.

Of course, that's one of the bad parts of this business in my experience: it's a business where you're allowed to keep doing it until you fail, and failure is generally not tolerated for very long in the newspaper business. You fail a couple of times and then you're off on something else. 'Oh, you're not doing this thing; you're not producing that. Well, that's fine, move along.' So you're right, you're great as long as you have a series, a string of successes. A lot of other fields are more tolerant of people having slow periods in their lives. I don't think the newspaper business is.

No, it's a very unforgiving business. Perhaps that's one of the reasons you get a lot of high achievers in it: the ones who are not as highly skilled and motivated just don't last long.

If you look at this series and at the Smokescreen series [see Chapter 12, 'Drive Clean Smokescreen'], they both probably exemplify the sort of key elements of investigative journalism. You've got to be relentless, and you've got to be tenacious. You've got to be skeptical, and push hard. And don't take no for an answer. In either of those series, you could have given up long before you'd won the race.

# Commentary

No matter how interesting the data or the patterns revealed by analyzing the data, stories always need a human face. It was the telling of people's individual stories—and the fact that this was news Hamiltonians could use—that boosted reader interest in Reservations, not the data analysis that the series relied on. Before the data could be analyzed, it had to be obtained, and again, it was the Vallance-Jones's principled persistence—not technology—that ultimately overcame official resistance to releasing the necessary records.

The Reservations series, then, exemplifies the use of computer-assisted reporting in the forging of the investigative report. It began with a battle to obtain data from a government department, proceeded with the reportorial expertise required to make sense of the data (literally to see the patterns by 'asking questions' of the data, as Vallance-Jones would put it)[12], and became a newspaper series through the fleshing out of facts with the dramatic telling of individual stories. The *Spectator* also posted online the database of inspection reports, allowing readers to see for themselves how Vallance-Jones had arrived at his conclusions. This is another major promise of computer-assisted reporting: its ability to bring greater transparency to the process of reportage.[13]

Computer-assisted stories can arise in various ways and from humble beginnings: a source's tip, a lead arising from ordinary beat or 'shoe-leather' reporting, the pursuit of a more general interest in an existing issue—all these and more can send the reporter seeking database information, usually in cases where the numbers involved are large enough to preclude the possibility of detecting patterns with the naked eye.

In the case of Reservations, however, the sequence was reversed. Although the series led with the story of guests at a wedding reception who got food poisoning from the catered fare, Vallance-Jones learned of the incident from the database research. He came across minimal detail in the database referring to the wedding reception, and from this scant information (no names, for example, were included), he traced the couple and learned their story.[14]

The series dealt of course with more than individual horror stories about being sickened by bad food;[15] it also targeted the system that allowed dirty eateries to continue to operate. It showed that Hamilton's health department wasn't doing the regular inspections required by law and wasn't taking appropriate action even when inspections revealed serious transgressions such as repeat offences. Without computer-assisted technology, Vallance-Jones would have been unable to show the systemic nature of the problem.[16]

Clearly, the provision of database analysis made the story too strong to dismiss as a matter of rare exceptions to a generally good food-inspection system. The series showed the system itself was flawed. Both under-resourced and understaffed, the public health department was unable to fulfill its responsibility to the public.

But computer-assisted reporting isn't just for documenting abuses or wrongdoing discovered through the more traditional reporters' means and against the claims of eventual critics or naysayers. The techniques of CAR can allow for new kinds of stories, ones that otherwise might not be told. And if you approach CAR as Vallance-Jones does, as 'a way of thinking', the story possibilities are endless.

Neither do you need to be an expert in CAR or employed at a large-circulation daily to begin to undertake computer-assisted investigations. In 2001, Barb Sweet, working at *The Telegram* (St John's), did extensive investigation into oil tanker safety at Placentia Bay, Newfoundland. Although the paper enjoyed only modest technical abilities in CAR and could not spare a reporter for days (let alone weeks) at a time, it had a will and found a way. Not content to rely on information supplied by Transport Canada, Sweet used ship information from websites and from an access-to-information request to build a database. The database revealed serious deficiencies in the aging tankers that plied Placentia Bay, a location deemed the likeliest place for an oil spill in Canada. Sweet began tracking the tankers by various means, including collecting daily port-entry logs, and then, having only limited software to work with, entered all the data by hand—some six hundred items of information on eighty-nine oil tankers. Sweet's two-story series sparked an investigation that revealed Transport Canada wasn't meeting its inspection targets.[17]

For Reservations, Vallance-Jones, having obtained the database of restaurant inspections, used relatively simple software to crunch the numbers and look for patterns in the two thousand pages of electronic records. Of the series, he wrote, 'The same data exist in dozens of cities, so it is a story ripe for the picking.'[18] He has repeatedly made the point that CAR can be undertaken by anyone willing to make a start up the learning curve. Along with other investigative reporters, he understands that unless CAR becomes part of the big picture, undertaken by reporters in general, not just by stars among the ranks, its great potential cannot be fulfilled.[19]

On the other hand, expertise can make all the difference. The system for keeping track of restaurant inspections in Hamilton included paper records and a database designed to allow reporting by municipalities to the provincial health ministry. The problem was that ministry staff in Hamilton 'had no idea how to make a copy of the underlying data they had themselves entered'. Vallance-Jones did.

Having already made extensive use of the provincial reporting system software (Microsoft FoxPro), Vallance-Jones knew that 'it should be straightforward to write a query to produce the data'. From the database he was able to compile a list of dirty restaurants (those cited for critical violations or those that had repeatedly failed inspections); and from the list, he was able to obtain the paper records for each establishment. 'Without the data, we never could have zeroed in so well on premises that consistently had problems,' he noted in an article for *The IRE Journal*. 'The database allowed us to see both the big picture, and the detail that mattered.'[20]

Editors at the *Hamilton Spectator* had for some time been considering a series on food safety; they had seen similar CAR treatments of the issue by newspapers in other North American cities. Robert Cribb's nearly year-long series on food safety, called Dirty Dining, had begun running in the *Toronto Star* early the previous year and won accolades.[21] The series sparked a minor sensation and was largely responsible for the institution of a 'pass' system in the city's restaurants. Any place that serves food in Toronto now is required to 'advertise' its health status with an official sticker at its entrance (green for pass, orange for problems, red for no go). Vallance-Jones refers to Cribb's series—and its impact—in one of his own stories for Reservations.[22]

In Hamilton, an industrial city of nearly half a million people roughly an hour's drive southwest of Toronto, reader response to Reservations was also strong; in fact, unprecedented. The paper and Vallance-Jones were inundated with letters, phone calls, and email responses. Local politicians and officials demanded action to rectify the situation. Before the stories had finished running, plans were made to clean up the city's food-handling practices and hire more inspectors.[23] Health department officials even promised action on a permanent posting system, like the one instituted in Toronto, to identify Hamilton's substandard eateries.

Yet although Reservations did spark the city's hiring of more inspectors and did lead to a remodelled inspections system, the temporary disclosure system it instituted was rudimentary and flawed. It issued certificates only to those restaurants that passed inspection and failed to provide full disclosure to the public.[24]

The difference in impact between the results of Vallance-Jones's Reservations in Hamilton and Robert Cribb's Dirty Dining in Toronto can probably be attributed to at least two factors: the size difference in the cities themselves (Toronto, with its much larger population and greater pool of restaurant-goers and tourists) and the length of time the series ran (Dirty Dining for a year and Reservations for a week). Nevertheless, both raised awareness of the health and political issues involved, and both were carried out by exceptionally talented investigative reporters working at the top of their craft.

One last lesson to be taken here is that of the close connections between so-called spot or hard news and investigative or issues reporting. One case of food poisoning might be 'news'. When Cribb and Vallance-Jones took on the story of dirty restaurants in their respective cities (Cribb, ironically, in response to a personal bout of food poisoning, compliments of a restaurant he unlovingly referred to as 'Chez Disgusting')[25] they were engaged in classic investigative reporting. Their work led to revelations of systemic problems (such as the absence or failure of safeguards that were supposed to protect people). This amounted to putting the 'issue' on the table and any follow-up stories can also be considered issues reporting.

# Endnotes

1.  'Hamilton's silent epidemic', *Hamilton Spectator* (26 November 2001), A7.

2.  'Food for thought', *Hamilton Spectator* (24 November 2001), A6.

3.  'Recipe for disaster', *Hamilton Spectator* (24 November 2001), A1.

4. 'City to beef up food checks', *Hamilton Spectator* (26 November 2001), A1.

5. The site was launched in October 2005 to address the dearth of Canadian materials (including downloadable databases) for Canadian reporters interested in learning computer-assisted reporting. At the time of this writing, Fred Vallance-Jones was also working on a book about computer-assisted reporting along with another CAR heavy hitter: the CBC's David McKie.

6. Philip Meyer, *Precision Journalism: A Reporter's Introduction to Social Science Methods* (Lanham, MD: Rowman & Littlefield Publishers, Inc., 2002), vii.

7. You use simple spreadsheet software (like Microsoft Excel) and simple database software (like Microsoft Access), to work with numbers and begin to learn computer assisted reporting. Both set up information in tables, with vertical columns and horizontal rows. The 'fields' are the vertical columns that set out the parameters of the search. The horizontal rows list the individual items being compared. Here's a simple example: If you wanted to compare the individual salaries in a given company or organization for this year and last year, you would list the individual names of the salary earners in horizontal (numbered) rows, and the basic parameters of the search in vertical (lettered) columns: A. Name of salary earner; B. Last year's salary; and C. This year's salary. You could then use the spreadsheet's mathematical functions to perform various calculations (such as the percentage differences from the first year to the next).

8. The rim is the copy-editing section of the print newsroom. In the days before computers, the section comprised a desk in the shape of a horseshoe. The most senior editor sat in 'the slot'—a desk on the inside of the rim— and handed out copy-editing assignments to the editors sitting around the outside of the rim.

9. See Peter Gorrie's comments on newspaper circulation in Chapter 4, 'Asbestos, Again'.

10. Vallance-Jones did wade into the ongoing debate about journalism schools in an article for *Media* magazine. See 'A meeting place for professionals and mentors: When journalism schools get it right, they can be indispensable', *Media* 10.2 (Fall 2002), 18, 32.

11. Tom Goldstein, a former dean of the Columbia University School of Journalism, argued that the downturn in the newspaper business (where most graduates of journalism schools used to get their start) makes journalism schools only more necessary. 'We're going back to a freelance culture,' Goldstein is quoted as saying in James Ledbetter's 'The Slow, Sad Sellout of Journalism School', *Rolling Stone* 771 (November 1997), 73. See also Tom Goldstein's 'A Lover's Judgment', *Columbia Journalism Review* 40.4 (November/December 2001), 34.

12. Fred Vallance-Jones, 'Do you want to produce stories that demand attention? Then learn how to ask questions of your data', *Media* 8.2 (Summer 2001), 28.

13. Fred Vallance-Jones, 'Database reporting reveals food-handling gone wrong', *Investigative Reporters and Editors, Inc. The IRE Journal* 26.1 (January/February 2003), 36–38. Here, you can read the reporter's first-person account of the work that went into the series.

14. Because online information is much less accessible in Canada than it is in the United States, Canadian reporters are often forced to reverse the pattern of their searches. What information is released to Canadian reporters must first be rendered anonymous, according to the Canadian politicians and bureaucrats who oversee Access to Information regimes. See Fred Vallance-Jones, 'The fight for data continues . . . and we do experience success along the way', *Media Magazine* 11.4 (Winter 2006), 23. Commenting on CAR in Canada, Vallance-Jones wrote, 'We analyze the anonymized data for trends, then go looking after the fact for people to put a human face on what we uncover. We've become great at stories that reveal big, broken systems. If we can't find sex offenders, at least we can out the bureaucrats or the cops or the drug companies.'

15. 'When dining is risky', *Hamilton Spectator* (26 November 2001), A1.

16. Several of the stories in the series dealt with the systemic nature of the problem. See the following: 'Hunt for hazardous food preparation has health inspectors going from hot to cold', *Hamilton Spectator* (26 November 2001), A7; 'Dirty city restaurants receive light penalties', *Hamilton Spectator* (27 November 2001), A1; and 'Plenty of room for errors', *Hamilton Spectator* (27 November 2001), A4.

17. Barb Sweet, 'Sailing for disaster', *The Telegram* (St. John's) (16 November 2001), A1; and 'Safety standards often ignored', *The Telegram* (St. John's) (17 November 2001), B1.

18. Fred Vallance-Jones, 'Database reporting reveals food-handling gone wrong', op. cit., 38.

19. In September 2006, the *Edmonton Journal* launched a series on restaurant food safety called 'Behind the Kitchen Door'. See the carincanada.ca website for details.

20. 'Database reporting reveals food-handling gone wrong', op. cit., 38.

21. Robert Cribb, 'Special Report—Dirty Dining: City's health inspection system for restaurants a menu of failure and inaction, a Star investigation reveals', *Toronto Star* (19 February 2000), A1.

22. 'Toronto diners not left in the dark', *Hamilton Spectator* (28 November 2001), A1; and 'Taking danger out of dining', *Hamilton Spectator* (28 November 2001), A8.

23. 'Mayor vows food checks', *Hamilton Spectator* (27 November 2001), A1.

24. Fred Vallance-Jones, 'Database reporting reveals food-handling gone wrong', op. cit., 38. '. . . As we reported in April [2002], the system is flawed because even when critical violations are found, the signs are issued anyway, so long as the problems are corrected by the time the inspector leaves. Not one single premise has been denied a sign and the public is still given no information about the problems that are found. In fact, Hamilton still requires members of the public to put in a special request to the health department to see inspection reports.'

25. Robert Cribb, 'Dirty dining', *Media* 8.2 (Summer 2001), 12–13.

# Chapter 12

# Drive Clean Smokescreen

In 1999, the Ontario government introduced a program, called Drive Clean, of mandatory emissions tests for road vehicles. Like such programs in other North American cities, Drive Clean required motorists to have their vehicles tested for the volume of pollutants they emitted. If a car's pollutants reached a certain level, the vehicle flunked the test, and its owner would have to pay for repairs before he could renew the car's registration. These mandatory emissions tests were supposed to keep polluters off the road. The government's official Drive Clean website stated that the program was working to plan; it even reported on the estimated volume of pollutants the program had spared the environment.

But rumours were afoot about Drive Clean, and CAR expert Fred Vallance-Jones of the *Hamilton Spectator* decided to check them out. His efforts led to the paper's ten-story series, Smokescreen, published in the fall of 2004. Vallance-Jones filed a freedom-of-information request with the Ministry of the Environment for a database that contained over twelve million Drive Clean test results for southern Ontario between 1999 and early 2004. A three-year battle ensued with ministry bureaucrats, but finally the database was released (as usual in Canada, without the names of individual drivers or other information that could identify them). In his column the day the series began, editor Dana Robbins noted how hard the provincial government had worked 'to prevent the *Spectator* from telling you this story'.[1]

After the database was secured, Vallance-Jones was joined in the massive CAR project by veteran investigator and *Spectator* colleague Steve Buist.[2] The two proceeded to analyze the database and track down sources by conventional and undercover means.[3] Soon they were able to reveal the Drive Clean program's shortcomings in the

Smokescreen series. It was the largest data investigation the *Spectator* had ever undertaken, wrote managing editor Casey Korstanje, calling Drive Clean a system 'tailor-made for hustlers and cheaters'.[4]

The series showed that the Drive Clean program, which required vehicles to be tested every two years, was not only wasteful and unreliable, but also plagued with fraud. Clean vehicles that passed the test would get stickers of approval renewed; those that flunked were supposed to be repaired and then tested again, returning to the road only after earning a passing grade and a sticker to prove it. The tests would also be used to document Drive Clean's environmental benefits, or so at least the plan proposed.

The benefits, it would turn out, were much overrated.

In reality, drivers of newer cars regularly shelled out money for tests that were little needed. Meanwhile, drivers of older, more polluting vehicles resorted to unscrupulous garages to get their Drive Clean pass certificates and their polluting vehicles back on the road. Sometimes the tests themselves gave false results, but, more often, crooked dealers were 'fixing' the test results and issuing fake pass certificates for a price—higher than the $35 cost of the test itself, but lower than the cost of the repairs that would have been required to halt the rush of toxins from the cars' tailpipes. Under the government's Drive Clean program, the mandatory tests were carried out by private garages for a cut of the profits. The scenario was ripe for corruption, and the corruption proved widespread.

Vallance-Jones and Buist revealed that in some categories more than 98 per cent of cars were passing the Drive Clean test on the first try; as well, pass rates had risen dramatically over the preceding years and were continuing to rise.[5] The technology, too, was wanting. Test results could vary widely for the same car tested again only minutes after a first try, and the computer models used to assess the overall benefits of reduced pollution—benefits presented as fact—were in fact unreliable at best.[6] With no central command and no independent oversight to verify and monitor test results, the Drive Clean program practically invited fraud; and while the program failed to get polluters off the road, the doctored test results gave a falsely rosy picture of its anti-pollution effectiveness.

In short, while non-polluters were continuing to shell out for tests, polluters were easily eluding the system. In addition to the illegal means of evading detection was a perfectly legal one: cars that needed pricey repairs could be issued 'conditional' passes that allowed them to remain on the road until the repairs could be completed. In an article for *Media Magazine* about the series, Vallance-Jones called these conditional passes 'get-out-of-jail-free' cards.[7]

Those scamming the system used various techniques to profit from selling fake pass certificates at a substantial profit—in some cases more than ten times the cost of the test.[8] Honest brokers, on the other hand, even those doing brisk business in testing, had trouble barely meeting the costs of buying and running the necessary equipment.[9]

The series provoked almost immediate government response and elicited promises to review and revise the fraud-prone program. The day after the first piece ran, a provincial cabinet minister said she was 'appalled' to learn the extent of Drive Clean fraud from the *Spectator* series. She vowed to raise the issue with the province's environment minister[10] (who promised in turn to 'crack down on corrupt garages'). The story noted that in the previous two years, the government had suspended an average of two garages per month from participation in the program for such dishonest dealings.[11]

Plans were initiated to overhaul Drive Clean. The revised measures would target likely polluters, exempt newer cars with little potential to pollute, and put an end to conditional passes. Provincial police were encouraged to lay fraud charges against those who profited from cheating the system, and an internal government review launched two months after the *Spectator* series 'identified many of the same problems found by the newspaper'.[12]

Smokescreen's ten stories ran from 18 to 23 September 2004.[13]

# The Interview: **Fred Vallance-Jones**
(8 April 2006)

Fred Vallance-Jones initiated this CAR project with a freedom-of-information request after hearing stories about Drive Clean around town and at the urging of a *Spectator* editor. After completing the information request, he had plenty of time to mull the situation over.

> There had been some stories about high pass rates in Drive Clean and minor irregularities. One of my editors suggested we file a freedom-of-information request. I asked for the Drive Clean database in December 2000.

The battle for the database would take three years and include two freedom-of-information appeals. A less experienced and determined reporter might have given up soon after he began, but Vallance-Jones is an unusual man: he's able to combine insatiable curiosity and a passionate belief in the value of the work with a mild-mannered approach that puts people at ease. He also knew how to bide his time, maintaining his interest while he waited for authorities to give up the database. What kept him going?

> Just the knowledge that the story was there. It took us three years to get the Drive Clean data . . . three years of appeals and arguments before the Ontario information commissioner—written arguments. It was just because I knew it was important that the public be allowed to see the actual results of these tests. Because all we had before that was a ministry website that said Drive Clean works: 'Don't worry; all fraud is weeded out, the integrity of the program is absolutely the most important thing; and it works fine and the auditors say it's great.' Really the website for Drive Clean was a form of modern-day propaganda. And I knew that we had to dig on this to find out what was really going on.

It didn't take long for Vallance-Jones to realize that people's misgivings about the program were well-founded. He began the database research by running 'some simple queries' that confirmed 'very high, and with time, rising pass rates'.

> Once I delved more deeply into the data, I discovered some cars were passing tests only moments after failing. This led to a further freedom-of-information request for enforcement information. My colleague Steve Buist, meantime, investigated the scientific underpinnings of Drive Clean, and found them suspect.

The defining moment for the reporters came soon after the arrival of the hard-won government statistics. When Vallance-Jones was finally able to scour the database, he noticed almost immediately a pass rate so elevated that it screamed for scrutiny.

> That was the first query of the day. I went to a colleague and said, 'Look at this . . . 99 per cent of the cars are passing.' And right there, I knew absolutely we had a story. And then I dug into it a little bit more and found out other things about it. The most fun was taking the time of the tests for the same cars, and, of course, the cars weren't identified specifically because of the privacy laws.
>
> At the time, they weren't giving me the VINS [vehicle identification numbers]. So I had to work out the actual identity of the cars by using a combination of fields, the make and model, and the year, and the odometer readings. In putting it all together, I could tell [for example] that a 1996 Corolla with 96,000 kilometres on it had been tested two minutes later with 96,001 on it, at the same garage. You knew that the odds of there being two Corollas at the same garage at the same time of day were minimal. Eventually, I did win the VINS. They had to hand them over—but long after the series was published.[14]

Vallance-Jones has elsewhere commented on the state of access-to-information laws in Canada. In a piece for *Media* magazine, he compared the relatively easy availability of public data in the United States to the 'state-secrets' approach of Canadian authorities. He railed against bureaucratic intransigence, Canadian style: 'Because of our privacy laws, data here have to be "anonymized", with any details that would reveal an individual's identity scrubbed out, ostensibly to protect the individuals, but mostly to protect bureaucrats who might otherwise have to account for the failings in the programs they administer.'[15]

After winning the FOI battle, Vallance-Jones faced his next major hurdle: analyzing millions of test records with no names and no vehicle identification numbers. Fortunately, his technique of using a combination of fields to determine the cars' identities 'had been fairly effective'.

> That was where I got the break, [thinking] that, well, cars are passing within less than a minute, or a minute or two or three or four, and how is that possible? I mean, if it's a polluter one minute, how can it not be a polluter two minutes later? And sometimes the answer was that the test results were variable. From one minute to the next, the car could have different emissions. But often the reason was that they were cheating. They were testing the car and finding it failing but giving it a pass certificate anyway.

In an important 'shoe-leather' segment of the work, the reporter interviewed a former mechanic who had been charged (and convicted) of fraud for cheating, and then pocketing the profits, on Drive Clean tests at the garage where he worked. Vallance-Jones noted that he tracked down that source 'through old fashioned journalism'. The initial clue, however, came from the government documents that he'd flushed into the public arena with his FOI fight.

> I had received some documents from the government on the garages that had been disciplined under the program, and I happened to call one of them. I was talking to them and I think they were doing what many people would hope to do in a situation like that: they were trying to divert this reporter off onto somebody else.

In an attempt to free themselves from press scrutiny, the people Vallance-Jones spoke to at the garage decided to feed him the errant mechanic and (now legally compromised) former employee. They gave Vallance-Jones his name and a past court date.

> So I started chasing that down and calling the courthouse, and eventually found the information and I went to court on his next court date. He was charged by the police after the ministry had done an investigation, but he was actually turned in by the garage. The government didn't find him. Just going back to the memory bank here . . . he had been into the garage—he was working an overnight shift where he would test a number of cars at this used-car dealership. They discovered a bunch of printouts, the morning he was fired, for tests on cars he wasn't supposed to be testing. So he was caught by the garage, not by the government's computers.

Vallance-Jones mentions this facet of the story to stress that part of the problem with Drive Clean was lax enforcement. Some of the series' most compelling reads came not from database analysis, but from people's descriptions of how the scamming worked. For example, when Vallance-Jones approached the mechanic outside the court, the latter commented on how easy it was to cheat the system. 'It's not rocket science,' he told the reporter. 'You could sit there and make it look good on paper. As long as it looks good on paper, they don't give a shit.'[16]

> We were sitting outside the courthouse at that point. What happened was that I saw him in court, and after court I sat down beside him and started chatting. It was just the normal kind of procedure. You talk to somebody; you slowly gain their trust. And he was kind of a chatty guy.

The mechanic might have been chatty by nature, but Vallance-Jones is also the kind of reporter who inspires confidence. He's aggressive but never off-putting. Did the mechanic talk to him to relieve his guilty feelings?

> I don't know how deeply he thought about it. But sometimes it's in the readers' interest, so we chatted some more outside and eventually he told me the whole story of how it happened. That was a great break, but there was nothing special about it. It was just a case of following up a tip and finding out when the guy was going to be in court and making a point of being there when he was there, and then talking to him. There was a side request for discipline actions, which is how I found this guy, because they did have a surveillance system that went after garages they suspected of cheating. But there were an awful lot they didn't catch.

The provincial government policed the program, but not very effectively.

> Not as well as they could have, I don't think. But they were telling the public this. This is the thing. Once in a while the Ministry of Environment would put out a low-profile press release, saying [for example] such and such a garage has been charged with two counts under the Environmental Protection Act. Usually, it was under the Environmental Protection Act—there were two or three different offences they could be charged with. But these press releases, like the standard sort of informational press releases, completely went under the radar screen. Nobody really picked up on the amount of fraud that was going on. And it just took somebody digging into it to find it. But meanwhile, the [government] website never said any of this. [According to it,] everything was just fine, was operating as it was supposed to, and was successful. 'Go on and get your car tested, because you're doing good things for the environment.' In fact, it was largely a waste of money, and riddled with fraud.

Part of the problem was the large number of garages involved in the program, all offering the certification tests.

> One of the reasons they had so many garages doing it, we were told, was that they wanted to ensure there were lots of places, but they also wanted to have this as an incentive for the garages, so that they would sign on to Drive Clean. So they never capped the number of garages that could participate.

That made honest profits for individual garages harder to come by, and effective implementation and oversight of the testing even more unlikely.

> It just made it bigger and meant none of them could make very much money out of the program. So that was the problem: nobody made much money, except the ones that were doing a lot of tests—and there were a few of those. But the average garage, spending $60,000, $70,000, $80,000 on the testing machine, wasn't making its money back. The test was $35.

The system was supposed to work by allowing the garages to make up their investment in Drive Clean by charging for tests and certification papers as well as for required repairs.

> They would make money on the tests. They got a piece of that. And then they also would make money, supposedly, on the repairs. And they did. There were various scams under Drive Clean to repair cars that didn't need to be repaired and so on. It was an enormous system [the government] decided to set up, with private garages doing the testing; there had been all kinds of studies that showed this kind of decentralized testing system was prone to fraud because the garages would want to bend things their way. But the provincial government still went ahead and did it that way; they just said that was their philosophy. They wanted to have a free-enterprise system as widely available as possible, not something run by the government.
>
> The database was extremely large—more than three gigabytes of data. The computer program I usually use to analyze data, Microsoft Access, could not cope with such a large file. I had to obtain and learn how to use MySQL, a much more powerful database program. And to see if fraud existed in Hamilton, we launched an elaborate undercover operation involving the temporary purchase of a motor vehicle, and clandestine visits to garages and used-car dealerships.

There is only thing he would have done differently in retrospect: file his freedom-of-information requests much earlier, 'so as to avoid slowing the project later'. Still, the impact of the series was immediate. Days after the first story ran, government officials promised a complete review of Drive Clean (a review that did proceed early in 2005). Vallance-Jones kept the heat on.

> There were many follow-ups in the period immediately following the story as I chased reaction and reported on audits released in an FOI request we didn't get on time for the original publication. I continue to follow up occasionally. The government made changes to the program in the fall of 2005 but some elements are still out for public discussion.

Not generally attached to labels such as *investigative reporter*, Vallance-Jones allows that regardless of terminology, this kind of in-depth reporting always appealed to him. He loves to dig and considers the search for truth the highest value in journalism. He offered crisp advice to the aspiring reporter: 'Be persistent. Follow the loose ends and inconsistencies. Follow your nose.'

# The Interview: **Steve Buist**
(6 August 2006)

Steve Buist joined the Smokescreen project after the database was in hand.

> I actually joined the project after it had been in the works for some time. This all started with a fairly lengthy fight to get information from the provincial environment ministry, which is responsible for the Drive Clean program here in Ontario. Fred had been fighting for a matter of years to get them to release the test results for each car. And so he finally was successful at winning that fight and they turned over ultimately something like twelve million test results, and basically said, 'Here, have fun.'
>
> Fred was able to put all the results through some fairly sophisticated computer analysis by car model type, the age of the car, the different pollutants that were being measured [and so on]. . . . I expect they have in BC a similar type of thing where if you fail then you can have some work done and then have the car retested. That process had been under way for a few years. Fred was successful. He put it through a bunch of computer analyses, and then at that point I think the project had become a little bit daunting, so I was asked to jump in and give Fred a hand.

Buist specializes in large investigative projects and has done several multi-part series. Teaming the two reporters worked out: their different styles proved complementary.

Vallance-Jones tends to notice the fine details, while Buist likes to scout out the larger landscape.

> It was a mutual decision, where everyone realized that this had the potential to overwhelm just one person. And it actually worked out well, because I think Fred and I have different skill sets that meshed well. Fred is very good at looking at things through . . . a microscope. I am more the other way; I look at things through a telescope. So I'm the one who was stepping back and saying, 'What's the big picture?' And Fred is very good at looking at the minutiae, the intricate details.

With research, the intricate details began to add up and an 'aerial' view started to emerge.

> What we were finding was that there didn't seem to be a lot of rationale for this program. What were touted as being the successes for this program weren't being borne out by what we were finding in the numbers. And I don't necessarily attribute this to any sort of malice on the part of the provincial government. I just think it's one of those things where it was a program that everyone wanted to believe in and thought at face value was good. I mean, who's going to argue against trying to reduce pollution? It's like mom and apple pie. So everyone thought this was a good thing. I don't think anyone ever thought to actually put it to some high-level scrutiny to see if it was actually doing what it said it was doing. What we were finding was, in fact, that it wasn't as successful as people thought or hoped it would be.

Buist thinks that because people *wanted* to believe in emissions testing and its value, they were easily deceived. He remembers well his own date with Drive Clean.

> You take your car for a test. You sweat and sweat. I think the reason a lot of people didn't think too much about it is that you had to do it. You didn't have much choice, so there was no sense bellyaching about it. So you take your car in and all you care about is getting your pass. And then you do [get your pass], which, as we showed, was the case with an overwhelming majority of cars. You get your pass and you think, 'Thank goodness my car is okay.' And if you're one of the small minority of people that don't pass, you think, 'Oh my god, I'm a bad person. My car is polluting the environment.' You get it fixed, it gets its pass, and then you think, 'Okay, now I'm a good person. I did a good thing. I helped improve the environment.' But as we were showing, even [older] cars . . . were passing at 95 or 96 per cent. So it makes you wonder what the value is in this. How much more pollution were we adding to the environment by making millions of [newer] cars go and get a test every year, driving to and from the centres?

And, perhaps, obtaining fraudulent certificates that in effect authorized even more pollution.

> I think the most telling statistics we stumbled on were [those that showed] how the system works: If you fail your test, you have to have work done on your car up to a maximum amount of money, and then you have a retest. If you pass the retest, you get your sticker. Even if you don't pass your second test, you can get what's called a conditional pass, so basically you can just go on your merry way anyhow. When we compared the conditional pass numbers—basically a car that had flunked twice but had had some work done on it—we were able to show that [such] cars more often than not were polluting *even more* than they were on the first test. This work was supposed to be making these cars somewhat better, but more than 50 per cent of the time the cars were performing worse on the second test. So you could make the ridiculous argument that you were actually hurting the environment by trying to repair these cars. No sense.

Both reporters were struck by the extent of the problems and by how long the irregularities had escaped notice.

> What surprised us about the program was that there had been so little official scrutiny. And again, I don't attribute that to any sort of maliciousness on the part of the government. But it had just really become one of those things . . . it has to be working because everyone thinks it's working. And we did compare other jurisdictions to Ontario and what they were doing. BC has its own version of this [called Air Care], and so do several US states.
>
> The results seem to be fairly uniform across North America, showing that this particular type of testing program, where you stick a car on a treadmill and put a probe up its rear end, wasn't the most effective way. And we weren't taking advantage of advances in technology. It was prone to corruption, and so much of the program depends on computer modelling. So when you hear the government saying, 'Good news everyone, the Drive Clean program has reduced automobile emissions by X per cent and taken X million tonnes of smog-causing pollution out of the air,' when you actually look at how they arrive at those numbers, much of it is just done on computer modelling.
>
> So the government says that if your car went in and had this reading, and then it was repaired and then it had this different reading, ergo, we calculate here's how much pollution is being reduced in the environment. But it's all based on computer models, and if the models aren't particularly accurate or effective, then you've got a whole lot of meaningless numbers. As we were showing, there were lots of times when the car was doing worse on the second test, so in fact you could argue that Drive Clean was *adding* pollution to the air.
>
> We were also able to show that the computer modelling being used by the province to come up with these calculations for benefits, had, in fact, been debunked as an inaccurate model in other jurisdictions. Basically, it was junk in,

junk out, and people were taking it as gospel. You'd see these numbers getting thrown around by the government and then, of course, getting picked up by news organizations and getting spewed out again.

Buist, like the *Toronto Star*'s Jim Rankin, holds a bachelor's degree in human biology. He's used to the idea of analysis and proof.

That's why I gravitated to medical stuff. The science world is very rigid in terms of 'show me the numbers'. Whether that helps or not [in journalism] I don't know. But, yeah, I've come up through science.

The defining moment on the Smokescreen project for Buist was the insight he gained through personal experience with the testing system, some of it coming even before he began working on the series with Vallance-Jones.

In Ontario, the program requires cars to be tested for the first time when they reach three years of age. So you spend your thirty-five bucks and you go get your car tested at age three. And I remember that I had a leased car, and I still had to do it when it turned three, and you sweat, you worry about it. That had happened before we did this series.

And now I understood why I had so much wasted energy over this. We noticed that for three-year-old cars that were getting tested for the first time, the pass rate was I think 99.3 or 99.7 per cent. So, basically, 7 cars out of 1,000 weren't passing, which means 993 cars out of 1,000 were passing. So you have to ask yourself, 'What possible value is there to society to test 1,000 cars and find out that 993 of them pass, other than the fact that garages have grabbed $35 from each of those people to conduct the test?' And for the 7 that failed, did the government reduce pollution in the province enough by fixing 7 cars—maybe—that it overcame the pollution caused by requiring 993 other cars to find one of these sites and go and get tested? [Especially when people] drive around for 20 minutes, like you're told to, so that you get your engine warm enough and burn off all the junk that's in your tailpipe. If everyone's like me, they learn the secret is you drive around for 20 minutes. Now you've added who knows how many times the amount of pollution to the air that you're 'fixing' by catching seven cars.

Buist's go-round with Drive Clean gave him some understanding of the program long before he worked on the Smokescreen series. That understanding played into his dawning awareness of some of the story's less obvious aspects. It also highlights one of the joys of journalism that doesn't often get mention: the way reflecting on personal experience can bring flashes of insight to a professional investigation.

> I was just like everyone else. All I cared about was getting the pass. I didn't want
> to have to spend any money on my car. What if something went wrong with the
> test and my car came up with a bad reading? So, for me, that was the defining
> moment—when we realized the absurdity of the situation.

If getting hold of the database presented the initial obstacle, seeing past the rose-
coloured windshield of Drive Clean through to its dubious merits was the second.

> Yes. And then taking that to the next level: What does this mean to you and me,
> and what does it mean to the environment? Ultimately, that's what this program
> was supposed to be all about. And coincidentally or not, following the series—I
> believe Fred can confirm this—the government decided to raise the limit for the
> first test to five years.[17] We're pretty confident that this was based on our series.

Having promoted the program to private garages, the government found itself in a
tight spot once the series started to run.

> The other problem for the government is that they were kind of backed into a
> corner because they had to convince all of these garages to buy expensive
> equipment to conduct the tests. So they couldn't just scrap the whole program,
> because then you'd have thousands of garages saying, 'You forced us to go out
> and spend eighty to a hundred thousand dollars to buy the equipment, and we're
> getting back X per cent of each test, so you're leaving us high and dry with this
> useless equipment.' They were caught between a rock and a hard place. On the
> one side, they would have the garages screaming at them about having to fork
> out money for equipment, and on the other side, they would have drivers who
> were angry because they were taking meaningless tests.

Follow-up stories show the series alerted the public to the issues and moved the
provincial government to revamp Drive Clean.[18] Those are results Buist can live with,
and looking back, he can't think of what the reporters might have done differently.

> You have to keep in mind this wasn't something that was life or death to people.
> It wasn't like anyone was going to die if we didn't do this story. We followed it up
> when the government decided they were going to revamp the program, and we
> kept following that. We're in a bit of a lull now, because the government is at a
> point where they are going to decide whether to pull the plug formally on it.

Buist did note that elsewhere in the world there are live emissions-monitoring systems that actually work to reduce pollution.

> Virtually every state in the United States has some form of emissions monitoring in place, but most of them now use the on-board computer in cars. So you just tap in to the on-board computer as opposed to using an old-fashioned probe up the tailpipe. Some places have also gone to kind of a novel way of doing it using a machine much like a radar gun, to detect speed on the highway. This [device] is pointed at the air and when the car drives by, the device can measure the emissions that are left behind. So they can just set them up at roadside.

Even the technical limitations of Ontario's Drive Clean program rendered it susceptible to cheaters. A favourite scam of unscrupulous operators was known among the initiated as 'clean piping'.[19]

> The program works on the basis that you punch the VIN for a car into the computer. That's what makes the computer think it's your car. What's actually on the treadmill could be anything. The computer knows only what you enter into it. So you could have a twenty-year-old clunker and put that VIN into the system, but have a brand new shiny Cadillac on the treadmill. As far as the computer knows, that's a twenty-year-old car on the treadmill, and that's the easiest way around the system. From the tailpipe of a brand new car, of course you're going to get a very good reading.

Buist doesn't mind being called an investigative reporter—'that's what they call me here'—but neither did he plan for the unofficial title.

> I did a lot of jobs here before. I started as a sports reporter; I was the assistant sports editor. I've also worked at the *Sault Star* in Sault Ste Marie. As the assistant sports editor, I did a number of different editing roles here, and then I decided to go back to reporting. That was a time when we were doing a lot of features and large lengthy projects and it evolved from there.

He never attended journalism school and is 'proud of it'. His attraction to newspaper journalism began in university, in his 'jock' days, and his entrance into the profession was 'a fluke, basically'.

> I went to the University of Guelph. That's where I got my science degree. I was a sports nut, a jock. Guelph has quite a good student newspaper, even though it doesn't have a journalism program. I used to read the paper every week at university and I remember thinking, 'I can do this as well as they can.' I submitted something and they published it. Within a matter of weeks, the sports editor quit, and I inherited [the role] by default. But I was just doing that more as a lark, because I knew I was going away to university to do my graduate work. I was basically doing it for beer money. I had a scholarship to go to the University of

Missouri to do graduate work in neurophysiology. I went down, hated it, was terribly homesick. I came back home and was going to reapply to a Canadian school, but I had to wait for the cycle to come around again.

Born in Hamilton and raised in Burlington, Buist never did complete that master's degree.

No. I went down for a brief period of time and hated it. My old job as sports editor at the Guelph student newspaper was still open, so I was just doing it as something to do, and then I thought, 'Gee, I'm going to see what happens.' So I sent out something like two hundred resumés to basically every newspaper in Ontario. And I guess my resumé just happened to land on the sports editor's desk at the *Sault Star* the same day that someone was quitting. He called me, offered me the job over the phone, and that was it.

Buist's background expertise in science and his hard-evidence approach to stories have proven something of a mixed blessing.

I think a lot of people don't bother to do basic preparation before they start a story, and for someone who deals in science a lot of the time, I spend a whole lot of my time trying to undo damage that reporters have done before me. I'll call up a professor and he's resistant to talk to me because the last journalist he dealt with botched the story. So I spend a lot of my time just saying, 'Look, my background is in science, I came up through the system, you can use big words with me.'

I do spend a lot of my time trying to convince [sources] that they can talk to me and not worry that somebody misquoted them or didn't understand them, or said, 'Here's the next cure for cancer.' So I guess I would say I fully prepare to speak to sources—and then *listen* to what they say. So often, people are just sitting there thinking of the next question they're going to ask without really listening to what they're being told.

His only advice for aspiring reporters is time-tested and shopworn: break into the business and then do a good job.

Get your foot in the door any way you can, because editors are no different from any other part of the species: they will take the path of least resistance. And if you're there in front of them and doing the job [they'll be glad of it]. I mean, I used to be an editor, and I used to have to deal with freelancers, and you knew which ones were dependable, you knew which ones if you were in a pinch you could pick up the phone and say, 'I really need you.' That's how you get into the business—get your foot in the door. Once you've got your foot in the door, I guess what I would say is that right now with the explosion of information that's available at your fingertips, there's no excuse for any reporter in the world to be poorly informed about what the story assignment is.

# Commentary

If only it were possible to bottle the scientific mindset of the insightful Steve Buist and the passionate determination of the indefatigable Fred Vallance-Jones—I'd hand out free vials to all the young hopefuls in the first journalism class of every semester. On the other hand, these ace reporters came by their sterling qualities honestly.

For starters, 'valiant' doesn't half describe the concerted measures Vallance-Jones took to acquire the database for Smokescreen—from December 2000 to its eventual release nearly three years later. When the provincial government turned down his first request for Drive Clean test results in 2000, he swiftly appealed to Ontario's information commissioner. In December 2001, the government released fifty test results—minus the names of the garages who conducted the tests. Again Vallance-Jones appealed, and again the information commissioner ruled in favour of the newspaper. In the fall of 2003, the government did give up the information, including the names of participating garages, but for results only until December 2000—the date of the original access request! Vallance-Jones had to file one last request to finally receive the up-to-date database in November of 2003.[20]

Thus, as is routinely the case in computer-assisted reporting, a database struggle with government authorities preceded actual reportage. The database had existed for years before the *Spectator* series, but had never before been analyzed because it had never before been released. Vallance-Jones has elsewhere commented eloquently on the importance of fighting for such data and wrestling public-interest information into the public realm: 'One big, broken system is at least partially fixed,' he noted, 'because journalists keep fighting for data.'[21]

Computer-assisted reporting presents a potentially revolutionary advance in the arts of reportage. This series is classic CAR, since the twelve million Drive Clean test results could hardly have been analyzed—or even compiled—using only pencil, paper, and brainpower. The reporters could not have hoped to collect so many records and then make sense of them by 'eyeballing' for trends and discrepancies. This CAR story, then, involved a large database and the battle to get it released along with the results of computer-enhanced analysis—both par for the course in CAR projects.

But it involved other more traditional elements as well. Before Steve Buist became involved in the story, he'd noted his own overreaction to the Drive Clean test, a mental note that led to his insight about the psychology of denial underlying a widespread misconception that somehow the program *must* work. Before Vallance-Jones set out to procure the database, he listened to what people were alleging about Drive Clean and asked himself how he might go about finding the truth.

The investigation was prompted by the existence not of a database but of rumours that suggested Drive Clean was not working, that it was in fact being abused. Note how the rumours were lent credibility by the lack of information on the government's own website. This is, of course, how rumours usually circulate—in a deficit of reliable information. Yet rumours are not always borne out, and this is part of what makes investigative journalism a sometimes dicey and always expensive commitment.

Here, as in virtually all investigative work, the old shoe-leather journalism paid off for the reporters, who, at one point in the investigation, went undercover. Posing as prospective used-car buyers, they had the car in question, a 1993 Plymouth Sundance, tested at four garages in the Hamilton-Burlington area—and got highly variable results at each, from 'near failures to a comfortable pass'. Test scores for the same car on the same day, they reported, could 'go up and down like a yo-yo'.[22]

And, of course, the series involved the extensive observation and interviewing of traditional reportage, including especially, as Steve Buist noted, the ability to hear what is being said to you. In fact, the art of listening would appear to be a critical piece of standard equipment in the method of the investigative reporter, for whom 'information' is contestable and facts remain, theoretically at least, provisional. The story is not in the numbers but in the questions you think to ask of the numbers.

Great reporters have always been great questioners. They've always fought for information, followed the money, crunched the numbers to substantiate allegations, and gone the extra mile for the story. Not surprisingly, the greatest reportorial rigour tends to net the greatest stories.

But the potential of CAR is finally of a piece with the potential of investigative reporting. In fact, computer-assisted reporting is best viewed as the latest advance in investigative journalism; it amplifies *and* advances the investigator's attempts to probe beneath the surface of the facts and events we call 'news'. Remember that Vallance-Jones employed traditional means to track down the mechanic who was charged with and convicted of Drive Clean fraud. But his first clue to that source came from government information he acquired by making 'a side request for discipline actions'.

Here is one case where the impact of an investigative series is easy to see, for it was sure and swift. It included (about a week after the series ran) government action to crack down on garages that cheated and to post their names on the Internet. Plans were initiated to exempt newer cars from the tests and eliminate the 'conditional pass' category.[23] The series also underlines the need for follow-up stories. In one of his regular columns for *Media* magazine, Vallance-Jones noted that the impact of this series was further strengthened by the paper's keeping tabs on the issue with timely follows.[24]

At the very least, the series made public the faulty science that underlay the testing and the previously unsubstantiated rumours of irregularities and wrongdoing. In effect, it forced Ontario's provincial government to act.[25] On a deeper level, the series made visible the absurdity of a situation already mired in the context of everyday consumer capitalism. It revealed, among other choice facts, that over the five years motorists had been fulfilling their civic duty and getting their cars tested, the Drive Clean program had cost them more than a billion dollars—all this with vastly overstated and largely unproven environmental benefits.[26]

Even more disconcerting was the discovery late in the series that newer cars had been included in the Drive Clean plan partly *in order* to make the program 'financially viable'.[27] Smokescreen, then, exemplifies how far past the common wisdom CAR can transport enterprising reporters, and by extension, their readers.

# Endnotes

1. Dana Robbins, 'Smoke and mirrors', *Hamilton Spectator* (18 September 2004), A2. In this column, Robbins went into some detail about the battle Vallance-Jones waged to have the records released and the nearly endless obstructions bureaucrats placed in his path.

2. In 2003, Buist had been named Journalist of the Year at the Ontario Newspaper Awards for his exposé of a chain of nursing and retirement homes. In his column, editor Dana Robbins called Buist 'one of our most veteran investigative reporters.' ('Smoke and Mirrors', op. cit.)

3. Steve Buist and Fred Vallance-Jones, 'Your car failed Drive Clean? Try, try, try again', *Hamilton Spectator* (21 September 2004), A1.

4. Casey Korstanje, 'Drive clean smokescreen', *Hamilton Spectator* (20 September 2004), A17.

5. Steve Buist and Fred Vallance-Jones, 'A billion dollars up in smoke', *Hamilton Spectator* (20 September 2004), A1.

6. Steve Buist and Fred Vallance-Jones, 'Is Drive Clean merely bad science?' *Hamilton Spectator* (22 September 2004), A8.

7. Vallance-Jones, 'The fight for data continues', op. cit.

8. Steve Buist and Fred Vallance-Jones, 'Drive Clean's dirty secrets', *Hamilton Spectator*, (18 September 2004), A1.

9. Steve Buist and Fred Vallance-Jones, 'Garage owners say it's tough to profit from Drive Clean', *Hamilton Spectator* (21 September 2004), A6.

10. Fred Vallance-Jones, 'Drive Clean enforcement needs beefing up: MPP', *Hamilton Spectator* (20 September 2004), A7.

11. Rob Ferguson, 'Minister vows to clean up dirty Drive Clean operations', *Hamilton Spectator* (21 September 2004), A7.

12. Fred Vallance-Jones, '2004 was a good year for CAR', *Media* 11.1 (Winter 2005), 18.

13. While the series proper consisted of ten stories, three more are referred to here and listed in Appendix A. See the following: Dana Robbins, 'Smoke and mirrors', *Hamilton Spectator* (18 September 2004), A2; Casey Korstanje, 'Drive clean smokescreen', *Hamilton Spectator* (20 September 2004), A17; Rob Ferguson, 'Minister vows to clean up dirty Drive Clean operations', *Hamilton Spectator* (21 September 2004), A7.

14. Late in 2005, the government's persistent attempts to withhold the database's vehicle identification numbers were quashed by the province's information and privacy commissioner, who ruled that this data too should be released. See Fred Vallance-Jones, 'The fight for data continues', op. cit. 'Just recently, the Ontario government lost the last of three appeals launched by the *Spectator* over the Drive Clean data. The government had been holding out that the vehicle identification numbers of cars constituted the personal information of vehicle owners because for $12, you can look up the name, but not the address, of a vehicle at a transport ministry office. The information and privacy commissioner dismissed that argument, and the VINs are now public along with the rest of the data.'

15. Fred Vallance-Jones, 'The fight for data continues . . . and we do experience success along the way', *Media* 11.4 (Winter 2006), 2.

16. Steve Buist and Fred Vallance-Jones, 'Cheat took cash for fake test results', *Hamilton Spectator* (18 September 2004), A1.

17. Fred Vallance-Jones, 'Drive Clean changing gears', *Hamilton Spectator* (19 November 2005), A3. The lead of the story confirms the Ontario government did revise the rules to have cars tested at five years, not three.

18. An independent review of Drive Clean about a year after the series ran recommended a scrap-and-rebuild operation for the entire emissions-testing program. See Meredith Macleod, 'Drive clean overhaul in the works', *Hamilton Spectator*, (12 September 2005), A1.

19. Steve Buist and Fred Vallance-Jones, 'Drive Clean's dirty secrets', op. cit.

20. For more details, see the article by editor Dana Robbins, 'Smoke and Mirrors', op. cit. Robbins paid both reporters high praise and attributed the *Spectator*'s growing reputation for computer-assisted reporting to Vallance-Jones: 'The fact that the *Spec* has a national reputation in this highly specialized field is a tribute to Fred.'

21. 'The fight for data continues', op. cit.

22. 'Your car failed Drive Clean?' op. cit.

23. Steve Buist and Fred Vallance Jones, 'What's ahead for Drive Clean', (23 September 2004), A1.

24. 'The fight for data continues', op. cit.

25. Steve Buist, '*Spec* series could spark speedy review', *Hamilton Spectator* (23 September 2004), A1.

26. Steve Buist and Fred Vallance-Jones, 'A billion dollars up in smoke', op. cit.

27. Fred Vallance-Jones, 'Drive Clean founder: Put on the brakes', *Hamilton Spectator* (22 September 2004), A1. Datelined Toronto, the story quoted the man who designed Drive Clean. He advised that mandatory emissions testing be phased out, starting with newer vehicles: 'Norm Sterling, environment minister in Tory premier Mike Harris's cabinet, also made the startling revelation yesterday that newer cars were included partly to make Drive Clean "financially viable".'

# Chapter 13

# Singled Out: An Investigation into

# Race and Crime

It goes by various names: racial bias, targeting, institutionalized racism, skin-colour prejudice, and racial profiling. It isn't supposed to happen here, in Canada's largest and most ethnically diverse city. But for years, Toronto's black citizens had complained that the city's police force routinely discriminated against them. For just as long, police had denied the allegations.

At the *Toronto Star*, a team of five led by reporter/photographer Jim Rankin decided to find out the truth. The result was the controversial series Singled Out in the fall of 2002.[1] In the process, the reporters became the first journalists in Canada to bust open a long-time taboo and use computer-assisted reporting to bear out the black community's claims. It took a landmark CAR case, one of the largest and most controversial ever conducted in Canada, to put the facts on the record. The series shows just how far computer-enhanced investigative techniques can take motivated reporters in dissecting a public interest issue.

In March of 2000, the *Star* filed a formal information request for the Toronto police database of arrests made and charges laid. Called the Criminal Information Processing System (or CIPS), the database was normally used for tracking people through the justice system. It included details of police ticketing, arrests, and charges for both criminal offences (like assault) and non-criminal ones (like lapsed car insurance).

A little more than two years later, in June 2002, the database was ordered released by a ruling of the provincial information and privacy commissioner. A modified version of the CIPS database, contained on a single CD, it excluded personal information to protect privacy rights and detailed over a 6-year period (1996 to 2002) some 480,000 incidents of arrest or ticketing, and almost 800,000 cases where charges were laid. Names were removed, but other characteristics of the individuals involved, including skin colour, were not. The database specified skin colour for more than 93 per cent of drug and Criminal Code of Canada offences. The police department might well have noticed the problem in its midst had it analyzed its own data. But to do so would have crossed a line drawn in an undeclared race war that began more than a decade earlier.

In 1989, a police officer spoke publicly about his belief that race and crime were connected. The officer was Julian Fantino, who had yet to become chief of police and was at that time a staff inspector in North Toronto. Fantino released race-based stats at a public meeting, with the 'explanation' that blacks accounted for most of the crime in a certain poverty-stricken, high-crime area of the city. Then all hell broke loose. The officer's comments unleashed the anger of critics and community activists, and the police department was forbidden to analyze the statistics on race and crime readily available in its own database.

The ban imposed by the board that governed Toronto police was ostensibly meant to keep such statistics from being used by bigots to negatively stereotype groups of people. In the commotion, critics went unheard who argued that the injunction against statistical evidence would also tend to protect any officer who did practise racial discrimination from ever being found out, let alone held to account. Police departments in the United States and Britain routinely keep and analyze records that include the skin colour of those stopped, arrested, and charged precisely in order to screen for evidence of racial bias and discriminatory policing among members of the force.

By 2002, the officer who had provoked the 1989 ban had become Toronto's chief of police, and the ban against analyzing race-based stats remained firmly in place. But while police intelligence was forced into the shadows by a kind of mandated ignorance, the *Toronto Star* was under no such constraints.

With the database in hand, and the help of an in-house data specialist, Jim Rankin used Microsoft Access to set about analyzing the information for evidence of racial profiling—a discriminatory practice of stopping black people more often than whites or treating blacks in custody more harshly than whites in custody—both on the assumption of guilt based on the officers' own skin-colour prejudice. After the analysis was completed, the *Star* had the findings checked by a top statistician at York University, Michael Friendly, who pronounced them valid.[2]

The study focused on two areas where evidence of racial profiling could be detected. In the first, it compared what happened to white and black suspects when they were arrested on the same charge of simple drug possession—a 'high-discretion' offence where decisions such as whether to grant bail or retain a suspect in custody are left to the arresting officer. It found that in ten thousand cases over the six-year period, more whites than blacks were released at the scene on a promise to show up in court (76.5 per cent, compared to 61.8 per cent). Of those taken into custody, blacks were kept behind bars awaiting hearings about twice as often as whites (15.5 per cent of the time compared to 7.3 per cent).[3]

The second area of analysis put the same question about racial bias to data on routine traffic stops. The examination of traffic-violation data focused on disparities in so-called 'out-of-sight' offences—those, such as driving without insurance, that officers could discover only after pulling over the motorists in question, presumably at random. But the data showed that police did stop more black drivers than white drivers, providing evidence of racial profiling, defined in the series as the practice of 'targeting racial minorities on the assumption they commit more crimes'.[4]

Based on 7,500 'out-of-sight' violations between 1996 and 2002, the analysis found that blacks were overrepresented—they accounted for nearly 34 per cent of those charged with out-of-sight violations even though they comprised only 8.1 per cent of the city's population. Whites, meanwhile, represented 52.1 per cent of motorists charged while comprising 62.7 per cent of the city's population. The numbers indicated that black men between the ages of 25 and 34 were especially vulnerable. They received 39.3 per cent of tickets issued for out-of-sight violations in the 25–34 age group but made up only 7.9 per cent of Torontonians in the same age group. Black motorists, in other words, were being pulled over for the undeclared 'crime' of 'driving while black'.[5]

Both areas of analysis—drug possession charges and out-of-sight offences—showed clear evidence of racial discrimination: Toronto police, whether consciously or subconsciously (that is, whether or not they intended to do so or were aware that they did so), were targeting blacks. A complaint once regarded as merely anecdotal, now had numbers—the police department's own—to substantiate the claim.

In their work to put human faces to the story, the reporters consulted black community leaders, police representatives, lawyers, academics, and rights advocates. Of course, they also traced and interviewed victims of police discrimination, most of whom requested anonymity for fear of police reprisals.

Not so Jason Burke, a young black man pictured on the front page that kick-started the Singled Out series. Burke had been falsely charged with drug dealing and ultimately released with no charges laid. He wanted to sue police for pepper-spraying him and holding him for three days on charges that finally had to be dismissed for lack of evidence. But the young man held out little hope for change in the system any time soon, maybe ever. 'I don't think a day will come,' he told the reporters, 'when I won't be profiled.'[6]

Graphs, charts, and other visual aids supplemented the crime-data analysis and interviews to draw an uncompromising picture of unequal justice for Toronto's blacks. In a restrained piece that ran with the first story, long-time *Star* managing editor Mary Deanne Shears (who left the paper in 2005) wrote that she hoped the work would lead to action and improved race relations. She explained how the series had begun two years earlier with an access request and, while acknowledging police efforts to address racism on the force, firmly noted that the problem remained.[7]

The series had barely made the stands when it ignited a controversy that smoulders still. While black leaders and rights advocates spoke words of praise, the city's police association sent notice of intent to launch a $2.7 billion class-action suit for defamation. The *Star* never backed down; it continued to stand behind the story, countering police anger and criticism with the facts the reporters and the database analysis had unearthed. The lawsuit was eventually dismissed.[8]

Ten main stories ran from 19 to 26 October 2002—five on 19 October, three on 20 October, and two on 26 October.

# The Interview: **Jim Rankin**
(6 April 2006)

This series arose out of the desire on the part of the reporters to find the truth about the allegations of racial bias and profiling that Toronto's black community had spoken out against for years. They knew that since 1989 the police force had been forbidden to keep race-based records, so to begin with, they didn't realize that a database even existed.

Then they got a lucky break, compliments of a police department clerk who issued a press release with a fortuitous error. The gaffe—a badly worded description of a suspect as 'yellow-skinned'—caught hell from Torontonians. And it got the reporters thinking. The press release and its error suggested that data on race and crime did indeed exist, even if police were mandated not to analyze it (and, in effect, to act as if it didn't exist). Rankin recalls how the reporters got their chance to address the issue.

> It's a neat story. Over the years, there had been a lot of stories, well documented in the local media, about problems Toronto's black communities had had with

police. And I say 'communities' because it's really not fair to say there's one black community in Toronto. You've got people emigrating from Africa; you have people who have been in Canada for generations; and you have people coming from the Caribbean. They're really not one group; they have different problems and different issues. They're just like anyone else in Canada; you can't group them together.

So we knew there were a lot of stories out there. It was in February 1999 that Toronto police erroneously put out a news release in which they described a suspect as having yellow skin. And it caused a stink. There were apologies almost immediately from the police saying it was a mistake [made by] a clerk who should have substituted 'Asian' for 'yellow-skinned'. They said they had a computer code in one of their databases that had skin colour, and yellow meant Asian, and it never should have come out in a public press release.

So it got us thinking about what kind of things the police did document. We were well aware that dating back to the late '80s in Toronto, the police had been officially forbidden from analyzing anything that had to do with race and crime. So we started thinking, 'Well, they have the data, though. They could do it if they wanted to. What if we got hold of that data and had a look at it? What would it show?'

They spent roughly a year making informal, and futile, efforts to get hold of what they believed were two databases. Then, in March 2000 they filed a formal freedom-of-information request stressing that they 'didn't want any personal information, which would hold up the release, and didn't want names'.

The police denied access to both of them and this was the beginning of a two-and-a-half-year FOI battle with the police to get—what ended up being—one database. We appealed a couple of times; they came back with some fee estimates that were kind of outrageous. In one instance, we asked for just a list of the kinds of information that's in the database—a list of fields, we call it. The police said that it would cost us $7,440.

It was never clear why it would cost so much, but by my estimates it should have cost less than a dollar in photocopying fees—it was just a list. And so the information and privacy commissioner got back to us and agreed, saying it should cost 60 cents. And the police released the list eventually.

The number-crunching research began with the database—the single CD containing arrest data from 1996 to 2002. Before the team of reporters ultimately assigned to the series got involved in fleshing it out with interviews and traditional reportage, the data had to be analyzed for correctness and the initial interpretations needed to be sound. The reporting phase was completed only in the last month before the series ran. But in a sense, Singled Out began with that simple sheet of information, called a police arrest form.

> On police arrest forms we ended up looking at the kinds of information that are recorded in an arrest, and skin colour was one of them. That was the impetus. Then it was just a matter of getting the data and getting it in cleanly in a way that wouldn't infringe on people's personal information.

The research required that the reporters look to the UK and the US to compare how these countries—and their newspapers—dealt with racial profiling in their police forces. Did they keep race-based statistics and review them?

> In the US, this is nothing new . . . they review it without much controversy. They use it as a tool to look for patterns of potentially biased behaviour by officers. In a lot of places, this stuff is not remotely controversial. In the UK, they release data every year showing who police stopped, by skin colour, and reasons why, and it's really progressed way beyond where we're still at today in Canada.
>
> We looked at how other papers in different jurisdictions—in the UK and the US—had gone about things, what kind of problems they had encountered, and learned from that, and we certainly did a lot of reading of anecdotal stories and looking for people who had been on the receiving end of some biased policing.

The series also took the reporters back in time to the 1989 incident that provoked the order to refrain from keeping records on race and crime. When Julian Fantino let drop his take on race-based stats at a public meeting, a *Star* reporter was there. When Fantino's comments appeared in the *Toronto Star*, an uproar of criticism ensued and the ban was born.

> That happened because Julian Fantino, who back then was not yet chief but with a division in North Toronto, revealed at a public meeting some race-based crime data that showed who was being arrested for certain crimes in that area. In the audience was a *Toronto Star* journalist, Royson James, and the next day or shortly thereafter, he wrote up the whole meeting and the fact that race-based stats had been released. And this ignited a huge controversy in the city and this paper for one advocated on the editorial pages that we shouldn't keep race-based stats, we shouldn't be looking at them, it's dangerous, they could get into the hands of people who will use them to push their racist agendas and say that [a given] community is more responsible for certain kinds of crime. So that was the genesis of the ban.

But wasn't it damning in itself that Toronto police didn't want to release the database in the first place? Doesn't it suggest that they knew they had a problem and just didn't want anybody else to know about it?

> Well, who knows if they ever looked at it themselves to see what it showed before they released it to us? The concern was genuine. The police board in 1989 issued this edict that they're not to analyze race-based data. 'You can't do it, you're not allowed,' the board said.

The idea of race-based statistics hit a raw nerve, but by the time of Rankin and company's Singled Out series on race and crime, things had changed. Support had grown for the idea of keeping such stats precisely in order to gauge for police bias.

> People had come around to thinking, 'Well, what's the harm with just looking, and using it as a tool to gauge for potential bias?' And in a lot of jurisdictions they had already reached that conclusion much earlier. But in Canada they hadn't, and they still haven't really. So that was a reason why they were probably hesitant to give us the data, too—they weren't supposed to look at it.

The defining moment for Rankin came when the database analysis began to yield its telling disproportions, in the process vindicating the black community. To the trained eye, certain patterns stood out.

> You just eyeball the gaps. We knew there were big differences that the data couldn't explain away.

But the statistical analysis was so complex—and the results so potentially explosive—that the *Star* sought the help of a newsroom specialist and a statistical expert at York University before publishing.

> We knew that it would be very controversial. We did the initial analysis completely in house—it was me and a database specialist in the library, who in a previous job had done a lot of work with big databases—and we spent the better part of the summer cleaning up the data, asking questions of it, trying to find answers for why we were seeing what we were seeing, and trying to find factors within the data that would explain the differences we were seeing. In the end, we took our findings package and methodology to Professor [Michael] Friendly at York University. The main goal was to have him review it and look at the methodology and give us a yea or a nay on whether or not it was sound. And he did do that.
>
> Friendly just used more sophisticated software than we have to look at probabilities. For instance, he did a regression analysis to look for possible things that we couldn't see with the naked eye that might explain the patterns. We published after that and he did a more extensive review afterwards.

Ultimately, five reporters worked on Singled Out: Jim Rankin, John Duncanson, Scott Simmie, Michelle Shephard, and Jennifer Quinn. But it started out with just two, Rankin and Duncanson, who had worked together before on another piece.

> We actually did an earlier police series in '96 or '97—another analysis. So for a while there, although we had to wait a long time, and it was a battle, it wasn't too labour-intensive. We just had to wait for the process to work its way through. Once we had a copy of the data in hand, everyone else got involved. We got five reporters together: two former police-issues reporters, two crime reporters, and feature writer Scott Simmie. And we needed that many.
>
> Part of the problem was we had to analyze it all first, and then start the reporting that would flesh it out and put a human face on it. We didn't want to go around telling everybody we had analyzed this data and found X when we weren't finished it yet. We had to wait until the final numbers were in and then we went knocking on doors. The actual reporting phase at the end took only a month.

The battle for data, on the other hand, consumed a lot of time.

> It was a win in the end that we got the stuff, but it actually came to us through the mediation phase. We were in a back-and-forth, quite co-operative conversation with the Toronto police at the end, and it was mainly because we had to deal with issues of privacy: How do we make sure there are no names in there? How do we make sure we can't take an exact criminal charge—say it's a bizarre one, like sticking your dog with a fork, and there's only two of them in the whole database—and protect that person from being identified? You could potentially go to the court and say, 'Tell me the people who have been charged with sticking their dog with a fork,' and we would know who it is.
>
> So there were a lot of those sorts of issues that had to be ironed out. And there was a lot of co-operation, too, with the police in the end before they handed the database to us. It was in electronic format. This would not have worked on paper . . . we're talking about a massive database.

As Rankin says, the major obstacles for the reporters included getting the database in the first place (that occurred two years after the initial freedom-of-information request, when the province's information and privacy commissioner ruled in the *Star*'s favour and a mediator was appointed to deal with privacy concerns), doing the complex analysis required, and then finally dealing with the police fallout—including the force's threat of a $2.7 billion libel lawsuit against the paper.

If he had it all to do over again, Rankin said, he would have got the website up faster and more completely, both for greater transparency and to dispel more readily the charges by opponents that the reporters had 'cherry-picked' the data.

> What we should have done was get everything ready to go up online when we published—everything—showing the raw data, the complete methodology. People who wanted to could go see how we did it; it would be more transparent.
>
> We had that on the Internet, but it wasn't in-depth to the level that we thought we needed it to be. We thought it was good . . . and then we realized after the stories ran and the shit hit the fan that we had to get more up there, show them the raw data. There's a lot of work involved just getting that ready for public consumption. You have to pretty much publish a guide so people know what they're looking at, and it would have taken probably another month to get it ready for that kind of presentation.

The impact was immediate and explosive. Thanks poured in from the vindicated black communities and demands came from several quarters for inquiries and action plans. On the downside, the police union threatened a $2.7 billion class-action libel suit on behalf of its more than seven thousand members. The reporters were prepared for some heat, but not for the firestorm of protest that they got from police.

> We knew there'd be a pretty emotional reaction to it, we just didn't know how big. It was a big issue overnight, and it wasn't an issue that was new either, I mean to the black communities.

Though the controversy was long-standing, the *Toronto Star* series made the issues addressable by naming them and documenting the facts.

> Well, it made it mainstream, tangible. There had been plenty of academic studies—in Ontario, in Toronto, in Canada—that pointed to the same kind of problems, and they received a lot less attention because, probably, they were academic in nature.
>
> There was a landmark study in Ontario, the Ontario Commission into Systemic Racism in the Justice System. It involved all kinds of stakeholders and academics, who had access to raw police and court data. It was very expensive and it pointed to systemic racism. It came out, and got some pretty good media coverage. And then the government of the day, the NDP, were voted out in 1995, and that report got lost. It came out at the end of the NDP government's reign, and it got put to the back burner.
>
> Our series examined stuff that's been brought up in the past, but it was packaged in a newspaper format, and in a way that allowed people to really connect with it. And it involved an analysis of a pretty huge chunk of data.

The series relied on computer-assisted reporting and on the existence of a large database. In the case of Singled Out, the data 'was there, it was already recorded, and in electronic format.' But there are still many occasions, Rankin noted, where no database exists and reporters are forced to build their own. Such was the case, for instance, with the series Nobody's Children.

Rankin embraced CAR when he built his own database for the earlier police series he wrote with Duncanson.

> For the last police story I worked on before this one, I ended up with a database of five hundred Toronto officers who had had some form of trouble. We made that. We got hold of paper documents that related to police disciplinary hearings, the complaint system, and instances where judges had spoken from the bench in a critical way of police conduct. So we actually had to assemble the database. It wasn't a matter of asking for it, the thing didn't exist. And that's how I got started.

A self-confessed and unabashed investigative reporter on the *Star*'s I-team, Rankin believes that anyone can engage in computer-assisted reporting with a little help from colleagues and experts.

Rankin started at the *Star* as a photographer, then went back to school for a journalism degree. He enjoyed his tour of duty in journalism school.

> It was the best of the six years I spent in university—a lot of fun. Though I still think there's a great value in having a degree in something other than journalism as well.

After journalism school, Rankin became a two-way (both photographer and reporter) at the *Star*. It took several years into his time at the paper before Rankin got interested in investigative journalism and developed his keen ability in computer-assisted reporting. His advice on investigative reporting and CAR is to the point: 'Do your homework and continually question.'

One of the problems, or potential brakes, on the use of computer-assisted reporting is widespread innumeracy among reporters. Rankin concedes it's common but believes that lack of math skills shouldn't stop a good reporter from chasing down a story; it should urge him or her to get help. Ultimately, the solution is to address the basic problem of innumeracy, and in the meantime to remember that 'you can really be taken advantage of if you don't understand how things work.'

Still, you don't have to be adept at CAR to begin to use it, he maintained. You can get help with the heavier mathematical stuff as long as you understand the basic principles, the kinds of questions to ask—and these are the same things required in all good reporting.

You don't have to know how to do it to benefit from it. You have to understand what you can do with it. And once you understand that, if you're at a newspaper that has resources, you can ask for the data. And when you land it, get someone to help you with it. So you don't have to be a computer genius to do this stuff. You have to think like a reporter, and a lot of it isn't that complex. It's about counting, but the computer allows you to do it much quicker.

The race and crime one [Singled Out] was different; it was a pretty deep analysis that involved all kinds of parameters. It wasn't a simple matter of counting and it was a lot more involved. And you need to have people who specialize in that kind of stuff to get you through.

Computer-assisted reporting also isn't exclusive to large investigative projects; it can be incorporated into daily reporting technique to good effect.

If you think of it as a tool that will help you, say, review the budget, you can take the budget and stick it into a spreadsheet and see if everything adds up. And if it doesn't add up, ask some questions. It's pretty basic—you can do that on paper.

The techniques of computer-assisted reporting can allow journalists to finally go beyond 'attributive' stories—the he-said-she-said variety—to devise their own research questions and paths, to crunch their own numbers, and do their own analyses from the perspective of the public interest.

It allows you to shed some light on things that previously probably wouldn't have been looked at by journalists. The software has allowed us to do a different kind of investigative reporting. It's still just a tool, and you still have to find people to illustrate your stories. I mean, looking at data all day is not too exciting.

In the end, it all comes down to some well-worn words of advice for aspiring reporters: take it slow and steady, but take it. Seek out expertise. And don't forget the old standby, reproven at every turn: assume nothing.

It's so true . . . assuming makes an ass out of you and me. You can't really take anything on its appearance and say that this must be so. You have to continually question what you're looking at. And particularly when it comes to data-related projects, you always have to ask yourself, 'Well I'm seeing this but what can explain *why* I'm seeing this, and who do I have to talk to, to explain it for me?' That's crucial. It's also important to get the ear of a few people who really know the topic you're looking at, even if you don't intend to quote them. Just get in and use them as a mentor and—this has been said, too—just sit at their feet for a while and listen. You have to do that, to get familiar with a topic, especially when

> you're becoming a quasi-expert at something and every year there's a new topic
> that comes along. You really have to listen hard and be open.

As for investigative reporting, you don't have to be at the *Toronto Star* to engage.

> I think there's a misconception that only the big papers can do this stuff, and it's
> just not true. In a small town, you can ask your city hall for data and take it and
> look at it, and come up with a story. You don't have to have a lot of money to do
> it and you don't have to have a lot of people.

You have to have the brains, the talent, and the motivation.

# Commentary

It would be difficult to find a better example than the *Star*'s Singled Out series to exemplify the elements of the classic investigative project. Pulling it off took the dedicated perseverance of five reporters and two database analysts, not to mention the paper's commitment of money, time, and unflagging moral support. It illustrates the power and potential of computer-assisted reporting, whose advent has raised the journalistic bar and made social-science research methods part of the mix for reporters' repertoires. To the sense of mission and the perseverance to overcome obstacles characteristic of the investigative reporter, CAR brings a new element: an operational question.

In the end, Singled Out was not only about institutionalized racism, it was also about the newspaper's staking of a claim to authority in defending the public's right to know. There had been previous studies that arrived at conclusions similar to those of the *Star*'s investigation, documenting consistent, even 'normalized' racial discrimination within the police force, and there had been efforts by the police and others to address the issue. But never before had a local newspaper held its local police force—and its entire community, finally—to such clarion account. In a city much touted for its ethnic diversity, the series asserted not only the public's *right* but also its *responsibility* to know about the racial profiling going on under its nose.

As soon as Singled Out began to run, letters and calls of commendation and support poured in from the vindicated black communities. Officials were deluged with demands for action from all corners. A former Ontario lieutenant-governor called for a summit meeting; the provincial human rights commission announced an inquiry into racial profiling; the solicitor-general said the public process for complaints against police—widely denounced as toothless at best—would be reviewed. The rush

of commentary continued for months in letters to the editor, columns, and news stories, all reflecting a gamut of response from the impassioned support of the vindicated to the calls for change of the newly outraged.[9]

The editorial ink flowed from the pens of columnists, including Royson James,
the *Star* reporter who had covered the 1989 meeting that sparked the ban on race-
based statistics.[10] By the end of 2002, the statistician who had pronounced on the
series was featured as a kind of hero ('the man behind the numbers')[11], critics were
urging a new policy for traffic stops (including surveillance cameras in police cruis-
ers),[12] and yet another rights group announced it would undertake a study.[13]

The impact of the Singled Out series extended to police officials in Kingston,
Ontario, who in the spring of 2003 announced they would consider their own study
to determine whether police there engaged in racial profiling. The plan met with concerted opposition from the head of the Ontario Association of Chiefs of Police,[14] but
that summer the Kingston force defied the association and said it would proceed to
gather race-and-crime statistics.[15]

By June 2005, the Kingston force had completed its study, finding ample evidence
of racial profiling. Editorials urged the Toronto force to follow in the progressive
footsteps Kingston had forged and finally look at the human devastation behind the
numbers indicating racial bias among its officers.[16] In 2006, provincial legislation was
introduced to restore civilian oversight of the police complaints process introduced a
decade earlier, a procedure that had police overseeing their own complaints process.[17]

But closer to home, the police reaction was less enlightened. The Toronto force
responded badly to the example set by its counterpart in Kingston. From the first,
Toronto police officials had flatly denied the existence of racial profiling and fiercely
resisted all evidence unearthed. The police chief of the day, Julian Fantino, called
almost immediately for what he termed an 'independent' race-relations probe.[18] He
railed against the study, claiming the *Star*'s findings didn't 'make any sense'. When
the *Star* presented its research to the police chief at a fall 2002 interview that was supposed to last an hour and was attended by senior police officials and the force's
lawyer, the chief cut short the meeting after twenty minutes. Later that day, in a
police memo, he charged the *Star* with dubious motives and accused it of engaging
itself in 'racial profiling for its own private agenda'.[19]

Barely three months later, early in 2003, with the controversy still roiling, the
police union announced its intention to sue the *Star* for libel in a $2.7 billion class-
action suit on behalf of its 7,200 members.[20] Attacks on the accuracy of the series'
findings continued, and despite the rigour of the investigation and the verification of
findings by external experts, police critics dismissed the study as 'junk science'.[21]

The *Star* stood fast, countering criticism with the evidence hard-won by its
reporters. It published a response to its angry critics[22] and found some comfort

several weeks later in its nomination for the prestigious Michener Award for Meritorious Public Service Journalism. In an article brimming with pride, the paper reported that the effects of Singled Out were still reverberating.[23] The story did end up winning the Michener as well as the National Newspaper Award for investigative reporting in 2002.[24] The race probe that had been announced soon after the series ended got under way with much publicity,[25] and the lawsuit was ultimately dismissed, though not for lack of effort on the part of the police union.[26]

One of the things the database analysis had shown was a disproportionately high rate of blacks charged with violent crimes, especially among the city's Jamaican ex-pat community, a finding that could not be explained by racial profiling or other forms of police bias. The data showed that nearly half of the violent-crime charges in Toronto were laid against people born in Canada; the next highest category was people born in Jamaica (who accounted for only 2.4 per cent of the population, but 9.5 per cent of the violent-crime charges).[27] In cases of violence, police officers have little discretionary leeway—they aren't deciding by their own lights whom to pull over, but are intervening in ongoing violent disputes or charging someone after the fact of a violent crime. In other words, in the matter of this finding, there was little room for officers to exercise a racial bias, again either conscious or subconscious. In the city's Jamaican community, the high rate of violence turned out to have more to do with poverty and gun laws than police discrimination. It is a further tribute to the series, the reporters, and the *Toronto Star* that they did not try to whitewash this finding by ignoring or downplaying it.

The numbers told a story, one that could not be ignored. Now that evidence had been produced, the controversy unleashed, and the public made aware—the rivers of ink seemed to suggest—the appropriate authorities would have to move from denying the problem to dealing with it. Public officials would be held to account. In study after study, commission after commission, and report after prestigious report, the existence of racism in the police force had been documented and decried.

University of Toronto criminologist Scot Wortley, an expert in racial profiling widely quoted in the series, said the *Star*'s research findings had simply documented what many other studies had suggested, and what many people had long believed. Wortley's 1997 study, 'The Usual Suspects: Race, Police Stops and Perceptions of Criminal Justice', was among the most thorough and detailed work ever done on racial profiling in Canada. Another of his studies, co-authored by Gail Kellough of Toronto's York University and published in 2002 in the *British Journal of Criminology*, found that in two Toronto bail courts blacks were 1.5 times more likely to be kept behind bars than whites. The study, which had benefited from access to notes written by arresting officers, also pointed out that police officers were likelier to judge blacks more harshly than whites when they wrote up their suspect-assessment reports. The more negative the arresting officer's assessment, the less likely the accused would be to make bail, and the more likely to plead guilty to the charges. Even earlier, the landmark 1995 Commission on Systemic Racism in the Ontario Criminal Justice System concluded on the basis of Toronto police files from 1989 and 1990 that the city's blacks were three times more likely to be refused bail than whites facing the same charge.

One of the stories carried a photo of Wortley. It showed him in his office, sitting on a stool beside a large poster depicting Martin Luther King on the left and Charles Manson on the right, under a three-deck banner headline announcing that the black civil rights leader is seventy-five times more likely to be stopped by police than the white convicted murderer.[28]

Of course the investigation's findings came as no surprise to members of the black communities. One black leader noted that there had already been numerous studies documenting racial discrimination in the force. What was needed was not another study, she urged, but action to redress the wrong. 'I've been in Canada for thirty years and have heard about the problem with racial bias and policing every year for thirty years,' said Valarie Steele. 'This is not news to us.'[29]

Indeed, the unsavoury findings stretched back in a long line of studies. They included a 1992 Stephen Lewis report on 'two-tier' policing several years before the already-mentioned Commission on Systemic Racism in the Ontario Criminal Justice System. In fact, the *Star* series was but the latest in a long line of probes to uncover racial discrimination in policing, although the first to do so in the form of a newspaper series accessible to 'average readers'.

Over and over again, the charge that police practised racial profiling was proven. A few years after Singled Out, Jim Rankin returned to the issues briefly in the pages of the *Star*[30] to comment on a new book entitled *The Colour of Justice: Policing Race in Canada*. Its author, University of Windsor law professor David Tanovich, used hundreds of news articles, academic studies, and commissioned reports to show that racial profiling was routinely practised by police forces across the country to target blacks and virtually all people of colour.[31]

Yet no matter how many times the charge of institutionalized racism was reiterated, it appeared in some sectors to fall silent on the deaf ears of dogma, oblivious to evidence.

The thinking around racial profiling could become a self-fulfilling prophecy. The series repeatedly cited criminologists to make the point that the vast majority of individuals in any community, regardless of skin colour, obey the law, in order to counteract an opposing 'argument' that higher crime rates among blacks 'justify' racial profiling. But if the majority in all groups is law-abiding, then nothing justifies profiling—it's merely another name for racial prejudice in action. If police officers assume that blacks are inherently violent, they will subject them to greater surveil-lance, which in turn will result in a greater number of arrests, reinforcing the preju-dice. And although the police force had called for race-relations programs over the years, it never aggressively recruited black or other minority officers to try to address the problem within. (For example, in October 2002 when Singled Out ran, only 11 per cent of police recruits were visible minorities.)

The series cited a chilling example, courtesy of Scot Wortley, of the kind of circu-lar thinking that perpetuated the racism: 'We know as criminologists that the vast majority of all communities are law-abiding,' Wortley said. 'We also know that most pedophiles are white [males]. Does that mean that every time there's a case of such a crime that all white males deserve to be stereotyped, and stopped, and searched?'[32]

Perhaps the greatest service of Singled Out was to show how a refusal to see racism had become an unspoken order to say nothing about it—a denial of the evidence that amounted to blaming both victim and messenger while perpetuating the idea that some forms of racism are somehow acceptable.

# Endnotes

1. For this chapter's examination, the five reporters agreed to let *Star* veteran Jim Rankin speak for the group.

2. 'Treatment differs by division', *Toronto Star* (19 October 2002), A12.

3, 'Singled out: *Star* analysis of police crime data shows justice is different for blacks and whites', *Toronto Star* (19 October 2002), A1.

4. Ibid.

5. 'Police target black drivers: *Star* analysis of traffic data suggests racial profiling', *Toronto Star* (20 October 2002), A1.

6. 'Singled out', op. cit.

7. 'Our duty: Examine all issues', *Toronto Star* (19 October 2002), A2.

8. The police union was unable to carry through with its threat to sue the paper because the group was too large to allow for any single officer to be identified as racist. The civil offence of defamation requires the individual plaintiff to be identifiable as the subject of the allegations.

9. See the following: Nick McCabe-Lokos, 'Tougher watch on police urged: Council weighs in on race-crime row', *Toronto Star* (1 November 2002), A21; Scott Simmie and Jennifer Quinn, 'Complaint system under fire: Lack of faith seen in police complaint system', *Toronto Star* (21 November 2002), B1.

10. See especially the following: Royson James, 'Statistics only lend weight to experience', *Toronto Star* (23 October 2002), B1; 'Racial data a hot potato: Even among activists an old debate rages: Can statistics do good as well as harm?' *Toronto Star* (26 October 2002), B4; Royson James 'Old reactions to race, crime won't work', *Toronto*

*Star* (28 October 2002), B1; John Deverell, 'Racial profiling seen as crime: Race-relations group weighs in on controversy', *Toronto Star* (29 October 2002), B5.

11. Betsy Powell, 'Man behind the numbers: Statistics expert played key role in race, crime series', *Toronto Star* (11 December 2002), B1.

12. John Duncanson, 'Police may need policy for traffic stops', *Toronto Star* (4 December 2002), B1.

13. Scott Simmie and Michelle Shephard, 'Rights group set to probe profiling', *Toronto Star* (10 December 2002), A1.

14. 'Kingston police may keep notes on race', *Toronto Star* (17 May 2003), A21.

15. Sonia Verma, 'Kingston police to gather race data', *Toronto Star* (19 July 2003), A1.

16. 'Follow Kingston's lead', *Toronto Star* (28 May 2005), F6; and 'Race-based data tells human tale', *Toronto Star* (2 July 2005), F6.

17. 'Overseeing the police', *Toronto Star* (21 April 2006), A18. In 1997, the Ontario government disbanded an independent body, the Public Complaints Commission, leaving people with complaints the single option of taking their allegations of misconduct directly to police, an option widely regarded as toothless at best.

18. Michelle Shephard and Jennifer Quinn, 'Police chief calls for race-relations probe: Justice Dubin to study treatment of black suspects', *Toronto Star* (26 October 2002), A1, A15.

19. '"There is no racism. We do not do racial profiling"', *Toronto Star*, (19 October 2002), A14. The *Star* ran a selected transcript of the interview with then Toronto police chief Julian Fantino.

20. Peter Small, 'Police union sues *Star* over race-crime series: 7200-member group seeks $2.7B damages in class-action lawsuit', *Toronto Star* (18 January 2003), A6.

21. Paul Moloney, 'Police attack *Star*'s race articles: Lawyer calls articles "junk science"', *Toronto Star* (21 February 2003), A1.

22. 'The *Star*'s response to the critics', *Toronto Star* (1 March 2003), A27.

23. Philip Mascoll, '*Star*'s race and crime series gets Michener nomination', *Toronto Star* (19 March 2003), A2.

24. Stan Josey, '*Star* wins prestigious awards: Race and crime series honoured for investigations', *Toronto Star* (3 May 2003), A3.

25. Catherine Porter, 'Race probe has busy opening', *Toronto Star* (19 February 2003), B2.

26. The libel suit was first dismissed in 2003, but the police union didn't give up until after its third try in 2005. See the following: Tracey Tyler, 'Police lawsuit against the Star dismissed', *Toronto Star* (25 June 2003), A1; and Nicolaas van Rijn, 'Ruling favours *Star*: Highest court kills $2.7 B class-action libel suit: Toronto Police Association's third straight loss', *Toronto Star* (28 January 2005), A2.

27. 'Black crime rates highest', *Toronto Star* (26 October 2002), A1, A14.

28. 'Police target black drivers: *Star* analysis of traffic data suggests racial profiling', *Toronto Star* (20 October 2002), A9.

29. 'Black crime rates highest', op. cit.

30. Jim Rankin, 'Justice is white: A new book says racial profiling is a sad fact of Canadian life', *Toronto Star* (26 March 2006), D4. See also Philip Mascoll and Jim Rankin, 'Racial profiling exists: Promises of internal probe fell flat', *Toronto Star* (31 March 2005), A1.

31. David Tanovich, *The Colour of Justice: Policing Race in Canada* (Toronto: Irwin Law, 2006).

32. 'Black crime rates highest', op. cit.

Part Three

# Talking Investigative Journalism

Chapter 14

# Conversations with Canadian

# Journalists

## Julian Sher
(23 May 2006)

A long-time investigative reporter, Montreal-based Julian Sher is also the creator and webmaster of JournalismNet.com, a site much consulted by students and professionals for its tips on using the Internet to do investigative work. He has been associated with investigative reporting for decades and was a founding member of the Centre for Investigative Journalism (the precursor to the Canadian Association of Journalists). Though he was with the CBC for a number of years, Sher has tended to move from medium to medium with ease as a freelancer. He's produced television documentaries, written newspaper articles, and authored books.[1]

---

Among Sher's newspaper achievements was a series of articles on the Hells Angels motorcycle gang. Sher worked on the award-winning 2004 biker series, The Power of the Patch,[2] with two *Globe and Mail* reporters, Michael den Tandt and Tim Appleby. Sometimes Sher pitches stories to newspaper editors. For the Hells Angels project, given his track record covering the notorious band of bikers, the paper sought him out.

> The *Globe and Mail* approached me; it was a proposal by Michael [Den Tandt], actually. He was interested in doing something about the bikers, and since it would be a long-term investigative feature they thought they would need my contacts and my expertise. We also wanted to convince the executives at the *Globe* to spend the time, the money, and especially give up the actual pages for a major investigative piece.
>
> They wanted to beef up their investigative work, and I had already done some stuff for them. There was a bit of lobbying because the topic was important. But we also had to convince the *Globe* to set aside four or five spreads, often double-page spreads, for several days in a row. And that's asking a lot of a daily newspaper.
>
> Investigative journalism is costly. They had to set aside the time. They had to free up two reporters. I was freelance, so they had to pay me a lot of money for a freelancer, because it's not a one-up [a single-story assignment]. I was working there for about four to six weeks. So they had to free up two journalists, a lot of editors and photographers, and then they had to free up the real estate of those pages.

Real estate?

> That's what it is. They can put ads there or 'prime-minister-sneezes' stories, but they do have to keep up their daily commitment as well.

Sher wanted to ensure that the paper was committed to the story, and would apportion it sufficient resources as well as good editorial attention and play.

> One of the things we had agreed on was we weren't going to start the project without the commitment of resources. We actually knew who our editor was going to be and it was somebody that I trusted quite a lot. I was less worried about the editor than with making sure that the commitment was there. And that's the first basic point I always make: investigative journalism can't be done without commitment by the person who's doing it, the actual grunt, but especially commitment by whoever your media boss is.

The *Globe and Mail* did commit to the story for various reasons.

> I think my credentials, Mike and Tim's enthusiasm, the fact that it was a hot story, that they did want to increase their crime coverage . . . it didn't take a lot of arm-twisting. We just had to lay it out. I had one of those rare—I don't want to

say pedigrees—but I had written a book, I'm well known for my TV work. I'd also written for newspapers, so they could lasso me in.

By this time, Sher was a fixture in Canadian journalism, a widely known and highly regarded entity.

But an entity who had already written for newspapers. So we came up with a plan right away. We began to outline some of our targets, and we even outlined what the story would look like if we could get all the stuff and, of course, it evolves and changes. And that was it. It was history.

It was also a great read with undeniable impact. As soon as the last piece in the series ran, things began to happen.

The next week the attorney general announced that he was going to set up a special squad to help prosecutors fight organized crime, and he explicitly referenced the *Globe and Mail* series. And that's rare, to have such a strong impact right away.

Sher had been covering the Hells Angels for years. By the time of the *Globe* series, he had already published *Road to Hell: How the Biker Gangs Are Conquering Canada*, a text that helped turn the tables on the group and bring media scrutiny to their activities.

I think it's indisputable—not vanity or anything—that *Road to Hell* changed the political and journalistic landscape in terms of the bikers. In BC, after publication of *Road to Hell* the media took up the battle against the Hells Angels. And the *Vancouver Sun*, especially, and also the *Province* began doing investigative stuff on their own, taking on the bikers. The bikers were getting an easy ride from politicians, the police, and the media in BC for the longest time. After the book came out, the RCMP, some of the top brass, were not very pleased and, in fact, launched a bit of an investigation to try to find out who had been talking to me. But in the end the RCMP reorganized itself. The book was very critical of senior management of the RCMP and said that they had dropped the ball very seriously in trying to get the bikers. But some in the RCMP agreed, and the book was one of the contributing factors to a reorganization of how the police looked at the bikers in BC. It was also a direct contributor to Revenue Canada's decision to go after the Hells Angels financially in British Columbia. It's rare you see a book playing such a direct role. And because it was a best-seller, it changed, I think, the way the public looked at the bikers as well.

Books do not, of course, reach as many people as newspaper articles, but in terms of measurable societal influence, they can pack a bigger punch.

> A newspaper reaches [farther]—the *Globe and Mail*, you're talking 500,000 [in circulation]; the *Toronto Star* is 800,000; a book, if you're lucky, sells 30,000, 40,000, 50,000—that's a huge best-seller in Canada.[3] But it doesn't matter. A book is permanent, it stays on; it's passed around. Books have a permanency and a long-term impact that newspapers and TV don't.

Having published *Road to Hell*, Sher had already done much of the necessary research for the newspaper series, and even more importantly, he had already paved the way for access to the right people, including top RCMP officials. The initial difficulty was gaining the same high-level access for the newspaper reporters.

> I put together a list of some of the best cops to speak to. We then actually organized a formal meeting with the biker enforcement unit, and we sat down with them and began laying out our project, and also began getting a lot of questions. That was a crucial meeting because we had to win over the trust of the biker cops. They knew me; they didn't know the other guys. The BEU [Biker Enforcement Unit] is a very tight organization, so you have to go in through the front door, and from the top down. You can't just get low-level, front-line cops. You've got to go through their bosses first.
>
> I had already earned their trust through *Road to Hell*. And then I just had to say, 'Look, trust me. Trust these guys. Here's what we want to do.' But at the same time, we had to make clear there were no deals, they were not going to see any of our stuff ahead of time, we were not going to pick favourites. We had to lay out the rules, and they had to lay out their rules. They were not going to give us any information about any ongoing cases or name any individuals.
>
> And that was actually important because one of them, the top BEU guy, later on was called to testify about the series when the anti-gang trial was going on. Don Bell was put on the stand and asked about why he co-operated with journalists. And he was able to say, 'I just answered their questions, they're investigative journalists, that's their job.' But because we had set out clear ground rules, we were able to show that everything was above board and ethical. I mean we didn't know that a few months later, he would actually have to testify about that meeting. But he did, in a biker trial. So that's why it's important to set the ground rules.

When he began working on the newspaper series, Sher wondered whether there would be anything new to uncover, anything he hadn't already addressed in *Road to Hell*. He wouldn't be disappointed.

I knew a lot about it. But it was interesting—the good thing about journalism is you almost always are surprised, and if you're not surprised, you're in trouble, you're doing something wrong. Because you certainly want to surprise the reader or the viewer, but you also want to surprise yourself. So the good thing about it is that I was surprised; I said to myself, 'I've written the book on this already, literally.' I didn't think I would learn new stuff.

But, in fact, you do, partly because it's going to be updated, but you wind up finding out much more. We had surprising access with the prosecutors. We got an interview with Donny Peterson. We got much more colour about what it was really like in London, Ontario, and in St Catharines. So the series wound up being much richer, and the informant, Bill—I'd never had an on-the-record interview where we actually ran a photograph of an informant. So in that sense we were exceptionally pleased.

The Power of the Patch series began with the story of an ordinary man who had been threatened by the Hells Angels over a business dealing after having gradually become ensnared in their criminal activities. The beautifully crafted story juxtaposed two worlds, a 'normal' one where violence is an aberration, and the world of the biker gang, where it was a way of doing business. This jarring disconnect makes the point that what happened to the ordinary man victimized by the Hells Angels could happen to anybody because the Angels are not an alien entity—they live among the so-called normal, not in a separate or foreign world. Did Sher think about that during the writing of the piece?

Yeah. I mean, almost all good journalism is a postcard from somewhere. It's either a postcard from Darfur: wish you were here, or wish you weren't here. Or it's a postcard into somebody's head: here's what the prime minister is thinking about as he wrestles with this dilemma. You're taking the readers somewhere they haven't been, sometimes into their own souls, if you're making them begin to think about their ethics.

So it's a postcard. And to some degree this was going to be a postcard from hell, and tell you about towns and people that had been terrorized in one way or another by the bikers. But you also had to make the bikers real—these are not demons, they're regular guys. So we had to get a sense of them.

Though Sher was an old hand at newspaper writing and faced no major obstacles in writing the series, he was nonetheless operating outside of his true element, which is broadcast journalism.

I guess in any medium, there's a fair amount of lobbying and politicking that goes on, and this was foreign territory for me. When I work for the CBC, I know where my documentary is going to get aired, I know the people, I know the game. And when you're writing a book, your publisher wants the book in stores. With the *Globe and Mail*, it took me a while to figure out the playing field, and the efforts that had to be made to make sure that the story got the treatment it deserved. But they were behind it from the start, so that really helped. I've always had a good relationship with them.

Sher didn't know the two reporters before he began working with them on the series project, but he knew their copy.

I was lucky, because both of them are excellent reporters and fine writers. Tim has covered crime for a long time, and has a real sense for the grit of the streets. And Michael is actually quite a stylist, so he brought to it a kind of literary approach. I was really lucky, and we're still quite close.

The *Globe and Mail* reporters continued to pursue the story with follow-ups after the series ran.

As a result of that series, Tim, in particular, has repeatedly broken stories because of the contacts he was able to nurture. And then I was front-paged in the *Globe and Mail* during the Bandidos massacre a couple of months ago.[4] So because of the track record I have with the *Globe* on that, I ended up doing multiple stories for them.

Sher knew early on that he wanted to be a journalist, but it would take some years as a professional before his interest turned to investigative work.

I knew from the time I was in high school I wanted to become a journalist. I started working on the student paper. I never had any other [career goals]—I just wanted to be a journalist. God knows why. I didn't think about investigative journalism. This was before Watergate, plus I was just a kid. I thought it would be exciting to drive around and cover the news. I just wanted to be a journalist. I remember the first story I ever did was an interview while I was in high school with the prime minister at the time [1968], Pierre Trudeau. I wrote away and I got an interview with him. It was by mail; it wasn't live.

So I wrote to the Prime Minister's Office and I got some answers to questions. And I thought, 'This is pretty cool . . . you can interview the prime minister.' So I knew from the start. And then I went to McGill because it had a daily newspaper. I walked into the *McGill Daily*, way before classes started, and never left the basement. I graduated with honours in history and did fine in school, but my only interest was in writing for the newspaper. So I always knew I wanted to be a journalist.

Then I got my first summer job. I walked into UPI [United Press International]—at the time they had an office in Montreal—and I said, 'I'd like to work for you for the summer.' And they said to me, 'Can you write?' I said, 'Absolutely.' And they gave me an Air Canada press release, I remember, and I sat down at a typewriter and rewrote it. They looked at it and said, 'Good, you're hired.'

That's what it was like then. I worked for them for two summers—big time, right? And I would get news clippings from around the world, with my byline. So it was great. All of that was important. For most of my twenties, I worked for a left-wing paper [in Montreal, called *The Forge*] and made money as an editor for a local community paper.

Sher enjoyed working at *The Forge*, where he exercised the investigative bent that would come to characterize his later work.

I liked it, because you're going against the grain. And I remember we won—it was before the CAJ, it was called the CIJ [the Centre for Investigative Journalism]. It didn't have awards, they didn't give out prizes, but they listed some of the best investigative journalism, and we beat out *The Globe and Mail* on a story about an immigrant. So it was a thrill. I was just working for a small paper, but right away you know that good writing can go anywhere.

Then I started at CBC Radio, worked in radio, and then TV, and it was when I moved to TV that I began for the first time to do investigative stuff. I never did news; I've always covered current affairs. I've never been interested in daily news. I've always thought daily news to some degree was a fiction invented by advertisers who have to sell soap every day. There's news, but even an earthquake or fire really didn't just happen that day. Three people died in a fire today, yes, but something happened earlier on to set in motion that fire.

I started in radio when I was 30, so that was 1983, and I moved to TV by about 1987, I believe, and then started doing investigative stuff. We did a story on fire traps in the city. It exposed fire traps and got a lead editorial in *The Gazette* [Montreal]. And we did a story on killer roads. In fact, to this day I'm proud that I still drive on the roads and see how they've redone some of them and put in protective barriers as a result of the story.

Years later, Fred Vallance-Jones would write a three-part investigative series for the *Hamilton Spectator* on highway safety in Ontario. Called Speed, the series ran in the summer of 2005 and relied on a freedom-of-information request and the computer analysis of more than a million traffic tickets. It pointed out patterns even provincial police were unaware of and has been credited with helping to change the way Ontario police enforce the rules.

When Sher wrote his killer roads story for CBC, computer-assisted reporting had yet to become part of the journalistic landscape. Sher 'went through piles and piles of paper police reports, manually.' Of course, a million records are too many to han-

dle 'manually'—another example of how CAR amplifies work that is otherwise tradi-
tionally journalistic. The essentials of CAR are the same as those of investigative
reporting and indeed all good reporting: the same questioning at the core of the
work, the same enterprise to unearth the salient facts, and the same passion for truth.

Sher's investigative leanings blossomed when he was hired to work on *The Fifth
Estate*, the investigative unit at CBC Television. After that, he 'never looked back' and
tended to gravitate toward other reporters of investigative stripe. His two books on
the Hells Angels were co-written with *The Gazette* (Montreal)'s William Marsden,
who initially was a potential rival in the field.

> Bill and I knew each other in Montreal. The investigative world is small; to some
> degree, we were competitors. We had both worked on the tobacco-smuggling
> story. So there was sort of friendly competition. He had done a series of articles
> on why prosecutors were burning out in Quebec and the bikers were literally get-
> ting away with murder. Based on that, he approached *The Fifth Estate* to do a
> documentary. And I was free; I had left the CBC at the time. They said, 'Why don't
> you team up with Julian to do it?' Because he wanted to learn how TV could be
> done, we teamed up on that. And then he came up with the idea of doing a book.

Sher says the first thing to do on a major project is come up with a title.

> Before you do anything, think of a title, because it will summarize. So I came up
> with the idea of *Road to Hell* as a title for the documentary. And then after the
> documentary aired to some success, Bill said, 'Let's do a book on this.' My ini-
> tial reaction was surprise. I said, 'Gee there's so much written already, and we
> did this documentary. Is there really that much more to say?' And again, I was
> quite surprised—there was tonnes to say. Absolutely.

Contrary to some of the popular wisdom on investigative reporting and reporters, the
love of the work comes from the satisfaction of curiosity, from *not* knowing it all.
Sher came to understand that while working on a documentary about the Steven
Truscott case.

> I had the absolute privilege to work on the Steven Truscott documentary—prob-
> ably one of the finest pieces of work I've done—for two years at the CBC.[5] Now
> where are you ever going to get a chance to work on something for two years?
> We produced an hour-long documentary called *His Word Against History*, which
> changed history. Steven Truscott came forward for the first time. That documen-
> tary made him a hero again to a whole new generation of Canadians. One-point-
> four million people watched the documentary every time we aired it. It then
> sparked a reopening of his case and helped contribute to the justice minister
> ordering a new court hearing that's going to come up [19 June 2006][6]—on a case

that had been settled fifty years ago and had gone all the way to the Supreme Court.[7]

So it had tremendous impact. I had the absolute luxury that you can only get at *The Fifth Estate* of spending two years doing an investigation. After it was finished, Random House called me up and asked if I'd like to do a book. And I said yes, but I figured I'd have to dig a little more and find out more stuff. After two years, I was the walking expert on Steven Truscott. And the amount of stuff we found out in the book just made the documentary pale in comparison.

That's the value of digging: never, never stop.

For aspiring reporters, Sher's advice is to know your own mind.

The first thing you have to decide is where you are going to get your jollies. Are you going to get more of a kick doing daily news versus investigative reporting? Do you prefer one-night stands or a long-term love affair? Both are equally valid, but you have to decide, because you can't do both. You certainly can't do both well over long periods.

Now I've done the reverse. Most people start in daily news and then get more experience and get the urge and then move on to investigative journalism. I've done it backwards. I've always done investigative journalism and now recently with some of my newspaper work, I find myself in daily news. And I can see the attraction, because it's fast, it's quick. You get addicted to the pace, and you get instant satisfaction. If you make a mistake or it doesn't work, the next day it's another story. New journalists really have to decide.

Books appear to offer more 'space' to tell a story, but Sher calls that 'a real misunderstanding by journalists'.

Investigative journalism has nothing to do with the length of the final product; it does have to do with length of time you get to work on it. It's much more [a question of] complexity, commitment, the fact that you are going to live and breathe this story for months and months and months.

So it takes an ability to organize complex investigations. Again, it's the difference between being a traffic cop and a homicide detective, between being a beat cop and a major undercover operative. Both are equally valuable for the public, both require certain talents—they're just different jobs. A homicide cop would probably cause a major pileup if he were given to do traffic at a major intersection. Investigative journalism is sometimes seen as the summit, the real goal. Well, it depends what you want to do. I personally love investigative. I couldn't see myself doing anything but.

The value of investigative journalism, I would argue, is that it is in the end what real journalism is about. It's almost inconceivable that you could get more than a stab at the truth on a daily schedule. You're at the mercy of news conferences, press releases, and spin doctors. And you have to become an instant expert. It's one thing if you're a beat reporter, that's different. A beat reporter basically winds up becoming almost an investigative journalist on a daily basis. But just being thrown into the mix, general assignment, you'll get some of the facts right, but you can rarely probe beneath the surface.

Investigative reporting also involves an element of risk because it proceeds against opposition from those with secrets to keep. Beat reporters deal with a different sort of difficulty: the risk of a kind of enculturation, in which beat reporters come to identify so closely with the people they're covering that they fail to see the countercultural stories at hand. On the beat, in other words, familiarity can breed blindness. Of course, the best beat reporters understand the danger and withstand the temptation (think of Lindsay Kines and his thoughtful approach to this aspect of beat reporting).

As for the future of investigative reporting, Sher says, there's good news and bad news.

It goes up and down. The bad news is that a lot of media owners are reluctant to spend the money that's required to do good investigative journalism. So in the States and in Canada we've seen huge layoffs of staff; in the States and in Canada we have seen the abolition or the dismantling of what investigative teams there were. And then the newspapers especially are looking over their shoulders, and they see TV, twenty-four-hour cable news services, and the Internet as their competition. So you get the dumbing down and the unwillingness to invest in investigative journalism. And newspaper readership is plummeting, with few exceptions. That's the bad news.

Now, the good news, I would argue, is that newspaper readership is plummeting in part because people are getting their daily fix of news from CNN and the Internet. There was one study showing that when Belinda Stronach resigned, or crossed the floor, 67 per cent of *Globe and Mail* readers had heard about it and knew about it before they were going to read their morning paper. So telling people that Belinda Stronach resigned, crossed the floor, is not going to tell anybody anything they don't already know. What they're turning to the *Globe and Mail* for is the behind-the-scenes look.

What is the biggest boom right now in print? Non-fiction books. If you look at the success of non-fiction investigative books. The behind-the-scenes, real story of the Iraq war; the real story of some of the corporate shenanigans. And look at the popularity of documentary. It's because people are getting their daily fix of news from the Internet and from CNN. We're never going to miss any news about six more bodies in Iraq or the price of gold.

That's what people are thirsting for. So newspapers, if they're smart, they will deliver it. The newspapers may not be delivering it, but I think the market shows—the success of books, the success of documentary filmmaking—that the audience is demanding serious investigative, probing journalism.

And when people ask if the Internet spells the death of journalism, I say it spells the rebirth of journalism, because we'll finally be able to get away from doing the kind of daily drudgery that the Internet does fine. And even the Internet provides great resources for people to do investigative stuff. You're getting a lot of investigative sites—The Smoking Gun, for instance. In that sense, I'm optimistic. Put it this way: I'm optimistic about my future as an investigative journalist. I will get my stuff out; it will be published; there will be documentaries.

What about newspapers?

I think if newspapers are smart, they will realize that they have to compete with the Internet and the twenty-four-hour cable news by offering something different. At a minimum, it means insight, which more and more of them are doing, rather than the daily news. It also means breaking something new on your front page that nobody else has.

Like a lot of self-made journalists, Sher is suspicious of journalism schools. When he speaks to students at universities, he makes no bones about that.

The first thing I tell them is don't go to journalism school, because I'm convinced that journalists are born, not made. If you're not born with it, if you don't have that curiosity and that skepticism and that drive and that passion, no number of courses is going to make you into a journalist. If you have that, then a journalism school can help you hone your skills. I also tell them if they're in journalism school, go do something else as well. In other words, take economics or history, some real area of academics rather than journalism. Otherwise they're giving you the recipe, but you don't have any of the ingredients. Because journalism just teaches you how to apply what you know to the world, and if you don't know anything, then it's not going to teach you anything.

The key to getting a job is having the 'clips' (the published work) that show you can do the work. Sher believes that potential employers don't care about academic credentials.

What they look at is the portfolio. [They won't be impressed] if you graduated from Harvard's School of Journalism and you haven't a single thing to show. If you graduated from no school or the journalism school of Timbuktu, but you took down your local mayor by exposing corruption, you're going to get hired. People look at your portfolio.

So even if you're at journalism school, go out and write, write, write, write. Write from the beginning; write on your school newspaper; start freelancing for the local paper. Then go get a job at a daily; work your butt off, where you're at bat three, four times a day. Because even if you're lucky to get a job at some major paper, you're not going to get the playing time to do the work. You want to practise. Before you start hitting home runs, you have to learn how to pick a pitch to hit. Go work for some small paper or get a basic job at the CBC.

Sher has maintained the website JournalismNet.com for about a decade.

I was lucky to catch the wave of the Internet before it actually became a wave. It was still black and white and text. I was waylaid in bed for a week back in '97, and I thought I should check out this Internet thing. So I started reading about it and playing with my computer. I started developing the site originally to avoid a long list of bookmarks, and then started sharing it with people at the CBC, and then started training people. It was exploding, and people wanted training.

It just grew from there. . . . [The website is] up there with the *Columbia Journalism Review* and most of the major journalism foundations—and it's just me. It's a hugely popular site. I do it, really, to give back to the journalism community. And I get a lot of feedback from people around the world, and often get story ideas. So it's a lot of fun.

It obviously takes courage to go after a story about a notoriously violent biker gang. But Sher wouldn't call himself fearless.

I'm not sure if I'm fearless—I'd say dogged. I don't think you want to be fearless. Fear is a good thing. Fear doesn't mean panic. You should be fearful of fire, and then you decide, 'Am I going to run through these flames in order to save that child or not? Can I build a fire and control it?' Fear means you should take precautions before you knock on the Hells Angels clubhouse, but do knock on the Hells Angels clubhouse, and go through the door and do your interviews.

And sometimes, too, it means backing off.

I've cancelled interviews. We were in Pakistan [working on a story for the *New York Times*]. We'd finally negotiated to meet with a terrorist, and we were quite willing to do it. But in the end, we decided not to do it, because we looked at the pros and cons, and it just wasn't worth the risk. So I'll go to Pakistan, and I'll take risks. I've gone to Beirut and I've covered civil wars. And I probably would go to Baghdad if I was asked. But fear is a good thing. It forces you to decide whether the story is worth it. Is it worth dying for?

# Endnotes

1.  Sher has published four books. His first, *White Hoods: Canada's Ku Klux Klan*, was published by New Star Books in 1983, and his second, *'Until You Are Dead': Steven Truscott's Long Ride into History*, by Knopf

Canada in 2001. The last two books, about the Hells Angels, were co-authored by veteran investigative reporter William Marsden of the *Gazette* (Montreal). Both volumes, *The Road to Hell: How the Biker Gangs Are Conquering Canada* and *Angels of Death: Inside the Bikers' Global Crime Empire*, were published by Knopf Canada, in 2003 and 2006 respectively. Seal Books published a mass-market edition of *The Road to Hell* in 2005.

2. The series ran 17, 20, and 24 July 2004.

3. Given the size of the Canadian market, this country's authors are doing well when their books sell one-tenth of the number of copies (in the 3,000-to-5,000 range) that Sher cites (30,000 to 50,000 copies) as constituting a 'huge best-seller'.

4. Julian Sher, 'We had no reason to be worried', *Globe and Mail* (17 June 2006), A1.

5. Sher co-produced the television documentary 'His Word Against History' for the CBC's *The Fifth Estate*. It first aired in March 2000.

6. Sentenced to be hanged at the age of 14 for the murder of 12-year-old Lynne Harper in Clinton, Ontario, Steven Truscott became this country's youngest death row inmate in 1959, in a case so controversial it is credited with helping end the death penalty in Canada. Truscott, who has always proclaimed his innocence, saw his death sentence commuted to life imprisonment and was paroled in 1969. But it wasn't until October 2004 that then federal justice minister Irwin Cotler ordered a judicial review of the case. In 2006, the Ontario Court of Appeal conducted the review, hearing witnesses between 19 June and 7 July 2006. In the early months of 2007, Crown and defence lawyers made oral presentations of their arguments. At the time of this writing, in the summer of 2007, a decision was still pending. Then, on August 28, just as this book was going into production, Steven Truscott was acquitted of the crime, finally clearing his name nearly a half century later. See Julian Sher's article in the 29 August 2007 edition of the *Globe and Mail*, titled '"It's my name"—and new he's got it back'.

7. A much earlier book written by Isabel LeBourdais (*The Trial of Steven Truscott*, McClelland & Stewart, 1966) had led the Liberal government of Lester Pearson to order a Supreme Court review of the Truscott case, but the judges ruled 8–1 to uphold the guilty verdict.

# Cecil Rosner
(10 August 2006)

Cecil Rosner has spent thirty years in print and broadcast journalism and is now managing editor in Winnipeg for CBC Manitoba. His own investigative work and his consistent efforts on behalf of investigative journalism generally make him one of the most insightful Canadian commentators on the subject. Rosner teaches a course in investigative reporting at the University of Winnipeg and when we spoke was at work on a Canadian history of the craft. He's confident, despite obstacles, about the future of the field.

Is the future of investigative journalism threatened?

It will always be there; there will always be individuals who really want to do this. And in a way, with the Internet and blogs and alternative kinds of organizations, it's becoming easier for really motivated individuals to do this type of thing. Before, you had to have support from some giant organization.

Especially in TV, because it's so expensive.

Exactly. Now if you look around the landscape, obviously you still need good resources to do good work. So I think in the long run, there will always be very motivated people who want to do this, and now they have better access to do it.

Several investigative reporters I've talked to say the idea that everybody wants to 'graduate' to this line of reportage is a myth—that it's just too demanding.

You know what's interesting, as I'm doing my stuff [for the book], and I'm talking to people who did projects in the '60s and '70s—I'm finding some of them use the phrase 'burned out'. It can burn you out. Because it's such an intense thing and sometimes people want to go away from it just to recover, because you're living under a lot of very intense pressure, and not a lot of people can do that their whole lives.

Well, it certainly takes the courage to persevere. Maybe it also takes a special kind of craziness to believe that you can see it through to the end, to publication. Especially for newspapers, with the downturn in the business, with the advent of convergence (which I think of as concentrated ownership on steroids).

There are the two things. What do the large organizations want? And the individuals who go into journalism and become interested in journalism or passionate about it—what do they want? These are always two separate things. Sometimes, if you look historically, you'll find at some newspapers without the least interest in investigative journalism, one or two odd characters there doing some very good work.

What about computer-assisted reporting? When you started working on the David Milgaard story, most newsrooms didn't even have computers.[1]

Well, I used to be at the *Winnipeg Free Press*. So I actually first met Joyce [Milgaard] in 1980. She was just starting her campaign to get her son freed and she was starting to publicize it so she wandered into the newsroom at the *Winnipeg Free Press*. And this is very typical: the city editor saw me idle and said, 'Go talk to this lady.' So I went and talked to the lady and I did a story at the time but that was it. That was as far as it went.

I thought, 'Okay, this is kind of interesting. I have no real way of knowing whether she's right or wrong, whether her son really is innocent, but she seems very passionate.' So it was a one-off. And I did not take it further than that at the time. I think the only one, journalistically, who did was this guy called Peter Carlyle-Gordge, who served as a *Maclean's* correspondent in Manitoba at the time. I think of all the journalists in that era, he took the most interest in it.

He lives in Winnipeg. He's always been a freelancer, worked for the *Globe* for a bit, worked for *Maclean's* for a bit. He testified at the Milgaard inquiry recently. That's another story altogether: They were going after journalists [at the inquiry], if you can believe it. It was very bizarre. It's still going on, it's going to resume in September [2006]. Carl Karp, who wrote the Milgaard book with me—his name was on the witness list, but somehow mine wasn't. I don't know what they were thinking . . . but we were kind of strategizing as to how to get to go testify at this thing, because they were turning it against anyone who did any-thing to get Milgaard's case any attention. This whole inquiry seems to be some sort of payback. It's very bizarre if you look at some of the transcripts.[2]

But anyway, I got back into the story in the late '80s, like '89, '90, when it had already geared back up. And he was still in jail—it was well before the Supreme Court [ruling].[3] So it was still early days and there still wasn't a lot of other evidence, but the big thing for me was the suggestion that now there was some information about who might really have committed the murder. For me, that took it from some inconsistencies in the timing and other smaller issues to suddenly there being a possibility now of really breaking this case open if you could point the finger. That's when I got re-excited about the thing. It was that fact.

So that's kind of what [inspired the book]. I've been trying to figure this out: In all the cases of journalistic involvement in wrongful convictions, how much of the contribution came from journalists, and how much came from lawyers or other activists? It's interesting to parse that. And I think my contribution on the Milgaard front came in all the stuff surrounding Larry Fisher and doing the research that pointed to him, and finding out stuff that the Milgaards and their whole team didn't know.

That was gratifying. I felt that there was a useful journalistic contribution [made in this case]. Rather than just—you know there are instances of lawyers feeding stuff to reporters and reporters regurgitating it. And that's not real inves-tigative journalism.

It seems the most important thing is the independence of mind that allows for a jour-nalist to conceive of and pose the questions that no one else is asking.

Yeah. And this is interesting, too: As we were doing the book, we kept an open mind throughout. It was funny, but [publisher] McClelland & Stewart, their first proposal to us for what the book should be called was Free David Milgaard Now. They wanted a sort of advocacy book [arguing] that he should be freed. Now, we had looked at all the evidence and we actually came to the conclusion he was innocent, but still we kept an open mind throughout the entire process. For instance, I came across this guy who had been a prison guard of Milgaard's and I heard from someone else that another guy was claiming Milgaard had confessed to him. So then I had this guy's name, and I spent weeks trying to find him. And I finally did. I tracked him down and I went and interviewed him and he said yup, and he gave me this whole story about how David Milgaard had confessed to him. So then we started investigating that, and came to the conclusion that he was not credible.

But I just think that's an important principle. If you're going to treat journalism as a social science, you have to at all times have a completely open mind and be prepared to change your hypothesis based on whatever evidence it is you're collecting. Because I've seen journalists have as much tunnel vision as cops and prosecutors.

It's almost as if the true investigative reporter has got to be someone torn between opposite poles, someone who embodies qualities that don't usually go together, like the passion to make right what's wrong, and the dispassion or detachment to rely on the evidence.

Exactly. When I look at this historically, like in the nineteenth century even, you have a lot of very passionate journalists, but they're politicians.

And polemicists.

And sometimes they do very good work that you could consider good journalistic work, but sometimes they're blinded by whatever cause they happen to be espousing, and shut their eyes to evidence that might be there because it doesn't suit their political purposes. Yeah, I agree, that's a good way to characterize it: you do have to have both those qualities.

The journalistic nine-to-five is a lot easier. Investigative reporters take the high road, but it's also the hard road. Why do you think they do it?

It gets back to motivations. That's one of the questions I'm asking a lot of people. What are your motivations for doing this kind of work? And the replies can get interesting. I interviewed Michael McCauley—if you remember the Somali inquiry, he broke all those stories. There might not have been a Somali inquiry if not for a lot of his work. And he now is a foreign correspondent, he's posted for CBC Radio, and he says, 'That's what I actually prefer doing. I can't be a policeman all my life'—I think that's the way he put it. It was kind of an interesting perspective. So [investigative journalism] does motivate some people some-times, but others think in the end what they really enjoy doing is something else.

What about doing investigative journalism in order to see justice done, or at least be part of making that difference?

The motivations are different for different people. Here's an interesting perspec-tive I got the other day. I was talking to Phil Mathias, who has had a long inter-esting career. He started at the *Financial Post* [now the *National Post*] doing investigative stuff in the late '60s, and then *The Fifth Estate*, and he did all this Airbus stuff. He says if you look at a lot of investigative journalists, most of them are Catholics. This was his thesis: it's because of their moral sense of right and wrong.

So Catholics hold the keys to the kingdom of right and wrong?

I don't know. But he then did rhyme off a whole bunch of names of people who he claimed were Catholics and investigative journalists. Who knows? Interesting point of view anyway.

Then there is the law to worry about. And like the Rolling Stones song says, 'when the law gets ready' . . . stuff happens.[4]

It's important to [realize] that when you're taking on very powerful people, you have to have the same accurate standards that you would apply to any piece of work. But at the same time, you have to have confidence that it's possible to take on. I was reading recently about libel insurance in the States, about how your insurance company looks at you funny if you have more than three notices of libel against you. So the mere threat, merely initiating a suit, is enough to endan-ger your libel insurance. When you're in an atmosphere like that, then things get tough. The whole libel atmosphere is very, very troubling.

At the CBC, there were two separate suits by two doctors, and they both won. And then all the appeals were upheld and the Supreme Court wouldn't hear it, so the CBC lost. And if you add it up, it's close to three million dollars.[5]

That's enough financial damage to chill even the most courageous journalist or news organization.

It was about conflict of interest. What can a suit like that do if not inhibit people from writing or doing TV broadcasts about potential conflicts of interest? That can't be a good thing.

Some stories that seem to reporters clear-cut have met with threats of libel suits in recent years.

> Even slam-dunk stories, we are still fighting. In the first year of [CBC TV's] *Disclosure*, we did a story about a chiropractor. Using a hidden camera, we produced a story about the chiropractor that resulted in his regulatory body cancelling his licence. So he's out of business as a direct result of our story. This was in . . . it might have been early 2002. He's suing us. And it's still going on, and it may well go to trial next year.

On what basis? How can such a suit for libel go forward?

> I don't know. If you have enough money, you can pursue a lawsuit and keep it going for a long, long time.
>
> The other suit hanging on from *Disclosure* is a story we did about a former Edmonton police chief. And what we found was there had been an investigation in the early '80s, an internal Edmonton Police Department investigation of allegations that some police themselves were shaking down prostitutes. There was an internal EPD investigation—they had suspects, interview statements, and all the rest of it. Then the lead investigator was told one day to stop. This is being shut down. You are not to investigate this any more. That is the end of it.
>
> That's what happened in around 1982. No word had ever been written or said about this; it was secret until we found out about it and did a documentary. We also reported the fact that one of the suspects at the time happened to be the Edmonton police chief.

When was this? How long had it been kept secret?

> Well we ran the story in 2004, so about twenty years. It's on our website, if you want to check it out. It's the subject of a gigantic lawsuit right now. This guy is retired, but he's now suing us for the story that we did. We did have a number of sources that we want kept confidential and he was trying to force us to name them. It went to a hearing in Edmonton last year.[6]

As part of the pre-trial discovery-of-records process, the retired chief demanded to see all 627 documents used to prepare the documentary. The CBC argued that the documents contained 'confidential source information, communication between solicitor and client, or irrelevant information.'[7]

> We redacted all that from our papers and they said, 'No, we need to see all this.' So it went to a hearing in front of a judge in Alberta and we won a pretty important minor victory. There's this precedent called the 'newspaper rule', and Alberta

had never acknowledged it but this judge basically did. It protects us up until the point of a trial.

At trial we have to argue it all over again on constitutional grounds, but the newspaper rule protects you up until the point of the trial. So we did win on that basis. We don't know whether he's funding this or he's getting help from other organizations to fund the suit. But it's going to carry on for a long, long time too.

In terms of whether investigative reporting will survive into the future—the whole libel issue is a major one, obviously, a big consideration for organizations contemplating doing this kind of work. It always has an effect in the backs of minds of senior managers. CBC has very good in-house lawyers; they're extremely, extremely good.

## Did you always want to be a journalist, since you were a kid?

No. It sort of occurred to me in university. I think it's mainly a mindset. I'm involved in a lot of hiring now too. And you try to gauge people's motivations, especially coming into a broadcast outlet—some people just want to be on TV.

## What advice would you give to aspiring journalists?

In terms of doing investigative work, the first thing is there's got to be a mindset. You have to have a kind of sceptical inquiring mind when it comes to all things. Because there's so much industry out there right now that is designed to get you to think in one way or another about everything. And so you have to have a desire to figure out ways to see behind that and beyond that. As you said, it's very easy just to come in and get your assignment or do something that's on the day's agenda and then go home. And, hopefully, you're on page one, or you're on TV. And if that's your desire in life, fine. But it's much more important and interesting and personally satisfying and useful to society if you say to yourself, 'Okay, how do I serve the public interest?'

And I think there's also an element of holding power to account. There are all kinds of elements in this world that wield power, and it should be part of journalism's function to hold those various elements to account. And that's the way aspiring journalists should think. They should look at the status quo and say, 'Okay, why should this be the status quo? Does this have to be the status quo? This is the conventional explanation for this thing, but maybe there are some alternative explanations.' Maybe in the late '60s or early '70s a lot more people naturally thought that way. And historically, based on what's going on in the world, I think when foundations of certain conventional truths are crumbling around you, you naturally start thinking that way. 'Oh, my president is going to jail because he's a crook even though he says he isn't? Okay, then why shouldn't I question everything?' That's how I think aspiring journalists need to think.

And then, if they buy into that or already have that mindset, then it gets back to what we were talking about at the beginning. You've got to have a devotion to seeking the truth, not just lazily acting as somebody's megaphone or puppet or the transmission belt for whatever press release that comes along. A devotion to really trying to find out the truth of the matter and going beyond just this person's opinion, that person's opinion.

Once you get to that realization, then you've got to have the skills to be able to do that. I do a lot of in-house training of investigative journalists and it's 90 per cent research. It's like, How do you test this statement? How do you find this piece of information out? How do you do it quickly if you're on a deadline? Because that is the big problem with journalism: it's constrained by deadlines. So these are skills that you need to try to get closer to the truth of any particular situation.

I agree with what you say about motivation. If there's no passion, the questions won't even arise. You can show an aspiring reporter who's got a question how to go about trying to answer that question with various research techniques. But you can't put the fire of the question into another unless that person is already prone to question.

It's true. And the politicians and powerful people are very savvy. They may make a statement that might be technically accurate, and then if a journalist doesn't ask a follow-up question to go one step beyond, they get away with it. Or there are a lot of examples of how some reporters will write or broadcast something and then whoever it's directed against will wait to see whether it is getting picked up by other people; if not, it dies. I've heard that from a lot of people I've talked to and, of course, I've seen it for myself. When you do a story and it gets roundly ignored, first you get discouraged that it's had no impact, and then it literally can die, even though it's very important.

Even if you look at big cases, if you look back to the My Lai Massacre . . . I was just reading your stuff about the My Lai incident and how it was mentioned by this person and then that person, but then it wasn't [picked up]. I saw something in your paper I've never seen before, I can't remember seeing before. You said a reporter that I've never heard of had referenced My Lai, like a month before Seymour Hersh's famous piece.[8]

And you see that a lot, actually, in different forms. You have to have the courage to keep on a story, too, because there can be powerful disincentives for you to carry on down a path. A guy like Andrew McIntosh, who was on Shawinigate, is a good example. Because he was with the *National Post*, a lot of people wrote it off, thinking, 'Oh, the *National Post*—they're just out to get the Liberals, it's Conrad Black.' And all that likely is true in the big picture. But then you have a very solid guy called Andrew McIntosh doing very solid journalism. I think a lot of his initial stuff was dismissed because of those other factors, all those things that go into the competitive world of breaking stories. Same with the [Quebec] sponsorship scandal. There were lots of early hints of various things going on, but [until Daniel LeBlanc got it together] it got glossed over.

That's the way it always is in journalism—like a relay race in a sense. And you want people to pick up on the story. You don't want to own the story; you want the story to go on. And the only way that can happen is if other people pick up on it. That's how it *should* work. But it seems to me Rosner's right—that something else has changed here. Something's different, and it has to do with the kind of impact he mentioned above: the chasm between the big takeout, and the impact that it has. It's as Rosner says. Now, those who ought to be held accountable just wait. All they have to do is let it ride. If people don't talk about it for a couple days, it's as if it never happened.

> Totally. Here's an example I'm referencing in my book. In Manitoba, we had this vote-rigging scandal in the '90s. In the 1995 provincial election, the Conservatives under Gary Filmon (who was the premier at the time) came up with this plan that they wanted to try to defeat the NDP in three key swing ridings. So this was their plan: Let's invent a *phony party*—I believe it was called the Native Voice Party. 'We'll recruit these Aboriginals. And we'll fund them secretly and they'll drain off some traditional NDP votes and our candidates will come up the middle and win.' It didn't work. The NDP won in all three ridings, but the Conservatives won the election anyway.
>
> So guess what? About a month later, there were a couple of stories about this, kind of 'page A9 stories', like somebody vaguely made this allegation. And then it died. And nothing more was heard about it until 1998, when Kurt Petrovic, the CBC Radio reporter, got hold of it, and dug and dug and dug, and then found one of the candidates with this party who came out and spilled the beans. And said, 'Yes, I was recruited by the Conservatives,' chapter and verse. Big scandal. Inquiry followed. The Conservatives were roasted for this, and it was one of the major factors in their losing the 1999 election. So it's an example of how things can get lost if they're not followed up. Silence can bury stuff. It just highlights the need to be dogged.

And that was twelve years ago. Now the technology has got away from us—it's scary to think about all the stories we're not reading, all the stuff we're not hearing about.

> When I was covering the Manitoba legislature, say for instance in the early '80s at the *Winnipeg Free Press*, we had six people at the legislature. I was one of four reporters, and we had two columnists. We had a lot of people scrutinizing what was going on with the provincial government. When did Canadian Press have their big purge in Ottawa . . . in the late '80s, or thereabouts? It seems to me that CP used to have quite a considerable presence in Ottawa, covering parliamentary committees and so forth. The level of scrutiny of these things is much lower now. And I think generally across newspapers that's probably the case, whether it's city halls or legislatures.

> If you never hear about things, how are you ever going to come to the point of thinking you ought to investigate them? So you need a lot of he-said-she-said journalism in order to give you the raw materials to know what is important to investigate.

That's really true. I never thought about it like that.

> When I do this investigative course [at the University of Winnipeg], one of the very first things I say is, 'I'm not here to "diss" daily journalism.' It's extremely important and it should be thorough and comprehensive. It's very difficult to get to the truth of the matter when you have a four- or six-hour deadline. In fact, you hardly ever do [have that many hours]. But at the same time, we need to know what key people in this world are saying. That provides you with the raw material to do some deeper thinking about these things, and then go one further level of analysis to investigation. As a lot of my editors have said over the years, 'All my reporters are investigative reporters.'

Well, it's true to a certain extent: all good reporting involves some investigation.

> But if you have to feed the daily deadline beast, the reality is you cannot do too much in-depth work.

There are individual differences among reporters—you know how one reporter will not even notice anything askew while the next will take off the first layer of skin to get to it. But the daily stuff means there is some sort of ongoing scrutiny.

> Exactly. It's the raw material for other stuff. If that's all there is, obviously that's not good enough.

I worry though, sometimes, when I see a kind of indifference among some of my students.

> Are they more conservative?

Well, they do seem a lot more conservative than we were when we were young. But the other thing is they seem to regard 'the media' as some sort of monolithic corporate entity. It's hard to get across how much personal responsibility matters in journalism, what a radical difference you can make, how when you write a story, especially an investigative story, you bring into being something that wasn't there before. It's difficult to impress on them that as a journalist, you've got to ask the questions, come up with the ideas, and be the one who notices that some things don't add up.

Well, what about the whole detective thing? Are any of them driven by that compulsion?

Yes, and it tends to pay off for them, even though like all J-schools we (at Thompson Rivers University) struggle for the right fit in the academy. But those who go for it find out that if only you scratch the surface, if you go looking, if you want to find out, chances are you will. They see that the world is full of stories.

Of course. You know, a lot of the American universities have these innocence projects going. New York had the first of them, but now there are about forty or fifty across the US, and it's where students under the supervision of a prof, either in the law department or in the journalism department, take on cases of wrongful conviction. There are quite a few of them now. The only one in Canada is the one at Osgoode, as far as I know, and I think the University of Montreal is trying to set one up.

But there's a process whereby you can really stoke some passion in students because there's a very tangible kind of goal in trying to demonstrate that somebody has been wrongfully convicted. That one at Northwestern in Chicago, they've got a dozen people off death row. You can imagine the level of satisfaction for both the teachers and the students in a program like that.

So what's the overall pattern that's emerging for your book?

Well, many of the reporters have mentioned the sea changes in the business over their careers. Paul McKay said he doesn't believe his 1988 story on Joseph Kirschbaum—in a forty-page supplement to the *Kingston Whig Standard*—would have a hope of running today. He said that illustrates what's happened to the business. But he also said if Neil Reynolds hadn't been the editor, it wouldn't have happened then either. So one important conclusion seems to be that individuals matter. A single individual can make a big difference, sometimes the critical difference, between a story seeing print or not.

Yeah, look . . . If Kevin Donovan and Rob Cribb decided to leave the *Toronto Star*, would the *Star* continue doing computer-assisted reporting?

Well, actually the *Toronto Star* is a bit of an exception. The whole investigative team at the *Star* is committed to the work and a lot comes down to their willingness to burn the midnight oil. On the other hand—and they all agree on this—the support from the top is indispensable. And of course the *Star* has been the most consistent among Canada's daily newspapers in supporting investigative journalism.

> Definitely.

Another thing I've learned is that given the often lonely nature of the work, most investigative reporters take heart and sustenance from the acknowledgment of their peers. It seems to counteract the high stress of the job.

> Yeah. I can't think of a time [without stress] when I was producing the pieces. Like the night before [an episode airs], you're in a sweat about, 'Did I get this? What if I got that thing wrong?' Especially at *Disclosure*—virtually every contentious story we did, we would have letters from lawyers in advance of our broadcast. So you're facing that all the time and a very easy thing is to pull the story down and run a rerun or just don't do it. That kind of stress is very high, which has led a lot of people to get out of it. Some persist, but others don't. And then the other feature is that it's a bit like walking a tightrope, because one wrong move can blow up your whole career.

I sometimes worry that investigative reports are having a dysfunctional effect on those who read or view them. Perhaps people are getting turned off because after the big takeout, nothing seems to change. Maybe they're thinking, 'Here's another problem that I can't do a thing about, much less solve.'

> Maybe. That's possible. It's made worse by the phony kind of investigative work that was in vogue in the mid-'90s, where everything was a hidden camera investigation that didn't deserve to be. There was a time when *Dateline NBC* was on four days a week, and *Prime Time Live*, and *20–20*. This era was kind of killed off by *Who Wants to Be a Millionaire* and then 'reality TV'. But from about '93 to '99, there was a gigantic explosion in the US network newsmagazine genre, and they were just pumping out these completely ridiculous things that they would call investigative journalism. And a lot of fatigue set in, I'm sure, amongst people just watching. How do you know what's important and what isn't important after consuming that day after day after day?

# Endnotes

1. Carl Karp and Cecil Rosner, *When Justice Fails: The David Milgaard Story* (Toronto: McClelland & Steward, 1991). A revised edition was issued in 1998.

2. Commission of Inquiry into the Wrongful Conviction of David Milgaard, Honourable Mr. Justice Edward P. MacCallum, Commissioner. The inquiry adjourned on 4 October 2006 after hearing witness testimony; it was

scheduled to resume on 11 December 2006. You can read online about the inquiry and see transcripts of the proceedings at the following URL: www.milgaardinquiry.ca.

3.  David Milgaard spent twenty-three years in prison for a murder he did not commit. He was sentenced to life in prison in 1970 for the rape and murder of Saskatoon nursing aide Gail Miller. In 1992, the Supreme Court of Canada overturned his conviction. Milgaard's name was finally cleared by DNA evidence in 1997. A man named Larry Fisher was convicted of the crime.

4.  The song, which came out in the 1970s, was entitled 'You Got to Move'. It tended to interpret the law as just another conspiracy against the counterculture of the 1960s. According to the song's chorus: 'You may be rich, you may be poor, but when the law gets ready, you got to move.'

5.  See *Myers v. Canadian Broadcasting Corporation* (1999) 47 CCLT (2d) 272 (SCJ) and *Leenen v. Canadian Broadcasting Corporation* (2000) 48 OR (3d) 656 (SC); aff'd. (2000), 54 OR (3d) 612 (CA).

6.  *Wasylyshen v. Canadian Broadcasting Corporation* ABQB 902. (30 November 2005; Docket Number 0403 08497), 9. Wasylyshyn's application for immediate disclosure of documents that would reveal the identity of the confidential sources was denied. The judge in the case noted, 'As I stated earlier, it is the assigned trial judge who will have the ultimate responsibility of determining whether or not the identity of the confidential sources should be disclosed.'

7.  *Wasylyshen v. Canadian Broadcasting Corporation*, op. cit., 2.

8.  Rosner was referring to my doctoral dissertation. See Maxine Ruvinsky, *The Underground Press of the Sixties*, Doctoral thesis (Montreal: McGill University, n.p., 1995), pp. 55–6. [Photocopy, Ann Arbor, MI: UMI Dissertation Services, 2000]
    'The "news" of the March 16, 1968 massacre of 347 unarmed South Vietnamese civilians . . . in what came to be known as My Lai . . . was not on the official record until close to two years after the event occurred, with the publication of . . . freelance reporter Seymour Hersh's book on the subject, in 1970. . . . It was not until September 1969 that the story first appeared on the front page of the *Columbus Enquirer* following the digging efforts of reporter David Leonard. Still, the overground press (including the news services) failed to pick up on the story. While this did not appear to surprise the media critics, it did the Pentagon, with one Pentagon lawyer commenting: "We were amazed that story never went any place—absolutely amazed." [*Los Angeles Times* (11 December 1969), IX: 8] . . . Hersh began investigating the story in October 1969. . . . When Hersh did manage to sell the story, it was to the Dispatch News Service, which ran the item on November 13, 1969. Even then, 13 of the 45 papers offered the story refused it. But this did constitute breaking the story, and virtually all major media competed to cover it once Dispatch News (long defunct) bought and ran Hersh's story. . . . Who broke the story of My Lai? The combined efforts of a virtual handful of people in opposition to forces of the government, the military establishment, and the major media combined.'

# Elaine Dewar
(8 August 2006)

The award-winning Elaine Dewar is a prominent magazine journalist as well as the author of three books.[1] She got her start at *Maclean's* in the early 1970s, as a researcher and editor. In the course of a freelance-writing career spanning decades, she has written for a host of Canadian magazines. Dewar was also a writer and story editor for the triple Emmy Award–winning TV series *Lorne Greene's New Wilderness* in the mid-1980s. At the time of our talk, she was at work on her first novel.

———————

Elaine Dewar represents a bit of a departure from the other interviewees in this book, which deals almost exclusively with newspaper writers. Despite her distinguished career as a magazine and book writer, Dewar never worked for a newspaper.

I think I wrote two book reviews, but that's it.

Did you always want to be a journalist?

Oh no. I always wanted to be a writer, but the reason I started at *Maclean's* was I needed a job and I thought the media might be somewhat more interesting than an art gallery, which is the kind of work I was doing before: I had started this art gallery with two or three other friends [in Toronto] and after the first six months picking the shows, it got so deadly boring I thought I was going to lose my mind.

So I started talking to my friends. Well all my friends were in journalism. Stephen [Dewar, her husband] was at CBC, Bill Cameron was at CBC, Geraldine Sherman was at CBC, Bob Fulford was at CBC, and Graham Fraser was going to go to the *Toronto Star*. We shared a house on Brunswick, Bill Cameron, Stephen, and me. And then when Bill moved out, Graham Fraser moved in. So that was the ambience, and when you're looking to find a job, well, you ask your friends.

As it happens, Bill had been hired as a writer at *Maclean's* about maybe six months before I decided I needed an actual job [in the late '60s]. He got me in there as a researcher on a project. There was this guy who was a former football player and by then a professor of English at Waterloo; he had theories about the Olympic Games in Montreal and how it was going to be a disaster. He had written this piece that was fact-free. So [*Maclean's* editor] Peter Newman decided there was something there and if this guy could just have a fact or two thrown into the piece, then maybe they could publish it. Bill Cameron said he had a friend who might be able to help him, and that was me.

So I go research this piece. I go to the library for a week and I'm reading everything there is to read about the Olympic Games. And every single Olympic Games since the first one had lost huge amounts of money. At this point, the mayor of Montreal, Jean Drapeau, was saying in print if these games go into debt, it's as impossible as him having a baby.

So I come back to [the writer] with umpteen thousand articles saying every single Olympic Games has run a deficit. And we started from there. Then they hired me full-time as a researcher. That was in '73. The real purpose of a researcher for them turned out to be that all of their articles were basically either fact-free or invented on the spot. They never fact-checked anything—this was before fact-checking. There were copy editors who read stuff and pointed out spelling errors and date errors and tried to correct basic improbabilities, but that was it.

I was set the task of actually looking at people's work before it went into print and maybe making a phone call or two. The first thing I worked on was a story about this guy who had been a minister of education in British Columbia. . . . Peter threw it to me and said could you kindly fact-check this. So I start calling around.

Well, the thing was just full of shit from stem to gudgeon. I mean no facts— it was made up. So I go back with my blue-pencilled copy to Peter and say, 'Well, okay, here's the problem: it's all wrong.' So Peter calls the guy and makes him fix it. And that was the beginning of fact-checking [at *Maclean's*].

## Didn't *Maclean's* know that fact-checking happened at other magazines?

They knew that the *New Yorker* sort of did it. But they thought it interfered with the autonomy of the reporter, and one of the first rules that were handed to me in this game was never check a quote, because people will always try to deny it. They will not remember exactly what they said. So if you have it in a notebook and it's verbatim or you have it on tape, then you run with the quote no matter what and you simply don't raise the issue in the fact-checking, you don't ask the question. You might raise the issue of a quote and give the guy or the gal a chance to make a correction about the fact contained in the quotation, but that's as far as it ever went. So, basically, my first job in journalism was to clean it up.

And it was incredibly interesting for me—as a person who thought somewhere deep down I really wanted to be a writer—to watch how other writers reacted to a junior snot-nose saying, 'I think you've got a problem here.' By and large, they were pretty good—I got threatened only a couple of times.

## When you started writing, did it help to have been an editor?

Absolutely. After the fact-checking job, I was made an assistant editor and I was given responsibility for the columns in the front and the back, running the columns and making sure that they were not libellous or otherwise bad. And then I started doing features. By the time I started doing features, my issues were not just fact and meaning and does the sentence work, but what's the story arc, what's the character development, how do you make it fit within the context of a magazine that has many facets to it in any given issue. How do you stay ahead of reality?

We had in those days a three-month lead time, which meant we were assigning stories sometimes six months in advance of when we planned to put them in print. And so it was really important to have a feeling for the zeitgeist— not the zeitgeist today, the zeitgeist six months from now—so that the story would appear at exactly the right time, it wouldn't be stale, it would be topical for that issue.

That became really fascinating to me. I mean, I walked into journalism with all kinds of lefty theories about how journalism was complete crap manipulated by corporate interests that bore no relation to reality. And I very rapidly fell in love with storytellers and storytelling. And saw no corporate anything, except once.

## What was the once?

It was a Heather Robertson column. There are two Heather Robertsons; this gal is about 62 now. She's a brilliant writer whose first book was called *Reservations Are for Indians*. So Heather is writing a column for *Maclean's* after that book came out and she's deemed to be this brilliant but odd person out in Winnipeg. And she's a Canadian nationalist and a leftist. So Peter, who was a nationalist, loved her international phase [when Robertson wrote about world politics, publishing, for example, a book about war called *A Terrible Beauty: The Art of Canada at War*], but was really scared about her socialist stuff. And she writes this column, a summertime column about how every time she gets on the road and drives to Manitoba on her vacation, sometimes she's so offended by Americans, she just wants to throw bombs at American licence plates.

And I look at this, and think, 'Yeah, I sometimes think that too—okay, fine, we'll print that.' I show it to Peter, and he says, 'Yeah, sometimes I think that too—we'll print that.' Well, the board at Maclean Hunter went insane. Insane. They wanted heads, the wanted blood, they wanted death. They wanted Heather fired, on the spot—off with her! And then they wanted me done, too.

So for three months, Peter apparently was trying to fire me but couldn't work up the nerve to walk into my office and say, 'Get out of here.' So he tried to do it through Mel Morris who was the managing editor then [1974]. He was a very interesting guy to work for. Anyway, Mel didn't tell me how much trouble I was in until the trouble passed, but at a certain point he let it be known that my head had been on the block and it was a damn sight of a mess that I didn't realize how much shit I was in for running that fact. But he was a great guy and a great supporter. And Heather and I became fast friends, friends ever since. So that's the only corporate influence that I remember: it was a board freak-out.

## When you left *Maclean's*, was it because you didn't want to edit people's copy any more? You wanted to write your own stories?

I didn't want to edit and manipulate copy. The magazine had changed from a monthly in which it was free range—you know everybody's voice was allowed—to a biweekly which was headed to a weekly which was going to be a *Newsweek* or *Time* facsimile, in which the discourse had to be reduced to a certain tone and certain phrases and certain scripted notions of what a magazine story must be. And the voice issues drove me insane. I couldn't stand it. It was like I could write this stuff rolling off a log, and I often did, because a lot of the writers I'd been using had trouble adapting to that new [more corporate, monotone] style. So when they couldn't deliver, I'd just rewrite their stuff: bing-bang, bing-bang. I was like a rewrite factory. And I hated it. I thought it was a complete waste of talent and I didn't like the new magazine. I didn't want to be there and I didn't know what to do. That was my last job [in 1977, after which Dewar started her full-time freelance career, concentrating on complex investigative work].

How would you define investigative reporting?

Well, usually, if nothing else: more time spent. Because investigative journalism means you go beyond the surface reportage of daily news. For me, it's looking at more fundamental questions than what happened today and what did he say at the press conference and what did she say in the scrum. It's about shaping a slice of reality and trying to trace its history and how it blossoms into the reality we all live with. So it goes beneath the surface.

How do you think it relates to issues reporting? Because I think the two are closely related, that they feed off each other and spur each other on.

I'm not sure what you mean by issues reporting.

Let's take for example your first book. You'd written about environmental stuff before, even though some of it was from a business perspective. And here was *Cloak of Green*, a gutsy exposé of environmental politics. So it's not like the environment just became news when you wrote *Cloak of Green*. The book was investigative because it brought out new information, but it was also issues reporting because that new information advanced the issue or at least the public debate around the issue.

That's right. And *Cloak of Green*, like every piece I've ever done, did not start as an investigation, as in, Let's go unearth the wrongdoing. It started as an inquiry, as in, Why am I seeing this strange phenomenon in front of my face? Where did this come from, what does this mean? And how does it fit into what is really concerning me at the present moment about the air I breathe and the water I drink and what's going to be with my kids?

So I was fascinated by this guy who suddenly appears in the middle of Toronto in November with parrot feathers in his hair, being treated as a kind of king among men, who's going to save us, and is presented to the community of environmentalists as the master of the rainforest environment in Brazil. This guy, if we gave him money, was going to protect the rainforest and keep us all from dying of global warming and a diminishing ozone layer.

And all of those issues were very much in the news that summer—1988 was a horribly hot summer, it was just vile. And the global warming issue was starting to get attention in its second, actually its third, cycle. I didn't know that at the time, I thought it was news. But it worried me. It seemed to me climate change was in front of my face and here's this guy, a Native person. And I knew bloody well, in my bones, that most of the people in that room would not have lined up to give a Canadian Native person money for any reason.

And yet here was this guy from the Amazon who they could not wait to give money to, without asking any questions. It was just, He's from the Amazon, the sky is falling, we can't breathe, it's too hot, and he's going to fix it.

So following that guy and those connections consumed five years. And it blew away all of my conceptions about the science of climate change, the politics of the environment, the history of the politics of the environment, the way my government employed the environment as a political tool in Canada's interests abroad, the way my government infiltrated the left and the centre in Brazil and gave it courage and support to help democratize Brazil. I mean none of these questions would even have occurred to me to ask if I hadn't set foot down that first part of the path and asked, 'How did these people connect with this guy?'

So that's how issues and investigation come together. The issue is there in front of your face, something happens, and you have to ask the question, How come? And you keep going and going and going until you satisfy yourself that you begin to understand how come, and why.

As opposed to just what?

That's exactly it. What is the beginning and the last question is why.

Wasn't there a magazine piece you published before you wrote the book?

There was. It was called 'Mr. Universe' and it was about Maurice Strong, who is the centrepiece for the last third of the book. Strong ran the Earth Summit at Rio [in 1992], and he also ran the first Environmental UN Summit in 1972. Strong turned out to be the link, the connector between all these different ideas and people and bodies. *Saturday Night* was where I first sold the idea. I said, 'You know, there's something going on here with this Brazilian guy and I'm really interested and will you take a flyer on me?' And they said, 'Oh yeah, sure.' Four years later [in 1991], I published the magazine story [in *Saturday Night*], and five years later, I published the book.

As a long-time magazine writer, what did you think about writing books when you finished *Cloak of Green?*

I thought it was a very strange book, in that it was incredibly intensely detailed and I felt like I was under the gun, like I had to get that book out. I could not shrug it off, do it in pieces, do it in three parts, as everybody kept urging me: You're trying to put too much together in one place, you can't do it, it'll kill you, blah, blah, blah.

I had to finish that project the way I wanted it done. Because I didn't think I'd ever get a chance to put those issues and those characters together in one context again, and I thought the whole point was how they connected. So it was a son of a bitch to do, it paid me so little money—I mean it was just pathetic. It was a good [author] advance in terms of book advances, but when you're spending six or seven years on a project, no advance is enough.

And it taught me a great deal about the making of a book. It taught me things that I didn't want to do in the next book. It also taught me that a book has a life that can't be predicted. I mean, I just sold that book to Brazil this year. And I couldn't sell the rights for love or money when it first was published and I couldn't understand it. It seemed to me obvious there should be a Brazilian audience for this book. I couldn't get anybody to pay attention. Go explain.

You can't explain it. I found that book connected with the [political] right in ways that I could never have predicted. I had much more interest from the right-wing nationalist ideologues in the United States and Canada than I could ever have predicted. They were interested in the whole issue of how international institutions like the UN are undermining national sovereignty and the whole notion of national sovereignty. That's what grabbed them about that book, the mechanism with which national sovereignty is being decimated in the interests of large multinationals.

I didn't know it was going to go that way but that's the way it went. So I kept getting phone calls from loony right-wingers. And I'd say, 'Why do you want to talk to me? I don't agree with you. You're nuts. Go away.' But it rang a bell. So I think the thing I understood from that was that there is no way you're ever going to understand who your reader might be. Don't worry about it, just go forward and say what you have to say and be done with it.

When you finished *Cloak of Green*, did you think, 'Okay this is the way to go, you write books because books can get beneath the surface'?

No. I couldn't wait to not write another book.

So you wanted to go back to magazine articles?

I wanted to go back to magazine articles because they give you such a rush of connections so fast and then it's over and you go on to the next. You don't stick there in that thing forever and ever. You're done, you get out. It's like having babies, if they hang around too long you've got to kick them out. Books take way too long.

So what brought you to *Bones* and *The Second Tree*?

Magazine stories. Always magazine stories. *Bones* started from a climate change story, because I didn't feel satisfied that I'd really dealt with the science of global warming in *Cloak of Green*.

## Had you studied sciences in university?

I studied arts in university. After first year, I never took another science course. But I was a really good science student in high school. I wanted to go into medicine until I was 17.

## Of course, your father was a physician.

Yeah, and I worked in his office. I was a sickly kid, so I was very interested in how the body works and why the body doesn't work. I did biology, chemistry, physics, and I did all the maths.

So when I came to university, the turning point was a general science course that we all had to take the first year at York that I flunked the last test in. I did an [arts] degree at U of T. I did two years at York and then switched to U of T. But I hated the course; I absolutely loathed it. There were ideas in the course I liked, but mostly I hated how they dealt with information in science. They did not inquire; you were expected to deliver. And I was totally uninterested in that. I realize now I wouldn't have felt comfortable in science until I got to a doctorate. I would have been in hell. Because what I was learning in my arts courses was how to ask questions, not take dictation.

## So you remained in arts. And after you finished *Cloak of Green* you were happy to go back to magazine articles—except they led you back to books.

I was interested in the science of global warming and I ended up talking to this guy named Doug Larsen at Guelph, who had what he thought was a wonderful climate-measurement device that went back six thousand years. It was basically tree rings, and he found that the tree rings in this specific location correlated perfectly with summer temperature and summer rainfall so you could, looking at the tree rings in any given year, establish how much rainfall, how much heat, etc. And that was like a thermometer, as he put it, right in the middle of the buttocks of North America that stretched back six thousand years. And no one doing the computer modelling of climate change wanted to talk to him. No one wanted to give him money, and I was just outraged because it was clear as a bell to me that you could indeed computer model it, but you needed real measurements to make and test those models to make them work.

So in the course of that story, he introduced me to an archaeologist whom he had consulted about the growing of corn on the escarpment in that area of Ontario, and how the climate warmed and warmed and warmed sufficiently for corn to be grown after about 500 AD. The corn culture basically moved into Ontario around 500 AD, moved up higher and higher and further and further north, and that, too, was an indication of climate change.

So I go to see this guy. I walk in the door, and he's in this museum that he's got outside of [the University of] Western Ontario in London and he sits me down and we're talking about this stuff, and all of a sudden I realize the corn culture that he's writing about in southern Ontario is identical to the Brazilian corn culture that I had read about in anthropological works. And I say, 'Did you realize they had the same culture?' And he said, 'No, I didn't know that.'

And then he turned to me and said, 'Do you realize how the archaeological heritage of this province is being treated like garbage by the government of Ontario?' And from there it was a hop and a skip and a jump to *Bones*. Because I was looking at the origins of Native culture in North America, and the reigning story was it had come over the Bering Strait and down south and conquered the Americas in one fell swoop, killing all the animals—a riotous killing from Alaska all the way to Tierra del Fuego, in something under a thousand years. Anyway, I'm looking at this story and the story doesn't work for me as it clearly didn't work for many others. And all of that was kicked off by a climate change story.

So the years go by, and all of a sudden I'm realizing that archaeology, which had fascinated me since I was a kid, was a science undergoing tremendous change and pressure, coming from an area that I would never have expected, which is genetics, that you could trace human populations through space and time by looking at relationships between quirks and twists in mitochondrial DNA in every cell. Okay, so it's now thirty years since I've been in a biology class, and of course mitochondria were never mentioned, and DNA was unknown territory. And the human genome . . . what was that?

None of that was in my head from school. So at a certain point while I was writing *Bones*, I did a chapter on the anthropological use of genetics. It was just like pulling teeth to try and read the papers and make sense of them and try and figure out whether they were reasonable or whether the anthropologists using this material were misusing it. None of them, for example, could tell me the history of the science they were using. They didn't know where it came from. So *The Second Tree* was an attempt to understand that, where it came from. And that took me to a history of biology in the modern era.

So when you finished *The Second Tree* . . .?

I said, 'I'll never do this again.' I said, 'I can't stand this. If I have to do one more project like this, I'm going to go insane.'

But it got some rave reviews, and it's such an accomplishment, and now it's there for all to read.

*The Second Tree* was the hardest thinking I have ever done in my life and I think I'm at a stage now where thinking hard is becoming so hard, so hard. You know all of the tricks, all of the facility that you pick up over years and years of writing, that's all there. But thinking skills—I was much smarter thirty years ago, and I can feel myself slowing down, I can feel the intellectual slowness now, and it was just killing me how long it was taking me to master this new material. It was killing me.

Well, it was a huge undertaking.

Yeah, okay. It was great, it was fun, it was a miracle cure—until I had to actually make sense of it. And then it was just hell on wheels. So I decided at the end of it that I really didn't want to do another project quickly. I just couldn't summon the energy. Then, of course, I get this agent who is suddenly pushing me to present a new project, and I'm reading about these little people in Indonesia found in an archaeological setting and suddenly I find myself really interested in the whole business of speciation and how it is we decide what's human. So I thought, 'Okay, I'll do a project on that.' And I couldn't do it. I made the proposal, I had all these offers, and at every turn I found a reason not to take it and switched to the novel.

How did the novel erupt into consciousness?

I sat myself in front the computer and said, 'Write. Without a notebook. You are going to write.'

And what made you sit yourself down and write without a notebook?

I had been writing from a notebook and suppressing myself for thirty-five years. Suppressing myself, suppressing the insight, suppressing the character study, suppressing the really funny bits because they were defamatory. Suppressing, suppressing, suppressing, and I couldn't stand it any more.

So when you sat down to write without a notebook and not suppress, did you say to yourself, 'I'm going to write a novel,' or did you just say, 'I'm going to write and to hell with what results and everything else'?

I said, 'I'm writing a novel but I don't know where it's going, and I don't care. I've got to get this out of me.'

That's less than a year ago, right?

Right. So now I'm on Chapter 19.

I just love it.

> Wait till you read it, maybe you won't love it. Maybe this is the biggest mistake of my life. And I've made some big ones.

Still, you sound positively gleeful about it, and you said it's the most fun you've ever had writing.

> Absolutely. Imagine not having to suppress everything. Now it may be that what I'm finding delicious will strike everybody else as boring, but I just enjoy getting it out. It's like it's been poisoning my system all these years, and I have to get it out.

But you still care about investigative reporting?

> I do, and I'm thinking that we need to do something about what's going on in the Middle East and there has to be proper reporting about that and we're not doing a very good job. And it scares me.

You were an investigative reporter basically before you knew you were. To me, it seems that investigative reporters are just people with a bad case of the smarts who can't stop asking questions.

> I think that's exactly true. They cannot stop asking questions and they get furious with people who lie—that's the other side. I get furious with people who lie and I will not quit until I've nailed them.

Don't you think an investigative reporter needs that sense of outrage at being lied to in order to hang in there and get through the work?

> But I don't know where the arrogance comes from that says, 'You owe me an answer.'

Maybe it isn't arrogance. If you're asking questions in the name of the public's right to know, it's not just for yourself, and it's not idle curiosity.

> I think that's a fiction. I think it's a very useful fiction, because the public certainly doesn't sit down there in the basement with me while I'm slamming it into words. The truth of the matter is we're satisfying our own sense of what it is that we want to know about how the world works. And the fact that we're doing it for a purpose broader than the gratification of getting it into print is wonderful, but I don't think it's the driver.

Both concentrated ownership and then convergence have eroded the journalistic base. What do you think is the future for investigative reporting, especially in newspapers, where most young journalists get their start?

> I see amazing investigative work coming out. It always surprises me, and I'm not sure why I'm surprised. There seems to be at least in some papers in this country a commitment to do it and to do it over time, to not give up and to make sure that they're actually doing stuff in the public interest.

So you think investigative reporting will survive because there are people still doing it and doing an amazing job?

> I think there are people absolutely determined to do it, and I think in a strange way convergence is helpful. I mean the technological innovation that allows you to turn your cell phone into a recording device—this is amazing stuff. People are able to wander here, there, and everywhere and get accurate reflections of what they see, and get them piped home in no time flat.
>
> I think that is changing the way we think about how we lay these stories down, but it isn't changing the most basic thing, which is to find what is hidden and bring it forward. And to try in some way to act on behalf of those who can't act for themselves. I see that impulse in just about every paper and every reporter who lasts longer than a couple of years.
>
> It's partly, I think, that people rely on that [the idea of working for the public interest] as the justification for their curiosity; I think most of us are embarrassed by our curiosity. And it's very helpful to feel that your curiosity can be put to a proper use, to a socially proper use. So I think that impetus is always going to be there and I think the corporate hounds will not care about that other than does it get them more readers or not, and I think it generally does. There's no reason to inhibit it, and there's every reason to promote it. Look how often the *Star* is running those group projects.

And check out the *Hamilton Spectator* with its series Blind Faith, about the pharmaceutical industry and its relationship with researchers in academia.

> I think it was the *Star*—it might have been the *Globe*—that did a takeout on an individual woman who was part of this Vioxx scandal. That was just amazing. And they basically said, in print, that this doctor who's a professor at U of T had a profound conflict of interest and never revealed it. It was an amazing piece of work. Very much to the point, it explained how the Vioxx scandal got up and walked, how they got so far down the road with such faulty data. It was really well done. And they've done a number of pieces like that. I don't think they do enough of that with political issues, but they certainly have been doing it on the social side and the *Star* has been doing an amazing job.

So I can't say that newspapers now are worse than they were. I think there was a period in the 1980s, maybe the early '80s, when the *Globe* was a better, tougher, more hard-hitting paper in its general coverage of all news than it is now, but I don't think they put any more—in fact I'm sure they put much less—in the way of resources into long investigative projects. But I think we're doing better in some ways.

**Computer-assisted reporting has done a lot to reinvigorate the investigative project, and there have been other important initiatives.**

Well, I'm thinking of John Sawatsky at Carleton. He had this really interesting idea of group journalism. I've done it as an editor but I've never done it as a writer—been part of a group going after a specific subject from many angles. What I liked about his idea was you could take all these students and give them a kind of matrix, and send them out to make sure that all basic questions were asked of everyone, not just one party, not doing it hit and miss. That really produced a huge network of information for him; it was really useful. I was quite impressed by that and, by the way, he used computers to organize that material.

I can remember the first time I worked on a computer was in 1985. *Toronto Life* said, You have to start using a computer because we're going computer and forget about it, we're not going to take your copy any other way, so here we'll give you a disk and you can get started. I had already started working on computers with Stephen at *New Wilderness*.[2] But I was really unhappy about it. I didn't like them; it took me a long time to get used to them. So I was really amazed that Sawatsky was so far down the road into understanding programming and the use of different programs to take different algorithms to get different swatches of information from what had been collected. I though that was really cool.

**What advice would you offer to aspiring journalists?**

Be happy.

**Don't worry, be happy?**

No, not *don't worry*. Worry—but be happy. Because there is no other profession on the planet where we are paid to inquire and satisfy our curiosity. Absolutely none. Nothing like it.

**Yeah, it's the best work in the world.**

It absolutely is. You know, I remember the first piece I did as a journalist. The first one—I thought I had died and gone to heaven. I could not believe that I was going to do this every day. They wouldn't have had to pay me! It was like, 'You mean I can sit here all day and read and think and then go and ask people questions? I can do that?' Oh, it was a revelation.

And then there was tremendous relief for me in getting out of the five-thousand-word box. I'd been pushing and pushing the margins for years—I mean I was doing ten thousand, and twelve thousand, and fifteen thousand, and then fifty thousand and one hundred thousand words. It's like I can clear my throat now, I can actually get things said here. There was tremendous relief in going to long form, and I obviously should have been in long form a lot earlier, but there's the fun factor, the quick turnaround.

I've had some really great editors who gave me my head and backed me in every corner you can imagine and were fun, were willing to take risks and just go with it and see what happens. And that too is something that I think we ought to look at: the relationship between the writer and the editor. Because you can't have good investigative journalism without an editor who's fulminating within the organization to make space for it and get money for it and who's willing to try out new aggressive young reporters and teach them and help them and support them and lead them. So I got very lucky in my whole career. I've had a real succession of interesting, gutsy editors who wanted to play in traffic.

# Endnotes

1. *Cloak of Green: The Links between Key Environmental Groups, Government and Big Business* (James Lorimer & Company, 1995 and 1998); *Bones: Discovering the First Americans* (Random House Canada, 2001; Carroll & Graf, 2002); and *The Second Tree: Of Clones, Chimeras, and the Quest for Immortality* (Random House Canada, 2004; Carroll & Graf, 2005).

2. In the mid-1980s, Dewar worked as a writer and story editor for the award-winning television series *Lorne Greene's New Wilderness*.

# David McKie
(10 August 2006)

The Ottawa-based and award-winning journalist David McKie is part of the CBC's investigative unit. A specialist in access-to-information and computer-assisted reporting, McKie also trains other journalists in these techniques. An inspired investigator and eloquent idealist, he teaches a course in investigative reporting with Jim Bronskill of the Canadian Press at the Carleton University's School of Journalism in Ottawa, and is one of the four authors of *Digging Deeper: A Canadian Reporter's Research Guide*.

---

Could you comment on the difference between investigative reporting in newspapers and investigative reporting for broadcast media?

> Well, a technique is a technique is a technique. There are stories that we've done over the past two years that have in many ways changed the landscape of the whole adverse-drug-reaction reporting schema. Faint Warning and Prescribed to Death—really these are techniques that can lead to stories in any medium. So the techniques and methodology really are irrespective of medium. I could be working for the *Globe and Mail* and still produce the same kind of stories.

Let's discuss the technique and methodology. Were you the producer for both those series?

> I was one of the main participants. I was one of the people who negotiated for the database, who began to analyze the database and to come up with the stories. I found most of the people who were in the stories that we did through using things like listservs and contacts. And at some point I then, too, became a reporter. So I wore many hats in the projects, but I was one of the main people.

Faint Warning was first, and then Prescribed to Death followed, right?

> That's right. And we did a series called Dying for a Job. And for that series and our continuing stories on workplace safety, we've raised the bar even higher, because we're not using one database, which was the case with Faint Warning. And for Prescribed to Death we were actually able to combine a bunch of databases. But now we are going after the databases of all the workplace-safety insurance boards across the country and ministries of labour for purposes of analysis.

So in terms of database analysis, the difference between Faint Warning/Prescribed to Death, and Dying for a Job is that Dying for a Job is the largest database project you've undertaken so far?

> Oh yeah, by far. I mean, it's taken us a few years but these are the databases that the workplace-safety insurance boards and ministries of labour use to determine who's getting sick and why, who's dying, who's being injured on the job and why, who should be compensated—all that kind of stuff. Not only are we getting these databases but we're getting prosecution databases as well. So we're getting all the administrative databases that allow us to say something fairly significant about the state of workplace safety not only in Ontario or BC, where you live, but

right across the country. So we are able to do something that no other news organization has done with regard to workplace safety and that is to talk about national trends.

Enough database material to be able to know you've pretty much got it all?

Well we did that for Dying for a Job. We identified two national trends, one with regard to violence: the fact that if you take a look at all the industries that are tracked through these databases, the workers in the social services and health-care industry are anywhere from six to twelve times more likely to file a claim for violence than workers in any other industry, including police. So we were the first ones to be able to quantify that nationally with data.

And then, of course, we told stories and we actually used BC as a base to tell a lot of our stories. We featured the case of the social services worker David Bland who was working in a mental health facility out in Richmond and he was stabbed to death by a former client. And we ended up telling that story as an indication of the kind of danger that people face, and this really fit into our trend. So that was one trend.

And the second trend we were able to identify was the fact that more than half of all claims made to all the boards across the country are for strains of all kinds—back strains, repetitive strain injuries, and whatnot—so when you have the data that institutions use for administrative purposes, you can analyze it and come up with trends, and then you find the stories. We found people and told their stories and their stories were emblematic of a broader trend. The point being—and we point this out in our book [*Digging Deeper*] as well—that you've got to find people to tell the stories. Numbers don't tell stories.

So irrespective of medium, if you find someone who's really interesting you can put them on the front page of the *Globe and Mail*, as they often do, or you can put them on *The National*, or you can put them on *The World at Six*, or *The Current*, or *Sunday Edition*. So you really do need to find the people, but the technique that we use goes beyond the anecdote and is pretty hard for authorities to refute. And that really is the power of computer-assisted reporting.

The people factor was always part of the news and will always be part of the news. In a way, computer-assisted reporting just amplifies what amounts to traditional journalistic thinking. On the other hand, database analysis obviously takes some finely honed mathematical skills, and many of my students shy away from it because of that.

I teach a couple of courses as well, third-year and master's students [at Carleton University's School of Journalism], and I go through the same thing. But even after four weeks, just doing a four-week module, three hours a pop, at the end of twelve hours, or four weeks, I can get them fairly comfortable with some basic numbers using spreadsheets. One of the exercises I do is to use a city budget. Now we all do budget stories, we all know that budget stories can be intimidating, and we also know that budget stories are incredibly political animals—that you could use numbers to tell people anything you want and you know that because journalists are so afraid of numbers, they're not necessarily going to challenge you. So what I do is get the summary budget information in spreadsheet format and I get it for a three- to four-year span so we can look at trends.

That way, we can just manipulate the numbers ourselves. One of the stories that the students inevitably end up doing is on how the city here [Ottawa] likes to crow about the fact that they are able to keep property taxes down. And they point to this as showing they are being stewards of the public purse and isn't this a wonderful thing. But take a look at some of the user fees—there's a column in the budget for revenues—and so if you're a city, the reason you generate revenues is that you're charging user fees. These are user fees or revenues: anything from having to pay to use an arena or a swimming pool to receiving your water—that's revenue, that's a user fee. Sewers—that's a user fee. And if you take a look at these user fees, they have increased tremendously over the past three or four years, at a far greater rate than taxes have, in some instances, an alarming rate. It's a hidden tax.

So that's the kind of story that you would not be able to tell if you were just using a flat file, reading through paper, and depending on city officials and politicians to tell you what the news was. This allows you to go beyond the anecdote, beyond the he-said-she-said journalism.

## Are you talking about relational databases now?

No, this is just a straight spreadsheet. You need the data in a spreadsheet so that you can see all the columns of information . . . so you can see that there are a certain number of services that actually generate revenues. All you do is use simple math. You just add the columns for the revenues and you do a simple formula to figure out the percentage increase, and you can see that the revenues for sewers and water—and I'm pulling this out of my hat, I don't have the exact figures—increased at a greater rate than taxes did. So taxes may have levelled off, but if you take a look at user fees for key services, they have increased certainly above the rate of inflation.

So then all of a sudden, just knowing first of all what to ask for, and having a certain comfort level working with a spreadsheet, which is doing the basic addition, subtraction, division—very easy stuff, grade 3 stuff—you could start to come up with stories using just very elementary computer-assisted reporting. We're not talking about relational databases, we're not talking about the projects that we do [at CBC]. We're talking about doing CAR on a daily basis in a small newsroom on a tight deadline.

## Did the series Dying for a Job require relational databases?

No, not for Dying for a Job. Because basically, we were able to negotiate with all the authorities across the country just to get flat files—and a flat file is just a table—so we would get one huge table with all kinds of fields in them and all kinds of codes.

## How would you put them all together?

Well we would just pull trends out of each one. You really have to break it down, if you're going to get people to understand this, you have to break it down. There are many levels of CAR. And the spreadsheet is the simplest thing. The nice thing about a spreadsheet is that you can get up and running—I can get students up and running in half an hour—and actually finding the stories.

## By asking questions of the data—is that what you mean by finding the stories?

Yeah, just doing simple math, adding columns together and figuring out percentages and seeing what is increasing more than something else. So if something is increasing more than something else, then you do the story about the thing that's increasing the most, and that's how we come up with stories such as taxes increasing at a higher rate, or services increasing at a higher rate compared to something else, and those are what we use to make headlines.

## And you don't have to attribute information to one or more experts.

Right, because you're using the institution's own data to pull information that you want to tell, and not that they want to tell. And so that's where the power comes from. But in order to get to that point, you have to realize that it's possible, you have to realize that institutions use data for administrative purposes, you have to know how to negotiate for it, and you have to know how not to take no for an answer. And then once you get it, the hard part's over.

## That's the hardest part, getting hold of the data, getting them to release it?

If you talk to people who do this all the time, they would say, and certainly this is my experience, that they spend an inordinate length of time right now negotiating for data.

## Do you teach your students that, too? How to negotiate for data?

Yes, because inevitably, you're asking people for information that they've never been asked for before. And usually you're dealing with a PR person who has no idea what you're talking about. So even a simple request like, 'I don't want the budget in paper format, I don't want a PDF, I want the information in a spread-sheet.' And they scratch their heads, they have no idea that the information even comes in that format because they don't deal on that level.

Yes, I remember that for one series—Fred Vallance-Jones's Reservations—the city didn't know how to extract the information, even though they'd recorded it. They'd made the database and put the information in, but they didn't know how to get it back out in certain formats.

That's part of the issue as well. In some cases, they're lying—just full of it. And in other cases, they really don't know. And that is what we're running into right now with our workplace-safety stuff. We are dealing with ministries of labour across this country and they honestly do not know how to extract the informa-tion, because the information systems they're using are so old. Generally speak-ing, the last thing that government is going to spend money on is its IT, its information storage system. Generally speaking, bureaucracies spend their time fighting fires, not being proactive. They spend their time reacting to things, so they are not going to use their databases. And this is what we found out with Faint Warning and Prescribed to Death—that institutions like Health Canada for the most part use their databases to look up problems, not to analyze trends.

But shouldn't they be?

They should be. So what happens is that people like Fred Vallance-Jones, peo-ple like Rob Cribb, people like David McKie . . . come along and they use these databases, and they say, Okay, well, we are going to look at trends, we are going to dig up trends, and then tell stories about those trends. And that's where the real power comes from—in our series, in the stuff that Fred has done, the stuff that Rob has done, the stuff we've all done. Because it's undeniable. What is an institution going to do? What is Health Canada going to do? It's their own data. That's why at the end of the day they were forced to put a searchable version of their adverse-drug-reaction database online, which is something we had done the previous year.

Well, you forced them to; you shamed them into it. How can they say there is no data or the data doesn't add up?

This is the real power of it. But the approach to it has to be systematic. I think we all agree that what we don't want to do is leave people with the impression that it's for big projects. It's not only for big projects. And increasingly, you'll hear that when you go to IRE conferences,[1] for example. You will hear in workshops that people talk about this; one workshop is fifty great CAR ideas that can be done quickly. And they will talk about certain stories having a CAR sentence or a CAR paragraph. In other words, it doesn't have to be the story; it can just be an element in the story.

So the budget example that I gave you is a way to integrate this technique into your everyday journalism. Because to actually do that story—I mean, these are assignments that my students end up doing and literally it takes an hour or two, once you're familiar with what the columns of information mean, which is what you have to do anyway—get someone to explain to you what the information means. I do that for them, but if I wasn't there what you would do is phone up a city official or bureaucrat and say, Well, I've got the spreadsheet now, I just want to make sure what the columns of information mean. And you're off to the races. And if you can't figure out how to add the columns and the like, what I did was I just went to the person who keeps our books here at the CBC, because I noticed one day when I was asking her about one of my time cards that she had a spreadsheet She consulted the spreadsheet, and obviously she knows how to use it. So I just asked her how to add and how to subtract. It took her fifteen minutes to show me.

Once you have the information in hand, there are people around who can help you if it's some of the higher-end stuff. As you get more comfortable with it, you start working with more complicated data sets. Certainly Fred, Rob and I, when we give workshops and stuff, we're always encouraging people to email us with questions, which people have done. The NICAR, the National Institute for Computer Assisted Reporting, which is an offshoot of the IRE, has a listserv and you can post questions there if you run into problems. So, really, there are all kinds of ways that you can get help fairly quickly to solve all kinds of problems.

Did you begin the Faint Warning series with the database? Or was it a case of thinking about the issue and then trying to figure out what kind of information and what databases you would need to tell the story?

Well, we didn't know what the story was. All we knew was that if we got a hold of a fairly substantial database, we would be able to look at it and figure out some trends and do some stories. So you get a database, as complete as you can, and to answer your question about relational databases, the CADRIS [Canadian Adverse Drug Reaction Information Service] is a relational database—databases made up of several tables linked together.

So you actually began the research with the database?

Yeah, but we didn't go into it saying we're going to get this or that story. You just don't know. You get data because you know that at some point there's probably going to be a trend in there. Sometimes there isn't.

But did something happen to get you to wonder about this particular database? I mean, there are a million databases you could go after.

> Well, we were always interested in dangerous drugs, and we were interested in Zyban, a smoking cessation drug, because we were hearing about lots of problems. I was interested in Propulsid, the drug that killed 15-year-old Vanessa Young a few years ago. We were interested in all kinds of drugs and we thought why not get a database that has all the adverse drug reactions, and we can see how these and other drugs are reacting. And then Health Canada said no, and we said, Well, we're not going to take no for an answer. Then Health Canada said, Why don't we send you a PDF [portable document format] file of adverse drug reactions for two years. And we said, Well, that's not good enough because we can't manipulate the information in a PDF to identify our own trends, which is what they don't want you to do. So we took the good fight to the information commissioner, and we won, eventually. To make a very, very long story short.

How long did it take to get the database for Faint Warning?

> It took about five years. And we are now probably headed to the Federal Court because Health Canada does not want to give us the fields in the CADRIS database that contain the provinces. So for example, in Prescribed to Death we did a story on the fact that many seniors are addicted to a benzodiazepine called Adavan. By some estimates, there are in BC alone, 175,000 people who are on this drug, which has been around forever, and are addicted to it. And Quebec is called the benzo capital of Canada: there's a higher percentage of Quebeckers on this drug than people anywhere else.
>
> Well we would love to do this kind of breakdown for all kinds drugs, to find out where the hot spots are in terms of prescribing and whatnot. You can't do that if you can't break the information down by province. And Health Canada refuses to give that information to us because they claim that if we had that information it would be easier for us to identify individuals.
>
> I just point that out because, as Fred will tell you, we're constantly fighting for data. It's non-stop, and it's an energy-sapping exercise—it really is. But at the end of the day, more often than not it's worth it. And what we're able to do, hopefully, is blaze a bit of a trail for others who will come along, for students we teach, maybe for your students, who will come along and all of a sudden bureaucrats will have heard of the stories that we've all done, and read the stuff that we've written and will understand that the default position does not have to be 'No'; [it can be] 'How can I help?' And now, the information commissioner's office actually has someone in there who knows a thing or two about databases because of the fights that we've waged. And institutions like Health Canada have access officers who now do nothing but database work.

Since when?

That's been a couple of years now. Certainly I've been through three or four different officers at Health Canada. We tend to burn them out, I don't know what happens to them, and they have told me that they end up handling all the database stuff. Because it takes them a while to get up to speed. They've got to have Excel and, more importantly, Access on their desktop. Many of them don't. Many of them don't even know how to open these programs or look at a table.

That's stunning.

So it's really still a bit of a pioneering effort, which is one of the reasons why Fred and I are going to be writing a book on CAR in Canada. Because you can get a sense from what I'm talking about that there's a lot that needs to be written. But there's no denying that it's a very powerful form of journalism. And I think for it to really take off it's got to become commonplace in newsrooms across the country where very simple things are done like asking for information in spreadsheet format instead of just getting it on paper and just being able to do your very quick calculations.

Let me ask you something about negotiating for information: Say I tell my students about Fred's Reservations series, and I say, 'Why don't we go out and see about the local restaurants in Kamloops. Why don't we call the city and see if they have inspections and ask them to send us their inspection reports.' What if the city says no? What's the next step?

First of all, they have to give it to you. The only reason they could refuse to give it to you is if it contained any personal information, but the reason that you go through the formal process of freedom of information at the provincial level or access to information at the federal level, is that they then go through the various and sundry requests, the documentation, and they expunge all personal references. So you're getting basically 'anonymized' data. And it's not a question of national security. There's no reason for them to refuse this other than when they're unfamiliar with something you ask for—and they're usually unfamiliar with databases—their natural default position is to say no. In many cases, journalists are intimidated by this and they go away.

Well, we don't go away. We fight back. And what your students can do is point to precedents, to stories that Fred has done, that Rob Cribb has done.

The key is to start small. What I will do is a half-hour brainstorming session with my students. Think about the city: You see all kinds of things. You see buses, you see roads, you see bridges, you see buildings, you see infrastructure, you see restaurants, you see swimming pools. What is the commonality among all those things? And the commonality is that they are to one degree or another overseen and regulated by the city. If they're regulated and overseen by the city, then the city has to keep track of that in terms of data, in databases. So from that you can extrapolate: Okay, well, according to the city's own information what is the most dangerous intersection, for example, in Ottawa or Kamloops? How many times are buses inspected? What state are the bridges in? How many times are the bridges inspected? So any inspection activity, anything like that at all—public health—just think of any area for which the municipality is responsible, and that activity is supported by data.

One of the first things I do is a huge brainstorming session. For example, say we're at a university here. Well, think of all the databases that this university would have. What kinds of things would they have to keep track of? A lot of it is just getting them [his Carleton students] used to a bureaucratic mindset. Think like a bureaucrat.

And when we talk about data, we have to be very clear that for the most part we're talking about institutions. We're generally not speaking about the private sector because the private sector can do a better job of protecting information using privacy laws, and they don't owe it to you.

But you can still use this technique to do good business stories, for example. There was a piece in the *New York Times* a couple of weeks ago about people who would return to the job market after being off for a spell. And they were able to compile information on that. You can go and get information from annual reports and determine things like how much money pharmaceutical companies are spending on marketing compared to research and development. Dump that stuff into a spreadsheet and do some nice little stories.

I tend to collect these examples for my classes and for the book to show that there are ways to use these techniques very quickly and very easily. But for the most part, we're talking about public institutions when it comes to data because we have more of a right to that stuff.

And there are organizations like Stats Canada, the provinces keep a lot of stats, the municipalities keep a lot of stats. With the recent census that stuff is broken down pretty intricately and you can get a slice for the Kamloops area and you can probably work with a statistician at Stats Canada.

You can get some pretty interesting stories, talk about who's commuting, where people are living, immigration patterns, and telework. Are more people working at home? Any kind of human activity that is surveyed, the number of same-sex couples, any kind of human activity that people are questioned about and they keep statistics for—you can get that for a specific area and design a little project. When I do workshops outside Ottawa, I usually end up using Stats Canada. I get some tailored statistics and we run through some exercises so the students can see how you can use this stuff, and there's a little bit of negotiation, but a lot of the stuff you can get free and easily. It's not rocket science, but again a lot of the reflex is just knowing what to ask for and when to ask for it.

And that comes from journalistic training.

And it comes from day one. A lot of my students now know how to ask for data. And they get it. And once they get it, if for whatever they can't figure it out, there's lots of help around.

Will the CAR book that you and Fred are writing be a how-to text?

It will be a bit of a how-to, some history, and it'll be very heavy on examples, just like *Digging Deeper* is, very anecdotal.[2] I like to say that when we were writing *Digging Deeper* it was part inspiration, part instruction. You have to be inspired first. You have to want to be able, after reading a story and learning how the reporter got it, to say, 'I want to do that.' You want to do that? Okay, here's how.

Do you consider yourself an investigative reporter?

Absolutely.

I found a lot of near sheepishness or embarrassment about the term in newsrooms. Some reporters think they shouldn't call themselves investigative reporters because it's somehow arrogant or egotistical. They feel as though they are putting on airs to so title themselves.

I used to think that, but it's a crock. There's a difference between what I do and what someone in daily news does, pure and simple. I mean the kind of information we get, the way we get it, the way we work sources—it's different, it's investigative. There's a methodology to it. We may use the he-said-she-said template as a starting point, but not an end point.

Did you always want to be a reporter since you were a kid?

Not really. I graduated from high school and I thought, 'What the hell do I want to do?' I ended up going to Carleton to play football. So I played football for four years, and they had a journalism school, so there were two reasons to go to Carleton.

Even then you thought journalism would be something you might be interested in?

Well, I just thought journalism sounded interesting. I wasn't a great reader of newspapers; I don't know that I was a particularly hyper-curious teenager or young adult. But journalism just sounded interesting. I enjoyed the course.

So by the time you were in journalism school, you sort of fell in love with it?[3]

No, I didn't fall in love with it. I started freelancing—radio, print, magazines—that's how I ended up doing the *Media Magazine* for the CAJ,[4] because I used to lay it out. I used to lay out magazines using PageMaker.

But I really started to fall in love with it when I saw the potential that journalism could have. I think I was probably in the business for five or six years when I started seeing the impact of stories by other investigative journalists. I remember going to CAJ conferences and listening to people like Jock Ferguson speak (he used to be an investigative reporter with the *Globe*), talking about great investigations to be done looking into areas like concrete. I'll never forget this . . . he said, 'Concrete: lots of money in concrete.' And just really being turned on by these people, and the work that they were doing.

So it was after you'd basically been in the business for a while, and it was CAR that turned you on?

Yeah, and just by going to CAJ conferences and talking to people like Fred and seeing the great stuff that they were doing and thinking, 'I want to do that. I want to be an investigative reporter, I want to break stories, I want to make a difference.' And this is a great technique; a great way to do it is to use this data. If I can learn this in a way that no one else can then it will give me an edge as well. Right now, one of my duties with the investigative unit at CBC news is to do the computer-assisted reporting stuff and all the access-to-information stuff.[5]

But I stress to people that I worked in daily news for over ten years, mainly radio. And that's where you really get an appreciation of a lot of issues. You cover everything; you get a sense of what's important and what's not. You're exposed to so much. You learn how to write quickly and precisely. You learn how a lot of things operate. I think what I would dissuade someone from is thinking that all of a sudden you can just fall into investigative journalism right out of school. You've got to go work in a daily newsroom and work there for a number of years for all kinds of reasons. And then after that, this is something that you evolve into. And all of us have been there.

Rob Cribb says people think everyone wants to be an investigative reporter, but nothing could be further from the truth. Most people just want to do their nine-to-five stint and call it quits.

Yes, you'd be surprised. I started to discover that. One of my jobs is to work with other reporters and help them file requests. I do a lot of teaching within the CBC, and it's just incredible how many reporters—and this not a value judgment, just an observation—who are happy doing the nine-to-five, happy doing the news conferences. And that's okay. But I always had the assumption that everyone wanted to do this. It's not the case. There could be all kinds of reasons for it—it's time-consuming, it's frustrating, you hit a lot of dead ends, you have to fight to get your stuff on the air, and in the paper to get the kind of placement that you want.

I remember that when we came out with the precursor to Prescribed to Death, we took a look at medical devices and we called the series that we did with marketplace A Matter of Trust. We took a look at clinical trials . . . [including] an illegal clinical trial that was taking place at the Children's Hospital of Eastern Ontario. We took a look at the lack of informed consent for clinical trials and at faulty medical devices based on the medical device adverse reaction database that I got from Health Canada, which really was the first CAR thing that I ever did. And we took a look at medical ghostwriting.

It was a fantastic series, but you know when it came out? It came out during the Iraq invasion. Which is all to say that you spend all this time and then the timing is just totally screwed up by something beyond your control. But I always say that really important stories will find an audience—they really will—and they will make a difference. I remember with Prescribed to Death we had to wait a week because the Pope had died. So the timing is always interesting, though if it's journalism that really matters I really do believe that it finds an audience. But it's not for everyone. The hours are incredibly long and it can be incredibly lonely because usually you are one of a few, if a few, people actually working on this stuff. Most people are doing the day-to-day stuff.

So you really have to be dedicated. And that's why people like me end up talking to people in other media like Rob and Fred. You form this kind of virtual community where you can commiserate and encourage each other and support each other.

### Do you find that the stories exert influence across media?

Oh yeah, I mentioned the stories that Margaret Monroe picked up from us on the faulty clinical trial at the Children's Hospital of Eastern Ontario. She did a whole bunch of stuff for the *Vancouver Sun* talking about these clinical trials, and she wrote about a trial gone wrong at the Children's Hospital. We had done the story. Now, we didn't get any credit for it, which was unfortunate, but we had done that story as part of the Matter of Trust series. She picked up on it. That's an example of a story that started in broadcast but ended up in print. When we did Faint Warning, the *Star* picked up on our stuff, got the same database, and did stories, and as a matter of fact, they were one of the CAR finalists last year along with us [at the 2005 Canadian Association of Journalists Awards, which has introduced a new category for computer-assisted stories].

So I think that really shows that the treatment is the same. Whether broadcast or print, you've got to find people and anecdotes, but those anecdotes don't exist in a vacuum. They're actually used to support a broader piece of analysis.

Computer-assisted-reporting techniques can be used to further the positive aspects of convergence, a phenomenon that I have generally regarded as just another way to erode the journalistic base. But the way you're talking about it, I can see a positive side—if the efficiencies gained and revenues saved by convergence were directed back into investigative projects, rather than at hiring fewer people to do more work across the various platforms.

> Absolutely. And I haven't spent any time talking about CBC.ca, which really, if it weren't for CBC.ca and the Web component, none of this stuff would have had the impact that it did. It was the ability to put the adverse-drug-reaction database online, to put a searchable version online, that netted us something like fifteen thousand visits in two days after we did the Faint Warning story. When we came up with Prescribed to Death, with a list of drugs that seniors are not supposed to take, we were able to put that list online and allow people to search themselves. That, you have to be able to do. The *Toronto Star* does that all the time. Fred does that. Really, for us the Web component is part and parcel. The *New York Times* is really focusing on that right now, the *Washington Post*, too. . . . We are fighting right now to make sure that the Web component really does get the funding that it needs to do this, because managers don't necessarily see it this way.
> So I think that really speaks to the need to have a multimedia approach. When I go out and do a story, I have a digital camera and I've got my microphone as well. Then we turn around and we're doing more stuff for TV. So really, within the CBC, you have to use all three media: radio, TV, and the Web.

I love CBC.ca because I can *read* it—it's as good as reading a hard-copy newspaper. Actually better, because I can search online.

> You got it. And you can read it, you can print it out. If you don't feel like watching *The National* tonight, you can watch it at 11:00 or 11:30, when they put it online. So it really does make sense, and I can't stress enough how important the online component is. For us, this stuff would not be as powerful without the online [possibilities]. I think it's really important for students, if they don't know this already, to have that appreciation. Again, when I go out to do a story, I've got all that stuff, so when I come back I'm thinking in terms of all three media, not just radio.

It seems that's where the future is for newspapers too: online. I can remember a time when the *Globe and Mail*, for one example among many, wasn't putting its stuff online. I guess it was a matter of managers figuring a free online version would hurt hard-copy sales.

> Now they're breaking stories online.
> A lot of [the stories they post online] is CP stuff, but that's okay. They tend to save their own people for the paper edition or for the later online editions, but at least they're putting stuff up there.

What do you think is the future for investigative reporting? Do you think it will gravitate toward online and so-called new or converged media?

> I hope so. I don't know if that will happen, but I certainly hope so. I don't think
> that the commitment will diminish. Certainly if you take him at his word, when
> David Asper [executive vice-president of CanWest Global] spoke at the CAJ con-
> ference in Halifax, he talked about the importance of investigative journalism and
> as proof of that he used a couple of court cases: the Juliet O'Neill case and the
> Andrew McIntosh case as two instances where they are spending a shitload of
> money to defend the principles that are really behind investigative journalism,
> which is the need to protect sources and to be able do that with impunity. So if
> you take him at his word, certainly that's the case.
>
> The CBC is spending money on investigative journalism. I'm doing what I'm
> doing because it's got a commitment to investigative journalism. And computer-
> assisted reporting and access to information is a huge part of that. Fred's doing
> what he's doing and Rob's doing what he's doing because their newspapers
> support it. And in terms of Torstar, it's the largest player in the game.

Well the *Toronto Star* is in a class by itself. If you look at its record of investigative
reporting, even before computers, it always led the pack. And even if you hear some
jealousy among reporters every once in a while about the *Star*, it seems to me their
sterling record is no reason to be jealous, it's just a reason to sit up and take notice
and learn a couple of things from a leader in the field.

> It's a great paper. And the *Globe and Mail* . . . the whole AdScam affair [the
> Quebec sponsorship scandal], they really dined out on that, and rightly so. But
> they continue to break stories and do some excellent work. And if you listen to
> [editor-in-chief] Eddie Greenspon, he is definitely a proponent of investigative
> journalism or deep-background enterprise reporting.
>
> So I think that as long as the major players and the people who are in charge
> continue to espouse this, I think it will be there. But I really do think that this has
> to be embraced by people in smaller newsrooms, and reporters. As I tell my stu-
> dents, you've got to start fighting for this stuff, and even if you've got to invest a
> little of your own time, it's an investment that pays off, because I did it, Fred did
> it, Rob did it, others have done it. We've invested our own time and now we're in
> a position where we've been able to prove ourselves. Our stories have had
> impact and we're able to do the kind of work that we want to do. But it doesn't
> happen overnight, and I think that commitment has got to be with the new gen-
> eration of reporters that are coming out of journalism schools. It really does have
> to be.
>
> I teach, Fred teaches, Rob teaches. I've spoken to other educators across
> the country and they're stressing this stuff as well, you're stressing this stuff with
> your students. So I'm optimistic. I think they're coming up, and the good ones
> are hungry and they've got a lot more tools to work with than we ever did.

Do you think that CAR will help to raise the bar generally? If it becomes more and more integrated and newcomers and students embrace it, do you think that will put an end to the strictly he-said-she-said variety of journalism?

I think the he-said-she-said stuff is going to be here with us to stay. That really bespeaks the whole notion of objectivity, which we've pooh-poohed now for what, the past fifty years? And it's still with us. If you read studies, which I did when I was doing my master's and my thesis, objectivity is pooh-poohed yet it's always our fallback position. Any time we come up with a new kind of journalism, be it literary journalism, or investigative journalism, or precision journalism, or computer-assisted reporting, or personal journalism, or public journalism, those are always kind of cast aside and we always come back to what we're familiar with. And funnily enough, what you find is that journalism is probably one of the most conservative institutions, more resistant to change than almost any other.

If you think of police and many other institutions that have gone to community-based models, and have totally rewritten the way they do things, journalism is pretty well acting in the same way it has for years. We tend to be very, very conservative. So I don't know that we're going to get away from the he-said-she-said stuff.

But are people reading it?

Not as much as they were before, but I think it's a little bit more complicated than the he-said-she-said dilemma. It speaks to different ways of consuming information. My kids, for example, get most of their information from the Net. This is the new generation; they're not reading newspapers [in hard copy or online]. And I don't know that if all of a sudden there's more investigative journalism they're going to start reading newspapers.

I think that what we have to do is—and maybe this is where the public journalism model fits in more—run those stories that resonate with younger people. We're not talking to them about what they find important. We're not engaging them. And to a degree I think that is a part of the problem.

Look, I don't think that investigative journalism is going to go anywhere. People like Andrew McIntosh might beg to disagree because one of the reasons he left Canada is that he couldn't do the kind of journalism he wanted to do, and he's in the States now [at the *Sacramento Bee*]. But I'm cautiously optimistic. I really do think the reason why I'm doing what I'm doing is that there's a recognition not only that this is important, but also that other people are doing it and we don't want to fall behind.

I don't intend to go anywhere; I know that Fred and Rob and others don't intend to go anywhere. We'll continue to ply our trade and we'll continue to teach, write, proselytize, and all that kind of fun stuff. You know, every year that I teach, there's usually a handful of students I work with who end up in newspapers and broadcast outlets who are doing really good investigative stuff. So you can multiply that. I know at King's College, for example, Dean Jobb is teaching out there, and he's got a couple of investigative courses and he's doing a great job. You're teaching people [at the Thompson Rivers University School of Journalism]; there are people at the University of British Columbia.

People are being turned out. So I think there's reason to be cautiously optimistic in spite of budget cuts. But it's really important that people realize that this doesn't have to be totally costly, doesn't have to be the megaproject. You can do it at a municipal level. If you just start small, you can start to do those little stories that will make a difference.

## So that would be your advice then to aspiring reporters?

Absolutely. Start small, work in a daily situation, and learn how to fight for this stuff. Learn how to do it efficiently, because then you'll be better equipped to handle the more complicated stuff.

## Could you say a few words about fighting more efficiently?

Make sure that your ATI or FOI requests are more tightly focused. Before you ask for a database, learn what it's called, what's in it. Get a record layout—in other words a template of what's in the database. Find out what the fields are. Do your homework. Because then you're in a position when you do ask for something to get the fields of information that everyone has agreed you can have, and therefore there's no muss, no fuss.

So do the upfront work. Take the time to find out what records institutions have—be it databases or whatever kind of documents they produce. When something goes wrong, what gets written down? How do they write it down? Where do they write it down? How do they use it? And if you have an idea of that, then you'll know what to ask for and you'll be in a better position to get it.

So between assignments you might have filed a request for a particular record and you get it and it's sitting there on your desk and you think, 'Okay, I've got X number of stories to do but I can probably convince my editor or my producer to give me a few hours at the end of the week to look at this.' You might do a little of this on your own time. And then you will realize, 'Yeah, there's a great story here, let me pitch it.'

And I say this because I did it for ten years. I did it. I was in a daily radio newsroom, I was filing every day, I was filing locally and nationally and doing docs—and I did it. I filed requests; I broke stories. The Matter of Trust stuff that I did with Bob Carty, who's now at *Sunday Edition*, and Erica Johnson, who's the co-host of *Marketplace*, I did that when I was working in daily news. So I have little sympathy for people who complain about the fact that they don't have enough time.

Either you want to do this stuff or you don't. And if you want to be stuck after fifteen, twenty years in the business doing he-said-she-said journalism, that's fine, if that's what you want. But if you want to do something different, then invest the time. It's like going to school—and your schooling really starts I think after you graduate, after you get that piece of paper. That's when you really start to learn. So grab on to a mentor. Read. Do the things you need to, make the kind of investments that you need to make in order to become the kind of journalist you want to become.

### Where did you take your first computer-assisted reporting course?

I did it out in Vancouver. I think it was in 1995; it was one of the [CAJ] workshops out there, and it was Fred who was leading it. And then I got really turned on, really turned on.

So I started about ten years ago, but I only really started getting into it seriously about four or five years ago, when I started negotiating for the Health Canada stuff and when I started getting into medical devices, because then the more you're into it, the more you want to learn. Then I started going to IRE conferences. A lot of it is just talking to people who are doing it and getting turned on by that. Once you're saying to yourself, 'I want to do it,' you're hooked. Because learning how to do it is the easy part, I think. Being committed to it and being committed to negotiating for the data and getting the data, that's the hard part, because that really requires a mental shift in the way that you do things. It's behaviour modification. The way I operate as a journalist now is totally different from the way I operated even three years ago.

### So computer-assisted reporting allows reporters to do their own research and their own thinking, and can enhance the results.

I tell my students it's the great equalizer, meaning that you don't have to work for the CBC, the *Star*, or the *Globe*. You can be doing this from your own desktop, or laptop, and you could be turning out first-rate work. I mean, one of the best investigative papers a while back was the *Eastern Graphic*—a little daily newspaper in PEI. It was just that the mentality of the paper was to break stories. So you don't have to be one of the bigfoots.

We won out over Fred for Prescribed to Death [at the 2005 CAJ Awards]. Our project was so large in scope—getting the database, putting it online. But the judge for the award made a specific mention of the fact that Fred without the same resources came very close. He's just doing phenomenal work.

But I just want to go back to something you said about journalists becoming their own experts. The analysis we ended up doing for Dying For a Job was quoted in publications like the *Toronto Sun* [which would write] 'according to the CBC analysis'.

That's where I think the real potential lies. No longer must journalists defer to 'experts'. Now they can assert a kind authority because it is authority based on demonstrable knowledge.

> I always tell my students to ask about the methodology [used in a study they are reporting on]. Otherwise, they may be giving it possibly unwarranted praise. And I tell my students about the most powerful question you can ask someone: How do you know that? Because I read through so many ministerial briefing notes where reporters were told all kinds of crap, but they echo those briefing notes. They're like parrots. They say what their officials tell them. I mean there's Stockwell Day, for example, standing up today talking about this latest terrorism threat [liquid explosives on planes]. Okay, how does he know all this stuff? Well, he's reading his briefing notes. How accurate are those briefing notes? How accurate is that information? And if we start asking such questions more, that speaks to an investigative/CAR mindset, because you're saying, 'Let me see the documentation that backs up what you're saying. Prove it.'

# Endnotes

1.  McKie and Vallance-Jones's book on CAR was due to be published in 2007.

2.  McKie graduated in 1982 with a bachelor's degree in journalism from Carleton, and in 2001 earned his master's in journalism, also at Carleton.

3.  He now edits *Media* magazine, the publication of the Canadian Association of Journalists, and a must-read for aspiring reporters.

4.  At the time of this writing, McKie had been on staff with the CBC for fifteen years and with the investigative unit for about five.

5.  IRE is the US group Investigative Reporters and Editors.

Chapter 15

# Conclusions

## The Future of Investigative Reporting

Increasing commercialization of the press and declining readership have characterized the newspaper industry over the last several decades. A focus on trying to maintain the profit margins of earlier decades has for most papers meant less money and fewer resources for expensive investigative projects. Except for a brief revival of interest in the craft during the days of the 1972–4 Watergate scandal in the United States, investigative reporting never returned to the kind of glory days that typified the muckrakers of the early twentieth century. Most of the journalists interviewed for this book—and most critics and onlookers generally—agree that the day of the great crusading daily is long gone. Paul McKay tipped his hat to a vanished era:

> In the great days of the muckraking era,[1] with Ida Tarbell and her exposé of Standard Oil[2] and Upton Sinclair's work on meat-packing plants in Chicago,[3] or tenement slum landlords in New York City, or who owned the oil companies— these exposés were required reading. People *wanted* to read them. People *raced* to read them and *talk* about them. As they did about the Watergate material [in the early 1970s]. I think that was the last great moment in the history of investigative journalism in North America, where everybody from the person in the coffee shop to the president of the United States read it. And waited for the next instalment.

According to most critics and commentators, the modern big-city daily, with its varied corporate interests outside newspapers and its emphasis on the bottom line and high profit margins, will find its ability to keep doing investigative work under new pressures from alternative news sources, especially online ones. The stage is set for newspapers to spend less on fewer resources of all kinds—from hiring staff to bankrolling investigative projects. One survey conducted by Arizona State University found that at a hundred of the largest US newspapers, resources were diminishing for investigative reporting as corporations cut budgets and other costs to maintain or increase profits.[4] Will investigative reporting vanish from newspapers and migrate to magazines, books, and online venues? Peter Gorrie believes so.

> I think the way the business is going, it is going to move away from papers just because a lot of things are moving away from papers. We just got the recent NADbank[5] figures for circulation and for all the papers—except the [*National*] *Post* on weekdays, which is going up a bit—the trend [across the country] is downward and it has been for several years. Especially in Toronto. Toronto is a very competitive market, so you'd think that the totals at least would go up. But it's still going down here.

The bottom line is that none of the papers in Toronto (Canada's most competitive newspaper market) is increasing circulation overall.

> The *Post* is way down on Saturdays. Among the four newspapers in Toronto [*Globe and Mail, National Post, Toronto Sun, Toronto Star*], the one that wins our so-called newspaper war is the one that goes down less than the others. It's just getting so fragmented. People are going to the Internet, but the Internet is not a place for investigative work, not that I've ever seen anyway. It's more a venue for people spewing.

Jim Bronskill believes the Internet can help newspapers reform themselves and win back readers. The new technology could be 'a way for journalism and this kind of [in-depth] journalism to develop.'

> The Internet is pretty amazing. It reaches people, and I think we can use it to expand and amplify what we do. It takes people, it takes energy, it takes commitment, and a bit of money, and vision, and coordination and planning. But hey, we should be able to do that. I think there's a hunger for it.

Paul McKay also sees newspapers as the best medium for investigative journalism. He believes that in-depth reporting is what people really want from a newspaper—'the full story with the whole context'—whether they read it in hard-copy form or, more likely, on a screen.

And that's what newspapers can do. Newspapers have space, and they have a legacy, a kind of cultural legacy that people are familiar with. Magazines can't do it as well, though they do it exceptionally well in some cases. So the daily newspapers, particularly the weekend Saturday or Sunday newspaper, are for all kinds of reasons the best place to have investigative reporting.

McKay noted that while there are a few magazines in the United States, and *The Walrus* in Canada, that do investigative journalism, they don't do it on the scale that the newspapers do. He doesn't see any smooth progression to a revived public-interest press either. He thinks the future for newspapers will be 'more fractured than that' and little interested in investigative reporting. And he believes that the torch will be carried by independent journalists publishing online. These quirky individuals will be more concerned with the cause than the cash.

I think it's going to be done by people who are basically going to take a vow of poverty, and are going to be fuelled mostly by a desire to dig and dig and dig, and come up and write important stories—stories that have to be told.

If the advent of the so-called free dailies is any indication of the direction newspapers are headed, McKay may well be right about the future of the investigative arts in journalism. The free dailies, mostly wire service copy sandwiched between ads, don't even pretend to offer the depth—the background, context, and insight—associated with traditional newspapers. These are the 'play-it-safe' newspapers that readers across the country may continue to peruse but otherwise pay little notice. For one critic, the free dailies shouldn't even be considered newspapers because 'real newspapers make readers think'.[6]

According to the hyper-authoritative *Economist*, the very survival of the newspaper as a news medium is threatened, not only in North America, but also in Latin America, Europe, Australia, and New Zealand.[7] A 2006 article predicted a continuing decline for hard-copy newspapers and lauded their anticipated replacement by online news sources. Yet, despite the sea change in the financial framework of the newspaper business since the end of the Second World War, much of the discussion about the press continues to focus on old assumptions. Paul McKay:

A lot of people haven't put two and two together, but the dilemma, I think, is that the major newspaper owners in Canada—CanWest, the *Toronto Star*, and the *Globe and Mail*—are all publicly traded companies. Now people would say, 'Well what does that have to do with the quality of news and the number of reporters they have in the newspaper and how much investigative journalism there is?' The brutal truth is that people buy or sell their shares of CanWest, for instance, on the basis of how big a return they're going to make how fast. And in this age of push-button share trading from your home, people are constantly scouting for where they're going to get the biggest, fastest return for their investment in shares. . . . That's a huge danger, because the interests of the reader, and even the interests of having a well-staffed newsroom, let alone investigative reporting, are not in the equation.

The future of the newspaper now rests in the hands of stockholders who have no interest in the quality and content of newspapers. So the fate of newspapers is really not in the hands of the editors or journalists at all. The financial premises behind what reporters and editors are doing these days are all wrong. They have nothing to do with the quality and content of newspapers.

In the days that McKay worked for a family-owned *Kingston Whig-Standard*, the newspaper still could make a profit, but the profit wasn't the point.

The point was quality and reputation—and it showed.

The problem of the newspaper's survival is generally discussed in terms of profits versus quality. But in his book *The Vanishing Newspaper*, Philip Meyer turns that reasoning on its head. The newspaper's sole chance of survival, Meyer contends, is to win back its public by paying attention to quality above all. According to the 'influence model' of the press, the financial health of a newspaper rests ultimately on that paper's ability to win the trust of its audience and to influence it. At stake in the loss of traditional newspapers is a society's 'ability to maintain a unified political culture with shared values,' Meyer argues, noting that the 'corruption of professional functions by corporations and partnerships has become quite visible in the more established professions such as accounting and medicine.' He suggests that journalism (like other professions such as accounting and medicine) has seen its professional function corrupted by corporations and commercialism, that it needs to be reformed, and that the people to do the reforming are journalists themselves, with core journalistic values in mind.[8]

Those of us who practise or teach journalism at ground level will make progress with greater speed and certainty if we also organize to reform ourselves. If we can do that, then the next generation of journalists will be ready to work when the process of natural selection chooses the new media forms where trust and social responsibility prevail.[9]

The new journalism, however, will not be as profitable as the old. Meyer argues that the profit margins of the twentieth-century newspaper industry were 'abnormally high', the result of an advantage newspapers no longer enjoy—'their near monopoly control over a retailer's access to their customers'—a loss exacerbated by the rise of

the Internet and online communications. But the financial downturn in the press—
the fact that the industry's profit margins have shrunk—is not the real problem,
Meyer maintains, and continuing to cut quality to save money is about the worst possible strategy newspapers can adopt.

> Cutting quality to maintain the accustomed profitability can postpone that
> adjustment, but such a strategy is very dangerous for existing companies. Lower
> quality will erode trust in the newspaper and create opportunities for what the
> business schools call bad competitors. What is a bad competitor? One who is
> willing to provide better service to customers at lower margins of profit. From the
> viewpoint of society, of course, the arrival of the 'bad' competitors might be a
> very good thing indeed.[10]

If Meyer is right, the media companies who understand the influence model and
apply it to the new communications environment will thrive, while those that cling
to cost-cutting to maintain profits will pass into history. The day of decommercial-
ization may be at hand. Paul McKay cited the non-profit *St Petersburg Times* in
Florida as an example of one alternative model for newspaper journalism.

> Its fiscal marching orders, if you will, are completely different. First of all, they're
> not subject to money being pulled en masse out of the newspaper for reasons
> that have nothing to do with the quality and content of the news product. It has
> stability. It makes money, but it doesn't have to make 50 per cent per year every
> year, year after year. To me it's a very intriguing thing, because part of the whole
> demise, the woeful direction of the business—a lot of it is finances.

A recent article in the *American Journalism Review* examined the trend and found
that non-commercial newspapers (including the *St. Petersburg Times*) 'have larger
news holes than papers of similar size, more local news and art, greater insulation
from economic downturns, and stronger focus on long-term goals.' Such media
could think 'more in terms of social responsibility, with less oppression from short-
term profit demands.'[11]

The June 2006 Senate report on the state of Canada's news media also deemed
commercialization a problem and recommended measures to turn back its effects,
including an ad-free CBC TV and limits on media ownership, with rules to prevent
domination by a single owner in a single market of newspaper, radio, and television
audiences.[12]

In both Canada and the United States, reporters say they have also been adversely
affected by commercialization. A panel study of Canadian journalists between 1996
and 2003 found that the reporters believed less importance was attached to tradi-

tional press values such as accuracy in reporting and promotion of free speech rights during the period.[13] In a survey of 1,149 US journalists, the reporters tended to be 'less satisfied if they work for organizations that they perceive to be strongly profit-oriented and more satisfied with their jobs if they perceive that their employers value good journalism.'[14]

According to one Norwegian study, severe commercialization of the press might even work to encourage investigative reporting. The study examined how commercial news criteria had affected investigative journalism since the 1980s. It concluded that 'commercial news criteria stimulate investigative journalism more than they restrain it, and that investigative journalism's contribution to democracy is more positive than negative.'[15]

## The Gap, the So-What Syndrome, and the Power of One

It was a single Children's Aid Society official who gave the *Toronto Star* permission to use photographs and publish the identities of the Crown wards profiled in the series Nobody's Children—and one photo was all the series needed. Only one reporter decided to cover an asbestos conference and ended up exposing a government/industry campaign to rehabilitate the deadly mineral. It took but one brave scientist in Anne McIlroy's Under Siege in the Ivory Tower series to put an important issue on the record. It was a single woman, Monia Mazigh,[16] whose persistence led to the eventual release of her husband from a Syrian jail. And it was a lone investigative reporter, CTV's Andrew Mitrovica, who pointed out the complicity of the press in the Maher Arar affair.[17]

The idea that an individual is powerless to effect change is widely believed even though it's patently false. It reflects a larger phenomenon, a kind of devaluing of the public sphere. Decades of privatization in once-public sectors have made this devaluation appear normal or inevitable—just a cost of doing business—but the effects have been disastrous, especially since a corresponding modern myth suggests that profitability is the final arbiter of value: if a product or service is any good, it should be able to operate as a business and make a profit.

Many of the stories profiled in this book show how common the dilemma is. In the series Nobody's Children, Crown wards remained Crown wards because it cost less to recycle kids through the system than to find homes for them. In the series about Vancouver's missing women, the initial police investigation faltered because it lacked anything like sufficient resources. Reinventing Our Wheels showed the profit motive at the core of the automobile industry as Death Wish showed it on a global scale for dirty industries generally. Blind Faith laid bare the financial dependence of university medical researchers on private pharmaceutical companies.

The press, like virtually all contemporary institutions, is caught on the horns of this dilemma. Charged with an ostensibly public-interest purpose, it too must operate at a profit to stay in business. If profit is its only motive, however, a newspaper loses its reason for being. In an article for *Media Magazine*, Neil Reynolds once argued for a need in the newspaper business to embrace the 'moral dynamic of investigative journalism'. It is moral judgment, Reynolds maintained, that distinguishes all journalism from 'mere information'.

> Many newspapers are embarrassed these days by the moral assessments inherent in journalism, which explains why so many of them have defined themselves simply as suppliers of information. These newspapers have cast aside their only essential *raison d'être*.[18]

Newspaper and other media reports can alert us to a problem, and they can prick the public conscience. But they cannot by themselves effect change or undo underlying assumptions. It seems, increasingly, that there's a gap between the revelations of an investigative article or series and action to redress the wrong exposed. More and more often, the investigative project appears to net only an immediate impact, and no matter how startling the revelations or well done the story, the ills exposed continue unabated as soon as the initial fuss dies down. No one is held accountable, and once the media glare subsides, things go back to 'normal'.

What if this syndrome has a dysfunctional effect in the wider society? What if it is part of the reason people are abandoning newspapers? What if the big investigative project that doesn't ultimately change anything is contributing to this dysfunctional effect, in a sense helping to normalize the ill or wrongdoing in question?

If the gap between the investigative story and the change the story is meant to provoke reflects the deeper loss of the public sphere, then what's wrong with the press is the same thing that's wrong with the government, the electoral process, the healthcare system, the educational system, the social-welfare system, and virtually every other 'system' of public life. But if there's a gap between telling the truth and making the change that should be the result of the truth being known, then what's the point in writing investigative stories? And if the press generally is remiss, and even the best investigative reporting has only passing impact, then why bother?

Because every difference, no matter how small, makes a difference.

Investigative work is not the exclusive province of large dailies. It can be undertaken by small papers and individual reporters with few resources, something to which numerous examples cited throughout this book attest. Two students at the Thompson Rivers University School of Journalism in Kamloops, BC, where I teach, distinguished themselves with stories before they had even graduated. In both cases, all the reporters had to go on was a breaking issue and some good questions.

Third-year student Melissa Lampman was interning at the *Kamloops Daily News* during the summer of 2006 and ended up covering an outbreak of the Norwalk virus at a downtown care facility.[19] When the virus attacked again at a nearby care facility only weeks later, Lampman started to dig. From local health officials, she got 'the usual answers: they said it was a closed area, like on a cruise ship, that it happens all the time, that it's commonplace, that because the facilities are near each other, it's hard to control.'

Lampman wasn't convinced. 'I thought, "But that's strange, hopping from one care facility to another. How'd that happen?"'

In conversation with sources, she learned that some nurses worked at more than one facility, 'going back and forth, back and forth, pulling double or triple shifts, working at one place and then going to another.'

Lampman wondered if the nurses could be cross-contaminating the care facilities.

About a half hour before deadline, she was able to confirm that there was no rule or policy in place to prevent nurses or other staff from working at more than one facility and no requirement that they inform authorities if they did so. A local health official conceded that cross-contamination wasn't impossible.[20]

Had Lampman been interning at a larger paper with more resources for investigative projects, she would likely have been teamed with a senior reporter to keep digging on the story and produce a definitive account, and the article would almost certainly have led to a policy change for the care facilities.

Juli Taylor was in her third year at Thompson Rivers University and her first year of the journalism program in 2005, when her pursuit of a story landed her in the thick of things with Betty Hinton, the Conservative MP for the federal Kamloops-Thompson-Cariboo riding. Hinton was in the habit of sending out informal surveys to gauge public opinion on various issues in the riding she represents.

Before voting against Bill C-38, the same-sex marriage bill, Hinton announced in the House of Commons that she'd done a survey of Kamloops that showed most of her constituents (82 per cent) were opposed to same-sex marriage.[21] That outraged some Kamloopsians, including a nursing professor at TRU, who wrote to the local *Daily News* calling Hinton's surveys biased and her use of them 'in speeches and advertising' an 'affront to democracy'.[22]

Taylor got hold of the survey and on the advice of her professor, Shawn Thompson (formerly of the *Kingston Whig Standard*), faxed copies of it to two independent experts in survey research—one at Ryerson University in Toronto and another at the University of Alberta in Edmonton. 'Shawn and I had talked a lot about it,' Taylor said. 'Because there were a lot of implications—libel and stuff—and we wanted to make sure we took every precaution.' She was able to decode the flawed methodology of Hinton's survey and nail down the story for the April 2006 issue of the J-school publication *Newsbreak*.

Hinton's Kamloops constituency office confirmed the survey had been sent to 44,688 households in the city and got 'several hundred' responses back. With 83,959 voters in the riding Hinton represents, there would have to be at least several thousand respondents for the survey results to be considered valid indicators of voter opinion. Taylor put these deficiencies to Hinton, who was not amused.

'She wrote me back and said she didn't care whether the experts approved, she was still going to use her surveys,' Taylor said. 'It's not a valid indicator of the riding and she shouldn't be using it, but she said she didn't think that was a concern.'

Did it bother Taylor that nobody in the press picked up on the story?

'It bothered me a bit, and it bothers me now that . . . I wasn't trying to criticize her, I asked her a question. Why doesn't she care about making sure that she has the opinion of the riding? Why doesn't she want to make sure that she has everybody's views?'

## The Personal and the Political

Investigative journalism is still worth the doing even if it cannot single-handedly solve the social problems it uncovers. The phenomenon of a gap—the apparently severed link between the investigative story and the appropriate remedial action by responsible officials that the story is meant to spark—can also point to solutions, to a reportorial future with a sense of history, to 'newspapers' with strong investigative units and a renewed public-interest ethic, and to a journalism noted more for its consistent high quality than for its stars.

Sometimes work on a story can connect to other work, past and future, in unpredictable ways. When David Pugliese talked about the Panama story and how a single line in John Bryden's book *Deadly Allies* sparked the idea for the series Criminalizing Dissent, a rush of memory swept me back to the year 1989. Then working for the Montreal bureau of the Canadian Press, I interviewed Bryden in order to review his book. I remember asking him how he managed to get hold of some of the documents that allowed him to write about and document Canada's crucial Second World War role in the development of chemical and biological warfare agents.

Bryden described the low-tech strategy he employed. This was still at least six years before CAR took off in Canada, but all of the necessary documents were available in Ottawa's National Archives. He explained how he would show up there every day, and, finally, officials at the archives got used to seeing him and stopped checking every single document he photocopied or accessed. Even the ATI officials didn't know for sure what those documents contained—what had been excised from the files and what had escaped the axe. There was simply too much information for any one individual or even department to control. Bryden's slow and careful cultivation of the archives staff enabled his accumulation of the documents essential to the book.

Nearly two decades have passed since Bryden conducted his seminal research. Since then, the volume of information has swelled, making its management by government an even more daunting task. Those who work at the National Archives still have no way of knowing which documents contain 'sensitive' information. Blacking out most information in most documents and flat refusals to release documents became the government's surest defences against inquiries, especially those from journalists.

The connections extend even further back. I had wanted to review *Deadly Allies* because I had some background on the issue. In 1985, as a reporter for the *Medicine Hat News* in Medicine Hat, Alberta, I tried to investigate rumours I'd heard from townspeople that during the Second World War, work had been done on mustard gas at Defence Research Establishment Suffield (DRES), including experiments conducted on the soldiers at the base. I've long since lost or misplaced the taped interview I did with a local man, who had served at the base and had contracted a cancer that he at least believed was caused by his exposure to mustard gas at DRES. I attempted briefly to write an article about the subject for a magazine back east, which showed initial interest in the query letter I sent them. But one thing led to another, and I eventually abandoned the effort and returned home to Montreal where I went to work for the city's Canadian Press bureau.

I can still remember thinking when I read Bryden's book (which included a reference to the work done at DRES on mustard gas) that I ought to have pursued the matter more aggressively back in Medicine Hat. But I was much younger then, and much less inclined to understand that just because no one else had cottoned on to the story didn't mean there wasn't one.

The nice thing about connections is that they tend to multiply. Years later, having earned my Ph.D. and while working as a journalism professor at the Thompson Rivers University School of Journalism, I mentioned *Deadly Allies* to a photographer colleague (the gifted Eileen Leier) who was planning a working visit to Quebec City. Leier read the book, became fascinated with the story, and ended up visiting Quebec's Grosse Île. This is the island in the St. Lawrence River where, as Bryden's book detailed, a top-secret anthrax lab was constructed during the Second World War. Leier shot a series of remarkable black-and-white photos at Grosse Île that in addition to their considerable artistic merit, told the story of the island's use, from 1832 to 1937, as a quarantine station for immigrants. She showed the work in 2003 at an exhibit at Vancouver's Presentation House Gallery. That art now forms part of the historical record, helping to document more of the island's history, once shrouded in rumours about the 'no-go' areas of ground still contaminated from the war work on anthrax.[23]

Good reportage, like participatory democracy, involves a community of effort rooted in historical context. It militates against the star system in a 'culture of narcissism' on steroids—one that appears to be defining contemporary North American society.[24] No single reporter, sticking to his or her own stories and time frame, much less self-interest, can hope to advance the cause of good journalism as a cornerstone of democracy. The lesson for aspiring journalists is to bring your skills and your ideals to the work, but park your ego at the door to the story. Virtually all the reporters interviewed for the case studies in this book exemplify the ability to temporarily subjugate the (entirely normal) desire for personal recognition to absorption in and deference to the needs of the public-interest story. If these stalwarts of the profession appear discouraged from time to time about the impact of their work, it's not because the work failed to render them rich and famous, but rather because they are in a position to notice disturbing trends that might well escape the attention of the public at large, and sometimes they are hard put to tell all they know.

# How to Be an Investigative Reporter

- **Think for yourself.** This ability to think critically and independently is at the core of the investigative reporter. You can't double-click your way to insight. Insight is won the same way it's always been won—by hard work, by research, by knowing enough about the subject to be able to think about it and ask questions and finally arrive at conclusions. Computers can't come up with the questions.

- **Persist.** Just because an entire political ministry has apparently been unable to see the error of its ways doesn't mean the error doesn't exist. You can be right about a hunch even though no one else shares it; research is the only way to confirm or disprove your hunch. It is almost uncanny, sometimes, how events seem to transpire to support great stories, as if the stories cry out to be told.

- **Never stint on the research.** The daily, dogged, persistence of the reporter will pay off. More important than what you know about an issue is what you think to ask. The heart of an investigative story (or any sustained inquiry) is the research question itself. As in Zen Buddhism, so in journalism: 'Your question is your treasure.'[25]

- **Follow up.** In order for the effects of an investigative piece to 'take', it's essential for journalists to follow up on the wrongdoing, malfunction, or injustice they've uncovered. You have to trust that the work is not wasted, that the efforts of an individual reporter in the service of a democratic press are more like a relay race than an individual one.

- **Embrace the moral dynamic of investigative journalism.** Once you decide to follow a story, one thing will lead to another, and finally the truth will come out. Trust your own outraged humanity as enough of a place to begin. Once a good reporter's human conscience is fully engaged, the rest seems to follow and the universe, as they say, kicks in.

# Endnotes

1. The 'muckrakers' were a group of US journalists at the turn of the twentieth century who took on America's powerful business and other elites with their exposés (mostly in magazines) of corruption in high places. The muckrakers were investigative journalists supreme (see Appendix B for titles about them), but the term *muckrakers* appears to have been retired, likely because of its unsavoury connotations.

2. The exposé consisted of eighteen instalments in the monthly magazine *McClure's*, where Tarbell worked with another famous muckraker, Lincoln Stephens, to campaign against corruption in politics and business. The Standard Oil series ran in *McClure's* from 1902 to 1904; it first appeared in book form in 1904 as *The History of the Standard Oil Company* (New York: W.W. Norton, 1966). Tarbell was born in 1857 and died in 1944.

3. Upton Sinclair, *The Jungle* (Tucson, AZ: Sharp Press), 2003. The realist novel about Chicago's meat-packing plants and the plight of the poor who worked in them was originally published in 1906. Sinclair was born in 1878 and died in 1968.

4. Brant Houston, 'Service journalism vs. corporate profits', *IRE Journal* 29.4 (July/August 2006), 4.

5. NADbank (Newspaper Audience Databank) is an organization that represents newspapers, advertisers, and media-buying companies. It facilitates the buying and selling of newspaper advertising and conducts market research for its members.

6. Ken Alexander, 'The Shrinking News', *The Walrus* 3.5 (June 2006), 18–20. '. . . The latest example of "vertical integration" [is] the convergence between genuine newspapers and their vapid, freeze-dried, under-reported cousins, the free dailies now so popular on buses and found underfoot everywhere. Torstar, responsible for the *Toronto Star* (among other traditional dailies), has a partnership agreement with *Metro Toronto*, part of the "world's largest newspaper, with more than 18.5 million daily readers in 88 major cities in 19 countries," as it proudly states on its masthead. That is, this cancer has spread not just across Canada, but is a global chimera, news across all borders reduced to its component parts and presented without adjectives, invectives, or life.'

7.  'Who Killed the Newspaper?' *The Economist*, Vol. 380, Issue 8492 (26 August 2006), 9–10.

8.  Philip Meyer, *The Vanishing Newspaper: Saving Journalism in the Information Age* (Columbia, MO: University of Missouri Press), 245–6.

9.  Meyer, *The Vanishing Newspaper*, op. cit., 244.

10. Meyer, op. cit., 245–6.

11. Carl Sessions Stepp, 'Journalism Without Profit Margins', *American Journalism Review* 26.5 (October/November 2004), 36–43.

12. Standing Senate Committee on Transport and Communications. *Final Report on the Canadian News Media*. 2 volumes. June 2006.

13. David Pritchard, Paul R. Brewer, and Florian Sauvageau, 'Changes in Canadian Journalists' Views about the Social and Political Roles of the News Media: A Panel Study, 1996–2003', *Canadian Journal of Political Science* 38.2 (June 2005), 287–306.

14. Randal A. Beam, 'Organizational Goals and Priorities and the Job Satisfaction of U.S. Journalists', *Journalism & Mass Communication Quarterly* 83.1 (Spring 2006), 169–85.

15. Rolland Asle, 'Commercial News Criteria and Investigative Journalism', in *Journalism Studies* 7.6 (December 2006), 940–63.

16. Monia Mazigh is the wife of Maher Arar, the Canadian man wrongly accused of terrorist activities and sent in 2002 to Syria where he was imprisoned and tortured. Finally cleared by a federal inquiry in 2006, Arar moved with his family to Kamloops the same year. Monia Mazigh taught finance at the city's Thompson Rivers University. For more, see two articles by *Kamloops Daily News* feature writer Mike Youds: 'Shelter from the storm: Arar finds sanctuary in unexpected place', *Kamloops Daily News* (27 December 2006), A4; and 'Find media leak, says Maher Arar: Seeks independent inquiry, doesn't want horror repeated', *Kamloops Daily News* (9 December 2006), A4.

17. See the following pieces by Andrew Mitrovica: 'Hear No Evil, Write No Lies', *The Walrus* 3.10 (December 2006/January 2007), 37–42; and 'RCMP Follies', *Media* 10.3 (April 2004), 6–7.

18. Neil Reynolds, 'The moral dynamic of investigative journalism', *Media* 3.2 (Summer 1996), 15.

19. See Lampman's *Kamloops Daily News* articles: 'Virus strikes lodge again' (25 August 2006), A3; 'Pine Grove bitten by Norwalk bug: Ponderosa Lodge now clear of virus' (2 September 2006), A1; and 'Norwalk virus makes rounds at Pine Grove' (6 September 2006), A4.

20. The official said that although it was possible staff took the virus from one facility to the other, 'many facilities had the outbreak throughout the course of the year and it appears to come at different times.' See 'Pine Grove bitten by Norwalk bug', op. cit.

21. Bill C-38, the same-sex marriage bill, received royal assent and became law—the Civil Marriage Act—on 20 July 2005. The law extends to same-sex couples equal access to civil marriage. Hinton made her remarks in the House on 28 June 2005, several weeks before the vote. According to the *Hansard* record for that date, Hinton said, 'I sent out a ballot within my own constituency on this issue. Eighty-two per cent of my constituents told me to vote in favour of the traditional definition of marriage. I have done so.' *Hansard* (28 June 2005), 1300.

22. Penny Powers, 'Hinton's tactics an affront to citizens', *Kamloops Daily News* (8 December 2005), A6.

23. Eileen Leier, *Grosse Île: The Immigrant Quarantine Station.* Vancouver, BC: Presentation House Gallery, 2004.

24. The phrase culture of narcissism is borrowed from the title of a book by the late Christopher Lasch: *The Culture of Narcissism: American Life in an Age of Diminishing Expectations* (New York: Warner Books, 1979), originally published by Norton in 1978.

25. Albert Low, *Zengong* 4.2 (June 1995), 10. 'It is from wholeness making itself known that the hunger and thirst that we feel in practice originates. This is why the Christian mystic said, "Do not quench your thirst." It is also why a Zen master in reply to a monk who asked him, "Where is my treasure?" said, "Your question is your treasure."' See www.zenmontreal.ca/zengong/ZenGongVo104-2.pdf.

# Appendix A

# Story Citations

## Part One
## Tracking the Truth: The Litrature of Exposure

### Chapter 1   The Case of the Disappearing Women

*Unless otherwise indicated, the stories carried the bylines of the three reporters who worked on the series: Lindsay Kines, Lori Culbert, and Kim Bolan.

21 September 2001
- 'Investigation turns up startling new numbers: Police to announce expanded probe; Women have history of drugs, prostitution, and links to Downtown Eastside'. *Vancouver Sun*, 21 September 2001, A1.

22 September 2001
- 'Report details police short staffing: Lack of resources hurts ability to protect the public, says confidential internal document'. *Vancouver Sun*, 22 September 2001, A17.
- 'How the police investigation was flawed: Too few officers, police infighting and lack of experience undermined first probe into disappearances'. *Vancouver Sun*, 22 September 2001, A1.

25 September 2001
- 'Police didn't pick up suspect who later murdered woman: Family wants answers: "If they had arrested him earlier, maybe my sister wouldn't be dead right now"'. *Vancouver Sun*, 25 September 2001, A1.

26 September 2001
- 'Police chiefs make pitch for DNA bank: Blythe says police "have acted very responsibly"'. *Vancouver Sun*, 26 September 2001, A10.
- 'Ontario learned the hard way how to share: Systems put into place after Paul Bernardo helped police catch a rapist in record time'. *Vancouver Sun*, 26 September 2001, A11.
- 'B.C. slow to adopt lessons of Bernardo: Police face obstacles tracking down serial predators'. *Vancouver Sun*, 26 September 2001, A1.

27 September 2001
- 'B.C. plans to integrate policing: Solicitor-general will also review use of DNA samples'. *Vancouver Sun*, 27 September 2001, A1.

9 October 2001
- 'Police build a "bridge" to victims' families: Relatives of women missing from the Downtown Eastside invited to discuss case'. *Vancouver Sun*, 4 October 2001, B1.

23 November 2001
- 'Killer could be getting smarter. Profilers say he may have refined his technique, going from leaving bodies to hiding them'. *Vancouver Sun*, 23 November 2001, A10.
- 'DNA clears suspect in murders'. *Vancouver Sun*, 23 November 2001, A1.

24 November 2001
- Lori Culbert. 'Story of a shattered life. Part One: A single childhood incident pushed Dawn Crey into a downward spiral from which she would never completely escape'. Lori Culbert. *Vancouver Sun*, 24 November 2001, D3.
- Lori Culbert. 'Story of a shattered life. Part Two: A single childhood incident pushed Dawn Crey into a downward spiral from which she would never completely escape'. *Vancouver Sun*, 24 November 2001, D3.
- 'Task force meets with Green River detectives: Police investigate the possibility of serial killer'. *Vancouver Sun*, 24 November 2001, A1.

26 November 2001
- 'Portrait of a prostitute killer: Marvin Tom's life of tragedy: Born with fetal alcohol syndrome into an abusive home, he became a violent drunk—and a killer'. *Vancouver Sun*, 26 November 2001, B4.

- 'Police move 100 suspects to top of their list'. *Vancouver Sun*, 26 November 2001, A1.

27 November 2001
- 'Police consider taking DNA from prostitutes'. *Vancouver Sun*, 27 November 2001, A1.
- 'Missing women make Vancouver a grisly anomaly'. *Vancouver Sun*, 27 November 2001, B5.
- 'For prostitutes, fear rises as more and more go missing'. *Vancouver Sun*, 27 November 2001, B4.

28 November 2001
- 'Long-term detox centre for women planned for Downtown Eastside'. *Vancouver Sun*, 28 November 2001, A9.
- 'How to fix the street violence? Until Canada's prostitution laws are repealed women will still be victimized, experts warn' *Vancouver Sun*, 28 November 2001, A8.

## Chapter 2  Reinventing Our Wheels

*The stories cited below ran simultaneously in the *Vancouver Sun*.

19 May 2001
- 'The smog monster: Our love affair with cars is poisoning the planet. Smog alerts are a deadly summer routine in most cities and the pollution problem is getting worse, not better'. *Ottawa Citizen*, 19 May 2001, A1.
- 'Smog's heavy toll: Two renowned air pollution experts warn that exponential car growth in Canadian cities is causing lung damage and costing lives and billions in medical costs. A revised estimate puts the annual national toll at up to 16,000 deaths'. *Ottawa Citizen*, 19 May 2001, B1.

20 May 2001
- 'Refiners say they are on target to meet new standards: Esso, PetroCan deny their gasolines impair anti-pollution devices'. *Ottawa Citizen*, 20 May 2001, A10.
- 'Refinery margins provide Esso, PetroCan key profit centres: Big two refiners account for half of nation's gas sales'. *Ottawa Citizen*, 20 May 2001, A11.
- 'OMA pegs smog's cost at 1,600 lives, $500M in medical fees'. *Ottawa Citizen*, 20 May 2001, A11.

- 'Canada's dirty refiners: Canadians unwittingly gas up with some of the world's filthiest fuel. It sabotages emission-control devices and spews "fugitive" pollutants into the atmosphere'. *Ottawa Citizen*, 20 May 2001, A1.

21 May 2001
- 'Putting the lid on "cat" crackers. The federal government took 10 years to make Canada's filthy gas match car anti-pollution devices. Oil companies fought that regulation all the way'. *Ottawa Citizen*, 21 May 2001. A1.
- 'CAA tells oil firms to "speed it up": Refiners urged to cut sulphur levels in gas'. *Ottawa Citizen*, 21 May 2001, A12.

22 May 2001
- 'Inventing the unthinkable: A brash Vancouver start-up aims to transform big-rig power plants and end the reign of the world's 200 million dirty diesels'. *Ottawa Citizen*, 22 May 2001, A9.
- 'Big rigs: dirty by design. Big-rig engines are among the dirtiest on wheels. In the US, more than a million were secretly tampered with, spewing pollution equal to 65 million cars'. *Ottawa Citizen*, 22 May 2001, A1.

23 May 2001
- 'The green, green gas of home: Ottawa biotech company Iogen has made its mark, and a lot of money, enlisting enzymes for commercial use. Now it has a plan to make them run your engine—with farm-fresh fuel'. *Ottawa Citizen*, 23 May 2001, A1.
- 'The greenest gas in Canada: Little guy MacEwen Petroleum of Ottawa is selling what the "oil oligarchs" won't: High-oxygen ethanol and low-sulphur gasoline—at no extra charge'. *Ottawa Citizen*, 23 May 2001, A11.

24 May 2001
- 'Canada's fuel-cell revolution: A miraculous Canadian invention may transform how energy is made, sold, and consumed in North America, while making car pollution virtually vanish. Or it might amount to a mirage'. *Ottawa Citizen*, 24 May 2001, A1.

25 May 2001
- 'The hidden costs of plug-in cars: A powerful corps of companies wants to replace gas-powered cars with ones charged from electric grids. They say that will curb urban smog. But what's at the other end of the plug?' *Ottawa Citizen*, 25 May 2001, A1.

- 'Ford thinks it has a "bright idea"; Powered by 19 nickel-cadmium batteries, Ford says its zero-emission commuter car will make "the world a better place"'. *Ottawa Citizen*, 25 May 2001, A13.

26 May 2001

- 'The plot against big, dumb cars: An unlikely David is poised to topple the Goliath of the auto industry, pitting his smart, light cars against the lumbering fuel-guzzlers'. *Ottawa Citizen*, 26 May 2001, B3.

27 May 2001

- 'The trouble with light trucks: A decade-long surge in sales of gas-guzzling SUVs, pickup trucks and minivans has cost Canadians cleaner air. It's the auto and oil companies that are profiting'. *Ottawa Citizen*, 27 May 2001, A1.
- 'How rules were bent for the PT Cruiser: Chrysler got its oddball new car rated as a "fuel-efficient truck". It proved a profitable ploy'. *Ottawa Citizen*, 27 May 2001, A10.

28 May 2001

- 'Ford leads Big Three in green makeover: Henry Ford brought the world the internal combustion engine. His great-grandson may consign it to history—and help preserve the planet in the bargain'. *Ottawa Citizen*, 28 May 2001, A1.

29 May 2001

- 'Jetta beats the hybrids for clean driving: Using a turbo-diesel system, the Volkswagen Jetta TDI is quick, practical and amazingly fuel efficient'. *Ottawa Citizen*, 29 May 2001, A11.

30 May 2001

- 'The communal commute: Jack Bell spent $600,000 of his own money to help clear Vancouver's roads of congestion and reduce the city's smog problem. It's a good thing he didn't wait for government help'. *Ottawa Citizen*, 30 May 2001, A15.
- 'Pay only for what you need: The car-sharing co-op option'. *Ottawa Citizen*, 30 May 2001, A1.

31 May 2001

- 'How the continent's best transit works: A maverick city bus manager decided to do what virtually no other transit agency has done in North America: Ask riders what they want, then deliver it. The results are astounding'. *Ottawa Citizen*, 31 May 2001, A1.

2 June 2001

- 'How our transit lost its way: Nothing busts city smog and congestion better than a bus. So why are transit agencies starved for funds to buy and run them?' *Ottawa Citizen*, 2 June 2001, A1.

4 June 2001

- 'Federal government favours car commutes: OC Transpo has a simple, efficient, money-saving way to get 133,000 public servants to work. That's against federal policy'. *Ottawa Citizen*, 4 June 2001, A1.

5 June 2001

- 'Canada fails to green own fleet: The federal government talks a green game about reducing smog and greenhouse gases. But what happens when its own rubber hits the road?' *Ottawa Citizen*, 5 June 2001, A1.

6 June 2001

- 'Athlete walks the walk in clean-air campaign: Olympian swears off private automobiles'. *Ottawa Citizen*, 6 June 2001, A1.

7 June 2001

- 'Tele-commuting: Fast, cheap, smog-free: Nortel leads the way with 20,000 staffers working from home, 4,700 in Ottawa alone'. *Ottawa Citizen*, 7 June 2001, A9.
- 'A radical's ultimate mobility solution: Ottawa energy expert Ralph Torrie has a vision: Employment, shopping, education, and recreation available in every city neighbourhood'. *Ottawa Citizen*, 7 June 2001, A1.

8 June 2001

- 'Smarter fuels, vehicles, cities: In the finale to Reinventing Our Wheels, Paul McKay concludes that movement is not the same thing as action'. *Ottawa Citizen*, 8 June 2001, A14.

## Chapter 3   Death Wish

2 June 2001
- 'Death Wish: The human race looks like it's going the way of the dinosaurs: We're driving ourselves to extinction. Starting today, in a dramatic series of articles, *Globe and Mail* reporter Alanna Mitchell goes to the world's environmental disaster zones to find out just how desperate the situation is—and what might save us from ourselves'. *Globe and Mail*, 2 June 2001, F1.
- 'At least the dinosaurs had an excuse. A world-renowned Canadian has a fascinating new theory to explain why the great prehistoric beasts died out—and he can't help but wonder whether humanity will share their fate. Philip Currie shares his findings with Alanna Mitchell, and points out that . . . at least the dinosaurs had an excuse'. *Globe and Mail*, 2 June 2001, F4.

4 June 2001
- 'The world's "single biggest threat". Water—Canadians may take it for granted, but some countries will do almost anything to ensure an adequate supply. The Death Wish series resumes with Alanna Mitchell braving the heat of the Jordanian desert to visit Azraq, the legendary oasis that humanity bled dry'. *Globe and Mail*, 4 June 2001, A8.

5 June 2001
- 'How the North is getting burned. If you doubt global warming is serious, visit the Arctic with Alanna Mitchell. At first, the big melt confused the people of Sachs Harbour, who found themselves suddenly catching salmon and spotting bizarre bird species from the south. But now they're worried—the rising temperatures are wreaking havoc with the environment and with their way of life'. *Globe and Mail*, 5 June 2001,. A10.

6 June 2001
- 'The man with a plan to save the planet. Russell Mittermeier doesn't believe that life on Earth is doomed, but the clock is ticking. To conclude this series, the dynamic scientist and president of Conservation International takes Alanna Mitchell deep into South America's equatorial rain forest to demonstrate that, despite all the damage humanity has done, Homo sapiens can coexist with nature'. *Globe and Mail*, 6 June 2001, A10.

## Chapter 4   Asbestos, Again

22 November 2003
- 'Asbestos makeover reignites old battle'. *Toronto Star*, 22 November 2003, A1.


## Chapter 5   Criminalizing Dissent

*The stories appeared under the double bylines of Jim Bronskill and David Pugliese.

18 August 2001
- 'Keeping the public in check: Special Mountie team, police tactics threaten right to free speech and assembly, critics say'. *Ottawa Citizen*, 18 August 2001, A1.

19 August 2001
- 'Spying on the protest movement: Private e-mails find way into military hands'. *Ottawa Citizen*, 19 August 2001, A1.

20 August 2001
- 'Secret files chill foes of government: State dossiers list peaceful critics as security threats'. *Ottawa Citizen*, 20 August 2001, A1.

20 August 2001
- 'Under the Canadian spyglass'. *Ottawa Citizen*, 20 August 2001, A4.

21 August 2001
- 'How police deter dissent: Government critics decry intimidation'. *Ottawa Citizen*, 21 August 2001, A1.

22 August 2001
- 'Mounties in masks: A spy story: Undercover tactics go too far, critics say'. *Ottawa Citizen*, 22 August 2001, A1.


## Chapter 6   Dialling for Dollars

2 November 2002
- 'Toronto a hotbed for phone fraud: Telemarketers sell phoney credit cards to U.S., Europe'. *Toronto Star*, 2 November 2002, A1.

- 'High flyers thriving in a low-life industry: Telemarketers cash in on the poor and elderly'. *Toronto Star*, 3 November 2002, A1.

## Chapter 7   Under Siege in the Ivory Tower

14 April 2001
- 'Prozac critic sees U of T job revoked'. *Globe and Mail*, 14 April 2001, A1.

5 May 2001
- 'Hospital confirms MD's views cost him job'. *Globe and Mail*, 5 May 2001, A5.

8 September 2001
- 'Under siege in the ivory tower'. *Globe and Mail*, 8 September 2001, F4.

## Chapter 8   Blind Faith

*The stories appeared under the triple bylines of Steve Buist, Joan Walters, and Luma Muhtadie.

25 June 2005
- 'Risks, Rewards & Research'. *Hamilton Spectator*, 25 June 2005, A1.

27 June 2005
- 'Dangerous medicine'. *Hamilton Spectator*, 27 June 2005, A1.
- 'Like a punch in the gut'. *Hamilton Spectator*, 27 June 2005, A6.

28 June 2005
- 'Big Pharma showers Mac with cash'. *Hamilton Spectator*, 28 June 2005, A1.
- 'Connections and conflicts'. *Hamilton Spectator*, 28 June 2005, A6.
- 'Big Mac research: A snapshot of some of the publicly funded health research projects at McMaster University'. *Hamilton Spectator*, 28 June 2005, A8.
- 'One prof's venture into business'. *Hamilton Spectator*, 28 June 2005, A9.
- 'Biochemist says he's "small potatoes"'. *Hamilton Spectator*, 28 June 2005, A9.

29 June 2005
- 'A bitter pill'. *Hamilton Spectator*, 29 June 2005, A6.

- 'Worry grows as MDs prescribe drugs for unapproved uses'. *Hamilton Spectator*, 29 June 2005, A1.

30 June 2005
- 'Drug research: Conflicting interests'. *Hamilton Spectator*, 30 June 2005, A1.

# Part Two
# Documenting the Truth: Computer-Assisted Reporting

## Chapter 9   Nowhere to Go

27 October 2001
- 'Nowhere to go'. *Toronto Star*, 27 October 2001, A30.
- 'Portraits of courage'. *Toronto Star*, 27 October 2001, B1.
- 'Trapped: For 10 years, Arlene Kennedy was forced to call a psychiatric ward her home'. *Toronto Star*, 27 October 2001, A31.

28 October 2001
- 'Adults beaten in group homes'. *Toronto Star*, 28 October 2001, A1.
- 'Beaten bloody for bedwetting'. *Toronto Star*, 28 October 2001, A9.

29 October 2001
- 'Parents cajole for dollars'. *Toronto Star*, 29 October 2001, A1.

30 October 2001
- 'Public has a right to abuse records'. *Toronto Star*, 30 October 2001, A3.

## Chapter 10   Nobody's Children

*Except for Tanya Talaga's 'Baby sleuth eases parents' fears', the stories were triple-bylined: Leslie Papp, Tanya Talaga, and Jim Rankin.

29 September 2001
- 'Nobody's children'. *Toronto Star*, 29 September 2001, A1.
- 'Wanted: Babies'. *Toronto Star*, 29 September 2001, B1.
- 'Baby sleuth eases parents' fears'. *Toronto Star*, 29 September 2001, B3.

30 September 2001
- 'Chaotic system discourages adoption'. *Toronto Star*, 30 September 2001, A1.
- 'Matching system "archaic"'. *Toronto Star*, 30 September 2001, A9.

1 October 2001
- 'Toronto CAS eyes overseas adoption'. *Toronto Star*, 1 October 2001, A1.
- 'The birth of adoption's new deal? Ontario urged to let adopted wards keep in touch with birth parents'. *Toronto Star*, 1 October 2001, A10.

2 October 2001
- 'B.C. leads adoption challenge'. *Toronto Star*, 2 October 2001, A1.

## Chapter 11   Reservations: Recipe for Disaster

24 November 2001
- 'Recipe for disaster'. *Hamilton Spectator*, 24 November 2001, A1.
- 'Food for thought'. *Hamilton Spectator*, 24 November 2001, A6.

26 November 2001
- 'City to beef up food checks'. *Hamilton Spectator*, 26 November 2001, A1.
- 'Hunt for hazardous food preparation has health inspectors going from hot to cold'. *Hamilton Spectator*, 26 November 2001, A7.
- 'Hamilton's silent epidemic'. *Hamilton Spectator*, 26 November 2001, A7.
- 'When dining is risky'. *Hamilton Spectator*, 26 November 2001, A1.

27 November 2001
- 'Mayor vows food checks'. *Hamilton Spectator*, 27 November 2001, A1.
- 'Dirty city restaurants receive light penalties'. *Hamilton Spectator*, 27 November 2001. A1.
- 'Plenty of room for errors'. *Hamilton Spectator*, 27 November 2001, A4.

28 November 2001
- 'City set to take action'. *Hamilton Spectator*, 28 November 2001, A1.
- 'Toronto diners not left in the dark'. *Hamilton Spectator*, 28 November 2001, A1.
- 'Taking danger out of dining'. *Hamilton Spectator*, 28 November 2001, A8.

## Chapter 12   Drive Clean Smokescreen

\*The stories listed below were written by Steve Buist and Fred Vallance-Jones unless otherwise indicated. The series proper consisted of ten stories. Three more articles of related interest are listed below: a column by the *Spectator*'s editor-in-chief Dana Robbins the day the series launched; an editorial by managing editor Casey Korstanje the next day; and a related article by reporter Rob Ferguson on 21 September about the immediate government response (which came just several days after the series began to run) to Drive Clean Smokescreen's revelations.

18 September 2004
- 'Cheat took cash for fake test results'. *Hamilton Spectator*, 18 September 2004, A1.
- 'Drive Clean's dirty secrets'. *Hamilton Spectator*, 18 September 2004, A1.
- Dana Robbins. 'Smoke and mirrors'. Column. *Hamilton Spectator*, 18 September 2004, A2.

20 September 2004
- 'A billion dollars up in smoke'. *Hamilton Spectator*, 20 September 2004, A1.
- Fred Vallance-Jones. 'Drive Clean enforcement needs beefing up: MPP'. *Hamilton Spectator*, 20 September 2004, A7.
- Casey Korstanje. 'Drive Clean Smokescreen'. Editorial. *Hamilton Spectator*, 20 September 2004, A17.

21 September 2004
- 'Your car failed Drive Clean? Try, try, try again'. *Hamilton Spectator*, 21 September 2004, A1.
- 'Garage owners say it's tough to profit from Drive Clean'. *Hamilton Spectator*, 21 September 2004, A6.
- Rob Ferguson. 'Minister vows to clean up dirty Drive Clean operations'. *Hamilton Spectator*, 21 September 2004, A7.

22 September 2004
- Fred Vallance-Jones. 'Drive Clean founder: Put on the brakes'. *Hamilton Spectator*, 22 September 2004, A1.
- 'Is Drive Clean merely bad science?' *Hamilton Spectator*, 22 September 2004, A8.

23 September 2004
- Steve Buist. '*Spec* series could spark speedy review'. *Hamilton Spectator*, 23 September 2004, A1.
- 'What's ahead for Drive Clean?' *Hamilton Spectator*, 23 September 2004, A1.

## Chapter 13   Singled Out: An Investigation into Race and Crime

*In all but one case, indicated below, these stories carried the bylines of all five reporters on the investigative team. They are listed in the cover story in this order: Jim Rankin, Jennifer Quinn, Michelle Shephard, Scott Simmie, and John Duncanson.

19 October 2002
- 'Singled out: *Star* analysis of police crime data shows justice is different for blacks and whites'. *Toronto Star*, 19 October 2002, A1.
- 'Our duty: Examine all issues'. *Toronto Star*, 19 October 2002, A2.
- 'Treatment differs by division'. *Toronto Star*, 19 October 2002, A12.
- 'The story behind the numbers'. *Toronto Star*, 19 October 2002, A12.
- '"There is no racism. We do not do racial profiling"'. *Toronto Star*, 19 October 2002, A14.

20 October 2002
- 'Police target black drivers: *Star* analysis of traffic data suggests racial profiling'. *Toronto Star*, 20 October 2002, A1.
- 'Analysis raises board hackles'. *Toronto Star*, 20 October 2002, A9.
- 'Police and race'. *Toronto Star*, 20 October 2002, A12.

26 October 2002
- Michelle Shephard and Jennifer Quinn. 'Police chief calls for race-relations probe: Justice Dubin to study treatment of black suspects'. *Toronto Star*, 26 October 2002, A1.
- 'Black crime rates highest: "No one was born violent . . . What's causing these problems?"' *Toronto Star*, 26 October 2002, A01.

# Appendix B

# Recommended Reading

Aucoin, James L. *The Evolution of American Investigative Journalism.* Columbia, MO: University of Missouri Press, 2005.

Barnett, Tracy L., ed. *100 Computer-Assisted Stories.* Columbia, MO: Investigative Reporters and Editors, 1995.

Behrens, John C. *The Typewriter Guerrillas: Closeups of 20 Top Investigative Reporters.* Chicago, IL: Burnham, Inc., 1977.

Benjaminson, Peter, and David Anderson, *Investigative Reporting.* Ames, IA: Iowa State University Press, 1990.

Bernt, Joseph, and Marilyn S. Greenwald, eds. *The Big Chill: Investigative Reporting in the Current Media Environment.* Ames, IA: Iowa State University Press, 2000.

Bolch, Judith. *Investigative and In-Depth Reporting.* Winter Park, FL: Hastings House, 1978.

Bruzzese, Len, Brant Houston, and Steve Weinberg. *The Investigative Reporter's Handbook: A Guide to Documents, Databases and Techniques.* Boston: Bedford/St. Martin's, 2002.

Chepesiuk, Ronald, et al. *Raising Hell: Straight Talk with Investigative Journalists.* Jefferson, NC: McFarland & Company, 1997.

Colbert, Jan, Bruce Moores, and Steve Weinberg, eds. *IRE Top 100 Investigations: Selected 1989 Contest Winners.* Columbia, MO: IRE, 1990.

Colbert, Jan, and Steve Weinberg, eds. *The IRE Book II: Summaries of Many Top Investigations from 1984.* Columbia, MO: IRE, 1985.

Cook, Fred J. *Maverick: Fifty Years of Investigative Reporting.* New York: Putnam, 1984.

Coronel, Sheila S. *Betrayals of the Public Trust: Investigative Reports on Corruption.* Quezon City, Philippines: Philippine Center for Investigative Journalism, 2000.

Cribb, Robert, Dean Jobb, David McKie, and Fred Vallance-Jones. *Digging Deeper: A Canadian Reporter's Research Guide.* Don Mills, ON: Oxford University Press, 2006.

De Burgh, Hugo. *Investigative Journalism: Context and Practice.* New York: Routledge, 2000.

DeFleur, Margaret. *Computer-Assisted Investigative Reporting.* Mahwah, NJ: Lawrence Erlbaum Associates, 1997.

Dennis, Everette E. *Investigative Reporting: Why Practitioners Need the Academy.* New York: Gannett Center for Media Studies (Columbia University), 1986.

Dholkia, C.P. *Nature of Investigative Reporting.* Jaipur, India: A.B.D. Publishers, 2004.

Dygert, James H. *The Investigative Journalist: Folk Heroes of a New Era.* Englewood Cliffs, NJ: Prentice Hall, 1976.

Ettema, James S., and Theodore Glasser. *Custodians of Conscience: Investigative Journalism and Public Virtue.* New York: Columbia University Press, 1998.

Fenton, Tom. *Bad News: The Decline of Reporting, the Business of News, and the Danger to Us All.* Washington: Regan Books, 2005.

Fitzpatrick, Ellen F. *Muckraking: Three Landmark Articles.* New York: St. Martin's Press, 1994.

Fleeson, Lucinda S. *Dig Deep & Aim High: A Training Model for Teaching Investigative Reporting.* Washington: International Center for Journalists, 2000.

Fleeson, Lucinda S. *Ten Steps to Investigative Reporting.* Washington: International Center for Journalists, 2000.

Gaines, William. *Investigative Journalism: Proven Strategies for Reporting the Story.* Oxford, UK: CQ Press, 2007.

Gaines, William. *Investigative Reporting for Print and Broadcast.* Belmont, CA: Wadsworth/Thomson Learning, 1998.

Garrison, Bruce. *Successful Strategies for Computer-Assisted Reporting.* Mahwah, NJ: Lawrence Erlbaum Associates, 1996.

Garrison, Bruce. *Computer-Assisted Reporting,* 2nd ed. Hillsdale, NJ: Lawrence Erlbaum, 1998.

Golin, Milton. *Daring Docs: High Drama in Journal AMA Papers and Other Investigative Reporting.* Lincoln, NE: ASJA Press, 2006.

Harmening, Thomas E. *The Status of Investigative Reporting in American Daily Newspapers (Research Report).* Bloomington, IN: Center for New Communications, School of Journalism, Indiana University, 1977.

Harry, M. *Muckraker's Manual: How to Do Your Own Investigative Reporting*, 2nd ed. Port Townsend, WA: Loompanics Unlimited, 1984.

Herzog, David. *Mapping the News: Case Studies in GIS and Journalism*. New York: Esri Press, 2003.

Houston, Brant. *Computer-Assisted Reporting: A Practical Guide*, 3rd ed. New York: St. Martin's Press, 2004.

Koch, Tom. *The Message is the Medium: Online All the Time for Everyone*. Westport, CT: Praeger, 1996.

Koch, Tom. *Journalism for the 21st Century*. Westport, CT: Praeger, 1991.

Krajicek, David. *Scooped!* New York: Columbia University Press, 1999.

Lawler, Philip F. *Alternative Influence: The Impact of Investigative Reporting Groups on America's Media*. Lanham, MD: University Press of America, 1982.

Levy, Elizabeth. *By-Lines: Profiles in Investigative Journalism*. New York: Four Winds Press, 1975.

McDevitt, Daniel S. *Managing the Investigative Unit*. New York: Charles C. Thomas, Publisher, 2005.

MacPherson, Myra. *All Governments Lie: The Life and Times of Rebel Journalist I. F. Stone*. New York: Scribner, 2006.

Malarek, Victor. *Gut Instinct: The Making of an Investigative Journalist*. Toronto: Macmillan Canada, 1996.

Meyer, Philip. *Precision Journalism: A Reporter's Introduction to Social Science Methods*, 4th ed. New York: Rowman & Littlefield Publishers, Inc., 2002.

Miller, Lisa C. *Power Journalism: Computer-Assisted Reporting*. Fort Worth, TX: Harcourt Brace College Publishers, 1997.

Miraldi, Robert. *The Muckrakers: Evangelical Crusaders*. Westport, CT: Praeger Publishers, 2000.

Mitford, Jessica. *Poison Penmanship: The Gentle Art of Muckraking*. New York: Vintage, 1957.

Mollenhoff, Clark R. *Investigative Reporting: From Courthouse to White House*. New York: Macmillan, 1981.

Moorcroft, Marilyn. *Investigative Reporting*. London: Franklin Watts, 1981.

Northmore, David. *Lifting the Lid: A Guide to Investigative Research*. London: Cassell Academic, 1996.

Patterson, Margaret Jones. *Behind the Lines: Case Studies in Investigative Reporting*. New York: Columbia University Press, 1986.

Paul, Nora, ed. *When Nerds and Words Collide: Reflections on the Development of Computer-Assisted Reporting*. St. Petersburg, FL: Poynter Institute, 1999.

Paul, Nora. *Computer-Assisted Research: A Guide to Tapping Online Information*, 4th ed. St. Petersburg, FL: Poynter Institute/Bonus Books, 1999.

Pawlick, Thomas. *Investigative Reporting: A Casebook.* New York: R. Rosen Press, 1982.

Penn, Stanley. *Have I Got a Tip for You—and Other Tales of Dirty Secrets, Political Payoffs, and Corporate Scams: A Guide to Investigative Reporting.* New York: Dow Jones, 1994.

Pilger, John, ed. *Tell Me No Lies: Investigative Journalism That Changed the World.* New York: Thunder's Mouth Press, 2005.

Protess, David. *Muckraking Matters: The Societal Impact of Investigative Reporting.* (The Institute for Modern Communications Research monograph series.) Evanston, IL: Northwestern University, 1987.

Protess, David L. *The Journalism of Outrage: Investigative Reporting and Agenda Building in America.* New York: Guilford Press, 1991.

Protess, David L., Fay Lomax Cook, Jack C. Doppelt, James S. Ettema, Margaret T. Gordon, Donna R. Leff, and Peter Miller. *The Journalism of Outrage: Investigative Reporting and Agenda Building in America,* new ed. New York: Guilford Press, 2005.

Reavy, Matthew. *Introduction to Computer-Assisted Reporting: A Journalist's Guide.* Mountain View, CA: Mayfield Publishing Company, 2001.

Redfern, Walter. *Writing on the Move: Albert Londres and Investigative Journalism (European Connections).* Bern, Switzerland: Peter Lang Publishing, 2004.

Schwartz, Debra A. *Writing Green: Advocacy & Investigative Reporting About the Environment in the Early 21st Century.* Baltimore, MD: Loyola College/Apprentice House, 2006.

Scott, Andrew, ed. *IRE 101: Computer-Assisted Stories from the IRE Morgue.* Columbia, MO: Investigative Reporters and Editors, 1993.

Semonche, Barbara P. 'Computer-Assisted Journalism: An Overview' in *News Media Libraries.* Westport, CT: Greenwood Press, 1993.

Serrin, Judith, and William Serrin. *Muckraking! The Journalism that Changed America.* New York: New Press, 2002.

Shapiro, Bruce, ed. *Shaking the Foundations: 200 Years of Investigative Journalism in America.* New York: Thunder's Mouth Press/Nation Books, 2003

Spark, David. *Investigative Reporting: A Study in Techniques.* Oxford: Focal Press, 1999.

Thomas, Helen. *Watchdogs of Democracy? The Waning Washington Press Corps and How It Has Failed the Public.* New York: Scribner, 2006.

Ullmann, John. *Investigative Reporting: Advanced Methods and Techniques.* New York: St. Martin's Press, 1995.

Walton, Richard H. *Cold Case Homicides: Practical Investigative Techniques.* Boca Raton, FL: CRC, 2006.

Ward, Jean, and Kathleen A. Hansen. *Search Strategies in Mass Communications*, 3rd ed. New York: Longman, 1997.

Weinberg, Steve. *Telling the Untold Story: How Investigative Reports are Changing the Craft of Biography*. Columbia, MO: University of Missouri Press, 1992.

Weinberg, Steve. *The Reporter's Handbook: An Investigator's Guide to Documents and Techniques. (IRE Sponsorship)*, 3rd ed. New York: St. Martin's Press, 1996.

Weinberg, Steve, and Jan Colbert, eds. *The Investigative Journalist's Morgue: An Index to Thousands of Stories and Series from the Files of IRE*. Columbia, MO: IRE, 1986.

Weinberg, Steve, and Andrew Scott, eds. *IRE 100 Selected Investigations: From 1991 & 1992 Contest Entries*. Columbia, MO: IRE, 1992.

Weir, David, and Dan Noyes. *Raising Hell: How the Center for Investigative Reporting Gets the Story*. Reading, MA: Addison-Wesley, 1983.

Whitaker, Reg, and Steve Hewitt. *Canada and the Cold War*. Toronto: Lorimer, 2003.

Williams, Paul N. *Investigative Reporting and Editing*. Upper Saddle River, NJ: Prentice Hall, 1982.

Wolfe, Tom, and E.W. Johnson, eds. *The New Journalism*. New York: Harper& Row, 1973.

## Online Resources

CAR in Canada
    www.carincanada.ca
    Fred Vallance-Jones is the webmaster for this site.

The CAR/CARR Links Page
    www.ryerson.ca/~dtudor/megasources.htm
    Dean Tudor, Ryerson University

Depth Reporting
    http://depthreporting.com
    Mark Schaver, The Courier-Journal, Louisville, Kentucky

Online News and Computer-Assisted Reporting Research Project
    http://com.miami.edu/car
    Bruce Garrison, University of Miami

'The Development of Computer-Assisted Reporting'
  http://com.miami.edu/car/cox00.htm
  Melisma Cox, University of Miami, AEJMC Paper, 2000

The J-Files at VCU
  www.people.vcu.edu/~jcsouth
  Jeffrey C. South, Virginia Commonwealth University

Institute for Analytic Journalism
  www.analyticjournalism.com

Investigative Reporters and Editors, Inc. (IRE)
  www.ire.org
  Founded in 1975 by a small group of investigative journalists, IRE has become a grassroots network for journalists of all kinds from around the world.

National Institute for Computer-Assisted Reporting (NICAR)
  www.nicar.org
  NICAR is a non-profit educational program of IRE and the Missouri School of Journalism.

NICAR Net Tour
  www.ire.org/training/nettour

Power Reporting: Resources for Journalists
  http://powerreporting.com/
  Bill Dedman's site features resources and training in computer-assisted reporting and editing.

Statistics Every Writer Should Know
  www.robertniles.com/stats
  Robert Niles's introduction to statistics 'for journalists and other writers who might not know math'.

Syllabi on Computer-Assisted Reporting
  http://powerreporting.com/syllabi.html
  This list comes from Bill Dedman's Power Reporting: Resources for Journalists website.

The Scoop

www.thescoop.org

Derek Willis maintains this blog on investigative and computer-assisted reporting.

# Index